Dewey Decimal Classification and Relative Index

Dewey Decimal Classification and Relative Index

Devised by Melvil Dewey

EDITION 20

Edited by

John P. Comaromi, Editor

Julianne Beall, Assistant Editor

Winton E. Matthews, Jr., Assistant Editor

Gregory R. New, Assistant Editor

VOLUME 1

Introduction ■ Tables

FOREST PRESS

A Division of
OCLC Online Computer Library Center, Inc.
ALBANY, NEW YORK

1989

Library of Congress Cataloging-in-Publication Data
Dewey, Melvil, 1851-1931.
    Dewey decimal classification and relative index / devised by
Melvil Dewey. -- Ed. 20 / edited by John P. Comaromi, Julianne
Beall, Winton E. Matthews, Jr., Gregory R. New.
    Contents: v. 1. Introduction. Tables -- v. 2-3. Schedules -- v.4. Relative
index. Manual.
    1. Classification, Dewey decimal. I. Comaromi, John P. (John Phillip),
1937-   .   II. Beall, Julianne, 1946-   .   III. Matthews, Winton E.   IV. New,
Gregory R.   V. Forest Press.   VI. Title.
Z696.D519 1989   025.4'31--dc19   88-24629

ISBN: (set) 0-910608-37-7; v. 1 0-910608-38-5; v. 2 0-910608-39-3;
v. 3 0-910608-40-7; v. 4 0-910608-41-5

This edition
of the
Dewey Decimal Classification
is dedicated
to
John Ames Humphry

Executive Director of Forest Press
1977-1985
Chairperson, Forest Press Committee
1971-1977
Gentleman & Leader

Contents

Contents

Volume 2

Volume 3

Volume 4

Publisher's Foreword

The year 1988 witnessed two events which will have a profound effect on the future of the Dewey Decimal Classification and other general classification systems. Curiously, both events took place on the same day.

On July 29, a computer tape containing substantially all of the text of DDC 20 was delivered to a firm in Massachusetts to begin production of this edition. The intellectual content of that tape was the result of ten years of intensive effort by the editorial group at the Library of Congress, numerous committees and advisors, and input from DDC users throughout the world. The computer tape itself was produced by the editors using a sophisticated microcomputer-based editorial support system and the DDC Database.

On the same date, Forest Press and the Dewey Decimal Classification became a part of the OCLC Online Computer Library Center, the Ohio-based not-for-profit organization which provides computer services and products to more than 8,000 libraries through a network which extends to Europe and Asia. Joining the DDC with the talents and resources of OCLC will allow the development of the computer products and services which are needed by DDC users.

DDC 20 itself represents an effort to meet the requirements of today while preparing for the needs of the future. In compiling this edition, Forest Press has had the advice and assistance of many persons in the library community.

Until July 29, Forest Press was a division of the Lake Placid Education Foundation. Editorial work on DDC 20 was thus completed under the guidance of the Forest Press Committee, appointed by the Trustees of the Foundation. The Committee included, in addition to members representing the Foundation's Board of Trustees, the following members representing library concerns: Walter W. Curley, Chairperson, former President of Gaylord Bros., Inc.; Richard W. Gardner, Professor of Library and Information Science, University of Montreal; Joseph H. Howard, Director, National Agricultural Library; John A. Humphry, former Executive Director, Forest Press; J. Michael O'Brien, Executive Director, Suburban Library System, Burr Ridge, Illinois; Peter J. Paulson, Executive Director, Forest Press; David Penniman, Director, Libraries and Information Systems Center, AT&T Bell Laboratories; Thomas Sullivan, former Associate Director of Indexing Services, The H. W. Wilson Co.; and Elaine Svenonius, Professor, Graduate School of Library and Information Science, University of California at Los Angeles.

Forest Press and the Forest Press Committee are assisted in their editorial responsibilities by an advisory group known as the Decimal Classification Editorial Policy Committee. The Editorial Policy Committee represents the libraries that use Dewey, and usually meets twice a year on matters relating to the development of the Classification. The Committee is made up of professionals who have experience in a wide variety of libraries, here and abroad, and who are well versed in the theory and application of the Classification. The members of the Committee who served during the preparation of Edition 20 are listed in the Preface.

For the actual editing of the Schedules, Tables, Index, and Manual, Forest Press contracts with the Library of Congress, whose table of organization includes a Decimal

Classification Division within its Processing Services Department. The Decimal Classification Division is the largest user of DDC in the world, applying DDC numbers to over 100,000 Library of Congress bibliographic records annually. In this way, classification theory and practice are combined, allowing for continuous and thorough editorial review. The editor of this edition has been John P. Comaromi, assisted by Julianne Beall, Winton E. Matthews, Jr., and Gregory R. New.

The international acceptance of the Dewey Decimal Classification continues to grow. The British National Bibliography adopted Edition 18 in 1971, permitting British libraries and many others throughout the English-speaking world to apply Dewey numbers to their collections. The national bibliographies of Canada, India, Australia, Italy, Indonesia, Jordan, Kenya, Pakistan, Zimbabwe, and other countries also use Dewey numbers in their bibliographic publications. It is expected that other national bibliographies will adopt Edition 20, thus enhancing the Classification and its application and benefiting the users of libraries everywhere by helping to standardize the subject approach to library materials.

In June 1985, a change of administration at Forest Press took place, at which time the undersigned succeeded John A. Humphry as Executive Director. During John Humphry's eight-year tenure as Executive Director, the Press and all its publications enjoyed wide acclaim from the library community throughout the world, and international activities were greatly expanded.

Peter J. Paulson
Executive Director
Forest Press, a divison of
OCLC Online Computer
Library Center, Inc.

18 August 1988

DEWEY DECIMAL CLASSIFICATION, ADDITIONS, NOTES AND DECISIONS

To keep users of Dewey Decimal Classification Edition 20 up to date on developments regarding the Classification, *Dewey Decimal Classification, Additions, Notes and Decisions*, popularly known as *DC&*, is published at occasional intervals. All purchasers of Edition 20 are entitled to subscribe to DC& and may be placed on the mailing list for this publication by either returning the enclosed card or by writing to Forest Press, 85 Watervliet Avenue, Albany, New York 12206-2082, U.S.A.

Preface by the Decimal Classification Editorial Policy Committee

The Decimal Classification Editorial Policy Committee was established in 1937 to serve as an advisory body in determining the general direction and policies of the Dewey Decimal Classification (DDC). It was reconstituted as a joint committee of the Lake Placid Education Foundation and the American Library Association in 1955. Its constituency consists of libraries, information agencies, and users of the Classification in the United States and abroad. The current membership of the Committee consists of a diverse group of library and information professionals and is international in scope. Its membership of ten includes public, special, and academic librarians; library educators; representatives of the American Library Association, the Library of Congress, and Forest Press (publisher of the DDC); a representative of the (British) Library Association; and a Canadian library educator. The main function of the Committee is to work with the editors of the DDC and advise Forest Press in matters relating to changes, innovations, and the general development of the Classification.

Three separate publications issued between Editions 19 and 20 (*004–006 Data Processing and Computer Science*; *301–307 Sociology*; and the *Proposed Revision of 780 Music*) and other revisions and expansions in *Dewey Decimal Classification, Additions, Notes and Decisions (DC&)* illustrate the policy of continuous revision adopted by the Editorial Policy and Forest Press Committees. Continuous revision means that major changes in the schedules and tables in most need of urgent development are issued between editions. These revisions are implemented at once on Library of Congress bibliographic records, making the new concepts and notations readily available for librarians to use. Librarians are thus able to implement the revised schedules and tables on an ongoing basis, instead of in more massive projects after the publication of new editions.

In creating new schedules and revising existing ones, the Committee often calls upon the expertise of outside groups. For Edition 20, such groups included various committees of the American Library Association, library associations of other countries, the African Section of the Library of Congress, working classifiers, and experts in various subjects (such as computer science and music).

The completely revised 780 Music schedule, for example, took over ten years to develop and involved classification and music experts in the United States, United Kingdom, Canada, and Australia, as well as a special subcommittee of the ALA Resources and Technical Services Division Subject Analysis Committee. The new music schedule is particularly needed as a tool for online browsing and retrieval in a complex subject area. The Editorial Policy Committee approved the changes in music for inclusion in Edition 20 only after much deliberation.

Since major revisions and expansions present inevitable implementation problems for libraries, they are recommended by the Committee only in response to requests of DDC users and where great need exists. For example, the new and greatly expanded schedules for *004–006 Data Processing and Computer Science* and *301–307 Sociology* were published between Editions 19 and 20 (and are now included in DDC 20) because the need for expansion to deal with the existing literature was identified by users and perceived by the DDC editors.

In addition to the changes in the schedules, there is a complete revision of area —711 British Columbia and major expansions of areas —52 Japan, —669 Nigeria, —68 Southern Africa, and —95 Papua New Guinea in Table 2. The changes and expansions in the area table were made only when the previous tables were unworkable (areas —669, —711 and —95) or when local literary warrant made expansion necessary (areas —52 and —68).

Relocations proposed by the editors are carefully examined and weighed in terms of their implications for implementation. In the preparation of Edition 20, relocations were monitored: 1) to eliminate dual provisions; 2) to regularize the use of standard subdivisions; 3) to provide uniformity of development for parallel subjects; 4) to insure proper subject relationships; and 5) to rectify erroneous placement of subjects. Most relocations in Edition 20 fall into the first two categories. Many of the others are repercussions of the new schedule *004–006 Data Processing and Computer Science*. Many numbers throughout the schedules relating to the field of computer technology were affected by the numbers in the new schedule. In determining which relocations were to be made, the extent of their effect on library service was always considered.

With the prospect of the Dewey Decimal Classification serving as an online retrieval tool, the Committee also considered the implications of the DDC being used not only by classifiers, but also by library users. For example, in evaluating the terminology of the index, the Committee recommended that, wherever appropriate and feasible, proper names be indexed in AACR2 form, and entries from lists of subject headings be incorporated into the index. As the Dewey Decimal Classification enters the online age, the Committee will continue to monitor future developments of the Classification and to recommend policies that will help it become more adaptable and amenable to online information storage and retrieval.

Since the publication of Edition 19, many individuals have served on the Editorial Policy Committee, each making unique contributions to its deliberations. Following is a list of the members (with the positions they held or hold during their tenure on the Committee) who contributed to the preparation of Edition 20: Joanne S. Anderson, Coordinator of Reference Services, San Diego Public Library; Henriette D. Avram, Assistant Librarian for Processing Services, Library of Congress; Lizbeth J. Bishoff, formerly Principal Librarian for Support Services, Pasadena (California) Public Library, now Manager, Cataloging and Database Services, OCLC; Barbara Branson, Principal Cataloger, Perkins Library, Duke University; Lois Mai Chan, Professor, College of Library and Information Science, University of Kentucky; Margaret E. Cockshutt, Professor, Faculty of Library and Information Science, University of Toronto, Canada; John P. Comaromi, formerly Associate Professor, Graduate School of Library and Information Science, UCLA, now Editor of the Dewey Decimal Classification; Betty M. E. Croft, Technical Services Librarian, Northwestern Missouri State University; Joel C. Downing, Director of Copyright and English Language Services, The British Library; Joseph H. Howard, Assistant

Librarian for Processing Services, Library of Congress; John A. Humphry, Executive Director, Forest Press; Donald J. Lehnus, Associate Professor, Graduate School of Library and Information Science, University of Mississippi; Joan S. Mitchell, formerly Library Network Support Manager, AT&T Bell Laboratories, now Director, Instructional Technology, Carnegie Mellon University; Peter J. Paulson, formerly Director of the New York State Library, now Executive Director, Forest Press; Clare E. Ryan, Head, Technical Services, New Hampshire State Library; Marietta D. Shepard, Chief of the Library Development Program of the Organization of American States; Russell Sweeney, Head of Department of Library and Information Studies, Leeds Polytechnic, England; and Arnold S. Wajenberg, Principal Cataloguer, University of Illinois at Urbana-Champaign.

The Editorial Policy Committee wishes to acknowledge the assistance provided by many groups and individuals in the preparation of DDC 20, including those groups mentioned earlier and individuals too numerous to name here. The Committee recommends to you this new edition of the Dewey Decimal Classification, with a sense of pride that this edition represents the best efforts of many individuals and the awareness that it is still far from perfect. The continuing development and viability of the Dewey Decimal Classification will rely on the interest and concern of all users around the world. Your comments, advice, and suggestions are ever welcome.

> Lois Mai Chan
> *Chairperson* (1986–   )
>
> Margaret E. Cockshutt
> *Chairperson* (1980–1985)
> Decimal Classification
> Editorial Policy Committee

30 June 1988

Acknowledgments

Developing and maintaining the Dewey Decimal Classification involves a cast of hundreds. I acknowledge the assistance of the members of the cast whose number does not permit me to name them all here; acknowledge the debt to those who have gone before us and upon whose shoulders we stand; acknowledge the work of the staff of Forest Press who bring our efforts to final and published form; acknowledge the advice and assistance of the Decimal Classification Editorial Policy Committee, our sure guide; acknowledge the extensive assistance of the Subject Analysis Committee of the American Library Association; and acknowledge the work of the present and former staff who worked upon Edition 20 in various capacities and to varying degrees: Benjamin A. Custer, Editor; Julianne Beall, Winton E. Matthews, Jr., Gregory R. New, and Margaret J. Warren, assistant editors; and Melba D. Adams, Kenneth Austin, Frances A. Bold, Michael B. Cantlon, Della M. Chase, Rosalee Connor, Eve M. Dickey, Darlene Foster, Idalia V. Fuentes, Glenna Sue Garner, Tina Golden, Valexia Hall, William S. Hwang, Irma Lashley, Nobuko Ohashi, Letitia J. Reigle, Virginia Anne Schoepf, Ruth Ann Sievers, David A. Smith, Emily K. Spears, Cosmo D. Tassone, Marcellus S. Todd, Marisa C. Vandenbosch.

John P. Comaromi
Editor
Dewey Decimal Classification
Library of Congress

8 August 1988

New Features in Edition 20

The aim of Edition 20 is user convenience: clearer instructions, more explanations, greater accessibility through expanded summaries, elimination of duplicate provisions for classing single subjects, and the inclusion of a Manual to guide the classifier.

Manual

The most striking change in DDC 20 is the presence of a Manual to assist in its application. The Manual represents the core of a much larger body of notes first introduced in the separately published 1982 *Manual on the Use of the Dewey Decimal Classification: Edition 19*. The Manual describes policies and practices of the Decimal Classification Division of the Library of Congress, offers advice on classing in difficult areas, and explains how to choose between related numbers. The briefer notes of the 1982 Manual, and those that need to be used frequently, have been incorporated in the Schedules and Tables. The new notes and the Manual should help classifiers resolve problems and apply the DDC with greater consistency.

General Format

The number of summaries has been increased. Furthermore, a new type of summary that incorporates two levels of structure has been introduced to provide a more effective overview. An example of such a summary can be found at 370 Education.

There is a significant increase in the number of notes in the Schedules and Tables, beyond the incorporation of notes from the 1982 Manual. There are more class-elsewhere notes to explain the relationship between overlapping and closely related subjects. A new kind of note, the see-also note, informs the classifier about related subjects that may be overlooked. Every add instruction includes at least one example.

Option notes, now enclosed in parentheses, provide notation which may be used in place of the preferred standard notation.

Completely revised segments and international cooperation

The only completely revised schedule in Edition 20 is 780 Music, originally drafted in Great Britain by Russell Sweeney and John Clews. A detailed description of the changes in 780 is given under the heading of 780 in the Manual. Comparative and equivalence tables are found on pages 496-514 in this volume.

The complete revision of the area table for British Columbia (T2—711) was drafted by a Canadian team headed by David Balatti of the National Library of Canada.

The expansions of the area and history numbers for South Africa (T2—68, 968) were developed in cooperation with the South African Institute of Library and Information Science; the African Section of the Library of Congress; and the American Library Association RTSD Committee on Cataloging: Asian and African Materials.

Other instances of international assistance in the development of the DDC are the expansion and revision of the area table for Japan (T2—52) in cooperation with Genten Wakabayashi of the Private University Library Association of Japan, and the expansion of the table for Melanesia (relocated from T2—932–937 to T2—95) and Papua New Guinea (T2—953) in cooperation with Fraiser McConnell of the National Library Service of Papua New Guinea.

Important Areas of Revision in the Tables

Table 1. Standard Subdivisions

—011   Systems

A new number added to specify the systems of a subject

—028   *Auxiliary* techniques and procedures; apparatus, equipment, materials

Use of this number for basic techniques and procedures of the subject discontinued; class in 001–999 without adding notation from Table 1

—029   Commercial miscellany

Expanded to include product catalogs and directories; buyers' guides and consumer reports; evaluation and purchasing manuals; estimates of labor, time, materials

—07   Education, research, related topics (formerly Study and teaching)

Several revisions

—08   History and description with respect to kinds of persons

T1—08804–08808 relocated to T1—081–088

—092   Persons

Use of —0924 for individuals discontinued; they are now classed in —092

—093–099   Treatment [of the subject] by specific continents, countries, localities

A new table displays the standard subdivisions that may be added to the chronological period and geographical subdivisions

Table 2. Geographic Areas, Historical Periods, Persons

Names have been updated and changed, and parts of countries are now generally given in the language of the country, e.g., T2—4333 Lower Franconia district is listed as Unterfranken Regierungsbezirk (Lower Franconia district). The AACR2 form of place names is used in the Index; an anglicized or standard form is used where the AACR2 vernacular form is not readily recognizable. Diacritics have been provided for the following languages: Amharic, Chinese, Czech, Dutch, Finnish, French, German, Greek, Italian, Japanese, Portuguese, Spanish, and Urdu.

—43   Germany expanded and revised

—492   Netherlands expanded

—493   Belgium expanded

—494   Switzerland expanded

—52   Japan revised and expanded (published in 1985 in *DC&* 4:5)

—563	Turkey in Europe relocated to —4961
—669	Nigeria revised and expanded
—68	Southern Africa: South Africa expanded (published in 1985 in *DC&* 4:5); Botswana, Swaziland, and Lesotho relocated from —681 to —688
—69	South Indian Ocean islands revised
—711	British Columbia completely revised; see comparative and equivalence tables on pages 496-514 in this volume.
—714	New administrative regions of Quebec assigned numbers
—83	Chile revised to correspond to reorganization
—931	Comprehensive works on New Zealand moved to —93
—932–937	Melanesia relocated to —95 and expanded

Table 3. Subdivisions for Individual Literatures, for Specific Literary Forms

To render instructions less difficult to follow, Table 3 has been divided into three sub-tables:

3–A for works by or about individual authors
3–B for works by or about two or more authors
3–C for subdivisions to be added to 3–B numbers and 808–809

Table 5. Racial, Ethnic, National Groups

—96–98	Expansion for African and American native peoples

Table 6. Languages

—96	Expansion in African languages

Important Areas of Revision in the Schedules

001–006	The span of numbers covering knowledge, systems, and data processing has been extensively revised. The relocation and expansion of data processing and computer science that appeared in the 1985 publication *004–006 Data Processing and Computer Science and Changes in Related Disciplines* have been incorporated in DDC 20 with some changes. The corresponding standard subdivision T1—0285 for computer application to a subject extends this expansion and revision throughout the Schedules. In addition, 003 Systems was expanded, and 001.5 Cybernetics and related disciplines has been scattered as follows: interdisciplinary treatment of communication to 302.2, cybernetics to 003.5, artificial intelligence to 006.3.
207	Christian education and religious instruction relocated to 268 Religious education in order to distinguish Christianity as an academic subject (207) from instruction in Christianity as a way of life (268).

220	Apocalyptic literature provided for throughout the Bible.
232.6	The Second Coming and Judgment of Christ relocated to 236.9 Last Judgment
248.48	Guides to Christian life for specific classes of persons (e.g., the young) of specific denominations relocated from the denomination to the class of persons in 248.8
267.15	The Salvation Army, a Christian movement, relocated to 287.96.
281.93 283.3 284.1–.2	Specific national Eastern Orthodox, Anglican, Lutheran, and Reformed churches relocated to area subdivisions, e.g., 281.93 to 281.94–281.99.
288	The Unitarian Church relocated to 289.1 with the Universalist Church.
297.8	Religions originating in Islam (Babism, Bahaism) relocated to 297.9.
305	The effect of media (e.g., television) on social groups (e.g., children) now classed with the medium in 302.23, not with the group affected.
312	Demographic statistics relocated to 304.6021 and to the specific subject, e.g., statistics on deaths by crimes of violence 364.15021 (published in 1985 in *DC&* 4:5).
323.4	Comprehensive works on civil rights moved from 323.4 to 323.
324.1–.2	Numbers provided for comprehensive works on kinds of parties. In the table at 324.24–324.29, nationalist parties relocated from 03 to 083; other recent political parties not fitting the left to right continuum of political opinion now provided for, e.g., religious parties 082.
324.268	Political parties of South Africa regularized to fit the table at 324.24–324.29.
327.3–.9	Espionage and subversion by specific nations now classed at 327.12 rather than at foreign relations in 327.3–.9.
333.79	Energy revised and expanded.
362–363	Specific social problems and services significantly revised and expanded, e.g., 362.29 Substance abuse, 363.728 Waste disposal.
374	Adult education revised and expanded.
380.3	Comprehensive works on communications relocated to 384 in order to collocate general works and works on specific topics.
380.5	Comprehensive works on transportation relocated to 388 in order to collocate general works and works on specific topics.
384.55	Television substantially revised.
401.9	Sociolinguistics relocated to 306.44.
418	Reading provided for in linguistics at 418.4.
513.93	Business arithmetic relocated to 650.01513.

529.7	Time systems relocated from 529.75 to 389.17 under Metrology and standardization, time instruments from 529.78 to 681.11 under Precision instruments and other devices.
530.4	States of matter expanded.
604.6	Waste technology relocated to 628.4.
621.38	Electronics and communications engineering substantially revised.
621.38195	Computer engineering relocated to 621.39, and revised and expanded (published in 1985 *004–006 Data Processing and Computer Science*).
628	Sanitary and environmental engineering significantly revised to eliminate obsolete distinctions.
720–724 730–735	Use of chronological periods for Oriental architecture and sculpture (the major topics relocated) has been made consistent with Western architecture and sculpture.
738	Substantial revision of pottery and porcelain, especially with respect to brands, varieties, types, and products.
780	Music has been completely revised. A Comparative table showing the location in both editions of most of the major topics of 780 is found on pages 496-504. An Equivalence table showing the changes in music from Edition 19 to Edition 20 and vice versa is found on pages 506-513. The new development is described in the 780 section of the Manual.
782.1	Staging dramatic music (782 in Edition 19) relocated to 792.5–792.7 and substantially revised.
791.4	Extensive revision of motion pictures, radio, television.
794.8	Electronic and computer games revised and expanded.
796.4	Weightlifting, track and field, gymnastics revised and expanded; athletic exercise relocated to 613.71 Physical fitness.
797.17	Minor methods of navigation (e.g., surfing and water skiing) relocated to 797.3 Other aquatic sports (published in 1983/1984 in *DC&* 4:4).
971.501–.504	Historical periods of New Brunswick moved to 971.5101–971.5104.
972.8	Historical periods of Central America revised to reflect each country's history.

Lists of relocations and reductions, and also comparative and equivalence tables are found on pages 479-514 in this volume.

Relative Index

The Relative Index for Edition 20 is smaller than the Index for Edition 19. The elimination of many unlikely entries (such as mercury as a building material) and the removal of see references were the major factors in size reduction.

See references have been eliminated from the Index since each term now has a number (in many cases this is the interdisciplinary number). See also references lead to broader and related terms.

Proper names are indexed under their AACR2 form, and under other commonly used forms of the name.

The seven Tables are identified by T1, T2, T3, etc., e.g., the area number for the United States is T2—73, Faust as a topic in literature T3C—351.

Suggestions from Users

Suggestions for improving the Dewey Decimal Classification are always given serious consideration and effected if found reasonable and feasible. We welcome any suggestions for improving Edition 20 and developing Edition 21. Suggestions and questions should be directed to the following parties:

(1) For sales; format; workshops; aids for the classifier; copyright questions:
       Executive Director
       Forest Press/OCLC
       85 Watervliet Ave.
       Albany, New York 12206-2082 U.S.A.

(2) For editiorial policy matters, such as areas needing extensive revision or expansion, and indexing policy:
       Chairperson
       Decimal Classification Editorial Policy Committee
       c/o Forest Press/OCLC
       85 Watervliet Ave.
       Albany, New York 12206-2082 U.S.A.

(3) For corrections and questions on how to apply the Classification:
       Editor
       Dewey Decimal Classification
       Decimal Classification Division
       Library of Congress
       Washington, DC 20540 U.S.A

Introduction
to the
Dewey Decimal Classification

About the Introduction

1.1   This Introduction is written primarily for the novice or beginning classifier, although the experienced classifier may benefit from reviewing its contents.

1.2   The Introduction is meant to be used in conjunction with the Glossary (in this volume) and the Manual (in Volume 4). The Manual, which will be of interest to both beginners and experienced classifiers, contains additional and more detailed information about the use of the Classification, offers advice on classifying in difficult areas, and explains how to choose between related numbers. References to the Glossary appear throughout the Introduction.

Classification: What It Is and What It Does

2.1   *Classification* provides a system for organizing a universe of items, be they objects, concepts, or records.

2.2   *Notation* is the system of symbols used to represent the classes in a classification system. In the Dewey Decimal Classification system (DDC), the notation is expressed in Arabic numerals. The notation gives at once both the unique meaning of the class and its relation to other classes. It permits the searcher to find a specific item within the class to which it belongs and near related classes. No matter how words describing subjects may differ, the notation identifies the subject and class within which the item belongs.

2.3   Libraries usually arrange their collections according to the systematic structure of a library classification. Each item is assigned a *call number* (see **Glossary**), usually consisting of the notation for its class, accompanied by a book number or some other device to subarrange the items of a class. The call number provides a unique identifying code that is used as an "address" on the shelf, and as a tag for library record keeping in circulation and inventory control.

2.4   The *subject catalog* is the index to the contents of a library collection. It lists works, parts of works, and important essays or literary works in collections by topic. If arranged alphabetically by words, it is called an *alphabetical subject catalog* (the pre-eminent form in North America). If arranged by the notation of a library classification system, it is called a *classified catalog* (the pre-eminent form in Europe). In addition to providing the class number at which the item is shelved, classified catalogs provide numbers for other subjects in the work.

History and Current Use of the Dewey Decimal Classification

3.1   The Dewey Decimal Classification is the most widely used library classification system in the world. It is used in more than 135 countries, and has been translated into over 30 languages. In the United States, 95% of all public and school libraries, 25% of all college and university libraries, and 20% of special libraries use the DDC.

3.2   The DDC was conceived by Melvil Dewey in 1873 and first published in 1876. The first edition was 44 pages long: 14 pages of front and back matter, 12 pages of summaries and schedules, and 18 pages of index. In its 20th edition it has grown to a four-volume set.

3.3   The DDC is developed, maintained, and applied in the Decimal Classification Division of the Library of Congress (LC), where annually over 100,000 DDC numbers are assigned to works acquired by the Library. In the United States, DDC numbers are incorporated into machine readable catalog (MARC) records, and distributed to libraries by way of computer tapes, Cataloging-in-Publication (CIP) data, and LC cards. DDC numbers also appear in MARC records in 12 other countries and are used in the national bibliographies of the United Kingdom, Australia, Canada, India, Italy, Indonesia, Jordan, Kenya, Pakistan, Zimbabwe, and other countries. Various bibliographic utilities and services in the United States and elsewhere make DDC numbers available to libraries through online access, publications, and production of catalog cards.

Overview of the Dewey Decimal Classification

CONCEPTUAL FRAMEWORK

4.1   In the DDC, basic classes are organized by traditional academic disciplines or fields of study. No principle is more basic to the DDC than this: the parts of the Classification are arranged by discipline, not by subject.

4.2   The consequence of this principle is that there is likely to be no one single place for a given subject. Marriage, for example, has aspects which fall under several disciplines, such as music, philosophy, sociology, and law. Music for marriage ceremonies belongs in 781.587 as part of the discipline of music; ethical considerations in marriage in 173 as part of the discipline of philosophy; sociological studies of marriage in 306.81 as part of the discipline of sociology; and legal aspects of marriage in

346.016 as part of the discipline of law. The Relative Index assembles the disciplinary aspects of a subject in one place:

Marriage	306.81
citizenship issues	323.636
customs	392.5
ethics	173
religion	291.563
Buddhism	294.356 3
Christianity	241.63
Hinduism	294.548 63
Islam	297.5
Judaism	296.385 63
folklore	398.27
sociology	398.354
law	346.016
literature	808.803 54
history and criticism	809.933 54
specific literatures	T3B—080 354
history and criticism	T3B—093 54
music	781.587
personal religion	291.44
Buddhism	294.344 4
Christianity	248.4
Hinduism	294.544
Islam	297.44
Judaism	296.74
public worship	291.38
Christianity	265.5
Judaism	296.444
see also Public worship	
religious doctrine	291.22
Buddhism	294.342 2
Christianity	234.165
Hinduism	294.522
Islam	297.22
Judaism	296.32
social theology	291.178 358 1
Christianity	261.835 81

NOTATION

4.3
At the broadest level, the DDC is divided into ten *main classes*, which together cover the entire world of knowledge. These classes are further divided into ten *divisions* and each division into ten *sections*, although not all the numbers for the divisions and sections have been used. (The

word "class" is used generally to indicate divisions, sections, and any other notational level in the hierarchy.)

4.4   The ten main classes are:

        000   Generalities
        100   Philosophy, parapsychology and occultism, psychology
        200   Religion
        300   Social sciences
        400   Language
        500   Natural sciences and mathematics
        600   Technology (Applied sciences)
        700   The arts   Fine and decorative arts
        800   Literature (Belles-lettres) and rhetoric
        900   Geography, history, and auxiliary disciplines

4.5   Main class 000 is the most general class, and is used for works not limited to any one specific discipline, such as encyclopedias, newspapers, and general periodicals. This class is also used for certain specialized disciplines that deal with knowledge and information generally, such as information science, library science, computer science, journalism, and bibliography. The content of the other nine classes is self-explanatory.

4.6   The first digit in the numbers listed above indicates the *main class.* Although each number contains three digits, only the first digit is significant in this list. The remaining zeros fill out the notation to the required three digits.

4.7   Each main class consists of ten *divisions*, also numbered 0 through 9. The number of significant digits here is two, the second digit indicating the division. 6$\underline{0}$0 is used for general works on the applied sciences, 6$\underline{1}$0 for the medical sciences, 6$\underline{2}$0 for engineering, 6$\underline{3}$0 for agriculture.

4.8   Each division has ten *sections*, again numbered 0 through 9. The third digit in each three-digit number indicates the section. Thus, 63$\underline{0}$ is used for general works on agriculture, 63$\underline{1}$ for specific techniques, 63$\underline{2}$ for plant injuries, 63$\underline{3}$ for field and plantation crops.

4.9   A decimal point (see **Glossary**) follows the third digit, after which division by ten continues on down to as specific a degree of classification as may be desired.

PRINCIPLE OF HIERARCHY

4.10   Hierarchy in the DDC is expressed through both notation and structure.

4.11   *Notational hierarchy* is expressed by length of notation. As the following example shows, numbers at any given level are subordinate to a class whose notation is one digit shorter; coordinate with a class whose notation has the same number of significant digits; and superordinate to a class with numbers one or more digits longer. The underlined digits in the example below demonstrate this notational hierarchy:

6̲00	Technology (Applied sciences)
6̲3̲0	Agriculture and related technologies
6̲3̲6̲	Animal husbandry
6̲3̲6̲.7̲	Dogs
6̲3̲6̲.8̲	Cats

4.12   "Dogs" and "Cats" are more specific than (or subordinate to) "Animal husbandry"; they are equally specific as (or coordinate with) each other; and "Animal husbandry" is less specific than (or superordinate to) "Dogs" and "Cats."

4.13   Relationships among topics that violate notational hierarchy are indicated by notes and other devices. A *centered entry* often constitutes a major departure from notational hierarchy. A centered entry (so called because its numbers, heading, and notes appear in the center of the page) occurs when a span of numbers rather than a single number is used for a subject. In the DDC, centered entries are always flagged typographically by the symbol > in the number column.

4.14   *Structural hierarchy* means that aside from the ten main classes every topic is subordinate to and part of all the broader topics above it. The corollary is also true: whatever is true of the whole is true of the parts. This important concept is sometimes called *hierarchical force* (see **Glossary**). Any note regarding the nature of a class holds true for all the subordinate classes (including logically subordinate topics classed at coordinate numbers). Because of this, such notes are given only once—at the highest level of application. For example, the scope note at 700 applies to 730, to 736, and to 736.4. The words "Description, critical appraisal . . . " found in that scope note also govern 736.4 Wood [carving], which thus includes the critical appraisal of wood carving.

Classifying with the DDC

DETERMINING THE SUBJECT OF A WORK

5.1   Classifying a work properly depends upon determining the subject of the work in hand. Judicious use of the following sources is suggested:

(A)   The *title* is sometimes a succinct abstract of the subject of a work, but it must always be regarded with suspicion; *Zen and the Art of Motorcycle Maintenance* does not sound like a work on values, but it is.

(B) The *table of contents*, if genuinely descriptive, should display the main topics discussed.

(C) *Chapter headings* may make up for the lack of a table of contents. Chapter subheadings often prove useful.

(D) If an *introduction* (by someone other than the author) is provided, it should be perused. Such introductions are intended to assist the reader by indicating the subject of the work and suggesting the place of the work in the development of thought on the subject.

(E) A *preface* (or introduction by the author) usually provides original purposes and afterthoughts.

(F) A *bibliography, bibliographic footnotes,* and *references* are all valuable sources of information.

(G) *Cataloging copy* from centralized cataloging services is often helpful by providing subject headings, classification numbers, and notes. Such copy appears on the verso of U.S. and British books as part of Cataloging-in-Publication (CIP) data.

(H) The *text of the work* and *book reviews* can verify the conclusions reached by using the sources listed above.

(I) *Reference tools* or *knowledgeable people* often help define terms.

The steps above are necessary for works on technical, scientific, and historical matters; they are seldom necessary when classifying works of the imagination. In the DDC, works of the imagination are generally classified by literary form rather than by subject.

DETERMINING THE DISCIPLINE FOR A WORK

5.2   The classifier must then select the proper discipline, or field of study, of the work. Because discipline is the primary consideration in classifying a work, works that are used together are found together.

5.3   The guiding principle of the DDC is that a work is classed in the discipline for which it is intended, rather than the discipline from which the work derives. For example, a work by a zoologist on agricultural pest control should be classed in agriculture unless it concentrates on background biological data, in which case it should be classed in biology.

5.4   Once the subject has been determined, and information on the discipline has been found, the knowledgeable classifier will turn to the Schedules. The Summaries beginning on page ix of Volume 2 are a good means of mental navigation for beginners. The *Relative Index* may help by suggesting the disciplines in which a subject is normally treated (for a discussion of the Relative Index, see paragraphs 10.1-10.15).

5.5   Whether or not the Relative Index is used, the classifier must rely on the structure of the Classification, and various aids throughout, to arrive at the proper place to classify a work. Even the most promising Relative Index citations must be verified in the Schedules; the Schedules are the only place where all the information about coverage and use of the numbers may be found.

MORE THAN ONE SUBJECT

5.6   When two or more subjects are treated in a work, use the following guidelines:

(A)   Class a work dealing with interrelated subjects with the subject that is being acted upon. This is called the "rule of application," and takes precedence over any other rule. For instance, class an analytical work dealing with Shakespeare's influence on Keats with Keats.

(B)   Class a work on two subjects with the subject receiving fuller treatment.

(C)   If two subjects receive equal treatment, and are not used to introduce or explain one another, class the work with the subject whose number comes first in the DDC Schedules. This is called the "first-of-two rule." For example, a history dealing equally with the United States and Japan, in which the United States is discussed first and is given first in the title, is classed with the history of Japan because 952 precedes 973.

Occasionally, specific instructions are given to use numbers which do not come first in the Schedules, e.g., to class birds (598) and mammals (599) in 599, which is the comprehensive number for warm-blooded vertebrates. Also disregard the "first-of-two rule" when the two topics are the two major subdivisions of a subject. For example, water supply (628.1) and waste control (628.4) taken together constitute most of 628 Sanitary engineering; works on these topics are classed in 628 (not 628.1).

(D)   Class a work on three or more subjects that are all subdivisions of a broader subject in the first higher number that includes them all (unless one subject is treated more fully than the others). This is called the "rule of three." For example, a history of Portugal (946.9), Sweden (948.5), and Greece (949.5) is classed with the history of Europe (940).

MORE THAN ONE DISCIPLINE

5.7   Treating a subject from the point of view of more than one discipline is different from treating several subjects in one discipline. Use the guidelines in paragraphs 5.8-5.11.

5.8   Use the interdisciplinary number provided in the Schedules or Relative Index if one is given. An important consideration in using such an interdisciplinary number is that the work must contain significant material on the discipline in which the interdisciplinary number is found. For example, 305.231 (a sociology number) is provided for interdisciplinary works on child development. However, if a work that is interdisciplinary with respect to child development gives little emphasis to social development and a great deal of emphasis to the psychological and physical development of the child (155.4 and 612.65, respectively), class it in 155.4 (the first number in the Schedules of the next two obvious choices). In short, interdisciplinary numbers are not absolute; they are to be used only when applicable.

5.9   Class works not given an interdisciplinary number in the discipline that gives the subject fullest treatment. For example, a work dealing with both the scientific and the engineering principles of electrodynamics is classed in 537.6 if the engineering aspects are introduced primarily for illustrative purposes, but in 621.31 if the basic scientific theories are only preliminary to the author's exposition of engineering principles and practices.

5.10   When classifying interdisciplinary works, do not overlook the possibilities of main class 000 Generalities, e.g., 080 for a collection of interviews of famous people from various disciplines.

5.11   Any other situation is treated in the same fashion as those found above in the instructions at More Than One Subject (paragraph 5.6).

WHEN ALL ELSE FAILS

5.12   When several numbers have been found for the work in hand, and each seems as good as the next, the following considerations may prove useful:

5.13   *Rule of Zero*. Subdivisions beginning with zero should be avoided if there is a choice between 0 and 1-9 at the same point in the hierarchy of the notation. Similarly, subdivisions beginning with 00 should be avoided when there is a choice between 00 and 0. For example, a biography of an American Methodist missionary in China is classed in 266 Missions. The content of the work can be expressed in three different numbers:

266.0092	biography of a missionary
266.02373051	foreign missions of the United States in China
266.76092	biography of a United Methodist Church missionary

The last number is used since it has no zero at the fourth position.

5.14   *Table of last resort.* In the absence of any other rule, the following table (in order of preference) may be used with caution:

(1)   Kinds of things
(2)   Parts of things
(3)   Materials from which things, kinds, or parts are made
(4)   Properties of things, kinds, parts, or materials
(5)   Processes within things, kinds, parts, or materials
(6)   Operations upon things, kinds, parts, or materials
(7)   Instrumentalities for performing such operations

For example, surveillance by border patrols could be classed in either 363.285 Border patrols, or 363.232 Patrol and surveillance. Choose 363.285 since border patrols are a *kind* of police service, while patrol and surveillance are *processes* performed by police services. However, do not apply this table (or any other guidelines, for that matter) if it appears to flout the author's intention and emphasis.

How DDC 20 Is Arranged

6.1   DDC 20 is composed of six major parts in four volumes as follows:

Volume 1

(A)   Introduction: Introduces the user to the DDC and provides instructions on how to use it.

(B)   Tables: The seven numbered Tables provide notation that can be added to the class numbers in the Schedules to provide greater subject specificity.

(C)   Lists which compare Editions 19 and 20: Relocations and reductions; Comparative Tables for Music and British Columbia; Equivalence Tables for Music and British Columbia.

Volumes 2 and 3

(D)   Schedules: Knowledge organized from 001 to 999.

Volume 4

(E)   Relative Index: An alphabetical list of subjects found in the Schedules and Tables, including synonyms and selected terms in common use.

(F)   Manual: Provides advice for classifying in difficult areas, and describes policies and practices followed by the Decimal Classification Division at the Library of Congress. Information in the Manual is arranged by the numbers in the Schedules and Tables.

Key Features of the Schedules and Tables

SUMMARIES

7.1   Summaries provide an overview of the intellectual and notational structure of classes. Three types of summaries appear in the Schedules and Tables of the DDC:

(A)   The summaries of the Schedules as a whole are found at the front of the Schedules (Volume 2).

(B)   Single-level summaries in the Schedules and Tables provide an overview of classes (except main classes) that have subdivisions extending over more than two pages. For example, 649 Child rearing and home care of the sick and infirm has the following summary:

SUMMARY

649.1	**Child rearing**
.3	**Feeding**
.4	**Clothing and health**
.5	**Activities and recreation**
.6	**Training**
.7	**Moral and character training**
.8	**Home care of sick and infirm**

(C)   Multi-level summaries are provided for eight major divisions and the Area Tables for Europe and North America. See 370 Education for an example of a multi-level summary.

ENTRIES

7.2   Schedule and Table entries are composed of a DDC number in the number column (the column at the left margin), a heading describing the class that the number represents, and often one or more notes.

7.3   The first three digits of Schedule numbers (main classes, divisions, sections) appear only once in the number column (when first used). They are repeated at the top of each page where their subdivisions continue. Subordinate numbers (beginning with a decimal point) appear in the number column, with the initial three digits understood.   For example:

371   School organization and management; special education

>   Class here schools and school systems, school policy

>   Class government regulation, control, support of education in 379; schools of specific levels in 372-374, 378

.5   School discipline

>   Overseeing student conduct

>   *For classroom discipline, see 371.1024*

>   *See also 371.782 for school programs to reduce violence*

.59   Student participation in the maintenance of discipline

>   Examples: monitorial and prefectorial systems, honor systems, student government

7.4   Table numbers are given in full in the number column of the Tables, and are never used alone. They may be used only when appended or added to numbers from the Schedules. There are seven numbered Tables in DDC 20, as follows:

T1	Standard Subdivisions
T2	Geographic Areas, Historical Periods, Persons
T3	Subdivisions for Individual Literatures, for Specific Literary Forms
T3—A	Subdivisions for Works by or about Individual Authors
T3—B	Subdivisions for Works by or about More than One Author
T3—C	Notation to Be Added Where Instructed in Table 3-B and in 808-809
T4	Subdivisions of Individual Languages
T5	Racial, Ethnic, National Groups
T6	Languages
T7	Groups of Persons

Except for notation from Table 1 (which may be added to any number unless there is an instruction in the Schedules to the contrary), Table notations may be added only as instructed in the Schedules (for a detailed discussion of the use of the seven Tables, see paragraphs 8.3-8.14).

7.5   When a subordinate topic is a major part of a number, it is sometimes given as a part of the heading. For example:

—72	Middle America	Mexico
610	Medical sciences	Medicine

7.6   Some numbers in the Schedules and Tables are in brackets or parentheses. Numbers in brackets ([ ]) represent topics which have been relocated elsewhere or are unassigned. Bracketed numbers should never be used. Numbers and notes in parentheses provide options to standard practice (for a discussion of options, see paragraphs 11.1-11.4).

NOTES

7.7   Notes are important because they supply information that is not obvious in the notational hierarchy or in the heading with regard to order, structure, subordination, and other matters. The notes described below (A) define what is found in the class and its subdivisions; (B) identify topics in "standing room," i.e., topics with insufficient literature to have their own number; (C) describe what is found in other classes; and (D) explain changes in the Schedules and Tables. Other notes are described in the sections on number building (paragraphs 8.1-8.17), precedence and citation order (paragraphs 9.1-9.5), and options (paragraphs 11.1-11.4).

7.8 Notes in categories (A) and (C) have hierarchical force (i.e., are applicable to all the subdivisions of a particular number). Those in category (B) do not have hierarchical force except where noted.

(A) Notes That Describe What Is Found in a Class

7.9 *Definition* and *scope notes* indicate the meaning and scope of the class. For example:

> 004.7   Peripherals
>
>> Input, output, storage devices that work with a computer but are not part of its central processing unit or internal storage

7.10 *Former heading notes* are given only when a heading has been altered to such a degree that the new heading bears little or no resemblance to the old. There is usually no change in the meaning of the number. For example:

> 597.51   *Elopomorpha
>
>> Former heading: Apodes (Morays and true eels)

7.11 *Variant name notes* are used for synonyms or near synonyms. For example:

> 332.32   Savings and loan associations
>
>> Variant names: building and loan associations, home loan associations, mortgage institutions

7.12 *General aspects notes* enumerate aspects that are not found in the standard subdivisions of Table 1 but are applicable to all the subdivisions of a particular number. For example:

> 690   Buildings
>
>> General aspects: planning, analysis, engineering design, construction, destruction of habitable structures and their utilities

7.13 *Class-here notes* list major topics that are included in a class even though they may be broader or narrower than the heading, overlap it, or define another way of looking at essentially the same material. For example:

> 363.7   Environmental problems and services
>
> Class here environmental protection

Environmental protection overlaps 363.7 and is a large part of it. For instance, 363.728 Waste disposal is a service very important in environmental protection.

7.14   Class-here notes are also used to indicate where interdisciplinary and comprehensive works are classed. In the DDC, "interdisciplinary works" treat a subject from the perspective of more than one discipline. "Comprehensive works" treat a subject from various points of view within a single discipline. For example:

> 391   Costume and personal appearance
>
> > Class here interdisciplinary works on costume, clothing, fashion
>
> 025.213 Censorship
>
> > Class here comprehensive works on library policies and practices relating to intellectual freedom

(B) Notes That Identify Topics in Standing Room

7.15   Standing room notes identify topics that have "standing room" in the number where the note is found. Standing room numbers provide a location for topics with relatively few works written about them, but whose literature may grow in the future, at which time they may be assigned their own number. These notes are introduced by one of the following terms: "Including," "Contains," "Example(s)," and "Common names." Standard subdivisions cannot be added to topics in standing room, nor are other number-building techniques allowed.

7.16   *Including notes* list topics that are not obviously a part of the number. For example:

> 940.44   Air operations [of World War I]
>
> > Including antiaircraft defenses

Antiaircraft defenses are not strictly part of aerial operations, but it is logical to class them in the same number. Class 940.44 has eight subdivisions, one of which is 940.444 Events of 1914. However, the including note signals that works on antiaircraft defenses of 1914 are to be classed in 940.44, not 940.444.

7.17   *Contains notes* list all of the major components of the number that do not have their own subdivisions. For example:

> 583.976 Fagales
>
> > Contains Fagaceae (oak family), Betulaceae (birch family), Corylaceae
>
> —4955   Ionian islands
>
> > Contains Cephalonia, Corfu, Leukas, Zante nomes (provinces)

7.18   *Example notes* describe the contents of an abstract category when the specific contents may not be immediately apparent. For example:

    623.829   Hand-propelled and towed craft

            Examples: barges, canoes, coracles, lifeboats, rafts, rowboats, scows, towed canalboats

7.19   *Common name notes* are used only in biology. They list common English terms that are typical examples of the more carefully defined Latin taxonomic categories.

    595.7644 *Cantharoidea

            Common names: fireflies, glowworms, soldier beetle

When the English term covers most members of the taxonomic category, the instructions have hierarchical force.

(C) Notes on What Is Found in Other Classes

7.20   *Class-elsewhere notes* indicate where to class parts of a subject or topics related to it, if they do not class in subdivisions of the number at hand. All notes that begin with the word "class" are class-elsewhere notes, except when they begin with "class here."

    341.73   Peace and disarmament

            Class peaceful settlement of disputes in 341.52

    343.0944   Vehicles

            Class property laws relating to vehicles in 346.047, vehicle operation in 343.0946, vehicle product liability in 346.038, vehicle insurance in 346.086092, . . .

    028.1   Reviews

            Class reviews of computer programs in 005.30296; techniques of reviewing in 808.066028; reviews of works on a specific subject or in a specific discipline with the subject or discipline, e.g., reviews of works on chemistry 540, reviews of entertainment films 791.43, critical appraisal of literature 800

7.21   *See references* begin with the word "For." A see reference in the DDC signifies that the subject referred to is a part of the class from which the reference is made. For example:

    —4115 Highland Region

        Class here *Scottish Highlands

           For districts of Highland Region, see —4116–4119

7.22   *See-also references* refer to subjects tangentially related to the class in hand. They are reminders that minor differences in wording and context often imply major differences in classification. For example:

    641.22   Wine

              Class here grape wine

                 See also 641.23 for sake (rice wine)

(D) Notes Explaining Changes in the Schedules and Tables

7.23   *Revision notes* warn users that there have been changes in the subdivisions of a class since the previous edition. They range from a note explaining that there has been a complete revision (as with 780 Music) to a note explaining that a few minor boundary changes in the 1973 reorganization of Chile are not spelled out in subdivisions of notation 83 in Table 2. The revision note is always the first note under the heading of the class affected.

7.24   *Discontinued notes* indicate that a number from an earlier edition is no longer used, or that some part of the subject of a number has been moved to a shorter number. For example:

    523   Specific celestial bodies and phenomena

              Use of this number for comprehensive works on descriptive astronomy discontinued; class in 520

7.25   *Relocation notes* state that all or part of the contents of a number have been moved to a different number. For example:

    362.293   Narcotics

              Cocaine relocated to 362.298

    362.71   Direct relief

              Protection for abused and neglected children relocated to 362.768

The relocation note is usually restated at the new number, either in the heading or in the appropriate note:

    362.298   Cocaine [*formerly* 362.293]

    362.768   Remedial measures, services, forms of assistance

              Including protection for abused and neglected children [*formerly* 362.71]

Number Building

8.1 The classifier will sometimes find that to arrive at a precise number for a work it is necessary to build or synthesize a number that is not specifically printed in the Schedules. Such built numbers allow for greater depth of content analysis. They are used only when instructions in the Schedules make them possible (except for standard subdivisions which are discussed in paragraphs 8.3-8.4). Building numbers begins with a base number (always stated in the instruction note) to which another number is added.

8.2 Basically there are four ways to build numbers: (A) from standard subdivisions (Table 1); (B) from the other Tables (Tables 2-7); (C) from other parts of the Schedules; and (D) from add tables in the Schedules.

(A) Adding Standard Subdivisions from Table 1

8.3 Notation from Table 1 Standard Subdivisions may be added to any number in the Schedules unless there is a specific instruction to the contrary. A *standard subdivision* represents a recurring physical form (such as a dictionary, periodical, or index) or approach (such as history or research) and thus is applicable to any subject or discipline. Here are a few examples:

150.5	Periodical on psychology
203	Dictionary of Christianity
340.02573	Directory of American lawyers
507.8	Use of apparatus and equipment in the study and teaching of science, e.g., science fair projects
622.0285	Use of computers in mining
808.04205	Periodical on writing English

The number of zeros is always indicated in the Schedules; the classifier should never use more than one zero in applying a standard subdivision unless instructed to do so.

8.4 The most important caveat with respect to standard subdivisions is that in most cases they are added only for works that cover or *approximate the whole of the subject* of the number. For example, a work on black widow spiders of California should be classed in the number for spiders 595.44 (not 595.4409794, the number for spiders in California). The classifer should not attempt to specify California because black widow spiders do not approximate the whole universe of spiders in California. Further instructions on using Table 1 are found at the beginning of Table 1 and in the Table 1 section of the Manual.

(B) Adding from Tables 2–7

8.5   The classifier may be instructed to add a number from Tables 2–7 to a base number from the Schedules or to a number from a Table. A summary of the use of each Table follows.

8.6   *Table 2 Geographic Areas, Historical Periods, Persons.* Table 2 numbers are added through the use of one of several standard subdivisions from Table 1 (09, 025, 071, etc.), e.g., reading in the elementary schools of Australia is 372.40994 (372.4 reading in elementary schools + 09 Historical, geographical, persons treatment from Table 1 + 94 Australia from Table 2).

8.7   Area numbers are sometimes added directly to schedule numbers, but only when specified in a note.   For example:

> 373.3–373.9   Secondary education and schools by specific continents, countries, localities
>
> > Add to base number 373 notation 3–9 from Table 2, e.g., secondary schools of Australia 373.94

8.8   *Table 3 Subdivisions for Individual Literatures, for Specific Literary Forms.* These subdivisions are used only in class 800 as instructed, usually following numbers for specific languages in 810–890 (see the Table 3 section in the Manual).

8.9   *Table 4 Subdivisions of Individual Languages.* These subdivisions are used only in class 400 as instructed, following numbers for specific languages in 420–490 (see the Table 4 section in the Manual).

8.10   *Table 5 Racial, Ethnic, National Groups.* Table 5 numbers are added through the use of standard subdivision 089 from Table 1, e.g., Ceramic arts of Chinese artists the world over is 738.089951 (738 Ceramic arts + 089 [Racial, ethnic, national groups] + 951 Chinese from Table 5).

8.11   Numbers from Table 5 may also be added directly to schedule numbers, but only when specified in a note.   For example:

> 155.84   Specific racial and ethnic groups
>
> > Add to base number 155.84 notation 03–99 from Table 5, e.g., ethnopsychology of Afro-Americans 155.8496073

8.12   *Table 6 Languages.* The most important uses of these numbers are to provide the basis for building a specific language number in 490 (to which notation from Table 4 is sometimes added) and to provide the basis for building a specific literature number in 890 (to which notation from Table 3 is sometimes added). The numbers are also used in Table 2 under —175 Regions where specific languages predominate, and at various points in the Schedules.

8.13   *Table 7 Groups of Persons.* The most important use of these numbers is through the use of standard subdivision 024 from Table 1 (which indicates treatment of a specific subject for specific kinds of users). For example:

513.024694   Arithmetic for carpenters (513 Arithmetic + 024 Works for specific types of users from Table 1 + 694 carpenters from Table 7).

8.14   Another use involves the sociology of occupational groups. A note specifies that the numbers from Table 7 are added directly to the schedule number:

305.909–.999   Persons by occupation

Add to base number 305.9 notation 09–99 from Table 7, e.g., persons occupied with religion 305.92, postal workers 305.9383

The group of persons found in Table 7 may also be shown through the use of standard subdivision 088 (Specific occupational and religious groups), e.g., farmers in United States history 973.088631 (973 United States history + 088 with respect to occupational and religious groups + 631 farmers).

(C) Adding from Other Parts of the Schedules

8.15   There are many instructions to make a direct addition to a number from another part of the Schedules.   For example:

809.935   [Literature] Emphasizing subjects

Add to base number 809.935 notation 001–999, e.g., religious works as literature 809.9352, biography and autobiography as literature 809.93592

In this example, the 2 in 809.9352 comes from 200 Religion, the 92 in 809.93592 from 920 Biography, genealogy, insignia.

8.16   In many cases, part of a number may be added to another number upon instruction. For example:

373.011   Secondary education for specific objectives

Add to base number 373.011 the numbers following 370.11 in 370.112–370.118, e.g., education for social responsibility 373.0115

In this example, 5 comes from 370.115 Education for social responsibility. Sometimes numbers are taken from more than one place in the Schedules; in such cases the procedure for the second addition is the same as for the first.

(D) Adding from Tables Found in the Schedules

8.17 Add tables in the Schedules provide numbers to be added to designated Schedule numbers (identified by a footnote); these tables must be used only as instructed. For instance, the add table at 616.1–616.9 is used only for diseases tagged with an asterisk or in class-here notes under headings tagged with an asterisk. Notation from the add table, such as 061 Drug therapy, may be used for 616.521 Eczema (asterisked) but not for hives (found in an including note at 616.51 but not asterisked).

Number Building: Citation and Precedence Order

9.1 Precedence and citation order come into play when multiple aspects or characteristics of a subject (such as age, area, gender, historical periods, national origin) are provided for in the Classification, and a single work treats more than one of them.

CITATION ORDER

9.2 Citation order allows the classifier to build or synthesize a number using two or more aspects or characteristics as specified in instruction notes. Success in building a DDC number requires determining which characteristics apply to a specific work, and determining from the DDC the sequence in which the characteristics will be ordered.

9.3 Citation order is always carefully detailed in number-building instructions. For example:

> 330.91–.99   Geographical treatment (Economic geography)
>
> > Add to base number 330.9 notation 1–9 from Table 2, e.g., economic situation and conditions in France 330.944; then add 0 (except 00 for North and South America) and to the result add historical period numbers from appropriate subdivisions of 930–990, e.g., economic situation and conditions in France under Louis XIV 330.944033, in the United States during Reconstruction period 330.97308, in South America in 20th century 330.98003

The number-building instruction defines the limits of number building; in the above example the classifier can build no further than historical period because the instruction does not permit it.

PRECEDENCE ORDER

9.4 If there is no provision to show more than one of the aspects or characteristics, it is a matter of *precedence* (because one choice must be made among several characteristics). Precedence notes supply either an instruction or table establishing precedence. An example of a precedence instruction is found at 305.9:

> 305.9 Occupational and miscellaneous groups
>
>> Unless otherwise instructed, class complex subjects with aspects in two or more subdivisions of 305.9 in the number coming last, e.g., unemployed bibliographers 305.9091 (*not* 305.90694)

In this case, the base subject is a group of persons; the two characteristics are employment status and occupational status. The occupation of bibliographer (305.9091) comes after unemployed status (305.90694) in the classification hierarchy; following the instruction note, therefore, the characteristic which must be chosen is bibliographer (305.9091).

9.5 An example of a table indicating precedence order is found at 800:

> 800 Literature (Belles-lettres) and rhetoric
>
>> Unless other instructions are given, observe the following table of precedence, e.g., collections of drama written in poetry from more than one literature 808.82 (*not* 808.81)
>>
>>> Drama
>>> Poetry
>>> Fiction
>>> Essays
>>> Speeches
>>> Letters
>>> Miscellaneous writings
>>> Satire and humor

This list means that fiction written as poetry is classed in poetry, but humorous fiction is classed in fiction.

The Relative Index

10.1 The Relative Index is so called because it relates subjects to disciplines. In the Schedules, subjects are distributed among disciplines; in the Relative Index subjects are arranged alphabetically, with terms identifying the disciplines in which they are treated subarranged alphabetically under them. For example:

Hospitals	362.11
accounting	657.832 2
animal husbandry	636.083 2
architecture	725.51
armed forces	355.72

Hospitals (continued)	
Civil War (United States)	973.776
landscape architecture	712.7
liability law	346.031
Mexican war	973.627 5
social theology	291.178 321 1
Christianity	261.832 11
social welfare	362.11
South African War	968.048 7
Spanish-American War, 1898	973.897 5
United States Revolutionary War	973.376
Vietnamese War	959.704 37
War of 1812	973.527 5
World War I	940.476
World War II	940.547 6

In some cases the term implies rather than states the discipline. In the above listing, "armed forces" implies the discipline of military science, "Vietnamese War" the discipline of history.

HOW TO USE THE RELATIVE INDEX

10.2   Once the subject of the work in hand is determined and located in the Relative Index, the classifier may find it helpful to review the disciplines and DDC numbers listed in the Index under the subject term. In all cases, however, the discipline and number must be checked in the Schedules or Tables, where complete information about the number and what it includes can be found.

10.3   The Relative Index is primarily an index to the terminology of the DDC. If the term sought is not found, the classifier should try a broader term, e.g., Agricultural industries if Livestock industry is not found.

FORMAT AND ARRANGEMENT OF THE RELATIVE INDEX

10.4   Index entries are arranged alphabetically word by word, e.g., Birth order precedes Birthday, New York precedes Newark. Terms indented below the main headings are alphabetized in one group even though they may be a mixture of disciplines, topical subheadings, and words that, when combined with the main heading, form phrases or inverted phrases. Terms qualified by words in parentheses file following words that are not so qualified, e.g., Air transportation insurance (Inland marine) files after Air transportation insurance.

10.5   Class numbers are printed in groups of three for ease of reading and copying. The spaces are not part of the numbers and *do not represent convenient places to abridge the number.*

10.6   Both direct and indirect entries are used in the Index. For example:

Adult education
Cemeteries
   World War II
Programs
   television broadcasting

10.7   See-also references are used for synonyms, for references to broader terms (but only when three or more new numbers will be found at the broad term), and for references to related terms (which may provide only one or two new numbers).

10.8   Numbers drawn from Tables 1-7 are indicated by T1 through T7:

T1   Standard Subdivisions
T2   Geographic Areas, Historical Periods, Persons
T3   Subdivisions for Individual Literatures, for Specific Literary Forms (for use in 800)
   T3–A   Subdivisions for Works by or about Individual Authors
   T3–B   Subdivisions for Works by or about More than One Author
   T3–C   Notation to Be Added Where Instructed in Table 3–B and in 808–809
T4   Subdivisions of Individual Languages (for use in 400)
T5   Racial, Ethnic, National Groups
T6   Languages
T7   Groups of Persons

ORDER IN WHICH NUMBERS ARE DISPLAYED

10.9   The first class number displayed in an Index entry (the unindented term) is the number for interdisciplinary works. If the term also appears in the Tables, the Table numbers are listed next, followed by other aspects of the term. For example:

Young adults	305.235
	T1—083 5
	T7—055
etiquette	395.123
health	613.043 3
home care	649.125

INTERDISCIPLINARY NUMBERS

10.10   Interdisciplinary numbers are not provided in the Index in the following three instances:

(1)   When the unindented term is ambiguous, e.g.:

   Liquid phases
      liquid-state physics   530.424

(2)   When the unindented term has no disciplinary focus, e.g.:

Collecting	T1—075
biological specimens	579.6
descriptive research	001.433
museology	069.4
recreation	790.132

(3)   When the interdisciplinary number might be misleading, e.g.:

Poodle	
animal husbandry	636.72
see also Dogs	

Only the animal husbandry number for poodles is given in the Index because the literature does not warrant an interdisciplinary number for poodles in zoology.

For more information on interdisciplinary numbers, see paragraphs 5.8-5.12.

TERMS INCLUDED IN THE RELATIVE INDEX

10.11   The Relative Index contains terms found in the headings and notes of the Schedules and Tables, synonyms, and selected terms in common use.

10.12   The following types of names from Table 2 Geographic Areas are included in the Index: (A) names of countries; (B) names of the states and provinces of most countries; (C) names of the counties of the United States; (D) names of capital cities and other important municipalities; and (E) names of certain important geographic features.

10.13   Also included in the Relative Index are the following groups of persons: heads of state used to identify historical periods, e.g., Louis XIV; founders of religions, e.g., Muhammad; initiators of schools of thought, e.g., Adam Smith.

10.14   Place names and other proper names are generally given in the form specified by the second edition of the *Anglo-American Cataloguing Rules* (AACR2), based on the names established in the Library of Congress authority files. Where an established form of the name was not available, an AACR2 form was provided by the editors. Diacritics have been provided only for the following languages: Amharic, Chinese, Czech, Dutch, Finnish, French, German, Greek, Italian, Japanese, Portuguese, Spanish, and Urdu.

TERMS NOT INCLUDED IN THE RELATIVE INDEX

10.15   Terms usually not included in the Index are:

    (A)   Phrases (mostly in the arts) beginning with the adjective form of languages and countries, e.g., *American* short stories, *French* cooking, *Italian* architecture

    (B)   Phrases which contain general concepts represented by standard subdivisions such as education, statistics, laboratories, and management, e.g., Art *education*, Educational *statistics*, Medical *laboratories*, and Bank *management*.

Options

11.1   The recommended standard notation for English-language users of the DDC is provided in this Edition. At a number of places in the Schedules, options are provided for libraries whose needs are not met by the standard provisions.

11.2   Options are found in parentheses and, when they apply to a specific note, are indented under the note. International users find options particularly helpful. Some important options for these users include inserting letters in the notation or using briefer notation to give prominence to the religion, literature, and language of a particular country. Examples of inserting letters and using briefer notation are found at 292-299 Religions other than Christianity, as follows:

    (Options: To give preferred treatment or shorter numbers to a specific religion, use one of the following:

    (Option A: Class the religion in 230-280, its sources in 220, comprehensive works in 200; in that case class the Bible and Christianity in 298)

    (Option E: Place first by use of a letter or other symbol, e.g., Hinduism 2HO (preceding 220), or 29H (preceding 291 or 292); add to the base number thus derived, e.g., to 2H or to 29H, the numbers following the base number for the religion in 292-299, e.g., Shivaism 2H5.13 or 29H.513)

11.3   While options are printed in the DDC, they are not used in the centralized classification service supplied by the Library of Congress (except for a second number in law 340 and for biography), and are only occasionally supplied by other centralized services.

11.4   *Alphabetical-arrangement* and *chronological-arrangement notes* are not placed in parentheses, but are, in effect, options. They represent suggestions only; the material need not be arranged alphabetically or chronologically. An example of an alphabetical arrangement note is found at 005.133 Specific programming languages: Arrange alphabetically by name of programming language, e.g., COBOL.

Close and Broad Classification

12.1
One of the valuable features of the DDC notation is its adaptability to both close and broad classification. *Close classification* means that the content of a work is specified by notation to the fullest extent possible. *Broad classification* means that the notation places the work only in a broad class by the use of shorter notation. For instance, a work on French cooking is classed closely at 641.5944 (641.59 Cooking by place + 44 France from Table 2), broadly at 641.5 (cooking). Close classification is recommended for classes in which many works are found. How close or how broad the classification of a specific library should be depends on the size and diversity of the collection.

12.2
The classifier should reduce the number to produce a grouping useful to the patrons of the library. For instance, a work on the family behavior of siblings in Canadian society would be most usefully classed in 306.8750971 (the full number) in a research library with a large sociology collection, in 306.875 (sibling relationships) in a large public library, in 306.87 (intrafamily relationships) in a high school library. One aid to reducing DDC numbers is the segmentation device provided by the Decimal Classification Division of the Library of Congress and some other centralized cataloging services. A more detailed description of this device is provided in the Appendix to the Manual in Volume 4.

12.3
The classifier should never reduce the notation to less than the most specific three-digit number (no matter how small the library's collection). A number also must never be reduced so that it ends in a 0 anywhere to the right of the decimal point.

12.4
The abridged edition supplies reduction on a ready-made basis and is convenient for small libraries to use on that account. *Abridged Edition 12* is intended for school libraries and for public libraries with moderately developed collections. The editors have been guided in length of abridged edition numbers and inclusion of topics by the advice of a subcommittee of the Subject Analysis Committee of the American Library Association.

Book Numbers

13.1
Most libraries find that some sort of subarrangement of the classes of the DDC is necessary for the efficient shelving and retrieval of specific works.

13.2
A common filing device for small libraries is to give the first three letters of the main entry (usually the author) on the spine. For example:

937   Gibbon's *Decline and Fall of the Roman Empire*
Gib

Such libraries also often class all biography in a "B" collection, and all fiction in an "F" collection, still using three-letter book numbers for the subject and author, respectively. In the latter case a single letter may indicate a title by an author. For example:

B   A biography of Lincoln
Lin

F   *David Copperfield* by Dickens
DICd

13.3   For larger libraries and those expecting to grow, the Cutter-Sanborn tables (available from Libraries Unlimited, Littleton, Colorado) may be preferred over letters alone. Numbers from these tables provide the greater specificity needed to overcome the inevitable conflicts arising when several authors with the same last name write about the same topic, several biographies on the same person are acquired, several people with the same name write about an author, or the same person writes about an author more than once.

Selected Bibliography

14.1   Richard Hyman's *Shelf Access in Libraries* (Chicago: American Library Association, 1982) provides a full discussion of the role of library classification in accessing books. A good introduction to the nature and characteristics of specific classifications can be found in the most recent edition of A. C. Foskett's *The Subject Approach to Information* (Hamden, Conn.: Linnet Books, 1982) and in Lois M. Chan's *Cataloging and Classification* (New York: McGraw-Hill, 1981). For the history of the DDC, see John Comaromi's *The Eighteen Editions of the Dewey Decimal Classification* (Albany, N.Y.: Forest Press, 1976); a digested version appeared in *The Quarterly Journal of the Library of Congress* (33:311-331, October 1976), and was included in Bill Katz's *Library Lit. 8- ; the Best of 1977* (Metuchen: Scarecrow, 1978). For development of the Classification through Edition 19, see Jeanne Osborn's excellent account in *Dewey Decimal Classification, 19th Edition: A Study Manual* (Littleton, Colo.: Libraries Unlimited, 1982). Her work is valuable as a study guide to the structure of the DDC and as an introduction to the Classification, to the editorial practices that govern it, and to the publishing practices regarding it. Rosalind E. Miller's and Jane C. Terwillegar's *Commonsense Cataloging: A Cataloger's Manual*, 3rd edition (New York: The H.W. Wilson Co., 1983) provides a practical introduction to basic principles for the inexperienced classifier. For works on book numbers, see John Comaromi's *Book Numbers: A Historical Study and Practical Guide to Their Use* (Littleton, Colo.: Libraries Unlimited, 1981) and Donald Lehnus's *Book Numbers: History, Principles, and Applications* (Chicago: American Library Association, 1980).

Glossary

Add note.   A note instructing classifiers to append or add digits found elsewhere in the Classification to a given base number.

Add table.   *See* **Table (2).**

Application.   *See* **Rule of application.**

Approximate the whole.   When the topic of a work is approximately coextensive with the topic of a DDC heading, the work is said to "approximate the whole." The term is also used to characterize works that cover more than half the content of the heading, and works that cover representative examples from three or more subdivisions of a class. When a work approximates the whole of a subject, standard subdivisions may be added for it. Approximating the whole is the opposite of having standing room. *See also* **Standing room; Unitary term.**

Artificial digit.   A letter or other symbol used optionally as a substitute for digits 0–9 to provide a more prominent location or shorter notation for various languages, literatures, religions, cultures, ethnic groups.

Aspects.   Those approaches to a subject that belong to different disciplines, e.g., the *technical* or *economic* aspects of the manufacture of television sets.   *See also* **Discipline; Facet; Subject.**

Attraction.   *See* **Classification by attraction.**

Author number.   *See* **Book number.**

Base number.   A number to which other numbers are appended or added.   *See also* **Add note.**

Bibliographic classification.   A fully developed classification system that specifies categories down to the finest gradations; it provides the means to relate the categories and to specify in the notation all of the aspects and facets of a work. It may be used to organize classified subject catalogs as well as libraries.   *See also* **Aspects; Facet.**

Bibliothecal classification.   *See* **Library classification.**

Book number.   That part of a call number that designates a specific item within its class. A library using the Cutter-Sanborn system can have D548d indicate *David Copperfield* by Dickens (where D stands for the D of Dickens, 548 for "ickens", and d for *David Copperfield*).   *See also* **Call number.**

Broad classification.   The classification of works in broad categories even when more specific numbers are available, e.g., classing a cookbook of Mexican recipes in 641.5 Cooking (instead of in 641.5972 Mexican cooking).

Built number.   *See* **Number building.**

Call number.   A set of letters, numerals, or other symbols (in combination or alone) used by a library to identify a specific copy of a work. A call number consists of the class number, book number, and sometimes such other data as date, volume number, copy number, and location symbol.   *See also* **Book number; Class number.**

Centered entry. An entry representing a subject covered by a span of numbers, e.g., 372–374 Levels of education. The entry is called "centered" because the span of numbers is printed in the center of the page rather than in the number column on the left side of the page. Centered entries are identified by the symbol > in the number column.

Characteristic of division. *See* **Facet.**

Citation order. The order in which the facets or characteristics of a class are to be combined in number building. For example, juvenile court procedure in the United States is expressed in a notation built or synthesized from four facets: 345/.73/081/0269. The citation order for the discipline of law (34) is branch of the law (here criminal 5), jurisdiction (here United States 73), topic in the branch of law (here juvenile court 081), and standard subdivision (here 0269 procedure). Instructions for citation order are provided in the Schedules. When number building is not permitted or possible, an order of precedence with respect to the choice of facets or characteristics is provided. *See also* **Precedence order.**

Class. *(Noun)* (1) A group of objects exhibiting one or more common characteristics, usually identified by a specific notation. (2) One of the ten major groups numbered 0–9 of the DDC. Also known as **Main class.** (3) A subdivision of the DDC of any degree of specificity. *(Verb)* To assign a class number to an individual work. Also called **Classify.**

Class-elsewhere note. A note instructing the classifier to class parts of a class or topics related to it in numbers that are not subdivisions of the number at hand.

Class-here note. An instruction identifying subjects (both broader and narrower than the number) that are to be classed in the given number and in its subdivisions. The narrower subjects identified in class-here notes are said to "approximate the whole." *See also* **Approximate the whole.**

Class number. Notation that designates the class to which a given item belongs. *See also* **Call number.**

Classification. A logical system for the arrangement of knowledge.

Classification by attraction. The classification of a specific aspect of a subject in an inappropriate discipline, usually because the appropriate discipline contains no explicit provision for the subject in question. For example, in the 18th and earlier editions of the DDC, social services related to water pollution were not provided for in 363, so works on this subject were attracted to the engineering numbers in 628.168.

Classified catalog. A catalog arranged according to the notational order of a classification system (rather than alphabetically).

Classify. (1) To arrange a collection of items according to a classification system. (2) To assign a class number to an individual item. Also called *class.*

Close classification. (1) A classification providing for minute subdivision of topics. Also called **Bibliographic classification.** (2) Arrangement of works in conformity with the provisions of such a scheme.

Comparative table.   When complete or extensive revision has taken place, a comparative table lists in alphabetical order selected topics with their current number and the number used in the previous edition. Found in this edition on pages 496-505 in Volume 1.   *See also* **Equivalence table; Revision.**

Complete revision.   *See* **Revision.**

Complex subject.   A complex subject as used in the DDC is a subject that has more than one characteristic. For example, the subject "unemployed bibliographers" has more than one characteristic (employment status and occupation) and is therefore a complex subject.   *See also* **Precedence order.**

Comprehensive number.   A number (often identified by a comprehensive works note) that covers all the components of the subject treated within that discipline. The components may be in a span of consecutive numbers, e.g., Sociology 301–307 (comprehensive number 301); or distributed in the Classification, e.g., medical diagnosis 616.075, with diagnosis of specific conditions scattered in 616.1–618.   *See also* **Interdisciplinary number.**

Cross classification.   Placing works on the same subject in two different class numbers tends to occur when items deal with two or more characteristics of a subject in the same class. Instructions in the Schedules should prevent the inconsistency.

Cross reference.   *See* **Class-elsewhere note; See-also references; See references.**

DDC.   Dewey Decimal Classification.

Decimal point.   The dot that follows the third digit in a DDC number. In strict usage the word "decimal" is not accurate; however, common usage is followed in this edition's explanatory material.

Discipline.   An organized field of study or branch of learning, e.g., 200 Religion, 530 Physics, 364 Criminology. In the DDC, subjects are arranged by disciplines.   *See also* **Subject.**

Discontinued number.   A number from the preceding edition that is no longer used because the subject represented by the number is now classed in a more general number. Numbers are usually discontinued because they identify a topic with negligible current literature or represent a distinction no longer valid in the literature or common perception of the field.   *See also* **Schedule reduction.**

Division.   The first level of subdivision of the ten main classes, represented by the first two digits in the notation, e.g., 53 in 530. More often than not the division is a discipline, e.g., 530 Physics.   *See also* **Main class; Section.**

Entry.   (1) In the Schedules and Tables: a self-contained unit consisting of a number or span of numbers, a heading, and often one or more notes. (2) In the Relative Index: a term or phrase followed by a DDC number.

Equivalence table.   When a complete revision has taken place, an equivalence table lists in numerical order the classes of the current edition with the equivalent number in the former edition (and vice versa). Found in this edition on pages 506-514 in Volume 1.   *See also* **Comparative table; Revision.**

Expansion.   The development of a class in the Schedules or Tables to provide further subdivisions.   *See also* **Revision.**

Extensive revision.   *See* **Revision.**

Facet.   Any of the various categories into which a given class may be divided, e.g., division of the class "people" by the categories race, age, education, language spoken, and so on. Each category contains terms based on a single characteristic of division, e.g., children, adolescents, and adults are characteristics of division of the "ages" category.   *See also* **Citation order.**

First-of-two rule.   The rule instructing that works on two mutually exclusive subjects, whether in adjacent or widely separated numbers, are to be classed in the number coming first in the Schedules or Tables.

Heading.   The word or phrase used as the caption of a given class.

Hierarchical force.   The principle that the attributes of a class that are defined in the heading and in certain basic notes apply to all the subdivisions of the class and to all other classes to which reference is made.

Hierarchy.   The arrangement of a classification system from general to specific. In the Dewey Decimal Classification, the degree of specificity of a class is usually indicated by the length of the notation and the corresponding depth of indention of the heading.

Including note.   An enumeration of topics that are not obviously a part of the class and that have not been given separate provision. Standard subdivisions may not be added to the numbers for these topics.   *See also* **Standing room.**

Interdisciplinary number.   A number (often identified by an interdisciplinary works note) used for works covering a subject from the perspective of more than one discipline, e.g., the interdisciplinary number for marriage is 306.81 in Sociology. *See also* **Comprehensive number.**

Library classification.   A classification designed to arrange the physical items of a library collection. Also called *bibliothecal classification.*

Literary warrant.   Justification for the appearance of a class or a topic in the Schedules, Tables, or Index, based on the existence of a literature on the topic.

Main class.   One of the ten major subdivisions of the Dewey Decimal Classification, represented by the first digit in the notation, e.g., the 3 in 300.   *See also* **Division; Section.**

Manual.   A guide to the use of the DDC that is made up primarily of extended discussions of problem areas in the application of the Classification. In the Schedules and Tables, see-Manual notes indicate where relevant information is available in the Manual. The Manual is found in Volume 4.

Notation.   Numerals, letters, and/or other symbols used to represent the main and subordinate divisions of a classification scheme. In the DDC, Arabic numerals are used to represent the classes, e.g., notation —07 from Table 1 and 511.3 from the Schedules.

Number building.   Making a given Schedule number appropriately specific by adding notation from the Tables or other parts of the Schedules.   *See also* **Citation order.**

Number column.   The column of numbers printed in the left margin of the Schedules and Tables, and to the right of the alphabetical entries in the Relative Index.

Order of precedence.   *See* **Precedence order.**

Phoenix schedule.   No longer used.   *See* **Revision** *(Complete revision).*

Precedence order.   The order indicating which one of two or more numbers is to be chosen when the numbers represent different characteristics of a subject that cannot be shown in full by number building. A note (sometimes containing a table of precedence) always indicates which characteristic is to be selected for works covering more than one characteristic. When the notation can be synthesized to show two or more characteristics, it is a matter of citation order.   *See also* **Citation order.**

Precedence table.   *See* **Precedence order.**

Reduction of Schedules.   *See* **Schedule reduction.**

Relative Index.   The index to the DDC, called "Relative" because it relates subjects to disciplines. In the Schedules, subjects are arranged by disciplines. In the Relative Index, subjects are listed alphabetically; indented under them is an alphabetical list of the disciplines in which they are found.

Relocation.   The shifting of a topic in a new edition of the DDC from one number to another number which differs from the old number in respects other than length, e.g., the relocation of cocaine from 362.293 to 362.298.

Reuse of numbers.   A total change in the meaning of a given number from one edition to another. Normally numbers are reused only in complete revisions or when the reused number has been vacant for two consecutive editions.

Revision.   The result of editorial work that alters the text of any class of the DDC. There are four degrees of revision: *Routine revision* is limited to updating terminology, clarifying notes, and providing modest expansions. *Substantial revision* involves a class that requires major redefinitions and significant relocations. In this edition, the revision of 628 Sanitary and municipal engineering is an example of substantial revision. *Extensive revision* involves a major reworking of subdivisions but leaves the main outline of the schedule as it was. The changes are shown only through a comparative table rather than through relocation notes in the schedule or table affected. There are no extensive revisions in Edition 20. *Complete revision* (formerly called a *phoenix*) is a new development; the base number remains as in the previous edition, but virtually all subdivisions are changed. In this edition, only 780 Music and T2—711 British Columbia are complete revisions.   *See also* **Comparative table.**

Routine revision.   *See* **Revision.**

Rule of application.   The rule instructing that works about the application of one subject to a second subject are classified with the second subject.

Rule of three.   The rule instructing that works that give equal treatment to three or more subjects that are all subdivisions of a broader subject are classified in the first higher number that includes all of them.

Scatter note. A class-elsewhere or relocation note that does not lead to a single location, but rather to multiple locations, e.g., at 028.1 Reviews, the classifier is instructed to class reviews of works on a specific subject or in a specific discipline with the subject or discipline.

Schedule reduction. The elimination of certain provisions of a previous edition, resulting in discontinued numbers. *See also* **Discontinued number.**

Schedules. The series of DDC numbers 001–999, their headings, and instructions or notes. They are the core of the DDC and constitute Volumes 2 and 3.

Section. The third level of subdivision in the Classification, represented by a three-digit notation not ending in zero, e.g., 629. *See also* **Division; Main class.**

See-also references. Notes in the Schedules and Tables to classes that are tangentially related to the number and that therefore might be confused with it. See-also references in the Relative Index may be to a broader term, or simply to any related term.

See references. A note in the Schedules and Tables introduced by the word ''for'' that leads from the number in which a subject is classed to component parts of the subject located elsewhere. *See also* **Class-elsewhere note.**

Separates. Extensive segments of the DDC that are published between editions.

Standard subdivisions. Subdivisions found in Table 1 that represent frequently recurring physical forms (dictionaries, periodicals) or approaches (history, research) applicable to any subject or discipline. They may be added to any number in the Schedules unless there are instructions to the contrary.

Standing room. A term which characterizes topics that are considerably less extensive in scope than their class numbers; standard subdivisions cannot be added to these topics nor are other number-building techniques allowed. Topics listed in notes beginning with ''contains,'' ''examples,'' ''including,'' and (usually) ''Common names'' have standing room in the class number, as do other minor topics which are not named. To have standing room is the opposite of approximating the whole. *See also* **Approximate the whole.**

Subject. An object of study. It may be a person or a group of persons, a thing, place, process, activity, abstraction, or any combination of these. It is often studied in more than one discipline, e.g., gold is studied in prospecting, mineralogy, jewelry-making, minting coins, economics, and dentistry. A class may or may not be a subject. In the DDC subject is contrasted with **Discipline.** Also called *topic.*

Substantial revision. *See* **Revision.**

Summary. A listing of the chief subdivisions of a class. Summaries provide a brief overview of the structure of the class, and are printed immediately under the entry for the class. For the whole Classification, the first, second, and third summaries (of main classes, divisions, and sections) appear in Volume 2.

Synthesis of notation. *See* **Number building.**

Table. In the DDC, a table of numbers that may be added to other numbers in the Schedules to make a class number appropriately specific to the work being classified. The numbers found in a table are never used alone. There are two kinds: (1) Tables 1–7 (always referred to with a capital T) appearing in Volume 1 and representing such concepts as geographical area, language, ethnic group, and standard subdivisions. (2) Sets of tabulated numbers found in add notes under specific numbers throughout the Schedules and occasionally in Tables 1–7. These tabulated numbers are called *add tables*.

Table of precedence. *See* **Precedence order.**

Topic. *See* **Subject.**

Unitary term. A heading or term in a note containing two or more words joined by "and" that have such overlapping meanings that the literature on them is unlikely to be clearly separated. In the DDC, unitary terms are treated as single subjects, and standard subdivisions may be added for the whole term or for either of its parts. (That is, each part of a unitary term is regarded as approximating the whole.) The following are examples of unitary terms:

Religious congregations and orders
Economic development and growth
Disputes and conflicts between states
Educational tests and measurements

The following are not considered unitary terms:
Culture and institutions
Marriage and family
Interest and discount
See also **Approximate the whole.**

Index to the Introduction and Glossary

References to the Introduction are identified by paragraph numbers. References to the alphabetically arranged Glossary are identified by G.

Publishing History of the Dewey Decimal Classification

EDITION	DATE	PAGES	COPIES	EDITOR
1	1876	44	1,000	Melvil Dewey
2	1885	314	500	Melvil Dewey
3	1888	416	500	Melvil Dewey
4	1891	466	1,000	Evelyn May Seymour
5	1894	467	2,000	Evelyn May Seymour
6	1899	511	7,600	Evelyn May Seymour
7	1911	792	2,000	Evelyn May Seymour
8	1913	850	2,000	Evelyn May Seymour
9	1915	856	3,000	Evelyn May Seymour
10	1919	940	4,000	Evelyn May Seymour
11	1922	988	5,000	Jennie Dorkas Fellows
12	1927	1,243	9,340	Jennie Dorkas Fellows
13	1932	1,647	9,750	Jennie Dorkas Fellows
14	1942	1,927	15,632	Constantin Mazney
15	1951	716	11,200	Milton J. Ferguson
15 rev	1952	927	11,045	Godfrey Dewey
16	1958	2,439	31,011	Benjamin A. Custer
17	1965	2,153	38,677	Benjamin A. Custer
18	1971	2,718	52,892	Benjamin A. Custer
19	1979	3,385	51,129	Benjamin A. Custer
20	1989	3,388		John P. Comaromi

Tables

Use of the Tables

These are auxiliary tables, and are used only in conjunction with the Schedules. In some instances the numbers from one table may be added to those of another table, but in all cases the numbers from one or a combination of tables are to be used only with appropriate numbers from the Schedules.

The dash preceding each number merely shows that the number never stands alone. The dash is omitted when the table number is added to a schedule number to make a complete class number.

Instructions in the use of a particular table precede it. Important supplemental instructions for Tables 1, 3, and 5 are found in the Manual in Volume 4.

A number in square brackets [ ] is not currently in use.

A number in parentheses ( ) is an option to standard usage.

Table 1. Standard Subdivisions

The following notation is never used alone, but may be used as required with any number from the schedules, e.g., classification (—012 in this table) of modern Indic languages (491.4): 491.4012. When adding to a number from the schedules, always insert a decimal point between the third and fourth digits of the complete number

If at any given number there are subdivisions having a notation beginning with 0 for a special purpose, use 001–009 for standard subdivisions; if notations beginning with 0 and 00 both have special purposes, use 0001–0009 for standard subdivisions. In a few instances, e.g., at 535.01, there are contrary instructions

Unless other instructions are given, class works to which two or more standard subdivisions are applicable according to the following table of precedence, e.g., education and research for specific types of users —07 (*not* —024):

Special topics	—04
Persons	—092
Auxiliary techniques and procedures; apparatus, equipment, materials	—028
Drafting illustrations	—0221
Education, research, related topics	—07
(*except* —074, —075, —076, —077)	
Management	—068
Philosophy and theory	—01
(*except* —0112, —014)	
The subject as a profession, occupation, hobby	—023
Patents and identification marks	—027
Commercial miscellany	—029
Standards	—0218
History and description with respect to kinds of persons	—08
Treatment by specific continents, countries, localities; extraterrestrial worlds	—093–099
Treatment by areas, regions, places in general	—091
Historical periods	—0901–0905
Forecasting and forecasts	—0112
Works for specific types of users	—024
Museums, collections, exhibits	—074
Museum activities and services Collecting	—075
Review and exercise	—076
Programmed texts	—077
Miscellany	—02
(*except* —0218, —0221, —023, —024, —027, —028, —029)	
Organizations	—0601–0609
Language (Terminology) and communication	—014
Dictionaries, encyclopedias, concordances	—03
Historical and geographical treatment (without subdivision)	—09
Serial publications	—05

See Manual at Table 1

SUMMARY

—01   Philosophy and theory

Class here methodology

Class interdisciplinary works on philosophy in 100

See Manual at T1—01

—011   Systems

Class here operations research [*formerly* —072], models (simulation) [*formerly* —0724]

Add to base number —011 the numbers following 003 in 003.1–003.8, e.g., computer modeling and simulation —0113, forecasting and forecasts —0112; however, class forecasting and forecasts for a subject in a specific historical period or area with the subject in the period or area, adding notation 01 from the tables under —0901–0905 and —093–099, e.g., forecasts of U.S. agricultural exports 382.41097301

Class models (simulations) in study and teaching in —078

See Manual at T1—0113 vs. T1—0285; 003, T1—011 vs. 510, T1—0151

—012   Classification

—013   Value

—014   Language (Terminology) and communication

Including content analysis

Class interdisciplinary works on communication in 302.2, on language in 400, subject headings and thesauruses in information retrieval in 025.49001–025.49999

For dictionaries, see —03

See Manual at T1—014 vs. T1—03; T4—864 vs. T1—014

—[014 1]   Communication

Number discontinued; class in —014

—014 2   Etymology

—[014 7]   Nonlinguistic communication

Number discontinued; class in —014

—014 8   Abbreviations and symbols

> Class interdisciplinary works on abbreviations in 411, on symbols in 302.222; interdisciplinary dictionaries of abbreviations in 413.1, of symbols in 302.222

—015   Scientific principles

> Use of science to analyze and describe the subject, to support or attack its validity, to carry out operations in the subject, to provide information needed in a subject

> Add to base number —015 the numbers following 5 in 510–590, e.g., mathematical techniques —0151 [*formerly also* —072]

> The terms "scientific method" and "statistical method" refer to research methods, and are classed in —072

> *For psychological principles, see* —019

> *See Manual at T1—015 vs. T1—024; 003, T1—011 vs. 510, T1—0151; 510, T1—0151 vs. 004–006, T1—0285; 519.5, T1—015195 vs. 001.422, T1—072*

—(016)   Bibliographies, catalogs, indexes

> (Optional number; prefer 016)

> Preferred number for indexes relocated to 016

—[018]   Methodology

> Number discontinued; class in —01

—019   Psychological principles

> Use for applications of individual psychology only, not for applications of social psychology

> Class social psychology in 302, interdisciplinary works on psychology in 150

> *See Manual at T1—019*

—02   **Miscellany**

SUMMARY

—020 2   Synopses and outlines

> Examples: chronological outlines

> Use only for genuine synopses and outlines, not for works called synopses or outlines that are regular treatises or introductions to a subject

> Use of this number for manuals discontinued; class in 001–999 without adding notation from Table 1

—020 7   Humorous treatment

> Use only when the humor goes beyond what is normally used to enliven a subject, i.e., when an author is making fun of a subject or its practitioners without simultaneously explaining its serious import

> *See Manual at T3B—7 vs. T3A—8 + 02, T3B—802, T3B—8 + 02, T3B—807, T3B—8 + 07, T1—0207*

—020 8   Audiovisual treatment

—021   Tabulated and related materials

> Including statistics of a specific demographic topic [*formerly* 312], general statistics, statistical graphs

> Class interdisciplinary collections of statistics in 310

—021 2   Tables, formulas, specifications

> Use of this number for statistics discontinued; class in —021

—021 6   Lists, inventories, catalogs

> Not provided for elsewhere

> Class lists and catalogs of products and services offered for sale, lease, or free distribution in —029, directories of persons and organizations in —025, catalogs of collections and exhibits in —074, price trends for collectors in —075, bibliographic catalogs in 016

—021 8   Standards

> Class here standards in specific times and places [*formerly* —09]

> Add to base number —0218 notation 1 or 3–9 from Table 2, e.g., standards in Israel —02185694

> Class interdisciplinary works on standards in 602.18

> *For specifications, see —0212*

—022   Illustrations, models, miniatures

> Class humorous cartoons in —0207, statistical graphs in —021

—022 1   Drafting illustrations

> Class here drafting illustrations in specific times and places [*formerly* —09]

> Class interdisciplinary works on drafting illustrations in 604.2

—022 2   Pictures and related illustrations

> Class here drawings, pictorial charts and designs, sketches
>
> *See Manual at T1—0222 vs. T1—0223*

—022 3   Maps and related forms [*formerly* 912.1001–912.1889], plans, diagrams

> Class interdisciplinary maps and related forms, maps and related forms of general geography and travel regardless of area in 912; historical atlases in 911
>
> *See Manual at T1—0222 vs. T1—0223; T1—0223 vs. 912*

—022 8   Models and miniatures

> Class simulation models in —011

—023   The subject as a profession, occupation, hobby

> Class here vocational guidance, choice of vocation, career opportunities, occupational specialties, professional relationships; the subject as a profession, occupation, hobby for specific kinds of persons
>
> Add to base number —023 notation 1 or 3–9 from Table 2, e.g., the subject as a profession in Great Britain —02341
>
> Class interdisciplinary works on professional relationships in 331.7; on vocational guidance, choice of vocation, career opportunities, occupational specialties in 331.702; on hobbies in 790.13

—024   Works for specific types of users

> Add to base number —024 notation 03–99 from Table 7, e.g., works for engineers —02462
>
> *See Manual at T1—015 vs. T1—024; T1—024; T1—024 vs. T1—08*

—025   Directories of persons and organizations

> Class here directories of public officials and employees of specific occupational categories [*formerly also* 351.2]; membership lists containing directory information, e.g., employment and education
>
> Add to base number —025 notation 1 or 3–9 from Table 2, e.g., directories of Ohio —025771
>
> Class directories giving biographical information in —0922
>
> *See also —029 for directories of products and services*

—(026)   Law

> (Optional number; prefer 340)
>
> Add to base number —026 notation 1 or 3–9 from Table 2, e.g., law of Australia —02694
>
> A special development of —026 covering treaties and cases in international law is given under 341.026 for use with subdivisions in 341.2–341.7; another special development of —026 covering laws, regulations, cases, procedures, courts in noninternational law is given in the centered entry at 342–347 for use in subdivisions of 342–347

—027   Patents and identification marks

—027 2   Patents

Add to base number —0272 notation 1 or 3–9 from Table 2, e.g., patents of Japan —027252

Class interdisciplinary collections of patents in 602.72, interdisciplinary works on patents in 346.0486

>   —027 5–027 8   Identification marks

Class comprehensive works in —027

—027 5   Trademarks and service marks

Use 929.9 for interdisciplinary works; however, use 602.75 for comprehensive works on trademarks generally found on products rather than identifying services

—027 7   Ownership marks

—027 8   Artists' and craftsmen's marks

Class interdisciplinary works in 700.278

—028   Auxiliary techniques and procedures; apparatus, equipment, materials

Use of this number for basic techniques and procedures of the subject discontinued; class in 001–999 without adding notation from Table 1

Statistical method relocated to —072, laboratory manuals to —078

For drafting illustrations, see —0221

See Manual at T1—028

—028 5   Data processing   Computer applications

The current subdivisions of this standard subdivision were separately published in 1985

Class here data processing in research [*formerly* —072]

Unless it is redundant, add to base number —0285 the numbers following 00 in 004–006, e.g., digital microcomputers —0285416, but digital computers —0285 (not —02854)

Class interdisciplinary works in 004, computer modeling and simulation in —0113

See Manual at T1—0113 vs. T1—0285; T1—0285; T1—0285 vs. T1—068; 510, T1—0151 vs. 004–006, T1—0285

—028 7   Testing and measurement

Example: testing in research [*formerly* —072]

Class here laboratory manuals for testing

Class interdisciplinary works on measurement in 530.8, technology of testing and measuring instruments in 681.2, educational testing in —076

—028 8   Maintenance and repair

Use this subdivision only with numbers denoting fabrication, manufacture, construction, installation, not with numbers denoting use, operation, or application when these are different, e.g., maintenance and repair of textile manufacturing machinery 681.76770288 (*not* 677.02850288), of tools 621.900288

Class interdisciplinary works on maintenance and repair in 620.0046

See also —0682 for management of maintenance

—028 9   Safety measures

Use only for the technology of safety. Do not use in 300 except as instructed under 351.783 and 352.3. For other social science aspects of safety use regular subdivisions of safety in 363.1 and 363.3

Class interdisciplinary works on safety in 363.1, on personal safety in 613.6, on safety engineering in 620.86

—029   Commercial miscellany

Class here listings of products and services offered for sale, lease, or free distribution

House organs relocated to —05, investment prospectuses to 332.6

Class interdisciplinary commercial miscellany in 380.1029

See also —074 for listings of noncommercial collections and exhibits

See Manual at T1—0294 vs. T1—074

—029 4   Trade catalogs and directories

Listing of products and services without independent evaluations or comparisons

Including commercial circulars and advertisements

Class here product directories, price lists, listings of free products and services, prospectuses of products for sale or lease

Add to base number —0294 notation 4—9 from Table 2 for the area in which the products are sold, e.g., product directories for Mexico —029472

Class catalogs of bibliographic materials in 010, noncurrent offers for sale used primarily to illustrate civilization and customs of an earlier period in 909 and 930—990

See also —0296 for catalogs and directories with independent evaluations or comparisons

See Manual at T1—0294 vs. T1—074

—029 6   **Buyers' guides and consumer reports**

Listings of products and services with independent evaluations or comparisons

Including evaluations of single products

Add to base number —0296 notation 4–9 from Table 2 for the area in which products are sold, e.g., buyers' guides for Canada —029671

Class evaluation and purchasing manuals in —0297

—029 7   **Evaluation and purchasing manuals**

Manuals that explain how to evaluate and purchase products and services but do not contain listings of what is available

Class here price trends

Class interdisciplinary evaluation and purchasing manuals in 381.33; listings of products and services with independent evaluations or comparisons in —0296, without independent evaluations and comparisons in —0294; price trends for collectors —075

See also —0687 for procurement management

—029 9   **Estimates of labor, time, materials**

Class here quantity surveying

Class interdisciplinary works on quantity surveying in 692.5

—03   **Dictionaries, encyclopedias, concordances**

Class interdisciplinary dictionaries in 413, interdisciplinary encyclopedias in 030

See Manual at T1—014 vs. T1—03

—[032–039]   **By language**

Numbers discontinued; class in —03

—04   **Special topics**

Use this subdivision only when it is specifically set forth in the schedules. Add other standard subdivisions —01–09 to it and its subdivisions as required, e.g., participatory democracy in France 323.0420944

—05   **Serial publications**

Class here house organs [*formerly* —029]

Class interdisciplinary serial publications in 050; specific kinds of serial publications with the kind, e.g., directories in serial form —025, administrative reports of organizations —06

—06   **Organizations and management**

>   —060 1–060 9   Organizations

       General aspects: history, charters, regulations, membership lists, administrative proceedings and reports

       Class comprehensive works in —06; interdisciplinary organizations in 060; organizations engaged in education, research, and related topics in —07; business enterprises in 338.7; government administrative organizations in 350; membership lists with directory information in —025; nonadministrative proceedings and reports in main number

       See Manual at T1—0601–T1—0609; T1—0601–T1—0609 vs. T1—072

—060 1   International organizations

       Do not use for guides to national organizations of the world; class in —06

—060 3–060 9   National, state, provincial, local organizations

       Add to base number —060 notation 3–9 from Table 2, e.g., national organizations in France —06044

—068   Management

       The science and art of conducting organized enterprises and projects

       Do not use —068 for management in the sense of carrying out the ordinary activities of a subject, e.g., management of the classroom (when the reference is to teaching) 371.1024 (*not* 371.10068)

       (Option: Class management of specific enterprises in 658.9)

       Class interdisciplinary works in 658

       See Manual at T1—0285 vs. T1—068; 338.09 vs. 338.6042, 332.67309, 346.07, 658.11, 658.21, T1—068; 350–354 vs. 658, T1—068; 658 and T1—068; 658, T1—068 vs. 302.35

—068 1   Organization and financial management

       Including initiation of business enterprises

       Class procurement of equipment and facilities in —0682, of materials in —0687; management of wages and salaries in —0683

       For internal organization, see —0684

       See Manual at 658.15 and T1—0681

—068 2   Plant management

       Class here comprehensive works on energy management

       Including equipment and utilities; maintenance

       Class a specific aspect of energy management with the aspect, e.g., energy conservation in production management —0685

       See also —0288 for technology of maintenance

       See Manual at 647.96–647.99 vs. 658.2, T1—0682; 658.2 and T1—0682

—068 3   Personnel management

Including selection [*formerly also* 658.31129]; management of fringe benefits, in-service training and residency, wages and salaries

Class interdisciplinary works on labor relations in 331.88

See also —07155 for in-service training and residency, 331.21 for wages, 331.255 for fringe benefits

See Manual at 658.3 and T1—0683; 658.3 vs. 331

—068 4   Executive management

Including internal organization, safety management

Class a specific aspect of safety management with the subject, e.g., personnel safety —0683

—068 5   Management of production

Class factory operations engineering in 670.42

See Manual at 658.5 and T1—0685

—068 7   Management of materials

Examples: physical distribution, procurement of office equipment

See also —0297 for evaluation and purchasing manuals

See Manual at 658.7 and T1—0687

—068 8   Management of distribution (Marketing) [*formerly also* 658.809]

Including marketing research [*formerly also* 658.838]; personal selling, retail marketing [*both formerly also* 658.89]

Do not use for the results of market research; class in 380–382

Class financial aspects of marketing management in —0681

For physical distribution, see —0687; advertising, 659.1

See Manual at 380.1 vs. 658.8; 658.8 and T1—0688; 658.8, T1—0688 vs. 659

—07   **Education, research, related topics**

Including training teachers, practice teaching

Class here subject-oriented study programs, comprehensive works on resources for study and teaching

Do not use for textbooks; class textbooks in 001–999 without adding notation from Table 1

Class interdisciplinary works on education in 370; specific resources not provided for here with the subject, e.g., directories —025, bibliographies 016, libraries 026

See Manual at T1—07 vs. 016, 026; 407, T1—07 vs. 410.7, 418.007, T4—8007, 401.93

SUMMARY

—070 1–070 9	**Geographical treatment**
—071	**Schools and courses**
—072	**Research**
—074	**Museums, collections, exhibits**
—075	**Museum activities and services** **Collecting**
—076	**Review and exercise**
—077	**Programmed texts**
—078	**Use of apparatus and equipment in study and teaching**
—079	**Competitions, awards, financial support**

—070 1–070 9   Geographical treatment

> Add to base number —070 notation 1 or 3–9 from Table 2, e.g., education in France —07044

—071   Schools and courses

> Class financial support of schools and courses in —079, special education in 371.9, elementary education in 372

—071 01–071 09   Geographical treatment

> Add to base number —0710 notation 1 or 3–9 from Table 2, e.g., schools and courses in Argentina —071082

> **—071 1–071 5**   Specific levels

> Class comprehensive works in —071, specific activities at any level in —072–079, the subject at the elementary level in 372.3–372.8

—071 1   In higher education

> Add to base number —0711 notation 1 or 3–9 from Table 2, e.g., university courses in Japan —071152

—071 2   In secondary education

> Class here vocational schools in specific subjects [*formerly also* 373.246]

> Add to base number —0712 notation 1 or 3–9 from Table 2, e.g., secondary schools in regions of low economic development —07121724

—071 5   In adult education

> Class here schools and courses in specific subjects [*formerly also* 374.013], continuing education, extension departments and services

—071 52   Institutes and workshops

—071 53   Radio and television classes

—071 54   Correspondence courses

> Class radio and television correspondence courses in —07153

—071 55   In-service training and residency

> Class here on-the-job education
>
> Class management of in-service training and residency in commercial enterprises in —0683

—072   Research

> Class here comprehensive works on statistical method [*formerly* —028], on scientific method; laboratory manuals used in research
>
> Do not use for results of research; class results of research in 001–999 without adding notation from Table 1
>
> Operations research relocated to —011; specific research techniques not provided for here relocated to the subject, e.g., mathematical techniques —0151, data processing —0285, testing —0287
>
> Class interdisciplinary works in 001.4, scientific and statistical method used in systems analysis in —011, financial support of research in —079
>
> *See Manual at T1—0601–T1—0609 vs. T1—072; 519.5, T1—015195 vs. 001.422, T1—072*

—072 01–072 09   Geographical treatment

> Add to base number —0720 notation 1 or 3–9 from Table 2, e.g., research in England —072042

—072 2   Historical research

> Including use of case studies

—072 3   Descriptive research

> Class here surveys and survey methodology
>
> *See also —075 for collection of objects*

—072 4   Experimental research

> Models (simulation) relocated to —011

—[073]   Students, learners, apprentices, novices

> Novices relocated to —0880909, students and learners to —088375, apprentices to 331.55

—074   Museums, collections, exhibits [*formerly also* 069.9]

> Class here history and description; guidebooks, catalogs, lists regardless of whether or not articles are offered for sale
>
> Class interdisciplinary works in 069, comprehensive works on museology of a subject in —075
>
> *See Manual at T1—0294 vs. T1—074*

—[074 01–074 09]   Geographical treatment

> Relocated to —0741–0749

—074 1–074 9   Geographical treatment [*formerly* —07401–07409]

> Class here specific museums, collections, exhibits

> Add to base number —074 notation 1 or 3–9 from Table 2, e.g., museums of Pennsylvania —074748

—075   Museum activities and services [*formerly* 069]   Collecting

> Including price trends for collectors

> Class here museology

> Class interdisciplinary works on museum activities and services in 069, on museum collecting in 069.4, on recreational collecting in 790.132; activities and services of or relating to specific museums, collections, exhibits in —074; specific museological techniques not provided for here in —028, e.g., maintenance and repair of collected objects —0288

—[075 09]   Historical and geographical treatment

> Number discontinued; class in —075

—[075 092]   Collectors

> Relocated to —092

—075 3   Organizing and preparing collections and exhibits

> Including prevention of theft; recording, registration, storage, transportation

—075 5   Service to patrons

> Including regulation of patrons

—076   Review and exercise

> Examples: workbooks with problems, questions, answers; civil service examinations

> Including testing, test construction and evaluation

> Laboratory manuals in study and teaching relocated to —078

> Class interdisciplinary works on civil service examinations in 350.3, review and exercise involving use of apparatus and physical equipment in —078

—077   Programmed texts

> Class here programming of texts and their use

—078   Use of apparatus and equipment in study and teaching

> Class here laboratory manuals [*formerly also* —028, —076] student projects and experiments

> Class laboratory manuals for testing in —0287, for research in —072

—079   Competitions, festivals, awards, financial support

Examples: bursaries, fellowships and scholarships, grants-in-aid, honorary titles, prizes

Do not use for description of works that are entered into competitions and festivals, that receive awards, or that are the results of financial support; class in 001–999 without adding notation from Table 1

Add to base number —079 notation 4–9 from Table 2, e.g., competitions in California —079794

Class interdisciplinary works on awards in 929.81

—08   **History and description with respect to kinds of persons**

Unless other instructions are given, class complex subjects with aspects in two or more subdivisions of —08 in the one coming last, e.g., handicapped children —087 (*not* —083)

Class treatment of specific kinds of persons as individuals in —092

See Manual at T1—024 vs. T1—08

SUMMARY

—081	**Men**
—082	**Women**
—083	**Young people**
—084	**Persons in specific stages of adulthood**
—085	**Relatives Parents**
—086	**Persons by social and economic characteristics**
—087	**Handicapped, ill, gifted persons**
—088	**Occupational and religious groups**
—089	**Racial, ethnic, national groups**

>   —081–087 Specific miscellaneous kinds of persons [*formerly* —08804–08808]

Other than occupational, religious, racial, ethnic, national groups

Class comprehensive works in 001–999 without adding notation from Table 1

See Manual at T1—081–T1—087

—081   Men

Class here males

See Manual at T1—081, T1—082, T1—08351, T1—08352

—082   Women

Class here females

See Manual at T1—081, T1—082, T1—08351, T1—08352

—083   Young people

> Class here children

—083 2   Infants

> Children from birth to age two

—083 3   Children three to five

> Class here preschool children

—083 4   Children six to eleven

> Class here school children

—083 5   Young adults

> Aged twelve to twenty
>
> Class here comprehensive works on young adults aged twelve to twenty and over twenty
>
> Class young adults over twenty in —0842

—083 51   Young men

> *See Manual at T1—081, T1—082, T1—08351, T1—08352*

—083 52   Young women

> *See Manual at T1—081, T1—082, T1—08351, T1—08352*

—084   Persons in specific stages of adulthood

> Class comprehensive works on adults in 001–999 without adding notation from Table 1

—084 2   Early adulthood

> Over twenty years of age
>
> Class comprehensive works on young adults, young adults aged twelve to twenty in —0835

—084 4   Middle adulthood

—084 6   Late adulthood

—085   Relatives   Parents

> Class here adoptive and foster parents, stepparents

—085 1   Fathers

—085 2   Mothers

—085 3   Grandparents

> Including great-grandparents of any degree

—085 4   Progeny

> Use for children when considered in relation to parents

—085 5   Brothers and sisters

—086	Persons by social and economic characteristics
—086 2	By social and economic levels
—086 21	Upper classes
	Examples: royalty, nobility, elite, wealthy
	Class reigning monarchs and their regents in —0883511
—086 22	Middle classes (Bourgeoisie)
	Examples: well-to-do persons; professional, managerial middle classes
	For lower middle classes, see —08623
—086 23	Lower middle classes
	Examples: moderate-income persons, the working class in developed areas
—086 24	Lower classes
	For slaves, serfs, peons, see —08625
	See also —086942 for the poor
—086 25	Slaves, serfs, peons
—086 3	By level of cultural development
—086 31	High cultural development
—086 32	Medium cultural development
—086 33	Low cultural development
	Including nonliterates
—086 5	By marriage status
—086 52	Single persons
	For separated and divorced persons, see —08653; widowed persons, —08654
—086 523	Engaged persons
—086 53	Separated and divorced persons
—086 54	Widowed persons
—086 55	Married persons
	Including persons married in common law
	For polygamous persons, see —08659
—086 59	Polygamous persons
—086 6	By sexual orientation
	Including persons with no sexual orientation
—086 62	Heterosexuals
—086 63	Bisexuals

—086 64	Homosexuals
—086 642	Male homosexuals
—086 643	Female homosexuals (Lesbians)
—086 9	Of special social status
—086 92	Antisocial and asocial persons

Examples: vagrants, criminals and other offenders, convicts

—086 93	Members of nondominant racial, ethnic, national, socioeconomic, religious groups

Class members of specific nondominant racial, ethnic, national groups in —089; of specific nondominant religious groups in —0882

—086 94	Socially disadvantaged persons

Examples: war victims, unemployed persons

Class persons socially disadvantaged by reason of inclusion in nondominant racial, ethnic, national, socioeconomic, religious groups in —08693

—086 942	Poverty-stricken and destitute persons
—086 945	Illegitimate, abandoned, abused children; orphans
—086 947	Unmarried mothers
—086 96	Retired persons
—086 97	Veterans of military service
—087	Handicapped, ill, gifted persons

Class here physically handicapped persons

—087 1	Blind and partially sighted persons
—087 2	Deaf and hard of hearing persons
—087 3	Motor-impaired persons
—087 4	Mentally ill and mentally handicapped persons
—087 5	Persons with developmental disabilities

Class persons with mental developmental disabilities in —0874

—087 7	Ill and shut-in (house-bound) persons

Not provided for elsewhere

—087 9	Gifted persons
—088	Occupational and religious groups
—[088 04–088 08]	Specific miscellaneous kinds of persons

Relocated to —081–087

—[088 056]	Adults

Use of this number for comprehensive works on adults discontinued; class in 001–999 without adding notation from Table 1

—[088 081 2]   Physically healthy persons

> Number discontinued; class in 001–999 without adding notation from Table 1

—[088 082 2]   Mentally healthy persons

> Number discontinued; class in 001–999 without adding notation from Table 1

—088 09–088 99   Specific occupational and religious groups

> Add to base number —088 notation 09–99 from Table 7, e.g., the subject with respect to novices —0880909 [*formerly also* —073], with respect to students and learners —088375 [*formerly also* —073], with respect to lawyers —088344, with respect to Methodists —08827
>
> *See Manual at T1—0882 vs. T1—09*

—089   Racial, ethnic, national groups

> Add to base number —089 notation 03–99 from Table 5, e.g., the subject with respect to Chinese —089951, with respect to Chinese in the United States —089951073
>
> Class comprehensive works on nondominant racial, ethnic, national groups in —08693; treatment with respect to specific racial, ethnic, national groups in places where they predominate in —091 or —093–099; treatment with respect to miscellaneous specific kinds of persons of a specific racial, ethnic, national group in —081–088, e.g., Chinese children —083
>
> *See Manual at T1—089 vs. T1—09*

—09   Historical, geographical, persons treatment

> Standards in specific times and places relocated to —0218, drafting illustrations in specific times and places to —0221
>
> Class directories of persons and organizations regardless of time or place in —025; historical and geographical treatment of organizations in —0601–0609
>
> *See Manual at T1—0601–T1—0609; T1—0882 vs. T1—09; T1—089 vs. T1—09; T1—09*

SUMMARY

—090 1–090 5	**Historical periods**
—091	**Treatment by areas, regions, places in general**
—092	**Persons**
—093–099	**Treatment by specific continents, countries, localities; extraterrestrial worlds**

>   —090 1–090 5   Historical periods

        Add to notation for each term identified by * as follows:

01	Forecasting and forecasts
02	Statistics and illustrations
021	Statistics
022	Illustrations
05	Periodicals
07	Museums, collections, exhibits; collecting objects
074	Museums, collections, exhibits

              Add to base number 074 notation 4–9 from Table 2, e.g., collections in Pennsylvania —074748, collections of ancient objects in Pennsylvania —0901074748

075	Collecting objects

        Class comprehensive works in —09; historical periods in specific areas, regions, places in general in —091, in specific continents, countries, localities in —093–099

        See Manual at T1—0901–T1—0905

—090 1   *To 499 A.D.

        Use for the ancient period when the coverage is not limited to areas provided for in —093

—090 12   *To 4000 B.C.

—090 13   *3999–1000 B.C.

—090 14   *999–1 B.C.

—090 15   *1st-5th centuries, 1–499

—090 2   *6th-15th centuries, 500–1499

        Class here Middle Ages

        See Manual at T1—0902

—090 21   *6th-12th centuries, 500–1199

—090 22   *13th century, 1200–1299

—090 23   *14th century, 1300–1399

—090 24   *15th century, 1400–1499

—090 3   *Modern period, 1500–

        For 20th century, see —0904; 21st century, —0905

—090 31   *16th century, 1500–1599

—090 32   *17th century, 1600–1699

—090 33   *18th century, 1700–1799

—090 34   *19th century, 1800–1899

---

*Add as instructed under —0901–0905

—090 4   *20th century, 1900–1999

—090 41   *1900–1919

         Class here early 20th century

             For 1920–1929, see —09042; 1930–1939, —09043; 1940–1949, —09044

—090 42   *1920–1929

—090 43   *1930–1939

—090 44   *1940–1949

         Class here the period of World War II

         Class 1939 in —09043

—090 45   *1950–1959

         Class here late 20th century, the post World War II period

         Class 1945–1949 in —09044

             For 1960–1969, see —09046; 1970–1979, —09047; 1980–1989, —09048; 1990–1999, —09049

—090 46   *1960–1969

—090 47   *1970–1979

—090 48   *1980–1989

—090 49   *1990–1999

—090 5   *21st century, 2000–2099

—091   Treatment by areas, regions, places in general

         History and description

         Add to base number —091 the numbers following —1 in —11–19 from Table 2, e.g., the Torrid Zone —0913; then add as instructed under —0901–0905, e.g., statistics of the Torrid Zone —0913021

         Class persons regardless of area, region, place in —092; treatment by specific continents, countries, localities in —093–099; history and description with respect to kinds of persons in —08

*Add as instructed under —0901–0905

—092   Persons

Biography, autobiography, description and critical appraisal of work, diaries, reminiscences, correspondence of persons regardless of area, region, place who are part of the subject or who study the subject, e.g., criminals, victims of crime, criminologists

Including collectors [*formerly* —075092]

Class here treatment of individuals

(Option A: Class biography in 920.1–928.9)

(Option B: Class individual biography in 92, or B)

(Option C: Class individual biography of men in 920.71, of women in 920.72)

Class biography not clearly related to any specific subject in 920; belletristic diaries, reminiscences, correspondence in 800; treatment with respect to kinds of persons in —08

Observe instructions not to use —092 (or 92 or 2 when the standard subdivision has been displaced) that apply to 180–190, 232.9, 748.29, 748.59, 749.2, 759, 809, 810–890 (the instructions for 810–890 are found under notation 09 from Table 3–B)

See Manual at T1—092

—092 2   Collected treatment

(Option: Class collected biography in 92, or 920 without subdivision)

Add to base number —0922 notation 3–9 from Table 2, e.g., collected biography of a subject in Italy —092245

Class collected treatment of persons of specific areas when not limited to a specific subject in 920.03–920.09

See Manual at T1—0922; T1—0922 vs. T1—093–T1—099

—[092 4]   Individual treatment

Number discontinued; class in —092

—[092 6]   Case histories

Number discontinued; class in 001–999 without adding notation from Table 1

—093–099   Treatment by specific continents, countries, localities; extraterrestrial worlds

> History and description by place, by specific instance of the subject
>
> Add to base number —09 notation 3–9 from Table 2, e.g., the subject in United States —0973, in Brazil, —0981, in North America —097; then add further as follows:

01	Forecasting and forecasts
02	Statistics and illustrations
021	Statistics
022	Illustrations
05	Periodicals
07	Museums, collections, exhibits; collecting objects
074	Museums, collections, exhibits

> > Add to base number 074 notation 4–9 from Table 2, e.g., collections in Pennsylvania —074748, collections of Brazilian objects in Pennsylvania —0981074748

075	Collecting objects
09	Historical and geographical treatment

> > Add to 09 the numbers following 09 in notation 090–099 from Table 1, e.g., 20th century 0904, rural regions 091734
> >
> > Use 093–099 to add notation for a specific continent, country, locality when the first area notation is used to specify area of origin, while the second one identifies the area in which the subject is found or practiced, e.g., Polish political refugees 325.2109438, Polish political refugees in Canada 325.21094380971

In table above, observe precedence as given at beginning of Table 1, e.g., a periodical of statistics 021 (*not* 05); however, class museums, collections, exhibits of the subject in an area in 074 regardless of historical period, e.g., collections of twentieth century Brazilian art 709.81074 (*not* 709.810904)

(Option: Add historical period numbers that appear in subdivisions of 930–990, using one 0 in all cases except 00 for North America and South America, e.g., United States during the Reconstruction —097308, Brazil during the Empire —098104, North America in the 20th century —097005. If option is used, do not use notation 090 from the table above. An extra zero is used for the balance of the notation from the table above, e.g., statistics of Brazil —09810021)

Class persons regardless of area, region, place in —092; treatment by areas, regions, places not limited by continent, country, locality in —091; history and description with respect to miscellaneous specific kinds of persons in —081–087, with respect to occupational and religious groups in —088, with respect to specific racial, ethnic, national groups nondominant in their continents, countries, localities in —089

See Manual at T1—0902; T1—0922 vs. T1—093—T1—099; T1—093—T1—099 and T2—3—T2—9

Table 2. Geographic Areas, Historical Periods, Persons

The following notations are never used alone, but may be used as required (either directly when so noted or through the interposition of notation 09 from Table 1) with any number from the schedules, e.g., wages (331.29) in Japan (—52 in this table): 331.2952; railroad transportation (385) in Brazil (—81 in this table): 385.0981. They may also be used when so noted with numbers from other tables, e.g., notation 025 from Table 1. When adding to a number from the schedules, always insert a decimal point between the third and fourth digits of the complete number

SUMMARY

—01–05	Historical periods
—1	Areas, regions, places in general
—11	Frigid Zones
—12	Temperate Zones (Middle Latitude Zones)
—13	Torrid Zones (Tropics)
—14	Land and land forms
—15	Regions by type of vegetation
—16	Air and water
—17	Socioeconomic regions
—18	Other kinds of terrestrial regions
—19	Space
—2	Persons
—22	Collected treatment
—3	The ancient world
—31	China
—32	Egypt
—33	Palestine
—34	India
—35	Mesopotamia and Iranian Plateau
—36	Europe north and west of Italian Peninsula
—37	Italian Peninsula and adjacent territories
—38	Greece
—39	Other parts of ancient world
—4	Europe Western Europe
—409 1	Regional treatment
—41	British Isles
—42	England and Wales
—43	Central Europe Germany
—44	France and Monaco
—45	Italian Peninsula and adjacent islands Italy
—46	Iberian Peninsula and adjacent islands Spain
—47	Union of Soviet Socialist Republics (Soviet Union) Russia (Russian Soviet Federated Socialist Republic)
—48	Scandinavia
—49	Other parts of Europe

—5	Asia	Orient	Far East
—509 1	Regional treatment		
—51	China and adjacent areas		
—52	Japan		
—53	Arabian Peninsula and adjacent areas		
—54	South Asia	India	
—55	Iran		
—56	Middle East (Near East)		
—57	Siberia (Asiatic Russia)		
—58	Central Asia		
—59	Southeast Asia		

—6	Africa	
—609 1	Regional treatment	
—61	Tunisia and Libya	
—62	Egypt and Sudan	
—63	Ethiopia	
—64	Northwest African coast and offshore islands	Morocco
—65	Algeria	
—66	West Africa and offshore islands	
—67	Central Africa and offshore islands	
—68	Southern Africa	Republic of South Africa
—69	South Indian Ocean islands	

—7	North America	
—709 1	Regional treatment	
—71	Canada	
—72	Middle America	Mexico
—73	United States	
—74	Northeastern United States (New England and Middle Atlantic states)	
—75	Southeastern United States (South Atlantic states)	
—76	South central United States	Gulf Coast states
—77	North central United States	Lake states
—78	Western United States	
—79	Great Basin and Pacific Slope region of United States Pacific Coast states	

—8	South America
—809 1	Regional treatment
—81	Brazil
—82	Argentina
—83	Chile
—84	Bolivia
—85	Peru
—86	Colombia and Ecuador
—87	Venezuela
—88	Guiana
—89	Paraguay and Uruguay

—9	Other parts of world and extraterrestrial worlds	Pacific Ocean islands
—93	New Zealand	
—94	Australia	
—95	Melanesia	New Guinea
—96	Other parts of Pacific Ocean	Polynesia
—97	Atlantic Ocean islands	
—98	Arctic islands and Antarctica	
—99	Extraterrestrial worlds	

—01–05   Historical periods

Add to base number —0 the numbers following —090 in —0901–0905 from Table 1, e.g., 20th century —04

—1   Areas, regions, places in general

Not limited by continent, country, locality

(Option: Add to each number as follows:
    03–09   Treatment by continent, country, locality
              Add 0 to base number and then add notation 3–9 from this table, e.g., Torrid Zone of Asia —1305, rivers of England —1693042, Italian-speaking regions of Switzerland —175510494, cities of ancient Greece —1732038

Prefer —3–9)

Unless other instructions are given, class complexly defined areas with aspects in two or more subdivisions of this table in the number coming last in the table, e.g., forested plateaus in North Temperate Zone —152 (*not* —123 or —143)

Class persons regardless of area, region, place in —2; specific continents, countries, localities in —3–9

See Manual at T2—1; T2—2 vs. T2—1, T2—3–T2—9

SUMMARY

—11	**Frigid Zones**
—12	**Temperate Zones (Middle Latitude Zones)**
—13	**Torrid Zone (Tropics)**
—14	**Land and land forms**
—15	**Regions by type of vegetation**
—16	**Air and water**
—17	**Socioeconomic regions**
—18	**Other kinds of terrestrial regions**
—19	**Space**

—11   Frigid Zones

—113   North Frigid Zone

—116   South Frigid Zone

—12   Temperate Zones (Middle Latitude Zones)

—123   North Temperate Zone

—126   South Temperate Zone

—13   Torrid Zone (Tropics)

—14   Land and land forms

—141   Continents

              Including continental shelves

—142   Islands

              Examples: atolls, coral reefs

—143   Elevations

         Examples: mountains, plateaus, hills, slopes

—144   Depressions and openings

         Examples: canyons, chasms, gorges, gulches, ravines, valleys; caves, karsts

—145   Plane regions

         Examples: pampas, plains, prairies, steppes, tundras

—146   Coastal regions and shorelines

         Examples: beaches, deltas

—148   Soil

—15   **Regions by type of vegetation**

—152   Forests

—153   Grasslands

—154   Deserts

—16   **Air and water**

SUMMARY

—161	**Atmosphere**
—162	**Oceans and seas**
—163	**Atlantic Ocean**
—164	**Pacific Ocean**
—165	**Indian Ocean**
—167	**Antarctic waters**
—168	**Special oceanographic forms and inland seas**
—169	**Fresh and brackish waters**

—161   Atmosphere

—161 2   Troposphere

—161 3   Stratosphere

—161 4   Ionosphere

—162   Oceans and seas

         For Atlantic Ocean, see —163; Pacific Ocean, —164; Indian Ocean, —165; special oceanographic forms and inland seas, —168

         See also —182 for ocean and sea basins

—163   Atlantic Ocean

> See Manual at T2—163 and T2—164, T2—165; T2—163, T2—164, T2—165 vs. T2—182

SUMMARY

—163 1	**North Atlantic Ocean**
—163 2	**Arctic Ocean (North Polar Sea)**
—163 3	**Northeast Atlantic Ocean**
—163 4	**Northwest Atlantic Ocean**
—163 5	**South Atlantic Ocean**
—163 6	**Southwest Atlantic Ocean**
—163 7	**Southeast Atlantic Ocean**
—163 8	**Mediterranean Sea**

—163 1   North Atlantic Ocean

> *For Arctic Ocean, see —1632; northeast Atlantic Ocean, —1633; northwest Atlantic Ocean, —1634*
>
> *See Manual at T2—1631 and T2—1635*

—163 2   Arctic Ocean (North Polar Sea)

—163 24   European sector

> Including Denmark Strait; Greenland, Norwegian, Barents, White Seas

—163 25   Asian sector

> Including Kara, Laptev, East Siberian, Chukchi Seas
>
> *For Bering Strait, see —16451*

—163 27   American sector

> Including Beaufort and Lincoln Seas, seas of Canadian Arctic Archipelago, Hudson and Baffin Bays
>
> *For Bering Strait, see —16451*

—163 3   Northeast Atlantic Ocean

—163 34   Baltic Sea

> Including Gulfs of Bothnia, Finland, Riga; Great and Little Belts; Oresund, Kattegat

—163 36   North Sea and English Channel

> Including Skagerrak, Strait of Dover, Firth of Forth

—163 37   Western waters of British Isles

> Examples: Irish Sea, North and Saint George's Channels, Firth of Clyde, Solway Firth

—163 38   French and Spanish coastal waters to Strait of Gibraltar

> Example: Bay of Biscay
>
> *For Strait of Gibraltar, see —16381*

—163 4	**Northwest Atlantic Ocean**
—163 42	Davis Strait
—163 43	Labrador Sea
—163 44	Gulf of Saint Lawrence and coastal waters of Newfoundland and eastern Nova Scotia
—163 45	North American coastal waters from Bay of Fundy to Massachusetts Bay

> Example: Cape Cod Bay

—163 46	United States coastal waters from Cape Cod to Cape Charles

> Examples: Nantucket, Rhode Island, Long Island Sounds; Buzzards, Narragansett, New York, Delaware Bays

—163 47	Chesapeake Bay

> Including York River [*formerly* —7553]

—163 48	United States coastal waters from Cape Henry to Straits of Florida

> Examples: Albemarle, Pamlico Sounds; Raleigh, Biscayne Bays
>
> Including Biscayne National Park
>
> *For Straits of Florida, see* —16363

—163 5	**South Atlantic Ocean**

> *For southwest Atlantic Ocean, see* —1636; *southeast Atlantic Ocean,* —1637; *Atlantic sector of Antarctic waters,* —1673
>
> *See Manual at T2—1631 and T2—1635*

—163 6	**Southwest Atlantic Ocean**

> Class here west Atlantic Ocean
>
> *For northwest Atlantic Ocean, see* —1634

—163 62	Sargasso Sea
—163 63	Bahama waters

> Example: Straits of Florida

—163 64	Gulf of Mexico

> Including Yucatán Channel
>
> *For Straits of Florida, see* —16363

—163 65	Caribbean Sea

> Including Gulfs of Honduras, Darien, Venezuela
>
> *For Yucatan Channel, see* —16364; *Panama Canal,* —1641

—163 66	South American coastal waters from Gulf of Paria to Cape São Roque
—163 67	Brazilian coastal waters southward from Cape São Roque
—163 68	Uruguayan and Argentinian coastal waters

> Examples: La Plata estuary, Bahía Blanca, Bahía Grande, Gulfs of San Matías and San Jorge

—163 7   Southeast Atlantic Ocean

         Class here east Atlantic Ocean

           For northeast Atlantic Ocean, see —1633; Mediterranean Sea, —1638

—163 72   African coastal waters from Cape of Good Hope to Congo River

—163 73   Gulf of Guinea

         African coastal waters from Congo River to Cape Palmas

—163 75   West African coastal waters from Cape Palmas to Strait of Gibraltar

           For Strait of Gibraltar, see —16381

—163 8   Mediterranean Sea

—163 81   Western Mediterranean

         Strait of Gibraltar to Strait of Sicily

           For waters between Spain and Sardinia-Corsica, see —16382; Tyrrhenian Sea, —16383

—163 82   Waters between Spain and Sardinia-Corsica

         Including Balearic and Ligurian Seas, Gulf of Lions

—163 83   Tyrrhenian Sea

           For Strait of Messina, see —16386

—163 84   Eastern Mediterranean

         East of Strait of Sicily

           For Adriatic Sea, see —16385; Ionian Sea, —16386; Mediterranean east of Crete, —16387; Sea of Crete and Aegean Sea, —16388; Black Sea, —16389

—163 85   Adriatic Sea

         Including Gulf of Venice, Strait of Otranto

—163 86   Ionian Sea

         Including Strait of Messina, Gulfs of Taranto and Corinth

           For Strait of Otranto, see —16385

—163 87   Mediterranean east of Crete

           For Suez Canal, see —16533

—163 88   Sea of Crete and Aegean Sea

           For Dardanelles, see —16389

—163 89   Black Sea

         Including Dardanelles, Bosporus, Seas of Marmara and Azov

—164   Pacific Ocean

See Manual at T2—163 and T2—164, T2—165; T2—163, T2—164, T2—165 vs. T2—182

SUMMARY

—164 1	**Southeast Pacific Ocean**
—164 2	**East Pacific Ocean**
—164 3	**Northeast Pacific Ocean**
—164 4	**North Pacific Ocean**
—164 5	**Northwest Pacific Ocean**
—164 6	**West Pacific Ocean**
—164 7	**Southwest Pacific Ocean**
—164 8	**South Pacific Ocean**
—164 9	**Central Pacific Ocean**

—164 1   Southeast Pacific Ocean

American coastal waters from Strait of Magellan to Mexico-United States boundary

Including Gulfs of Guayaquil, Panama, Tehuantepec, California; Panama Canal

For Strait of Magellan, see —1674

—164 2   East Pacific Ocean

For southeast Pacific Ocean, see —1641; northeast Pacific Ocean, —1643

—164 3   Northeast Pacific Ocean

North American coastal waters from California to tip of Alaska

—164 32   United States waters

Examples: Monterey and San Francisco Bays, Strait of Juan de Fuca, Puget Sound

For Alaskan waters, see —16434

—164 33   Canadian waters

Examples: Strait of Georgia, Queen Charlotte and Hecate Straits, Queen Charlotte Sound, Dixon Entrance

For Strait of Juan de Fuca, see —16432

—164 34   Alaskan waters

Examples: Gulf of Alaska, Bristol Bay, Cook Inlet, Norton Sound, Shelikof Strait

For Dixon Entrance, see —16433

—164 4   North Pacific Ocean

For northeast Pacific Ocean, see —1643; northwest Pacific Ocean, —1645

See Manual at T2—1644 and T2—1648, T2—1649

—164 5	Northwest Pacific Ocean
—164 51	Bering Sea
	Including Bering Strait
—164 52	Coastal waters of southeast Kamchatka
—164 53	Sea of Okhotsk
	Including La Pérouse Strait
—164 54	Sea of Japan
	Including Tatar, Tsugaru, Korea Straits
	For La Pérouse Strait, see —16453
—164 55	Eastern coastal waters and inner seas of Japan
—164 56	Yellow Sea
—164 57	East China Sea
	Including Formosa Strait
	For Korea Strait, see —16454
—164 58	Philippine Sea
	Including Luzon Strait
—164 6	West Pacific Ocean
	For northwest Pacific Ocean, see —1645; southwest Pacific Ocean, —1647
—164 7	Southwest Pacific Ocean
—164 71	Inner seas of Philippines
	For Sulu Sea, see —16473
—164 72	South China Sea
	Including Gulfs of Tonkin and Thailand, Singapore and Karimata Straits
	For Formosa Strait, see —16457; Luzon Strait, —16458
—164 73	Inner seas of Malay Archipelago
	Including Sulu, Celebes, Molucca, Ceram Seas; Makasar Strait
	For seas adjoining southern Sunda Islands, see —16474
—164 74	Seas adjoining Sunda Islands
	Including Java, Bali, Flores, Savu, Banda Seas
	For Karimata Strait, see —16472
—164 75	Arafura Sea
	Including Gulf of Carpentaria
	For Torres Strait, see —16476

—164 76	Coral Sea and seas adjoining Melanesia
	Including Bismarck and Solomon Seas, Gulf of Papua, Torres Strait; eastern Queensland coastal waters
—164 77	Fiji Sea
—164 78	Tasman Sea
	Including New South Wales coastal waters, Cook Strait
	For Tasmanian coastal waters, see —16576
—164 79	Eastern coastal waters of New Zealand
—164 8	South Pacific Ocean
	For southeast Pacific Ocean, see —1641; southwest Pacific Ocean, —1647; Pacific sector of Antarctic waters, —1674
	See Manual at T2—1644 and T2—1648, T2—1649
—164 9	Central Pacific Ocean
	See Manual at T2—1644 and T2—1648, T2—1649
—165	Indian Ocean
	For Indian Ocean sector of Antarctic waters, see —1675
	See Manual at T2—163 and T2—164, T2—165; T2—163, T2—164, T2—165 vs. T2—182
—165 2	Southwest Indian Ocean
	Class here west Indian Ocean
	For northwest Indian Ocean, see —1653
—165 23	Eastern coastal waters of Madagascar
—165 24	Coastal waters of south and southeast Africa
	From Cape of Good Hope to and including Delagoa Bay
—165 25	Mozambique Channel
—165 26	Coastal waters of east Africa
	From Cape Delgado to Cape Guardafui (tip of the "Horn")
—165 3	Northwest Indian Ocean
—165 32	Gulf of Aden
	Including Bab el Mandeb
—165 33	Red Sea
	Including Gulfs of Aqaba and Suez, Suez Canal
	For Bab el Mandeb, see —16532
—165 35	Persian Gulf
	Including Strait of Hormuz

—165 36	Gulf of Oman
	For Strait of Hormuz, see —16535
—165 37	Arabian Sea
	Including Laccadive Sea, Gulf of Mannar
—165 6	Northeast Indian Ocean
—165 64	Bay of Bengal
—165 65	Andaman Sea
	Including Gulf of Martaban, Strait of Malacca
	For Singapore Strait, see —16472
—165 67	Coastal waters of southern Sumatra, Java, Lesser Sunda Islands
	For Timor Sea, see —16574
—165 7	Southeast Indian Ocean
	Class here east Indian Ocean
	For northeast Indian Ocean, see —1656; Arafura Sea, —16475
—165 74	Northwest Australian coastal waters
	From Melville Island to Northwest Cape
	Example: Timor Sea
—165 75	West Australian coastal waters
	From Northwest Cape to Cape Leeuwin
—165 76	South Australian coastal waters
	From Cape Leeuwin to Cape Howe
	Examples: Port Davey [*formerly also* —9462], Great Australian Bight, Bass Strait, Tasmanian coastal waters
—167	Antarctic waters
—167 3	Atlantic sector
	Including Drake Passage, Scotia and Weddell Seas
	For Strait of Magellan, see —1674
—167 4	Pacific sector
	Including Strait of Magellan; Bellingshausen, Amundsen, Ross Seas
—167 5	Indian Ocean sector
—168	Special oceanographic forms and inland seas
	Examples: saltwater lagoons, inland seas, coastal pools
	Caspian Sea relocated to —479
	Class specific inland seas in —4–9

—169	Fresh and brackish waters

> —169 2–169 4   Surface waters
> Class comprehensive works in —169

—169 2	Lakes, ponds, freshwater lagoons
—169 3	Rivers and streams
—169 4	Waterfalls
—169 8	Groundwaters (Subsurface waters)
—17	**Socioeconomic regions**
—171	By political orientation
—171 2	Noncontiguous empires and political unions

Add to base number —1712 notation 3–9 from Table 2 for ''mother country'', e.g., French Community —171244

Class Roman Empire in —37

—171 3	Western bloc
—171 6	Unaligned blocs
—171 65	Afro-Asian bloc
—171 7	Communist bloc
—171 8	Wartime groupings
—171 82	Belligerents
—171 83	Nonbelligerents and neutrals
—171 9	Nonself-governing territories
—172	By degree of economic development
—172 2	High degree

Independent of aid from other regions except in case of disaster

—172 3	Medium degree

Semi-independent regions needing aid only for special projects

—172 4	Low degree

Dependent on other regions for many types of aid

—173	By concentration of population
—173 2	Urban regions
—173 3	Suburban regions

—173 4	Rural regions
	Including rural villages
—174	Regions where specific racial, ethnic, national groups predominate
	Add to base number —174 notation 03–99 from Table 5, e.g., regions where Arabs predominate —174927
—175	Regions where specific languages predominate
	Add to base number —175 notation from 1–9 from Table 6, e.g., regions where Spanish language predominates —17561
—176	Regions where specific religions predominate
—176 1	Christianity
—176 12	Catholicism
—176 14	Protestantism
—176 2–176 9	Other religions
	Add to base number —176 the numbers following —29 in notation 292–299 from Table 7, e.g., regions where Islam predominates —17671
—177	Nations belonging to specific international organizations
	Example: nations belonging to Organization of Petroleum Exporting Countries
	Arrange alphabetically by name of organization
	Nations belonging to the Council of Europe relocated to —4
—18	**Other kinds of terrestrial regions**
—181	Hemispheres
	Class zonal, physiographic, socioeconomic regions in a specific hemisphere in —11–17
—181 1	Eastern Hemisphere
—181 2	Western Hemisphere
	Class works emphasizing North and South America in —7, geography of Western Hemisphere in 917, history of Western Hemisphere in 970
—181 3	Northern Hemisphere
—181 4	Southern Hemisphere
—182	Ocean and sea basins
	The totality of continents facing and islands in specific major bodies of water
	Class ocean and sea waters in —162; zonal, physiographic, socioeconomic regions in a specific ocean or sea basin in —11–17
	See Manual at T2—163, T2—164, T2—165 vs. T2—182

—182 1   Atlantic region   Occident

> *See also —729 for Caribbean Area*

—182 2   Mediterranean region

—182 3   Pacific region

—182 4   Indian Ocean region

—19   **Space**

> Class extraterrestrial worlds in —99
>
> *See Manual at T2—19 vs. T2—99*

—2   **Persons**

> Regardless of area, region, place
>
> Class here description and critical appraisal of work, biography, autobiography, diaries, reminiscences, correspondence of persons associated with the subject, e.g., elementary educators 372.92
>
> All schedule and Manual notes for notation 092 and its subdivision from Table 1 are applicable here
>
> *See Manual at T2—2 vs. T2—1, T2—3–T2—9*

—22   **Collected treatment**

> Add to base number —22 notation 3–9, e.g., collected biography of persons from Italy —2245

—[24]   **Individual treatment**

> Number discontinued; class in —2

—[26]   **Case histories**

> Number discontinued; class in 001–999 without adding notation from Table 2

\>   **—3–9 Specific continents, countries, localities; extraterrestrial worlds**

> Class here specific instances of the subject
>
> (Option: Class areas and regions limited by continent, country, locality in —1)
>
> An area is classed in its present number even if it had a different affiliation at the time under consideration, e.g., Arizona under Mexican sovereignty —791 (*not* —72)
>
> Class comprehensive works in base number; areas, regions, places not limited by continent, country, locality in —1; parts of oceans and non-inland seas limited by country or locality in —16; persons regardless of area, region, place in —2
>
> *See Manual at T1—093–T1—099 and T2—3–T2—9; T2—3–T2—9; T2—3 vs. T2—4–T2—9*

—3   The ancient world

Class a specific part of ancient world not provided for here in —4–9

(Option: Class specific parts in —4–9 as detailed below)

See Manual at T2—3 vs. T2—4–T2—9

SUMMARY

—31	China
—32	Egypt
—33	Palestine
—34	India
—35	Mesopotamia and Iranian Plateau
—36	Europe north and west of Italian Peninsula
—37	Italian Peninsula and adjacent territories
—38	Greece
—39	Other parts of ancient world

—31   China

(Option: Class in —51)

—32   Egypt

Including Alexandria, Giza, Memphis, Abydos, Karnak, Luxor, Thebes

(Option: Class Egypt in —62; Alexandria in —621; Giza, Memphis in —622; Abydos, Karnak, Luxor, Thebes in —623)

—33   Palestine

Including Israel, Judah; Galilee, Judaea, Samaria; Jerusalem

(Option: Class Palestine, Israel in —5694; Jerusalem in —569442; Galilee in —56945; Judah, Judaea in —56949; Samaria in —56953)

—34   India

(Option: Class in —54)

—35   Mesopotamia and Iranian Plateau

Contains Media, Elam (Susiana), Persia, Assyria, Babylonia, Sumer

Including Ecbatana, Susa, Pasargadae, Persepolis, Ashur, Nineveh, Babylon, Ur

Class here Seleucid Empire

(Option: Class Iranian Plateau in —55; Media, Ecbatana in —555; Elam [Susiana], Susa in —556; Persia, Pasargadae, Persepolis in —5572; Mesopotamia, Seleucid Empire in —567; Assyria, Ashur, Nineveh in —5674; Babylonia, Sumer, Babylon, Ur in —5675)

Class central Asia in —396

—36   **Europe north and west of Italian Peninsula**

Class here comprehensive works on Europe

(Option: Class in —4)

Class a specific part of Europe not provided for here with the part, e.g., Greece —38

—361   British Isles   Northern Britain and Ireland

(Option: Class British Isles in —41, northern Britain in —411, Ireland in —415)

Add to base number —361 the numbers following —41 in notation 411–419 of this table, e.g., ancient Border Country —36137

For southern Britain, see —362

—362   Southern Britain   England

(Option: Class in —42)

Add to base number —362 the numbers following —42 in notation 421–429 of this table, e.g., ancient Chester —362714

Class comprehensive works on British Isles in —361

—363   Germanic regions

Including Vindelicia, Noricum, Raetia

(Option: Class Germanic regions in —43; Vindelicia in —433; Noricum in —436; Raetia in —4364)

For British Isles, see —361

—364   Celtic regions

Including Germania Superior, Lugdunensis, Aquitania, Narbonensis, Germania Inferior, Belgica

Class here Gaul (Gallia Transalpina)

(Option: Class Celtic regions, Gaul [Gallia Transalpina] in —44; Germania Superior in —4438; Lugdunensis in —445; Aquitania in —447; Narbonensis in —449; Germania Inferior in —492; Belgica in —493)

For British Isles, see —361

See also —372 for Gallia Cisalpina

—366   Iberian Peninsula and adjacent islands

Including Tarraconensis, Baetica, Lusitania

(Option: Class Iberian Peninsula and adjacent islands, Tarraconensis in —46; Baetica in —468; Lusitania in —469)

—37   **Italian Peninsula and adjacent territories**

Class here Roman Empire

(Option: Class in —45)

Class a specific part of Roman Empire not provided for here with the part, e.g., Britain —361

—371   Liguria

(Option: Class in —4518)

—372   Gallia Cisalpina

(Option: Class in —451)

—373   Venetia and Istria

(Option: Class Venetia in —453; Istria in —4972)

—374   Region northeast of Rome

Including Umbria, Picenum; Volsinii (Orvieto)

(Option: Class Umbria in —4565; Volsinii [Orvieto] in —45652; Picenum in —4567)

—375   Etruria

(Option: Class in —455)

—376   Latium

Class here Rome

Including Volsinii Novi (Bolsena), Ostia, Veii

(Option: Class Latium in —4562; Volsinii Novi [Bolsena] in —45625; Ostia, Veii in —4563; Rome in —45632)

—377   Southern Italy

Contains Samnium, Campania, Apulia, Calabria, Lucania, Bruttium

Including Naples, Herculaneum, Pompeii, Stabiae, Brundusium

(Option: Class Southern Italy in —457; Samnium in —4571; Campania in —4572; Naples, Herculaneum, Pompeii, Stabiae in —4573; Apulia, Calabria, Brundusium in —4575; Lucania in —4577; Bruttium in —4578)

—378   Sicily and Malta

Including Syracuse

(Option: Class Sicily in —458; Syracuse in —45814; Malta in —4585)

—379   Sardinia and Corsica

(Option: Class Corsica in —44945; Sardinia in —459)

—38 **Greece**

Class here comprehensive works on Greece and the Roman Empire; the Hellenistic World

(Option: Class in —495)

Class the Roman Empire in —37; a specific part of Greece not provided for here with the part, e.g., Ionia —3923, Aegean Islands —391

—381 Macedonia

(Option: Class in —4956)

—382 Thessaly, Epirus, adjacent Ionian Islands

Class here comprehensive works on Ionian Islands

(Option: Class Epirus in —4953; Thessaly in —4954; Ionian Islands, northern Ionian Islands in —4955)

Class southern Ionian Islands in —386

For Ithaca Island, see —383

—383 Aetolia, Acarnania, Doris, Locris, Malis, Phocis; Ithaca Island

Including Amphissa, Delphi

(Option: Class Aetolia, Acarnania, Doris, Locris, Malis, Phocis, Amphissa, Delphi in —4951; Ithaca Island in —4955)

—384 Boeotia, Megaris; Euboea Island

Including Chalcis, Thebes

(Option: Class Boeotia, Euboea Island, Chalcis, Thebes in —4951; Megaris in —4952)

—385 Attica

Class here Athens

Including Marathon

(Option: Class Attica, Marathon in —4951; Athens in —49512)

—386 Peloponnesus and adjacent Ionian Islands

(Option: Class Peloponnesus in —4952; southern Ionian Islands in —4955)

For divisions of Peloponnesus, see —387–389

\> **—387–389 Divisions of Peloponnesus**

Class comprehensive works in —386

—387 Achaea and Corinth

(Option: Class in —4952)

—388   Arcadia, Argolis, Elis

         Including Mycenae, Olympia, Phigalia, Tiryns

         (Option: Class in —4952)

—389   Laconia and Messenia

         Class here Sparta

         (Option: Class in —4952)

—39   **Other parts of ancient world**

SUMMARY

—391	**Aegean Islands**
—392	**Western Asia Minor**
—393	**Eastern Asia Minor and Cyprus**
—394	**Middle East**
—395	**Black Sea and Caucasus regions**
—396	**Central Asia**
—397	**North Africa**
—398	**Southeastern Europe**

—391   Aegean Islands

         (Option: Class in —499)

—391 1   Northern islands

         Contains Imbros, Lemnos, Northern Sporades, Samothrace, Tenedos, Thasos

         (Option: Class Imbros, Tenedos islands in —562)

—391 2   Lesbos

—391 3   Chios

—391 4   Samos

—391 5   Southwestern islands

         Including the Cyclades, Naxos and Thera islands

—391 6   Rhodes and Southern Sporades

         (Option: Class in —4996)

—391 7   Karpathos

         (Option: Class in —4996)

—391 8   Crete

         Including Knossos

         (Option: Class in —4998)

—392   **Western Asia Minor**

Class here comprehensive works on Asia Minor

(Option: Class in —561)

For eastern Asia Minor, see —393

—392 1   **Mysia and Troas**

Including Pergamum, Troy

(Option: Class in —562)

—392 2   **Lydia**

Including Sardis

(Option: Class in —562)

—392 3   **Ionia**

Including Ephesus, Magnesia ad Maeandrum, Miletus, Smyrna

(Option: Class in —562)

For Aegean Islands, see —391

—392 4   **Caria**

Including Halicarnassus

(Option: Class in —562)

—392 5   **Bithynia**

(Option: Class in —563)

—392 6   **Phrygia**

(Option: Class in —562)

—392 7   **Pisidia**

(Option: Class in —564)

—392 8   **Lycia**

(Option: Class in —564)

—392 9   **Pamphylia**

(Option: Class in —564)

—393   **Eastern Asia Minor and Cyprus**

(Option: Class eastern Asia Minor in —561)

\>   **—393 1–393 6 Eastern Asia Minor**

Class comprehensive works in —393

—393 1   Paphlagonia

            (Option: Class in —563)

—393 2   Galatia

            (Option: Class in —563)

—393 3   Pontus

            (Option: Class in —565)

—393 4   Cappadocia

            (Option: Class in —564)

—393 5   Cilicia

            (Option: Class in —564)

—393 6   Commagene

            (Option: Class in —564)

—393 7   Cyprus

            (Option: Class in —5645)

—394   Middle East

            (Option: Class in —56)

            Class a specific part of Middle East not provided for here with the part, e.g., Egypt —32, Palestine —33

—394 3   Syria

            Including Antioch, Palmyra, Ebla, Ugarit, Damascus

            (Option: Class Antioch in —564; Syria in —5691; Palmyra in —56912; Ebla, Ugarit in —56913; Damascus in —569144)

               For Phoenicia, see —3944

—394 4   Phoenicia

            Including Coelesyria; Baalbek, Byblos, Sidon, Tyre

            (Option: Class in —5692)

—394 6   Edom and Moab

            (Option: Class Edom in —56949; Moab in —56956)

—394 7   Arabia Deserta

            (Option: Class in —567)

—394 8   Arabia Petraea

            Including Sinai Peninsula; Petra

            (Option: Class Arabia Petraea in —53; Sinai Peninsula in —531; Petra in —56957)

—394 9   Arabia Felix

      Class here comprehensive works on Arabia

      (Option: Class Arabia Felix, Arabia in —53)

      For Arabia Deserta, see —3947; Arabia Petraea, —3948

—395   Black Sea and Caucasus regions

      Including Sarmatia, Albania, Colchis, Iberia

      (Option: Class Black Sea region in —477; Sarmatia in —4771; Caucasus in —479; Albania in —4791; Colchis, Iberia in —4795)

—395 1   Scythia

      (Option: Class in —4983)

—395 5   Armenia

      (Option: Class in —5662)

—396   Central Asia

      Including Hyrcania, Ariana, Bactria, Margiana, Sogdiana; Parthia

      (Option: Class Hyrcania in —5523; Central Asia in —58; Ariana, Bactria, Parthia in —581; Margiana in —585; Sogdiana in —587)

—397   North Africa

      (Option: Class in —61)

      For Egypt, see —32

—397 1   Mauretania

      Contains Mauretania Caesariensis, Mauretania Tingitana

      (Option: Class Mauretania Caesariensis, comprehensive works on Mauretania in —65; Mauretania Tingitana in —64)

—397 2   Numidia

      (Option: Class in —655)

—397 3   Carthage

      (Option: Class in —611)

—397 4   Tripolis

      Contains Leptis Magna, Oea, Sabrata

      (Option: Class in —612)

—397 5   Cyrenaica

      (Option: Class in —612)

—397 6   Marmarica

      (Option: Class in —612)

—397 7   Gaetulia

(Option: Class in —657)

—397 8   Ethiopia

Class here Cush, Nubia

(Option: Class in —625)

—398   Southeastern Europe

Including Pannonia, Thrace, Illyria, Moesia, Dacia; Constantinople

(Option: Class Pannonia in —439; Thrace in —4957; southeastern Europe in —496; Constantinople in —49618; Illyria in —497; Moesia in —4977; Dacia in —498)

For Greece, see —38; Black Sea region, —395

> ## —4–9 The modern world; extraterrestrial worlds

(Option: Class here specific parts of the ancient world; prefer —3)

Class comprehensive works on specific physiographic regions or features extending over more than one country, state, county, or other unit and identified by * with the unit where noted in this table, e.g., Lake Huron —774, Appalachian Mountains —74. Class works on a part of such a region or feature with the specific unit where the part is located, e.g., Lake Huron waters and shores in Ontario —7132, Cumberland Mountains —7691, Cumberland Mountains in Bell County, Kentucky —769123

(Option: To give local emphasis and a shorter number to a specific country, place it first under its own continent or major region by use of a letter or other symbol, e.g., Pakistan —5P (preceding —51); then subarrange each such number like the corresponding number in this table, e.g., Peshawar —5P23. Apply like any other area notation, e.g., geology of Peshawar 555.P23, history of Pakistan since 1971 95P.05, history of medical sciences in Pakistan 610.95P)

Class comprehensive works in base number

See Manual at T2—3 vs. T2—4–T2—9; T2—4–T2—9

—4   Europe   Western Europe

Class here nations belonging to the Council of Europe [*formerly* —177], southern Europe

(Option: Class here ancient Europe, western Europe; prefer —36)

Class Eurasia in —5

SUMMARY

—409 1	Regional treatment
—41	British Isles
—411	Scotland
—412	Northeastern Scotland
—413	Southeastern Scotland
—414	Southwestern Scotland
—415	Ireland
—416	Ulster Northern Ireland
—417	Republic of Ireland (Eire)
—418	Leinster
—419	Munster
—42	England and Wales
—421	Greater London
—422	Southeastern England
—423	Southwestern England and Channel Islands
—424	Midlands of England
—425	East Midlands of England
—426	Eastern England East Anglia
—427	Northwestern England and Isle of Man
—428	Northeastern England
—429	Wales
—43	Central Europe Germany
—431	Northeastern Germany
—432	Saxony and Thuringia
—433	Bavaria
—434	Southwestern Germany
—435	Northwestern Germany
—436	Austria and Liechtenstein
—437	Czechoslovakia
—438	Poland
—439	Hungary
—44	France and Monaco
—441	Northwestern France Brittany (Bretagne) region
—442	Northern France Normandy (Normandie) region
—443	Northeastern France Champagne region
—444	Eastern France Burgundy (Bourgogne) region
—445	Central France Centre region
—446	Western France Poitou region
—447	Southwestern France Guyenne (Aquitaine) Region
—448	Southern France Languedoc region
—449	Southeastern France and Monaco Provence region

—45	Italian Peninsula and adjacent islands Italy
—451	Northwestern Italy Piemonte region
—452	Lombardy region
—453	Northeastern Italy Veneto region
—454	Emilia-Romagna region and San Marino
—455	Tuscany region
—456	Central Italy and Vatican City
—457	Southern Italy
—458	Sicily and adjacent islands
—459	Sardinia
—46	Iberian Peninsula and adjacent islands Spain
—461	Northwestern Spain Galicia autonomous community
—462	Western Spain León region
—463	Castile
—464	New Castile region Castilla-La Mancha autonomous community
—465	Northeastern Spain
—466	País Vasco autonomous community
—467	Eastern Spain and Andorra Cataluña autonomous community
—468	Andalusia autonomous community and Gibraltar
—469	Portugal
—47	Union of Soviet Socialist Republics (Soviet Union) Russia (Russian Soviet Federated Socialist Republic)
—472	Northern area of Russia
—473	West central area of Russia
—474	Baltic Sea area of Soviet Union
—475	Lithuania (Lithuanian Soviet Socialist Republic)
—476	Western Russia and Belorussia
—477	Black Sea area of Soviet Union
—478	Eastern area of European Russia
—479	Caucasus area of Soviet Union
—48	Scandinavia
—481	Norway
—482	Southeastern Norway
—483	Southwestern Norway
—484	Central and northern Norway
—485	Sweden
—486	Southern Sweden (Götaland)
—487	Central Sweden (Svealand)
—488	Northern Sweden (Norrland)
—489	Denmark and Finland
—49	Other parts of Europe
—491	Northwestern islands
—492	Netherlands (Holland)
—493	Southern Low Countries Belgium
—494	Switzerland
—495	Greece
—496	Balkan Peninsula
—497	Yugoslavia and Bulgaria
—498	Romania
—499	Aegean Islands

—[400 9]   Regional treatment

Relocated to —4091

—409 1   **Regional treatment** [*formerly* —4009]

> Add to base number —4091 the numbers following —1 in —11–18 of this table, e.g., parts of Europe with high economic development —4091722

—41   **British Isles**

> Class here Great Britain, United Kingdom
>
> (Option: Class here ancient British Isles, northern Britain, Ireland; prefer —361)
>
> *For England and Wales, see* —42
>
> *See Manual at T2—41 and T2—42*

SUMMARY

—**411**	**Scotland**
—**412**	**Northeastern Scotland**
—**413**	**Southeastern Scotland**
—**414**	**Southwestern Scotland**
—**415**	**Ireland**
—**416**	**Ulster Northern Ireland**
—**417**	**Republic of Ireland (Eire)**
—**418**	**Leinster**
—**419**	**Munster**

—411   Scotland

> *For northeastern Scotland, see* —412; *southeastern Scotland,* —413; *southwestern Scotland,* —414

—411 1   Northern Scotland

> *For divisions of northern Scotland, see* —4112–4119

>   —411 2–411 9   Divisions of northern Scotland
>
> Class comprehensive works in —4111

—411 2   Islands authorities

> *For Orkney and Shetland, see* —4113; *Western Isles,* —4114

—411 3   Orkney and Shetland Islands authorities

—411 32   Orkney Islands Authority

—411 35   Shetland Islands Authority

—411 4   Western Isles (Outer Hebrides) Islands Authority

> Class here comprehensive works on Hebrides
>
> *For Inner Hebrides, see* —4118

—411 5   Highland Region

> Class here *Scottish Highlands
>
> *For districts of Highland Region, see* —4116–4119

*Class parts of this physiographic region or feature as instructed under —4–9

>   —411 6–411 9 Districts of Highland Region

                      Class comprehensive works in —4115

—411 6   **Northern districts of Highland Region**

—411 62   Caithness District

                      Class here former Caithness county

                      Farr, Tongue relocated to —41165

—411 65   Sutherland District

                      Including Farr, Tongue [*both formerly* —41162]

                      Class here former Sutherland county

—411 7   **Central districts of Highland Region**

—411 72   Ross and Cromarty District

                      Class here former Ross and Cromarty county

                      Class a specific part of former Ross and Cromarty county not provided for here with the part, e.g., Kincardine —41165

—411 75   Inverness District

                      Class here former Inverness-shire; *Great Glen

                      Class a specific part of former Inverness-shire not provided for here with the part, e.g., Kingussie —41192

—411 8   **Western districts of Highland Region**

                      Class here Inner Hebrides

                      Class a specific part of Inner Hebrides not provided for here with the part, e.g., Mull —41423

—411 82   Skye and Lochalsh District

—411 85   Lochaber District

—411 9   **Eastern districts of Highland Region**

—411 92   Badenoch and Strathspey District

                      Class here *Spey River

—411 95   Nairn District

                      Class here former Nairnshire

—412   **Northeastern Scotland**

—412 1   **Grampian Region**

                      Class here *Grampian Mountains

                      For districts of Grampian, see —4122–4124

*Class parts of this physiographic region or feature as instructed under —4–9

>   —412 2–412 4 Districts of Grampian

     Class comprehensive works in —4121

—412 2   Northern districts of Grampian

—412 23   Moray District

      Class here former Morayshire

      Class a specific part of former Morayshire not provided for here with the part, e.g., Grantown-on-Spey —41192

—412 25   Banff and Buchan District

      Class here former Banffshire; *Deveron River

      Class a specific part of former Banffshire not provided for here with the part, e.g., Aberlour —41223

—412 3   Central districts of Grampian

—412 32   Gordon District

      Class here former Aberdeenshire; *Don River

      Class a specific part of former Aberdeenshire not provided for here with the part, e.g., Fraserburgh —41225

—412 35   City of Aberdeen

      Class here Aberdeen

—412 4   Kincardine and Deeside District

      Class here former Kincardineshire; *Cairngorm Mountains; *Dee River

      Class a specific part of former Kincardineshire not provided for here with the part, e.g., Nigg —41235

—412 5   Tayside Region

      Class here *Strathmore

      For districts of Tayside, see —4126–4128

>   —412 6–412 8 Districts of Tayside

     Class comprehensive works in —4125

—412 6   Angus District

      Class here former Angus county

      Class a specific part of former Angus county not provided for here with the part, e.g., Dundee —4127

—412 7   City of Dundee

      Class here Dundee

*Class parts of this physiographic region or feature as instructed under —4–9

—412 8   **Perth and Kinross District**

> Including former Kinross-shire
>
> Class here former Perthshire; *Ochil Hills; *Tay River
>
> Class a specific part of former Perthshire not provided for here with the part, e.g., Callander —41312

—412 9   **Fife Region**

> Former name: Fifeshire

—412 92   North East Fife District

—412 95   Kirkcaldy District

—412 98   Dunfermline District

—413   **Southeastern Scotland**

> Class here *Central Lowlands

—413 1   **Central Region**

> Class here *Forth River
>
> *See also —16336 for Firth of Forth*

—413 12   Stirling District

> Class here former Stirlingshire; *Lennox Hills
>
> Class a specific part of former Stirlingshire not provided for here with the part, e.g., Falkirk —41318

—413 15   Clackmannan District

> Including former Clackmannanshire

—413 18   Falkirk District

—413 2   **Lothian Region**

> *For districts of Lothian, see —4133–4136*

\>   **—413 3–413 6   Districts of Lothian**

> Class comprehensive works in —4132

—413 3   **West Lothian District**

> Class here former West Lothian county
>
> Class a specific part of former West Lothian county not provided for here with the part, e.g., Bo'ness —41318

—413 4   **City of Edinburgh**

> Class here Edinburgh

*Class parts of this physiographic region or feature as instructed under —4–9

—413 5   Midlothian District

　　　　Class here former Midlothian county; *Pentland Hills

　　　　Class a specific part of former Midlothian county not provided for here with the part, e.g., Musselburgh —4136

—413 6   East Lothian District

　　　　Including former East Lothian county

　　　　Class here *Lammermuir Hills

—413 7   Borders Region

　　　　Class here *Border Country, *Southern Uplands; *Tweed River

　　　　For districts of Borders Region, see —4138–4139

>   　　—413 8–413 9 Districts of Borders Region

　　　　Class comprehensive works in —4137

—413 8   Western districts of Borders Region

—413 82   Tweeddale District

　　　　Former name: Peeblesshire

—413 85   Ettrick and Lauderdale District

　　　　Including former Selkirkshire

—413 9   Eastern districts of Borders Region

—413 92   Roxburgh District

　　　　Class here former Roxburghshire

　　　　Class a specific part of former Roxburghshire not provided for here with the part, e.g., Melrose —41385

—413 95   Berwickshire District

　　　　Class here former Berwickshire county

　　　　Class a specific part of former Berwickshire county not provided for here with the part, e.g., Lauder —41385

—414   Southwestern Scotland

—414 1   Strathclyde Region

　　　　Class here *Clyde River

　　　　For districts of Strathclyde, see —4142–4146

　　　　See also —16337 for Firth of Clyde

*Class parts of this physiographic region or feature as instructed under —4–9

>	—414 2–414 6 Districts of Strathclyde
	Class comprehensive works in —4141
—414 2	**Northwestern districts of Strathclyde**
—414 23	Argyll and Bute District
	Class here former Argyllshire, former Buteshire
	Class a specific part of former Argyllshire, of former Buteshire, not provided for here with the part, e.g., Kinlochleven —41185
—414 25	Dumbarton District
	Class here former Dunbartonshire; *Loch Lomond
	Class a specific part of former Dunbartonshire not provided for here with the part, e.g., Clydebank —41432
—414 28	Inverclyde District
—414 3	**North central districts of Strathclyde**
—414 32	Clydebank District
—414 34	Bearsden and Milngavie District
—414 36	Strathkelvin District
—414 38	Cumbernauld and Kilsyth District
—414 4	**Central districts of Strathclyde**
—414 41	Renfrew District
	Class here former Renfrewshire
	Class a specific part of former Renfrewshire not provided for here with the part, e.g., Greenock —41428
—414 43	City of Glasgow
	Class here Glasgow
—414 46	Monklands District
—414 49	Motherwell District
—414 5	**South central districts of Strathclyde**
—414 51	Eastwood District
—414 54	East Kilbride District
—414 57	Hamilton District
—414 6	**Southern districts of Strathclyde**
	Class here former Ayrshire
—414 61	Cunninghame District
—414 63	Kilmarnock and Loudoun District

*Class parts of this physiographic region or feature as instructed under —4–9

—414 64	Kyle and Carrick District
—414 67	Cumnock and Doon Valley District
—414 69	Clydesdale District

Former name: Lanark District

Class here former Lanarkshire

Class a specific part of former Lanarkshire not provided for here with the part, e.g., Motherwell —41449

—414 7   Dumfries and Galloway Region

For districts of Dumfries and Galloway, see —4148–4149

See also —16337 for Solway Firth

>   —414 8–414 9   Districts of Dumfries and Galloway

Class comprehensive works in —4147

—414 8   Eastern districts of Dumfries and Galloway

Class here former Dumfriesshire

—414 83	Annandale and Eskdale District
—414 86	Nithsdale District

Class here *Nith River

—414 9   Western districts of Dumfries and Galloway

Class here former Galloway

Class a specific part of former Galloway not provided for here with the part, e.g., New Abbey —41486

—414 92   Stewartry District

Class here former Kirkcudbrightshire

Class a specific part of former Kirkcudbrightshire not provided for here with the part, e.g., Creetown —41495

—414 95   Wigtown District

Including former Wigtownshire

—415   Ireland

For divisions of Ireland, see —416–419

>   —416–419   Divisions of Ireland

Class comprehensive works in —415

*Class parts of this physiographic region or feature as instructed under —4–9

—416   Ulster   Northern Ireland

               Class here *Bann River, *Lough Neagh

>   —416 1–416 7 Northern Ireland

               Class comprehensive works in —416

—416 1   Northeast area

               Class here former Antrim county

               Class a specific part of former Antrim county not provided for here with the part, e.g., Portrush —41627

—416 12   Antrim Borough

—416 13   Ballymena Borough

—416 14   Ballymoney Borough

—416 15   Moyle District

—416 16   Larne Borough

—416 17   Carrickfergus Borough

—416 18   Newtownabbey Borough

—416 19   Lisburn Borough

>   —416 2–416 4 Western area

               Class comprehensive works in —4162

—416 2   Western area

               Class here former Londonderry (Derry) county; *Sperrin Mountains

                  For Fermanagh District, see —4163; West central area, —4164

—416 21   City of Derry

                  Class here Derry (Londonderry) [*formerly* —41623]

—[416 23]   Derry (Londonderry)

                  Relocated to —41621

—416 25   Limavady District

—416 27   Coleraine Borough

—416 29   Magherafelt District

—416 3   Fermanagh District

               Former county

—416 4   West central area

               Class here former Tyrone county

*Class parts of this physiographic region or feature as instructed under —4–9

—416 41	Strabane District
—416 43	Cookstown District
—416 45	Dungannon District
—416 47	Omagh District
—416 5	Southeast area
	Class here former Down county
—416 51	Castlereagh Borough
—416 53	North Down Borough
—416 54	Ards Borough
	Class here *Strangford Lough
—416 56	Down District
—416 57	Banbridge District
—416 58	Newry and Mourne District
	Class here *Mourne Mountains
—416 6	Southern area
	Class here former Armagh county
	Class a specific part of former Armagh county not provided for here with the part, e.g., Bessbrook —41658
—416 61	Armagh District
	Including Armagh [*formerly* —41662]
—[416 62]	Armagh
	Relocated to —41661
—416 64	Craigavon Borough
—416 7	City of Belfast
	Class here Belfast, Greater Belfast
	Class a specific part of Greater Belfast not provided for here with the part, e.g., Newtownabbey —41618
—416 9	Counties of Republic of Ireland in Ulster
—416 93	Donegal County
—416 97	Monaghan County
—416 98	Cavan County
—417	Republic of Ireland (Eire)
	Class here *Shannon River

For counties in Ulster, see —4169; Leinster, —418; Munster, —419

*Class parts of this physiographic region or feature as instructed under —4–9

—417 1	Connacht

For divisions of Connacht, see —4172–4176

>	—417 2–417 6 Divisions of Connacht
	Class comprehensive works in —4171
—417 2	Sligo County
—417 25	Sligo
—417 3	Mayo County
—417 4	Galway County
—417 45	Galway
—417 48	Aran Islands
—417 5	Roscommon County
—417 6	Leitrim County
—418	Leinster
	Class here *Barrow River
—418 1	Northwest Leinster
—418 12	Longford County
—418 15	Westmeath County
—418 2	Northeast Leinster
—418 22	Meath County
	Class here *Boyne River
—418 25	Louth County
—418 256	Drogheda
—418 3	Dublin County
	Class here *Liffey River
—418 35	Dublin
—418 38	Dún Laoghaire
—418 4	Wicklow County
—418 5	Kildare county
	Class here *Bog of Allen
—418 6	Offaly County
—418 7	Laois County
—418 8	Southeast Leinster

*Class parts of this physiographic region or feature as instructed under —4–9

—418 82	Carlow County
—418 85	Wexford County
—418 856	Wexford
—418 9	Kilkenny County
	Class here *Nore River
—419	Munster
—419 1	Waterford County
	Class here *Suir River
—419 15	Waterford
—419 2	Tipperary County
—419 25	Clonmel
—419 3	Clare County
—419 4	Limerick County
—419 45	Limerick
—419 5	Cork County
	Class here *Blackwater River
—419 56	Cork
—419 6	Kerry County
—419 65	Killarney
—42	**England and Wales**

(Option: Class here ancient southern Britain, England; prefer —362)

See Manual at T2—41 and T2—42

SUMMARY

—421	**Greater London**
—422	**Southeastern England**
—423	**Southwestern England and Channel Islands**
—424	**Midlands of England**
—425	**East Midlands of England**
—426	**Eastern England East Anglia**
—427	**Northwestern England and Isle of Man**
—428	**Northeastern England**
—429	**Wales**

>   —421–428 England

     Class comprehensive works in —42

*Class parts of this physiographic region or feature as instructed under —4–9

—421   Greater London

SUMMARY

—421 2	City of London
—421 3	West London
—421 4	North London
—421 5	Tower Hamlets London Borough
—421 6	South London
—421 7	Outer London
—421 8	Boroughs created from Middlesex
—421 9	Boroughs created from Surrey

—421 2   City of London

—421 3   West London

—421 32   City of Westminster

—421 33   Hammersmith and Fulham London Borough

—421 34   Kensington and Chelsea Royal Borough

—421 4   North London

—421 42   Camden London Borough

—421 43   Islington London Borough

—421 44   Hackney London Borough

—421 5   Tower Hamlets London Borough

—421 6   South London

—421 62   Greenwich London Borough

—421 63   Lewisham London Borough

—421 64   Southwark London Borough

—421 65   Lambeth London Borough

—421 66   Wandsworth London Borough

—421 7   Outer London

> *For boroughs created from Middlesex, see —4218; boroughs created from Surrey, —4219*

\>   —421 72–421 76   Boroughs created from Essex

Class comprehensive works in —4217

—421 72   Waltham Forest London Borough

—421 73   Redbridge London Borough

—421 74   Havering London Borough

—421 75   Barking and Dagenham London Borough

—421 76   Newham London Borough

>   —421 77–421 78 Boroughs created from Kent

                             Class comprehensive works in —4217

—421 77	Bexley London Borough
—421 78	Bromley London Borough
—421 8	**Boroughs created from Middlesex**

                             Class here former Middlesex

—421 82	Hounslow London Borough
—421 83	Hillingdon London Borough
—421 84	Ealing London Borough
—421 85	Brent London Borough
—421 86	Harrow London Borough
—421 87	Barnet London Borough
—421 88	Haringey London Borough
—421 89	Enfield London Borough
—421 9	**Boroughs created from Surrey**
—421 91	Croydon London Borough
—421 92	Sutton London Borough
—421 93	Merton London Borough
—421 94	Kingston upon Thames London Borough
—421 95	Richmond upon Thames London Borough
—422	**Southeastern England**

                             Class here Home Counties; *Thames River

                             Class a specific Home County not provided for here with the subject, e.g., Hertfordshire —4258

                             For Greater London, see —421

SUMMARY

—422 1	**Surrey**
—422 3	**Kent**
—422 5	**East Sussex**
—422 6	**West Sussex**
—422 7	**Hampshire**
—422 8	**Isle of Wight**
—422 9	**Berkshire**

—422 1	Surrey

                             Class London boroughs created from Surrey in —4219

*Class parts of this physiographic region or feature as instructed under —4–9

—422 11	Runnymede Borough
—422 12	Spelthorne Borough
—422 13	Surrey Heath Borough
—422 14	Woking and Elmbridge Boroughs
—422 142	Woking Borough
	Class here Woking
—422 145	Elmbridge Borough
—422 15	Epsom and Ewell Borough
—422 16	Guildford Borough and Mole Valley District
—422 162	Guildford Borough
—422 165	Mole Valley District
—422 17	Reigate and Banstead Borough
—422 18	Tandridge District
—422 19	Waverley Borough
—422 3	Kent
	Class here *North Downs
	Class London boroughs created from Kent in —42177–42178
—422 31	Dartford and Gravesham Boroughs
—422 312	Dartford Borough
—422 315	Gravesham Borough
—422 32	City of Rochester upon Medway and Gillingham Borough
—422 323	City of Rochester upon Medway
—422 325	Gillingham Borough
	Class here Gillingham
—422 33	Swale Borough
—422 34	City of Canterbury
—422 35	Dover and Thanet Districts
—422 352	Dover District
	Class here Cinque Ports
	Class a specific part of the Cinque Ports not provided for here with the part, e.g., Hythe —422395
—422 357	Thanet District
—422 36	Sevenoaks District
—422 37	Tonbridge and Malling, and Maidstone Boroughs

*Class parts of this physiographic region or feature as instructed under —4–9

—422 372	Tonbridge and Malling Borough
—422 375	Maidstone Borough
—422 38	Tunbridge Wells Borough
—422 39	Ashford Borough and Shepway District
—422 392	Ashford Borough
—422 395	Shepway District
—422 5	East Sussex

Class here former Sussex; the *Weald

For West Sussex, see —4226

—422 51	Wealden District
—422 52	Rother District
—422 54	Hove Borough

Class here Hove

—422 56	Brighton Borough

Class here Brighton

—422 57	Lewes District
—422 58	Eastbourne Borough

Class here Eastbourne

—422 59	Hastings Borough

Class here Hastings

—422 6	West Sussex

Class here *South Downs

—422 61	Crawley Borough

Class here Crawley

—422 62	Chichester District
—422 64	Horsham District
—422 65	Mid Sussex District
—422 67	Arun District
—422 68	Worthing Borough

Class here Worthing

—422 69	Adur District
—422 7	Hampshire
—422 71	Basingstoke and Deane Borough
—422 72	Hart District and Rushmoor Borough

*Class parts of this physiographic region or feature as instructed under —4–9

—422 723	Hart District
—422 725	Rushmoor Borough
—422 73	Test Valley Borough and City of Winchester
—422 732	Test Valley Borough
	Class here *Test River
—422 735	City of Winchester
—422 74	East Hampshire District
—422 75	New Forest District
—422 76	City of Southampton
	Class here Southampton
—422 77	Eastleigh and Fareham Boroughs
—422 772	Eastleigh Borough
—422 775	Fareham Borough
	Class here Fareham
—422 78	Gosport Borough
	Class here Gosport
—422 79	City of Portsmouth and Havant Borough
—422 792	City of Portsmouth
	Class here Portsmouth
—422 795	Havant Borough
—422 8	Isle of Wight
—422 82	Medina Borough
—422 85	South Wight Borough
—422 9	Berkshire
—422 91	Newbury District
—422 93	Reading Borough
	Class here Reading
—422 94	Wokingham District
—422 96	Windsor and Maidenhead Royal Borough
—422 97	Slough Borough
	Class here Slough
—422 98	Bracknell Forest Borough
	Former name: Bracknell District
—423	Southwestern England and Channel Islands

*Class parts of this physiographic region or feature as instructed under —4–9

SUMMARY

—423 1	**Wiltshire**	
—423 3	**Dorset**	
—423 4	**Channel Islands**	
—423 5	**Devon**	
—423 7	**Cornwall and Scilly Isles**	
—423 8	**Somerset**	
—423 9	**Avon**	

—423 1   Wiltshire

—423 12   North Wiltshire District

—423 13   Thamesdown Borough

—423 15   West Wiltshire District

—423 17   Kennet District

—423 19   Salisbury District

           Class here *Salisbury Plain; *East Avon River

—423 3   Dorset

           Class here *Stour River

—423 31   West Dorset District

—423 32   North Dorset District

—423 34   East Dorset District

           Former heading: Wimborne District

—423 35   Weymouth and Portland Borough

—423 36   Purbeck District

—423 37   Poole Borough

           Class here Poole

—423 38   Bournemouth Borough

           Class here Bournemouth

—423 39   Christchurch Borough

—423 4   Channel Islands

—423 41   Jersey

           For Minquiers, see —42348; Dirouilles, Ecrehous, Paternosters, —42349

—423 42   Guernsey

           For Jethou, see —42347; Lihou, Lihoumel, —42349

—423 43   Alderney

           For Burhou, see —42347; Casquets, —42348

*Class parts of this physiographic region or feature as instructed under —4–9

—423 45	Sark
	For Brecqhou, see —42347
—423 46	Herm
—423 47	Burhou, Brecqhou, Jethou
—423 48	Casquets, Chausey Islands, Minquiers
—423 49	Other islands
	Including Barnouic, Dirouilles, Ecrehous, Lihou, Lihoumel, Paternosters, Roches Douvres
—423 5	Devon
	Class here *Exe River, *Tamar River
—423 51	Torridge District
—423 52	North Devon District
—423 53	West Devon Borough
	Class here *Dartmoor
—423 54	Mid Devon District
	Former heading: Tiverton
—423 55	Teignbridge District
—423 56	City of Exeter
	Class here Exeter
—423 57	East Devon District
—423 58	City of Plymouth
	Class here Plymouth
—423 59	South Hams District and Torbay Borough
—423 592	South Hams District
	Class here *Dart River
—423 595	Torbay Borough
	Class here Torbay
—423 7	Cornwall and Scilly Isles

>	—423 71–423 78 Cornwall
	Class comprehensive works in —4237
—423 71	North Cornwall District
—423 72	Restormel Borough
—423 74	Caradon District

*Class parts of this physiographic region or feature as instructed under —4–9

—423 75	Penwith District
—423 76	Kerrier District
—423 78	Carrick District
	Class here *Fal River
—423 79	Scilly Isles
—423 8	Somerset
—423 81	Sedgemoor District
—423 83	Mendip District
	Class here *Mendip Hills
—423 85	West Somerset District
	Class here *Exmoor, *Quantock Hills
—423 87	Taunton Deane District
	Class here *Blackdown Hills
—423 89	South Somerset District
	Former heading: Yeovil
—423 9	Avon
	Class here *Lower (Bristol) Avon River
—423 91	Northavon District
—423 93	City of Bristol
	Class here Bristol
—423 94	Kingswood District
—423 96	Woodspring District
—423 97	Wansdyke District
—423 98	City of Bath
	Class here Bath
—424	Midlands of England
	Class here *Welsh Marches; *Severn River

For East Midlands, see —425

SUMMARY

—424 1	Gloucestershire
—424 4	Hereford and Worcester
—424 5	Shropshire
—424 6	Staffordshire
—424 8	Warwickshire
—424 9	West Midlands Metropolitan County Black Country

*Class parts of this physiographic region or feature as instructed under —4–9

—424 1	Gloucestershire
—424 12	Tewkesbury Borough
—424 13	Forest of Dean District
—424 14	City of Gloucester
	Class here Gloucester
—424 16	Cheltenham Borough
	Class here Cheltenham
—424 17	Cotswold District
	Class here *Cotswolds
—424 19	Stroud District
—424 4	Hereford and Worcester

Class here former Herefordshire, former Worcestershire; *Upper (Warwickshire) Avon River

Class a specific part of former Worcestershire not provided for here with the part, e.g., Stourbridge —42493

—424 41	Wyre Forest District
—424 42	Bromsgrove District
—424 43	Redditch Borough
	Class here Redditch
—424 44	Leominster District
—424 45	South Herefordshire District
—424 46	City of Hereford
	Class here Hereford
—424 47	Malvern Hills District
—424 48	City of Worcester
	Class here Worcester
—424 49	Wychavon District
—424 5	Shropshire
	Former heading: Salop
—424 51	Oswestry Borough
—424 53	North Shropshire District
—424 54	Shrewsbury and Atcham Borough
—424 56	The Wrekin District
—424 57	South Shropshire District

*Class parts of this physiographic region or feature as instructed under —4–9

—424 59	Bridgnorth District
—424 6	**Staffordshire**
—424 61	Staffordshire Moorlands District
—424 62	Newcastle-under-Lyme Borough
—424 63	City of Stoke-on-Trent
	Class here Stoke-on-Trent
—424 64	Stafford Borough
—424 65	East Staffordshire District
—424 66	South Staffordshire District
—424 67	Cannock Chase District
—424 68	Lichfield District
—424 69	Tamworth Borough
	Class here Tamworth
—424 8	**Warwickshire**
—424 81	North Warwickshire Borough
—424 83	Nuneaton and Bedworth Borough
—424 85	Rugby Borough
—424 87	Warwick District
—424 89	Stratford-on-Avon District
—424 9	**West Midlands Metropolitan County** Black Country
—424 91	Wolverhampton Metropolitan Borough
	Class here Wolverhampton
—424 92	Walsall Metropolitan Borough
	Class here Walsall
—424 93	Dudley Metropolitan Borough
—424 94	Sandwell Metropolitan Borough
—424 96	City of Birmingham
	Class here Birmingham
—424 97	Solihull Metropolitan Borough
—424 98	City of Coventry
	Class here Coventry
—425	**East Midlands of England**
	Class here *Chilterns; *Trent River

*Class parts of this physiographic region or feature as instructed under —4–9

SUMMARY

—425 1	**Derbyshire**
—425 2	**Nottinghamshire**
—425 3	**Lincolnshire**
—425 4	**Leicestershire**
—425 5	**Northamptonshire**
—425 6	**Bedfordshire**
—425 7	**Oxfordshire**
—425 8	**Hertfordshire**
—425 9	**Buckinghamshire**

—425 1   Derbyshire

> Class here *Derwent River of Derbyshire

—425 11   High Peak Borough

> Class here *Peak District

—425 12   Chesterfield Borough

—425 13   Derbyshire Dales District

> Former name: West Derbyshire District

> Class here *Dove River

—425 14   North East Derbyshire District

—425 15   Bolsover District

—425 16   Amber Valley District

—425 17   City of Derby

> Class here Derby

—425 18   Erewash Borough

—425 19   South Derbyshire District

—425 2   Nottinghamshire

—425 21   Bassetlaw District

—425 23   Mansfield District

—425 24   Newark and Sherwood District

> Class here *Sherwood Forest

—425 25   Ashfield District

—425 26   Broxtowe Borough

—425 27   City of Nottingham

> Class here Nottingham

—425 28   Gedling Borough

—425 29   Rushcliffe Borough

*Class parts of this physiographic region or feature as instructed under —4–9

—425 3	Lincolnshire

Class here *Lincoln Heath; *the Wash; *Witham River

—425 31	West Lindsey District

Class here former Parts of Lindsey

Class a specific part of former Parts of Lindsey not provided for here with the part, e.g., Scunthorpe —42831

—425 32	East Lindsey District

Class here *Lincoln Wolds

—425 34	City of Lincoln

Class here Lincoln

—425 35	North Kesteven District

Class here former Parts of Kesteven

For South Kesteven, see —42538

—425 37	Boston Borough
—425 38	South Kesteven District
—425 39	South Holland District

Class here former Parts of Holland; *Welland River

For Boston Borough, see —42537

—425 4	Leicestershire
—425 41	Blaby District
—425 42	City of Leicester

Class here Leicester

—425 43	Oadby and Wigston Borough
—425 44	Harborough District
—425 45	Rutland District
—425 46	Melton Borough
—425 47	Charnwood Borough
—425 48	North West Leicestershire District
—425 49	Hinckley and Bosworth Borough
—425 5	Northamptonshire

Class here *Nene River

—425 51	Corby District
—425 52	Kettering Borough
—425 54	East Northamptonshire District

*Class parts of this physiographic region or feature as instructed under —4–9

—425 56	Daventry District
	Class here *Northampton Uplands
—425 57	Northampton Borough
	Class here Northampton
—425 58	Wellingborough Borough
—425 59	South Northamptonshire District
—425 6	Bedfordshire
—425 61	North Bedfordshire Borough
—425 63	Mid Bedfordshire District
—425 65	South Bedfordshire District
—425 67	Luton Borough
	Class here Luton
—425 7	Oxfordshire
—425 71	West Oxfordshire District
—425 73	Cherwell District
—425 74	City of Oxford
	Class here Oxford
—425 76	Vale of White Horse District
—425 79	South Oxfordshire District
—425 8	Hertfordshire
—425 81	North Hertfordshire District
—425 82	Stevenage Borough
	Class here Stevenage
—425 83	East Hertfordshire District
—425 84	Dacorum District
—425 85	City of Saint Albans
—425 86	Welwyn Hatfield District
—425 87	Broxbourne Borough
—425 88	Three Rivers District
—425 89	Watford and Hertsmere Boroughs
—425 892	Watford Borough
	Class here Watford
—425 895	Hertsmere Borough

*Class parts of this physiographic region or feature as instructed under —4–9

—425 9	Buckinghamshire
—425 91	Milton Keynes Borough
	Class here Milton Keynes
—425 93	Aylesbury Vale District
—425 95	Wycombe District
—425 97	Chiltern District
—425 98	South Bucks District
	Former heading: Beaconsfield
—426	Eastern England East Anglia

Class here the *Fens; *Great Ouse River

SUMMARY

—426 1	**Norfolk**
—426 4	**Suffolk**
—426 5	**Cambridgeshire**
—426 7	**Essex**

>	—426 1–426 5 East Anglia

Class comprehensive works in —426

—426 1	Norfolk
	Class here *Yare River
—426 12	North Norfolk District
—426 13	King's Lynn and West Norfolk Borough
—426 14	Breckland District
—426 15	City of Norwich
	Class here Norwich
—426 17	Broadland District
	Class here *Norfolk Broads
—426 18	Great Yarmouth Borough
—426 19	South Norfolk District
	Class here *Waveney River
—426 4	Suffolk
—426 41	Waveney District
—426 43	Forest Heath District

*Class parts of this physiographic region or feature as instructed under —4–9

—426 44	Saint Edmundsbury Borough
	Class here former West Suffolk
	Class a specific part of West Suffolk not provided for here with the part, e.g., Mildenhall —42643
—426 45	Mid Suffolk District
—426 46	Suffolk Coastal District
	Class here former East Suffolk
	Class a specific part of East Suffolk not provided for here with the part, e.g., Lowestoft —42641
—426 48	Babergh District
—426 49	Ipswich Borough
	Class here Ipswich
—426 5	Cambridgeshire
—426 51	City of Peterborough
—426 53	Fenland District
	Class here former Isle of Ely
	See also —42656 for Ely
—426 54	Huntingdonshire District
	Former county
—426 56	East Cambridgeshire District
—426 57	South Cambridgeshire District
—426 59	City of Cambridge
	Class here Cambridge
—426 7	Essex
	Class London boroughs created from Essex in —42172–42176
—426 71	Uttlesford and Braintree Districts
—426 712	Uttlesford District
—426 715	Braintree District
—426 72	Colchester Borough and Tendring District
—426 723	Colchester Borough
—426 725	Tendring District
—426 73	Harlow District
	Class here Harlow
—426 74	Epping Forest District

—426 75	Chelmsford Borough and Maldon District
—426 752	Chelmsford Borough
—426 756	Maldon District
—426 76	Brentwood District
—426 77	Basildon and Rochford Districts
—426 772	Basildon District
	Class here Basildon
—426 775	Rochford District
—426 78	Thurrock Borough
	Class here Thurrock
—426 79	Castle Point District and Southend-on-Sea Borough
—426 792	Castle Point District
—426 795	Southend-on-Sea Borough
	Class here Southend-on-Sea
—427	Northwestern England and Isle of Man

Class here comprehensive works on northern England

For northeastern England, see —428

SUMMARY

—427 1	**Cheshire**
—427 3	**Greater Manchester Metropolitan County**
—427 5	**Merseyside Metropolitan County**
—427 6	**Lancashire**
—427 8	**Cumbria**
—427 9	**Isle of Man**

—427 1	Cheshire
—427 12	Crewe and Nantwich Borough
—427 13	Congleton Borough
—427 14	City of Chester
—427 15	Vale Royal Borough
—427 16	Macclesfield Borough
—427 17	Ellesmere Port and Neston Borough
—427 18	Halton Borough
—427 19	Warrington Borough
—427 3	Greater Manchester Metropolitan County
—427 31	Trafford Metropolitan Borough
—427 32	City of Salford

—427 33	City of Manchester
	Class here Manchester
—427 34	Stockport Metropolitan Borough
—427 35	Tameside Metropolitan Borough
—427 36	Wigan Metropolitan Borough
—427 37	Bolton Metropolitan Borough
—427 38	Bury Metropolitan Borough
—427 39	Rochdale and Oldham Metropolitan Boroughs
—427 392	Rochdale Metropolitan Borough
—427 393	Oldham Metropolitan Borough
—427 5	Merseyside Metropolitan County
	Class here *Mersey River
—427 51	Wirral Metropolitan Borough
—427 53	City of Liverpool
	Class here Liverpool
—427 54	Knowsley Metropolitan Borough
—427 57	Saint Helens Metropolitan Borough
—427 59	Sefton Metropolitan Borough
—427 6	Lancashire
	Class here former Lancashire
	Class a specific part of former Lancashire not provided for here with the part, e.g., Liverpool —42753
—427 61	West Lancashire District and Chorley Borough
—427 612	West Lancashire District
—427 615	Chorley Borough
—427 62	Blackburn and Hyndburn Boroughs
—427 623	Blackburn Borough
—427 625	Hyndburn Borough
—427 63	Rossendale Borough
—427 64	Burnley and Pendle Boroughs
—427 642	Burnley Borough
—427 645	Pendle Borough
—427 65	Blackpool Borough
	Class here Blackpool

*Class parts of this physiographic region or feature as instructed under —4–9

—427 66	Fylde and Preston Boroughs
—427 662	Fylde Borough
	Class here *The Fylde
—427 665	Preston Borough
—427 67	South Ribble Borough
—427 68	Wyre and Ribble Valley Boroughs
—427 682	Wyre Borough
—427 685	Ribble Valley Borough
	Class here *Forest of Bowland; *Ribble River
—427 69	City of Lancaster

—427 8   **Cumbria**

Class here former Cumberland, former Westmorland; Lake District; Cumbrian Mountains

—427 81	Barrow-in-Furness Borough
—427 83	South Lakeland District
—427 84	Copeland Borough
—427 86	Eden District

Class here *Eden River

—427 87   Allerdale District

See also —16337 for Solway Firth

—427 89   City of Carlisle

—427 9   **Isle of Man**

—428   **Northeastern England**

Class here the *Pennines

SUMMARY

—428 1	**West Yorkshire Metropolitan County**
—428 2	**South Yorkshire Metropolitan County**
—428 3	**Humberside**
—428 4	**North Yorkshire**
—428 5	**Cleveland**
—428 6	**Durham**
—428 7	**Tyne and Wear Metropolitan County**
—428 8	**Northumberland**

—428 1   West Yorkshire Metropolitan County

Class here former Yorkshire, former West Riding of Yorkshire

Class a specific part of former Yorkshire, of former West Riding, not provided for here with the part, e.g., Sheffield —42821

*Class parts of the physiographic region or feature as instructed under —4–9

—428 12   Calderdale Metropolitan Borough

—428 13   Kirklees Metropolitan Borough

—428 15   City of Wakefield

                  Class here *Aire River

—428 17   City of Bradford

—428 19   City of Leeds

                  Including Wetherby [*formerly* —42842]

—428 2   **South Yorkshire Metropolitan County**

—428 21   City of Sheffield

—428 23   Rotherham Metropolitan Borough

—428 25   Barnsley Metropolitan Borough

—428 27   Doncaster Metropolitan Borough

—428 3   Humberside

                  Class here former East Riding of Yorkshire; *Yorkshire Wolds; *Humber River

                  Class a specific part of former East Riding not provided for here with the part, e.g., Norton —42846

—428 31   Scunthorpe Borough

                  Class here Scunthorpe

—428 32   Glanford Borough

—428 33   Cleethorpes Borough

—428 34   Great Grimsby Borough

                  Class here Grimsby

—428 35   Boothferry Borough

—428 36   Beverley Borough

—428 37   City of Kingston upon Hull

                  Class here Hull

—428 38   Holderness Borough

—428 39   East Yorkshire Borough

                  Former heading: North Wolds

—428 4   North Yorkshire

                  Class here former North Riding of Yorkshire; *Yorkshire Dales; *Derwent River of Yorkshire, *Ouse River

                  Class a specific part of former North Riding not provided for here with the part, e.g., Middlesbrough —42853

*Class parts of this physiographic region or feature as instructed under —4–9

—428 41	Craven District
—428 42	Harrogate Borough
	Wetherby relocated to —42819
—428 43	City of York
	Class here York
—428 45	Selby District
—428 46	Ryedale District
	Class here *North Yorkshire Moors
—428 47	Scarborough Borough
—428 48	Richmondshire District
	Class here *Swale River, *Ure River
—428 49	Hambleton District
	Class here *Cleveland Hills

—428 5   Cleveland

    Including former Teesside

    Class here *Tees River

—428 51	Stockton-on-Tees Borough
—428 53	Middlesbrough Borough
—428 54	Langbaurgh-on-Tees Borough
	Former heading: Langbaurgh Borough
—428 57	Hartlepool Borough
	Class here Hartlepool

—428 6   Durham

    Class here *Wear River

—428 61	Teesdale District
—428 62	Sedgefield District
—428 63	Darlington Borough
—428 64	Wear Valley District
—428 65	City of Durham
—428 67	Easington District
—428 68	Derwentside District
—428 69	Chester-le-Street District

—428 7   Tyne and Wear Metropolitan County

    Class here *Tyne River

*Class parts of this physiographic region or feature as instructed under —4–9

—428 71	Sunderland Metropolitan Borough
—428 73	Gateshead Metropolitan Borough
—428 75	South Tyneside Metropolitan Borough
—428 76	City of Newcastle upon Tyne

                  Class here Newcastle upon Tyne

—428 79	North Tyneside Metropolitan Borough
—428 8	Northumberland

                  Class here *Cheviot Hills

—428 81	Tynedale District

                  Class here Hadrian's Wall

                  Class a specific part of Hadrian's Wall not provided for here with the part, e.g., in Carlisle —42789

—428 83	Castle Morpeth Borough
—428 84	Blyth Valley Borough
—428 86	Wansbeck District
—428 87	Alnwick District

                  Class here *Coquet River

—428 89	Berwick-upon-Tweed Borough
—429	Wales

                  Class here *Cambrian Mountains

SUMMARY

—429 1	**North Wales**
—429 2	**Gwynedd**
—429 3	**Clwyd**
—429 4	**South Wales**
—429 5	**Powys**
—429 6	**Dyfed**
—429 7	**Mid Glamorgan**
—429 8	**West and South Glamorgan**
—429 9	**Gwent**

—429 1	North Wales

                  For Gwynedd, see —4292; Clwyd, —4293; Montgomery, —42951

—429 2	Gwynedd

                  Class here former Caernarvonshire

—429 21	Ynys Môn Borough (Isle of Anglesey)

                  Former County of Anglesey

—429 23	Dwyfor District

*Class parts of this physiographic region or feature as instructed under —4–9

—429 25	Arfon Borough
	Class here *Snowdonia
—429 27	Aberconwy Borough
—429 29	Meirionnydd District
	Class here former Merioneth
	Class a specific part of former Merioneth not provided for here with the part, e.g., Edeyrnion —42937
—429 3	Clwyd
	Class here former Denbighshire
	Class a specific part of former Denbighshire not provided for here with the part, e.g., Llanrwst —42927
—429 31	Colwyn Borough
—429 32	Rhuddlan Borough
—429 33	Delyn Borough
	Class here former Flintshire
	Class a specific part of former Flintshire not provided for here with the part, e.g., Buckley —42936
—429 36	Alyn and Deeside District
—429 37	Glyndŵr District
—429 39	Wrexham Maelor District
—429 4	South Wales
	For Powys, see —4295; Dyfed, —4296; Mid Glamorgan, —4297; West and South Glamorgan, —4298; Gwent, —4299
—429 5	Powys
	Class here mid Wales; *Wye River
	Class a specific part of mid Wales not provided for here with the part, e.g., Aberystwyth —42961
—429 51	Montgomery District
	Former name: Montgomeryshire
	Class here *Severn River in Wales
—429 54	Radnor District
	Former name: Radnorshire
—429 56	Brecknock Borough
	Class here former Breconshire
	Class a specific part of former Breconshire not provided for here with the part, e.g., Brynmawr —42995

*Class parts of this physiographic region or feature as instructed under —4–9

—429 6	Dyfed
—429 61	Ceredigion District
	Former name: Cardiganshire
—429 62	Preseli District
	Class here former Pembrokeshire
	Class a specific part of former Pembrokeshire not provided for here with the part, e.g., Narberth —42963
—429 63	South Pembrokeshire District
—429 65	Carmarthen District
	Class here former Carmarthenshire
	Class a specific part of former Carmarthenshire not provided for here with the part, e.g., Burry Port —42967
—429 67	Llanelli Borough
—429 68	Dinefwr Borough
—429 7	Mid Glamorgan
	Class here former Glamorgan
	For West and South Glamorgan, see —4298
—429 71	Ogwr Borough
—429 72	Rhondda Borough
	Class here Rhondda
—429 73	Cynon Valley Borough
—429 75	Merthyr Tydfil Borough
	Class here Merthyr Tydfil
—429 76	Rhymney Valley District
—429 78	Taff-Ely Borough
—429 8	West and South Glamorgan
—429 81	West Glamorgan
	For City of Swansea, see —42982; Lliw Valley Borough, —42983; Neath Borough, —42984; Afan Borough, —42985
—429 82	City of Swansea
—429 83	Lliw Valley Borough
—429 84	Neath Borough
—429 85	Afan Borough
—429 86	South Glamorgan
	For City of Cardiff, see —42987; Vale of Glamorgan Borough, —42989

—429 87	City of Cardiff
	Class here Cardiff
—429 89	Vale of Glamorgan Borough
—429 9	Gwent

Class here former Monmouthshire

Class a specific part of former Monmouthshire not provided for here with the part, e.g., Rhymney —42976

—429 91	Newport Borough
—429 93	Islwyn Borough
—429 95	Blaenau Gwent Borough
—429 97	Torfaen Borough
—429 98	Monmouth District
—43	**Central Europe Germany**

Class here Federal Republic of Germany, Holy Roman Empire

(Option: Class here ancient Germanic regions; prefer —363)

Class a specific part of Holy Roman Empire not provided for here with the part, e.g., Lombardy —452

For Switzerland, see —494

SUMMARY

—431	**Northeastern Germany**
—432	**Saxony and Thuringia**
—433	**Bavaria**
—434	**Southwestern Germany**
—435	**Northwestern Germany**
—436	**Austria and Liechtenstein**
—437	**Czechoslovakia**
—438	**Poland**
—439	**Hungary**

> —431–435 Germany

Class comprehensive works in —43

> —431–432 East Germany (German Democratic Republic) and Berlin

Class comprehensive works in —431

—431	Northeastern Germany

Class here East Germany (German Democratic Republic)

For Saxony and Thuringia, see —432

—431 5	Brandenburg
	Former state of German Democratic Republic
—431 51	Cottbus Bezirk (district)
—431 53	Frankfurt Bezirk (district)
—431 532	Frankfurt an der Oder
—431 55	Berlin
—431 552	East Berlin
—431 554	West Berlin
—431 57	Potsdam Bezirk (district)
—431 572	Potsdam
—431 7	Mecklenburg
	Former state of German Democratic Republic
	Including German Pomerania
—431 72	Neubrandenburg Bezirk (district)
—431 74	Rostock Bezirk (district)
—431 76	Schwerin Bezirk (district)
—431 8	Saxony-Anhalt
	Former state of German Democratic Republic
	Including Prussian Saxony
—431 82	Magdeburg Bezirk (district)
	Class here *Harz Mountains [*formerly* —4359]
—431 822	Magdeburg
—431 84	Halle Bezirk (district)
	Including Anhalt [*formerly* —4319]
—[431 9]	Anhalt
	Relocated to —43184
—432	Saxony and Thuringia
—432 1	Saxony
	Former state of German Democratic Republic
—432 12	Leipzig Bezirk (district)
—432 122	Leipzig
—432 14	Dresden Bezirk (district)
—432 142	Dresden

*Class parts of this physiographic region or feature as instructed under —4–9

—432 16	Karl-Marx-Stadt Bezirk (district)
—432 162	Karl-Marx-Stadt (Chemnitz)

—432 2   **Thuringia**

         Former state of German Democratic Republic

         Including *Thuringian Forest

—432 22	Gera Bezirk (district)
—432 24	Erfurt Bezirk (district)
—432 26	Suhl Bezirk (district)

>   **—433–435   West Germany (Federal Republic of Germany)**

         Class comprehensive works in —43

         For West Berlin, see —431554

—433   **Bavaria**

         Class here *Danube River in Germany [*formerly* —4348]; *Franconian Jura

         (Option: Class here ancient Vindelicia; prefer —363

—433 1	Oberfranken Regierungsbezirk (Upper Franconia district)
—433 11	Coburg
—433 15	Bayreuth
—433 18	Bamberg
—433 2	Mittelfranken Regierungsbezirk (Middle Franconia district)
—433 22	Erlangen
—433 24	Nuremberg (Nürnberg)
—433 3	Unterfranken Regierungsbezirk (Lower Franconia district)
—433 31	Aschaffenburg
—433 36	Schweinfurt
—433 39	Würzburg
—433 4	Oberpfalz Regierungsbezirk (Upper Palatinate district)
—433 47	Regensburg
—433 5	Niederbayern Regierungsbezirk (Lower Bavaria district)

         Class here *Bavarian Forest

—433 55	Passau
—433 58	Landshut
—433 6	Oberbayern Regierungsbezirk (Upper Bavaria (Oberbayern) district)

*Class parts of this physiographic region or feature as instructed under —4–9

—433 62	Ingolstadt
—433 64	Munich (München)
—433 7	Schwaben Regierungsbezirk (Swabia district)
—433 75	Augsburg
—434	Southwestern Germany
	Class here *Rhine River, *Main River
—434 1	Hesse
—434 12	Kassel Regierungsbezirk (district)
—434 124	Kassel
—434 14	Giessen Regierungsbezirk (district)
	Class here *Lahn River
—434 16	Darmstadt Regierungsbezirk (district)
	Including *Taunus Mountains
—434 163	Offenbach am Main
—434 164	Frankfurt am Main
—434 165	Weisbaden
—434 167	Darmstadt
—434 2	Saarland
	Class here *Saar River
	Rhine Province (Rhenish Prussia) relocated to —4343
—434 21	Saarbrücken
—434 3	Rhineland-Palatinate
	Class here Rhine Province (Rhenish Prussia) [*formerly* —4342]; *Moselle River
	For North Rhine-Westphalia, see —4355; Saarland, —4342
—434 31	Trier Regierungsbezirk (district)
—434 313	Trier
—434 32	Koblenz Regierungsbezirk (district)
—434 323	Koblenz
—434 35	Rheinhessen-Pfalz Regierungsbezirk (district)
	Class here Palatinate
	For Upper Palatinate, see —4334
—434 351	Mainz
—434 352	Worms

*Class parts of this physiographic region or feature as instructed under —4–9

—434 353	Ludwigshafen am Rhein
—434 6	Baden-Württemberg

Class here *Black Forest [*formerly* —4348]; Baden

For Stuttgart and Tübingen Regierungsbezirke, see —4347

—434 62	Freiburg Regierungsbezirk (district)

Including *Lake Constance

—434 626	Freiburg im Breisgau
—434 64	Karlsruhe Regierungsbezirk (district)

Class here former Baden

Class former Baden in Freiburg Regierungsbezirk in —43462, in Stuttgart and Tubingen Regierungsbezirke in —4347

—434 643	Karlsruhe
—434 645	Heidelberg
—434 646	Mannheim
—434 7	Stuttgart and Tübingen Regierungsbezirke (districts)

Class here former Württemberg

Class former Württemberg in Freiburg Regierungsbezirk in —43462, in Karlsruhe Regierungsbezirk in —43464

—434 71	Stuttgart Regierungsbezirk (district)
—434 715	Stuttgart
—434 73	Tübingen Regierungsbezirk (district)

Including former Hohenzollern [*formerly* —4349]

Class here *Swabian Jura

—[434 8]	Black Forest

Black Forest relocated to —4346, Danube River in Germany to —433

—[434 9]	Hohenzollern

Relocated to —43473

—435	Northwestern Germany
—435 1	Northernmost states
—435 12	Schleswig-Holstein

Including North Friesland; *North Frisian Islands

—435 15	Hamburg
—435 2	Bremen
—435 21	Bremerhaven

*Class parts of this physiographic region or feature as instructed under —4–9

—435 5	North Rhine-Westphalia

          Class here *Ruhr River

              For Münster, Arnsberg, Detmold Regierungsbezirke, see —4356

—435 51	Cologne (Köln) Regierungsbezirk (district)
—435 511	Aachen
—435 514	Cologne (Köln)
—435 518	Bonn
—435 53	Düsseldorf Regierungsbezirk (district)
—435 532	Wuppertal
—435 534	Düsseldorf
—435 536	Duisburg
—435 538	Essen
—435 6	Münster, Arnsberg, Detmold Regierungsbezirke (districts)

          Class here Westphalia; *Lippe River

—435 61	Münster Regierungsbezirk (district)
—435 614	Münster
—435 618	Gelsenkirchen
—435 63	Arnsberg Regierungsbezirk (district)
—435 632	Bochum
—435 633	Dortmund
—435 65	Detmold Regierungsbezirk (district)

          Including *Teutoburg Forest

—435 655	Bielefeld
—435 9	Lower Saxony

          Harz Mountains relocated to —43182

—435 91	Weser-Ems Regierungsbezirk (district)
—435 911	Osnabrück
—435 914	Oldenburg
—435 917	East Friesland region

              Contains Aurich, Friesland, Leer, Wittmund Kreise; Emden, Wilhelmshaven cities

              Class here *East Frisian Islands

—435 93	Lüneburg Regierungsbezirk (district)

*Class parts of this physiographic region or feature as instructed under —4–9

—435 95	Hannover Regierungsbezirk (district)
—435 954	Hannover
—435 958	Hildesheim
—435 97	Braunschweig Regierungsbezirk (district)
—435 976	Braunschweig
—436	Austria and Liechtenstein

Class here Austrian Empire, Dual Monarchy of Austria-Hungary

(Option: Class here ancient Noricum; prefer —363)

Class a specific part of Austrian Empire, of Dual Monarchy, not provided for here with the part, e.g., Croatia —4972

—436 1	Northeastern Austria
—436 12	Niederösterreich Land (Lower Austria province)
—436 13	Wien Land (Vienna province)

Class here Vienna

—436 15	Burgenland Land (province)
—436 2	Oberösterreich Land (Upper Austria province)
—436 3	Salzburg Land (province)
—436 4	Western Austria, and Liechtenstein

(Option: Class here ancient Raetia; prefer —363)

—436 42	Tyrol Land (province)
—436 45	Vorarlberg Land (province)
—436 48	Liechtenstein

Independent principality

—436 5	Styria Land (province)
—436 6	Carinthia Land (province)
—437	Czechoslovakia
—437 1	Bohemia

Contains Jihočeský, Severočeský, Středočeský, Východočeský, Západočeský krajs (regions)

Including Sudetenland

—437 12	Praha (Prague)
—437 2	Moravia

Contains Jihomoravský and Severomoravský krajs (regions)

Including Czech Silesia

—437 3 Slovakia

> Contains Bratislava, Středoslovenský, Východoslovenský, Západoslovenský krajs (regions)

—438 Poland

—438 1 Northwestern Poland   Polish Pomerania

> Contains Gorzow Wielkopolski, Koszalin, Slupsk, Szczecin, Zielona Gora voivodeships (provinces)

> Class here Pomerania

> *For German Pomerania, see —4317*

—438 2 North central Poland

> Contains Bydgoszcz, Elblag, Gdansk (Danzig), Torun, Wloclawek voivodeships (provinces)

> Including West Prussia, Pomerelia

—438 3 Northeastern Poland

> Contains Bialystok, Lomza, Olsztyn, Suwalki voivodeships (provinces)

> Including East Prussia

—438 4 Central Poland

> Contains Biala Podlaska, Ciechanow, Kalisz, Kielce, Konin, Leszno, Lodz, Lublin, Ostroleka, Pila, Piotrkow Trybunalski, Plock, Poznan, Radom, Siedlce, Sieradz, Skierniewice, Tarnobrzeg, Warsaw, Zamosc voivodeships (provinces)

—438 5 Southwestern Poland

> Contains Czestochowa, Jelenia Gora, Katowice, Legnica, Opole, Walbrzych, Wroclaw voivodeships (provinces)

> Class here Silesia

> *For Czech Silesia, see —4372*

—438 6 Southeastern Poland   Polish Galicia

> Contains Bielsko (Bielsko-Biala), Krakow, Krosno, Nowy Sacz, Przemysl, Rzeszow, Tarnow voivodeships (provinces)

> Class here Galicia

> *For East Galicia, see —47718*

—439 Hungary

> (Option: Class here ancient Pannonia; prefer —398)

—439 1 Pest Megye (county) and Budapest

—439 12 Budapest

—439 7   Hungary west of Danube

Contains Baranya, Fejer, Gyor-Sopron, Komarom, Somogy, Tolna Megye, Vas, Veszprem, Zala megyek (counties)

For Pest Megye, see —4391

—439 8   Hungary east of Danube

Contains Bacs-Kiskun, Csongrad, Heves, Nograd, Szolnok megyek (counties)

For Pest Megye, see —4391; easternmost Hungary, —4399

—439 9   Easternmost Hungary

Contains Bekes, Borsod-Abauj-Zemplen, Hajdu-Bihar, Szabolcs-Szatmar megyek (counties)

—44   **France and Monaco**

(Option: Class here ancient Celtic regions, Gaul [Gallia Transalpina]; prefer —364)

Class a specific overseas department of France with the department, e.g., Martinique —72982

SUMMARY

—441	**Northwestern France**	**Brittany (Bretagne) region**
—442	**Northern France**	**Normandy (Normandie) region**
—443	**Northeastern France**	**Champagne region**
—444	**Eastern France**	**Burgundy (Bourgogne) region**
—445	**Central France**	**Centre region**
—446	**Western France**	**Poitou region**
—447	**Southwestern France**	**Guyenne (Aquitaine) region**
—448	**Southern France**	**Languedoc region**
—449	**Southeastern France and Monaco**	**Provence region**

—441   Northwestern France   Brittany (Bretagne) region

\>   —441 1–441 5   Former region of Brittany   Modern region of Brittany

Class comprehensive works on former Brittany, on modern Brittany in —441

—441 1   Finistère department

—441 2   Côtes-du-Nord department

—441 3   Morbihan department

—441 4   Loire-Atlantique department

Former name: Loire-Inférieure

—441 5   Ille-et-Vilaine department

—441 6   Mayenne department

      Class here former region of Maine, modern region of Pays de la Loire

      Class each other specific department of Maine, of Pays de la Loire with the department, e.g., Sarthe —4417

—441 7   Sarthe department

—441 8   Maine-et-Loire department

      Class here former region of Anjou

      Class each other specific department of Anjou with the department, e.g., Sarthe —4417

—442   Northern France   Normandy (Normandie) region

>   —442 1–442 5   Former region of Normandy   Modern region of Basse-Normandie

      Class comprehensive works on Normandy, on Basse-Normandie in —442

—442 1   Manche department

—442 2   Calvados department

—442 3   Orne department

—442 4   Eure department

      Class here modern region of Haute-Normandie

      For Seine-Maritime department, see —4425

—442 5   Seine-Maritime department

      Former name: Seine-Inférieure

      Class here Rouen

—442 6   Somme department

      Class here former and modern regions of Picardy (Picardie)

      Class each other specific department of Picardy with the department, e.g., Oise —4435

—442 7   Pas-de-Calais department

      Including former region of Artois

      Class here modern region of Nord-Pas-de-Calais

      For Nord department, see —4428

—442 8   Nord department (Former region of French Flanders)

—443	Northeastern France Champagne region

Class here *Marne River

>	—443 1–443 3 Modern region of Champagne-Ardenne

Class here former region of Champagne

Class comprehensive works on Champagne, on Champagne-Ardenne in —443, each specific department of Champagne not provided for here with the department, e.g., Yonne —4441

—443 1	Ardennes department
—443 2	Marne department
—443 3	Aube and Haute-Marne departments
—443 31	Aube department
—443 32	Haute-Marne department
—443 4	Former region of Ile-de-France

Class here *Seine River

Class each specific department of Ile-de-France not provided for here with the department, e.g., Seine-et-Marne —4437

—443 45	Aisne department
—443 5	Oise department
—443 6	Paris metropolitan area

Including former Seine department, former Seine-et-Oise department

Class here modern Région Parisienne

For Seine-et-Marne department, see —4437

—443 61	Paris department
—443 62	Seine-Saint-Denis department
—443 63	Val-de-Marne department
—443 64	Hauts-de-Seine department
—443 65	Essonne department
—443 66	Yvelines department
—443 67	Val-d'Oise department
—443 7	Seine-et-Marne department
—443 8	Lorraine and Alsace regions

Class here *Argonne; *Vosges Mountains

(Option: Class here Germania Superior; prefer —364)

*Class parts of this physiographic region or feature as instructed under —4–9

>	—443 81–443 82 Former and modern regions of Lorraine

Class comprehensive works in —4438, each specific department of Lorraine not provided for here with the department, e.g., Vosges —4439

—443 81	Meuse department
—443 82	Meurthe-et-Moselle and Moselle departments
—443 823	Meurthe-et-Moselle department
—443 825	Moselle department
—443 83	Former and moderns region of Alsace

For territory of Belfort, see —44455

—443 833	Haut-Rhin department
—443 835	Bas-Rhin department
—443 835 3	Strasbourg
—443 9	Vosges department
—444	Eastern France Burgundy (Bourgogne) region

Class here *Saône River

>	—444 1–444 4 Former region of Burgundy Modern region of Burgundy

Class comprehensive works on former Burgundy, on modern Burgundy in —444

Class each specific department of Burgundy not provided for here with the department, e.g., Nièvre —4456

—444 1	Yonne department
—444 2	Côte-d'Or department
—444 3	Saône-et-Loire department
—444 4	Ain department

Including former regions of Bugey and Dombes

—444 5	Former and modern regions of Franche-Comté, and Territory of Belfort

Class here *Jura Mountains in France

Class each specific department of Franche-Comté not provided for here with the department, e.g., Doubs —4446

—444 53	Haute-Saône department
—444 55	Territory of Belfort

*Class parts of this physiographic region or feature as instructed under —4–9

—444 6	Doubs department
—444 7	Jura department
—444 8	Savoie department

         Class here former region of Savoy

         Comprehensive works on Alps in France relocated to —449

           For Haute-Savoie department, see —4449

—444 9	Haute-Savoie department
—445	Central France Centre region

         Class here *Loire River

         (Option: Class here ancient Lugdunensis; prefer —364)

>   —445 1–445 5   Modern region of Centre   Former region of Orléanais

         Class comprehensive works on modern Centre, on former Orléanais in —445

         Class a specific department of Orléanais not provided for here with the department, e.g., Yonne —4441

—445 1	Eure-et-Loir department
—445 2	Loiret department
—445 3	Loir-et-Cher department
—445 4	Indre-et-Loire department

         Class here former region of Touraine

           For Indre department, see —44551; Cher department, —44552

—445 45	Tours
—445 5	Former region of Berry

           For Creuse department, see —4468

—445 51	Indre department
—445 52	Cher department
—445 6	Nièvre department (Former region of Nivernais)
—445 7	Allier department

         Class here former region of Bourbonnais

         Class each other specific department of Bourbonnais with the department, e.g., Cher —44552

*Class parts of this physiographic region or feature as instructed under —4–9

—445 8   Former region of Lyonnais

      Class here modern region of Rhône-Alpes; *Rhône River

      Class each specific department of Rhône-Alpes not provided for here with the department, e.g., Haute-Savoie —4449

—445 81   Loire department

—445 82   Rhône department

—445 823   Lyon

—445 9   Former and modern regions of Auvergne

      Class here *Massif Central

      For Allier department, see —4457; Haute-Loire department, —44813

—445 91   Puy-de-Dôme department

—445 92   Cantal department

—446   Western France   Poitou region

—446 1   Vendée department

>   —446 2–446 5   Modern region of Poitou-Charentes

      Class here former region of Poitou

      Class comprehensive works on modern Poitou-Charentes, on former Poitou in —446; Vendée department in —4461

—446 2   Deux-Sèvres department

—446 3   Vienne department

—446 4   Charente-Maritime department

      Former name: Charente-Inférieure

      Including former region of Aunis

      Class here former region of Saintonge

      Class each other specific department of Saintonge with the department, e.g., Charente —4465

—446 5   Charente department

      Class here former region of Angoumois; *Charente River

      Class each other specific department of Angoumois with the department, e.g., Deux-Sèvres —4462

—446 6   Haute-Vienne department

      Class here former and modern regions of Limousin

      Class each other specific department of Limousin with the department, e.g., Corrèze —4467

*Class parts of this physiographic region or feature as instructed under —4–9

—446 7   Corrèze department

—446 8   Creuse department

         Class here former region of Marche

            For Haute-Vienne department, see —4466

—447   Southwestern France   Guyenne (Aquitaine) region

         Class here *Garonne River

         (Option: Class here ancient Aquitania; prefer —364)

>   —447 1–447 6   Former region of Guyenne (Aquitaine)

         Class here modern region of Aquitaine

         Class comprehensive works on former Guyenne, on modern Aquitaine in —447; a specific province of modern Aquitaine not provided for here with the province, e.g., Landes —44772

—447 1   Gironde department

—447 14   Bordeaux

—447 2   Dordogne department

—447 3   Lot department

—447 4   Aveyron department

         Including former region of Rouergue

—447 5   Tarn-et-Garonne department

—447 6   Lot-et-Garonne department

—447 7   Former region of Gascony (Gascogne)

         Class each specific department of Gascony not provided for here with the department, e.g., Pyrénées-Atlantiques —4479

—447 71   Gers department

—447 72   Landes department

—447 8   Hautes-Pyrénées department

—447 9   Pyrénées-Atlantiques department

         Former name: Basses-Pyrénées

         Including former region of Béarn

—448   Southern France   Languedoc region

         Class here *Cévennes Mountains

            See also —16382 for Gulf of Lion

*Class parts of this physiographic region or feature as instructed under —4–9

>	—448 1–448 8 Former region of Languedoc

Class here modern region of Languedoc-Roussillon

Class comprehensive works on former Languedoc, on modern Languedoc-Roussillon in —448

> *For Tarn-et-Garonne department, see —4475; Pyrénées-Orientales department, —4489*

—448 1	Haute-Loire and Lozère departments
—448 13	Haute-Loire department
—448 15	Lozère department
—448 2	Ardèche department
—448 3	Gard department
—448 4	Hérault department
—448 5	Tarn department
—448 6	Haute-Garonne department

Class here modern region of Midi-Pyrénées

Class each other specific department of Midi-Pyrénées with the department, e.g., Aveyron —4474

—448 62	Toulouse
—448 7	Aude department
—448 8	Ariège department

Including former region of Foix

—448 9	Pyrénées-Orientales department (Former region of Roussillon)

Class here *Pyrenees Mountains in France

—449	Southeastern France and Monaco Provence region

Class here comprehensive works on *Alps in France [*formerly* —4448], *Riviera

(Option: Class here ancient Narbonensis; prefer —364)

> *For Italian Riviera, see —4518*

>	—449 1–449 3 Former region of Provence

Class here modern region of Provence-Côte d'Azur

Class comprehensive works on Provence, on Provence-Côte d'Azur in —449; a specific department of Provence, of Provence-Côte d'Azur not provided for here with the department, e.g., Alpes-de-Haute-Provence —4495

*Class parts of this physiographic region or feature as instructed under —4–9

—449 1	Bouches-du-Rhône department
—449 12	Marseilles
—449 2	Vaucluse department
	Including Valréas enclave
—449 22	Avignon
—449 3	Var department
—449 4	Alpes-Maritimes, Corse, Monaco
—449 41	Alpes-Maritimes department
	Including former region of Nice
—449 414	Nice
—449 45	Former and modern regions of Corsica (Corse)
	(Option: Class here ancient Corsica; prefer —379)
—449 452	Corse-de-Sud department
—449 456	Haute-Corse department
—449 49	Monaco
	Independent principality, enclave in Alpes-Maritimes
—449 5	Alpes de Haute-Provence department
	Former name: Basses-Alpes
—449 6	Former region of Dauphiné
	Class each specific department of Dauphiné with the department, e.g., Isère —4499
—449 7	Hautes-Alpes department
—449 8	Drôme department
	For Valréas enclave of Vaucluse department, see —4492
—449 9	Isère department

—45   **Italian Peninsula and adjacent islands**   **Italy**

Class here *Alps in Italy, *Apennines

(Option: Class here ancient Italian Peninsula and adjacent territories, Roman Empire; prefer —37)

*Class parts of this physiographic region or feature as instructed under —4–9

SUMMARY

—451	**Northwestern Italy**	**Piemonte region**
—452	**Lombardy region**	
—453	**Northeastern Italy**	**Veneto region**
—454	**Emilia-Romagna region and San Marino**	
—455	**Tuscany region**	
—456	**Central Italy and Vatican City**	
—457	**Southern Italy**	
—458	**Sicily and adjacent islands**	
—459	**Sardinia**	

—451   Northwestern Italy   Piemonte region

      (Option: Class here ancient Gallia Cisalpina; prefer —372)

—451 1   Valle d'Aosta region

      Class here Aosta

>   —451 2–451 7   Piemonte region

      Class comprehensive works in —451

—451 2   Torino (Turin) province

      Class here Turin

—451 3   Cuneo province

—451 4   Alessandria province

—451 5   Asti province

—451 6   Novara province

      Including *Lake Maggiore

—451 7   Vercelli province

—451 8   Liguria region

      Class here *Italian Riviera

      (Option: Class here ancient Liguria; prefer —371)

      See also —16382 for Ligurian Sea

—451 82   Genova (Genoa) province

      Class here Genoa

—451 83   La Spezia province

—451 84   Savona province

—451 87   Imperia province

—452   Lombardy region

      Class here *Po River

*Class parts of this physiographic region or feature as instructed under —4–9

—452 1   Milano (Milan) province

      Class here Milano

—452 2   Varese province

—452 3   Como province

      Class here Como

—452 4   Bergamo province

      Class here Bergamo

—452 5   Sondrio province

—452 6   Brescia province

      Including *Lake Garda

      Class here Brescia

—452 7   Cremona province

      Class here Cremona

—452 8   Mantova (Mantua) province

      Class here Mantua

—452 9   Pavia province

—453   Northeastern Italy   Veneto region

      (Option: Class here ancient Venetia; prefer —373)

      See also —*16385 for Gulf of Venice*

>   —453 1–453 7   Veneto region

      Class comprehensive works in —453

—453 1   Venezia (Venice) province

      Class here Venice

—453 2   Padova (Padua) province

      Class here Padua

—453 3   Rovigo province (Polesine)

—453 4   Verona province

      Class here Verona

—453 5   Vicenza province

      Class here Vicenza

—453 6   Treviso province

      Class here Treviso

*Class parts of this physiographic region or feature as instructed under —4–9

—453 7	Belluno province
—453 8	Trentino-Alto Adige region
—453 83	Bolzano province (Alto Adige)
	Class here South Tyrol
—453 85	Trento province
	Including Trento
—453 9	Friuli-Venezia Giulia region
—453 91	Udine province
—453 92	Gorizia province
—453 93	Trieste province
	Class here Trieste
—453 94	Pordenone province
—454	Emilia-Romagna region and San Marino
—454 1	Bologna province
	Class here Bologna
—454 2	Modena province
	Class here Modena
—454 3	Reggio nell'Emilia (Reggio Emilia) province
—454 4	Parma province
	Class here Parma
—454 5	Ferrara province
	Class here Ferrara
—454 6	Piacenza province
—454 7	Ravenna province
	Class here Ravenna
—454 8	Forlì province
—454 9	San Marino
	Independent state
—455	Tuscany region
	(Option: Class here ancient Etruria; prefer —375)
—455 1	Firenze (Florence) province
	Class here Florence
—455 2	Pistoia province

—455 3	Lucca province
—455 4	Massa e Carrara (Massa-Carrara) province
—455 5	Pisa province

    Class here Pisa

—455 6	Livorno province

    Including Capraia, Elba, Gorgona, Montecristo, Pianosa islands

—455 7	Grosseto province

    Class here *Maremma

—455 8	Siena province

    Class here Siena

—455 9	Arezzo province
—456	Central Italy and Vatican City

    Class here former Papal States (States of the Church)

    Class a specific Papal State with the place where located, e.g., Marches —4567

—456 2	Lazio (Latium) region

    (Option: Class here ancient Latium; prefer —376)

     For Roma province, see —4563

—456 22	Frosinone province
—456 23	Latina province

    Including Pontine Islands

    Class here Pontine Marshes

—456 24	Rieti province
—456 25	Viterbo province

    Class here Viterbo

    (Option: Class here ancient Volsinii Novi (Bolsena); prefer —376)

—456 3	Roma (Rome) province

    (Option: Class here ancient Ostia, Veii; prefer —376)

—456 32	Rome

    (Option: Class here ancient Rome; prefer —376)

—456 34	Vatican City

    Independent papal state, enclave in Rome

*Class parts of this physiographic region or feature as instructed under —4–9

—456 5	Umbria region
	(Option: Class here ancient Umbria; prefer —374)
—456 51	Perugia province
	Class here Perugia
—456 52	Terni province
	(Option: Class here ancient Volsinii [Orvieto]; prefer —374)
—456 7	Marches (Marche) region
	(Option: Class here ancient Picenum; prefer —374)
—456 71	Ancona province
	Including Ancona
—456 73	Macerata province
—456 75	Ascoli Piceno province
—456 77	Pesaro e Urbino province
—457	Southern Italy
	(Option: Class here ancient southern Italy; prefer —377)
	For Sicily, see —458
—457 1	Abruzzi and Molise regions
	(Option: Class here ancient Samnium; prefer —377)

>	—457 11–457 17 Abruzzi region
	Class comprehensive works in —4571
—457 11	Aquila (L'Aquila) province
	Including L'Aquila
—457 13	Chieti province
—457 15	Teramo province
—457 17	Pescara province
—457 19	Molise region
—457 192	Campobasso province
	Including Campobasso
—457 194	Isernia province
—457 2	Campania region
	(Option: Class here ancient Campania; prefer —377)
	For Napoli province, see —4573; Salerno province, —4574
—457 21	Avellino province

—457 23	Benevento province
—457 25	Caserta province
—457 3	Napoli (Naples) province

> Including Capri, Ischia Islands
>
> Class here Naples
>
> (Option: Class here ancient Naples, Herculaneum, Pompeii, Stabiae; prefer —377)

—457 4	Salerno province

> Class here Salerno

—457 5	Puglia (Apulia) region

> (Option: Class here ancient Apulia, Calabria, Brundusium; prefer —377)
>
> *For Gulf of Taranto, see —16386*

—457 51	Bari province

> Class here Bari

—457 53	Lecce province
—457 54	Brindisi province

> Class here Brindisi

—457 55	Taranto province
—457 57	Foggia province
—457 7	Basilicata (Lucania) region

> (Option: Class here ancient Lucania; prefer —377)
>
> *See also —16386 for Gulf of Taranto*

—457 71	Potenza province
—457 72	Matera province
—457 8	Calabria region

> (Option: Class here ancient Bruttium; prefer —377)
>
> *See also —16386 for Gulf of Taranto, Strait of Messina*

—457 81	Catanzaro province
—457 83	Reggio di Calabria province

> Class here Reggio di Calabria

—457 85	Cosenza province

—458	Sicily and adjacent islands
	(Option: Class here ancient Sicily; prefer —378)

>	—458 1–458 2 Sicily region
	Class comprehensive works in —458
—458 1	Eastern Sicily
—458 11	Messina province
	Including Lipari Islands
	Class here Messina
	See also —16386 for Strait of Messina
—458 12	Enna province
—458 13	Catania province
	Including Mount Etna
	Class here Catania
—458 14	Siracusa (Syracuse) province
	Class here Syracuse
	(Option: Class here ancient Syracuse; prefer —378)
—458 15	Ragusa province
—458 2	Western Sicily
—458 21	Caltanissetta province
—458 22	Agrigento province
	Including Pelagian Islands
	Class here Agrigento
—458 23	Palermo province
	Class here Palermo
—458 24	Trapani province
	Including Egadi Islands
—458 5	Malta
	Independent state
	(Option: Class here ancient Malta; prefer —378)
—459	Sardinia
	(Option: Class here ancient Sardinia; prefer —379)
—459 1	Cagliari province
	Class here Cagliari
—459 2	Nuoro province

—459 3	Sassari province
—459 4	Oristano province

—46   Iberian Peninsula and adjacent islands   Spain

(Option: Class here ancient Iberian Peninsula and adjacent islands, Tarraconensis; prefer —366)

SUMMARY

—461	Northwestern Spain Galicia autonomous community
—462	Western Spain León region
—463	Castile
—464	New Castile region Castilla-La Mancha autonomous community
—465	Northeastern Spain
—466	País Vasco autonomous community
—467	Eastern Spain and Andorra Cataluña autonomous community
—468	Andalusia autonomous community and Gibraltar
—469	Portugal

>   **—461–468 Spain**

Class comprehensive works in —46

For Canary Islands, see —649

—461   Northwestern Spain   Galicia autonomous community

>   **—461 1–461 7 Galicia autonomous community**

Class comprehensive works in —461

—461 1   La Coruña province

Including Santiago de Compostela

—461 3   Lugo province

—461 5   Orense province

—461 7   Pontevedra province

—461 9   Asturias autonomous community (Asturias province)

Former name for Asturias province: Oviedo province

Class here Oviedo

—462   Western Spain   León region

Class here Castilla-León autonomous community; *Cantabrian Mountains

For Burgos province, see —46353; Soria province, —46355; Segovia province, —46357; Avila province, —46359

*Class parts of this physiographic region or feature as instructed under —4–9

>	—462 1–462 5 León region
	Class comprehensive works in —462
—462 1	León province
—462 2	Palencia province
—462 3	Valladolid province
	Class here Valladolid
—462 4	Zamora province
—462 5	Salamanca province
—462 6	Extremadura autonomous community
	For Badajoz province, see —4627; Cáceres province, —4628
—462 7	Badajoz province
	Including Mérida
—462 8	Cáceres province
	Class here *Tagus River in Spain
—463	Castile
	For New Castile region, see —464
—463 5	Old Castile region
	For Palencia province, see —4622; Valladolid province, —4623
—463 51	Cantabria autonomous community (Cantabria province)
	Former name for Cantabria province: Santander province
	Including Santander
—463 53	Burgos province
	For Treviño, see —4667
—463 54	La Rioja autonomous community (La Rioja province)
	Former name of La Rioja province: Logroño province
	Including Logroño
—463 55	Soria province
—463 57	Segovia province
	Class here Segovia
—463 59	Avila province

*Class parts of this physiographic region or feature as instructed under —4–9

—464	New Castile region Castilla-La Mancha autonomous community
	Class here La Mancha
—464 1	Madrid autonomous community (Madrid province)
	Class here Madrid

>	—464 3–464 8 Castilla-La Mancha autonomous community
	Class comprehensive works in —464
—464 3	Toledo province
	Class here Toledo
—464 5	Ciudad Real province
—464 6	Albacete province [*formerly* —46771]
—464 7	Cuenca province
—464 9	Guadalajara province
—465	Northeastern Spain
	Class here *Ebro River
	For Catalonia region, see —467
—465 2	Navarra autonomous community (Navarra province)
	Including Pamplona
	Class here *Pyrenees Mountains
—465 5	Aragon autonomous community
—465 51	Teruel province
—465 53	Zaragoza (Saragossa) province
	Class here Zaragoza
—465 55	Huesca province
—466	País Vasco autonomous community
	Former names: Basque Provinces, Vascongadas
	Class here territory of the Basque people
	For Navarra province, see —4652; Pyrénées-Atlantiques department of France, —4479
—466 1	Guipúzcoa
	Class here San Sebastián
—466 3	Vizcaya (Biscay)
	Class here Bilbao
	For Orduña, see —4669

*Class parts of this physiographic region or feature as instructed under —4–9

—466 5	Alava
	Including Vitoria
—466 7	Treviño
	Enclave of Burgos province in Álava province
—466 9	Orduña
	Enclave of Vizcaya province between Álava and Burgos provinces
—467	Eastern Spain and Andorra Cataluña autonomous community

>	—467 1–467 4 Cataluña autonomous community
	Former name: Catalonia region
	Class comprehensive works in —467
—467 1	Gerona province
—467 2	Barcelona province
	Class here Barcelona
—467 3	Tarragona province
—467 4	Lérida province
—467 5	Baleares autonomous community (Balearic Islands)
—467 52	Minorca (Menorca)
—467 54	Majorca (Mallorca)
—467 542	Palma
—467 56	Formentera and Ibiza
—467 6	Valencia autonomous community
—467 61	Castellón province
—467 63	Valencia province
	Class here Valencia
—467 65	Alicante province
—467 7	Murcia autonomous community (Murcia province)
	Including Cartagena
	Class here former Murcia region
	For Albacete province, see —4646
—[467 71]	Albacete province
	Relocated to —4646
—[467 73]	Murcia province
	Number discontinued; class in —4677

—467 9	Andorra
	Independent state
—468	Andalusia autonomous community and Gibraltar
	Class here *Guadalquivir River
	(Option: Class here ancient Baetica; prefer —366)

>	—468 1–468 8 Andalusia autonomous community
	Class comprehensive works in —468
—468 1	Almería province
—468 2	Granada province
	Class here Granada
—468 3	Jaén province
—468 4	Córdoba province
	Class here Córdoba
—468 5	Málaga province
	Class here Málaga
	For Melilla, see —642
—468 6	Seville province
	Class here Seville
—468 7	Huelva province
—468 8	Cádiz province
	For Ceuta, see —642
—468 9	Gibraltar
	British crown colony
—469	Portugal
	(Option: Class here ancient Lusitania; prefer —366)
—469 1	Historic province of Entre Douro e Minho
—469 12	Modern province of Minho
	Contains Braga and Viana do Castelo districts
—469 15	Modern province of Douro Litoral
	Contains Porto district
	For Aveiro district, see —46935; Viseu district, —46931

*Class parts of this physiographic region or feature as instructed under —4–9

—469 2   Historic province of Trás-os-Montes   Modern province of
Trás-os-Montes e Alto Douro

Contains Bragança and Vila Real districts

For Guarda and Viseu districts, see —46931

—469 3   Historic province of Beira

*For modern province of Douro Litoral, see —46915; modern
province of Trás-os-Montes e Alto Douro, —4692*

—469 31   Modern province of Beira Alta

Contains Guarda and Viseu districts

For Coimbra district, see —46935

—469 33   Modern province of Beira Baixa

Contains Castelo Branco district

For Coimbra district, see —46935; Santarém district, —46945

—469 35   Modern province of Beira Litoral

Contains Aveiro and Coimbra districts

For Leiria district, see —46942; Santarém district, —46945

—469 4   Historic province of Estremadura

*For modern province of Beira Litoral, see —46935; modern
province of Baixo Alentejo, —46955*

—469 42   Modern province of Estremadura

Contains Leiria, Setúbal districts

—469 425   Lisboa (Lisbon) district

Class here Lisbon

—469 45   Modern province of Ribatejo

Contains Santarém district

Class here *Tagus River

For Portalegre district, see —46952; Lisboa district, —469425

—469 5   Historic province of Alentejo

—469 52   Modern province of Alto Alentejo

Contains Evora and Portalegre districts

—469 55   Modern province of Baixo Alentejo

Contains Beja district

For Setúbal district, see —46942

—469 6   Algarve province (Faro district)

*Class parts of this physiographic region or feature as instructed under —4–9

—469 8   Madeira (Funchal district)

      Islands in Atlantic Ocean

—469 9   Azores

      Islands in Atlantic Ocean

      Contains Angra do Heroísmo, Horta, Ponta Delgada districts

—47   **Union of Soviet Socialist Republics (Soviet Union) Russia (Russian Soviet Federated Socialist Republic)**

      Class here eastern Europe

       For Balkan Peninsula, see —496; Soviet Union in Asia, —57

SUMMARY

—472	**Northern area of Russia**
—473	**West central area of Russia**
—474	**Baltic Sea area of Soviet Union**
—475	**Lithuania (Lithuanian Soviet Socialist Republic)**
—476	**Western Russia and Belorussia**
—477	**Black Sea area of Soviet Union**
—478	**Eastern area of European Russia**
—479	**Caucasus area of Soviet Union**

—472   Northern area of Russia

      For Komi Autonomous Soviet Socialist Republic, see —4787

      See also —16324 for White Sea

—472 3   Arkhangelsk and Vologda oblasts (provinces), Murmansk okrug (region)

      Including Nenets National District; Kola Peninsula

       For Franz Josef Land, see —985; Novaya Zemlya, —986

—472 5   Karelia (Karelian Autonomous Soviet Socialist Republic)

      Including Lakes *Ladoga and *Onega

—473   West central area of Russia

—473 1   Industrial area

      Contains Ivanovo, Kostroma, Ryazan, Tula, Vladimir, Yaroslavl oblasts (provinces)

—473 12   Moscow oblast (province)

      Class here Moscow

—473 5   Central Black Earth Region

      Contains Belgorod, Kursk, Lipetsk, Orel, Tambov, Voronezh oblasts (provinces)

*Class parts of this physiographic region or feature as instructed under —4–9

—474	Baltic Sea area of Soviet Union
	Class here Baltic States
	For Lithuania, see —475
	See also —16334 for Baltic Sea
—474 1	Estonia (Estonian Soviet Socialist Republic)
	Class here Livonia
	For Latvia, see —4743
	See also —16334 for Gulf of Finland
—474 3	Latvia (Latvian Soviet Socialist Republic)
	Including Courland
—474 5	Leningrad, Novgorod, Pskov oblasts (provinces) of Russia
—474 53	Leningrad oblast (province)
	Class here Leningrad
—474 7	Kaliningrad oblast (province) of Russia
—475	Lithuania (Lithuanian Soviet Socialist Republic)
—476	Western Russia and Belorussia
—476 2	Western Russia
	Contains Bryansk, Kalinin, Kaluga, Smolensk oblasts (provinces)
—476 5	Belorussia (White Russian Soviet Socialist Republic)
	Variant name: White Russia
	Including *Pripet Marshes
—476 52	Western and central
	Contains Brest, Grodno, Minsk oblasts (provinces)
—476 56	Eastern
	Contains Gomel, Mogilev, Vitebsk oblasts (provinces)
—477	Black Sea area of Soviet Union
	(Option: Class here ancient Black Sea region; prefer —395)
	See also —16389 for Black Sea
—477 1	Ukraine (Ukrainian Soviet Socialist Republic)
	Variant name: Little Russia
	Including *Dnieper River
	(Option: Class here ancient Sarmatia; prefer —395)

*Class parts of this physiographic region or feature as instructed under —4–9

—477 14   Ukraine west of Dnieper River

Contains Cherkassy, Khmelnitski, Kiev, Kirovograd, Vinnitsa, Zhitomir oblasts (provinces)

For southern Ukraine, see —47717; western Ukraine, —47718

—477 15   Ukraine east of Dnieper River

Contains Chernigov, Kharkov, Poltava, Sumy oblasts (provinces)

For Donets Basin, see —47716; southern Ukraine, —47717

—477 16   *Donets Basin

Contains Dnepropetrovsk, Donetsk, Lugansk (Voroshilovgrad) oblasts (provinces)

Class here *Donets River

—477 17   Southern Ukraine

Contains Crimea, Kherson, Nikolayev, Odessa, Zaporozhye oblasts (provinces)

See also —16389 for Sea of Azov

—477 18   Western Ukraine

Contains Chernovtsy, Ivano-Frankov, Lvov, Rovno, Ternopol, Trans-Carpathian, Volyn oblasts (provinces)

Including North Bukovina

Class here East Galicia; *Carpathian Mountains, *Dniester River

—477 5   Soviet Moldavia (Moldavian Soviet Socialist Republic)

Class here Bessarabia

Class each specific part of Bessarabia not in Soviet Moldavia with the subject, e.g., Odessa Region of Ukraine —47717; comprehensive works on Moldavia in —4981

—477 7   Rostov oblast (province) of Russia

Class here *Don River

—478   Eastern area of European Russia

Class here *Volga River

—478 1   Upper Volga

Contains Gorki and Kirov oblasts (provinces), Mari and Udmurt Autonomous Soviet Socialist Republics

—478 3   Middle Volga

Contains Kuibyshev, Penza, Ulyanovsk oblasts (provinces); Chuvash, Mordovian, Tatar Autonomous Soviet Socialist Republics

*Class parts of this physiographic region or feature as instructed under —4–9

—478 5   Lower Volga

> Contains Astrakhan, Saratov, Volgograd oblasts (provinces); Kalmyk Autonomous Soviet Socialist Republic

—478 7   Ural Mountains region

> Contains Chelyabinsk, Orenburg, Perm, Sverdlovsk oblasts (provinces); Bashkir and Komi Autonomous Soviet Socialist Republics; Komi-Permiak National District

> Class here *Ural Mountains

—479   Caucasus area of Soviet Union

> Class here *Caspian Sea [*formerly also* —168]

> (Option: Class here ancient Caucasus; prefer —395)

—479 1   Soviet Azerbaijan (Azerbaijan Soviet Socialist Republic)

> Including Nakhichevan Autonomous Soviet Socialist Republic, Nagorno-Karabakh Autonomous oblast (province)

> (Option: Class here ancient Albania; prefer —395)

> Class comprehensive works on Azerbaijan in —553

—479 2   Soviet Armenia (Armenian Soviet Socialist Republic)

> Class comprehensive works on Armenia in —5662

—479 5   Georgia (Georgian Soviet Socialist Republic)

> Including Abkhaz and Adzhar Autonomous Soviet Socialist Republics, South Oset Autonomous oblast (province)

> (Option: Class here ancient Colchis, Iberia; prefer —395)

—479 7   Russian areas

> Contains Krasnodar and Stavropol Krays; Chechen-Ingush, Dagestan, Kabardino-Balkar, North Oset Autonomous Soviet Socialist Republics

> Including Adyge and Karachai-Cherkess Autonomous oblasts (provinces)

> *See also —16389 for Sea of Azov*

—48   **Scandinavia**

> Class here northern Europe

> *For northwestern islands, see —491*

—481   Norway

> *For divisions of Norway, see —482–484; Svalbard, —981; Jan Mayen Island, —983*

*Class parts of this physiographic region or feature as instructed under —4–9

>   —482–484   Divisions of Norway

         Class comprehensive works in —481

—482   Southeastern Norway

         Contains Akershus, Aust-Agder, Buskerud, Hedmark, Oppland, Ostfold, Telemark, Vest-Agder, Vestfold fylker (counties)

         See also —16336 for Skagerrak

—482 3   Oslo fylke (county)

         Class here Oslo

—483   Southwestern Norway

         Contains Hordaland, More og Romsdal, Rogaland, Sogn og Fjordane fylker (counties)

         Including Bergen

—484   Central and northern Norway

         Contains Nord-Trondelag, Sor-Trondelag fylker (counties)

—484 5   Northern Norway

         Contains Finnmark, Nordland, Troms fylker (counties)

         Including Lofoten, Vesteralen islands

—485   Sweden

         For divisions of Sweden, see —486–488

>   —486–488   Divisions of Sweden

         Class comprehensive works in —485

—486   Southern Sweden (Gotaland)

         Contains Alvsborg, Blekinge, Goteborg och Bohus, Gotland, Halland, Jonkoping, Kalmar, Kristianstad, Kronoberg, Malmohus, Ostergotland, Skaraborg lanet (counties)

         Including Oland Island

         See also —16334 for Baltic Sea, Kattegat

—487   Central Sweden (Svealand)

         Contains Gavleborg, Kopparberg, Orebro, Sodermanland, Uppsala, Varmland, Vastmanland lanet (counties)

—487 3   Stockholms lan (Stockholm county)

         Class here Stockholm

—488   Northern Sweden (Norrland)

Contains Jamtland, Norrbotten, Vasterbotten, Vasternorrland lanet (counties)

See also —16334 for Gulf of Bothnia

—489   Denmark and Finland

>   —489 1–489 5   Denmark

Class comprehensive works in —489

For Greenland, see —982

—489 1   Sjaelland (Zealand) island

Contains Frederiksborg, Roskilde, Storstroms, Vestsjaelland amts (counties)

For Maribo amt, see —4893

See also —16334 for Great Belt, Oresund; —4893 for Falster and Lolland islands

—489 13   Kobenhavns amt (Copenhagen county)

Class here Copenhagen

—489 2   Bornholm island (Bornholms amt [county])

—489 3   Falster and Lolland islands

Class here Maribo amt (county)

Class Storstroms amt in —4891

—489 4   Fyn and Langeland islands

Class here Fyns amt (county)

See also —16334 for Great and Little Belts

—489 5   Jutland peninsula

Contains Aahrus, Nordjyllands, Ribe, Rinkobing, Sonderjyllands, Vejle, Viborg amts (counties)

See also —16336 for Skagerrak

—489 7   Finland

See also —16334 for Gulf of Finland

—489 71   Southern Finland

Contains Kymi, Uusimaa läänit (provinces)

Including Helsinki

—489 73   Southwestern Finland

                   Contains Ahvenanmaa, Häme, Keski-Suomi, Turku ja Pori, Vaasa
                   läänit (provinces)

                   Including Aland Islands

—489 75   Southeastern Finland

                   Contains Kuopio, Mikkeli, Pohjois-Karjala läänit (provinces)

—489 76   Oulu lääni (province)

—489 77   Lappi lääni (province)

                   Class here Lapland

                        For northern Norway, see —4845; northern Sweden, —488;
                        Murmansk okrug of Russia, —4723

—49   **Other parts of Europe**

                        SUMMARY

                   —491   **Northwestern islands**
                   —492   **Netherlands (Holland)**
                   —493   **Southern Low Countries   Belgium**
                   —494   **Switzerland**
                   —495   **Greece**
                   —496   **Balkan Peninsula**
                   —497   **Yugoslavia and Bulgaria**
                   —498   **Romania**
                   —499   **Aegean Islands**

—491   Northwestern islands

—491 2   Iceland

—491 5   Faeroes

—492   Netherlands (Holland)

                   Class here comprehensive works on Low Countries, on Benelux countries

                   (Option: Class here ancient Germania Inferior; prefer —364)

                        For Surinam, see —883; Netherlands Antilles, —72986; southern Low
                        Countries, —493

—492 1   Northeastern provinces

—492 12   Groningen

—492 13   Friesland

                   Including *West Frisian Islands

—492 15   Drenthe

—492 16   Overijssel

                   Including North East Polder

*Class parts of this physiographic region or feature as instructed under —4–9

—492 18	Gelderland
	Including Arnhem, Nijmegen
	Class here *IJssel River
—492 2	**Flevoland (Zuidelijke IJsselmeerpolders) and Markerwaard**
	Including Almere, Dronten, Lelystad, Zeewolde
	Class here *IJssel Lake (Zuider Zee)
—492 3	Northwestern provinces
—492 32	Utrecht
	Class here Utrecht
—492 35	North Holland
	Including Haarlem; Wieringermeer
—492 352	Amsterdam
—492 38	South Holland
	Including Delft, Leiden
—492 382	The Hague
—492 385	Rotterdam
—492 4	Southern provinces
	Class here *Meuse (Maas) River
—492 42	Zeeland
—492 45	North Brabant
	Including Eindhoven
—492 48	Limburg
	Including Maastricht
—493	**Southern Low Countries Belgium**
	(Option: Class here ancient Belgica; prefer —364)

>	**—493 1–493 4 Belgium**
	Class comprehensive works in —493
—493 1	**Northwestern provinces of Belgium**
	Class here Flanders
	For French Flanders region, see —4428
—493 12	West Flanders
—493 122	Bruges (Brugge)

*Class parts of this physiographic region or feature as instructed under —4–9

—493 14	East Flanders
—493 142	Ghent (Gent)
—493 2	**Northern provinces of Belgium**
—493 22	Antwerp (Anvers)
—493 222	Antwerp
—493 24	Limburg
—493 3	**Brabant province**
—493 32	Brussels
—493 4	**Southern provinces of Belgium (Wallonia)**
—493 42	Hainaut
—493 44	Namur
—493 46	Liège
	Class here *Meuse (Maas) River in Belgium
—493 48	Luxembourg
	Class here *Ardennes
—493 5	**Luxembourg**
	Grand duchy
—494	**Switzerland**
—494 3	**Jura region cantons**
	Class here *Jura Mountains
	Vaud relocated to —49452
—494 32	Basel-Stadt (Bâle-Ville)
	Class here former Basel canton
	For Baselland, see —49433
—494 33	Baselland
—494 35	Solothurn
—494 36	Jura
—494 38	Neuchâtel
—494 5	**Swiss Plateau (Mittelland) cantons**
—494 51	Geneva
	Class here Geneva
—494 52	Vaud [*formerly* —4943]
	Class here *Lake Geneva

*Class parts of this physiographic region or feature as instructed under —4–9

—494 53	Fribourg (Freiburg)
—494 54	Bern
	Class here *Bernese Oberland
—494 542	Bern
—494 55	Luzern
	Class here *Lake Lucerne
—494 56	Aargau
—494 57	Zurich
	Class here Zurich
—494 58	Schaffhausen (Schaffhouse)
—494 59	Thurgau
	Class here *Lake of Constance in Switzerland
—494 7	Alpine region cantons
	Class here *Alps
—494 71	Appenzell
—494 712	Appenzell Ausser-Rhoden
—494 714	Appenzell Inner-Rhoden
—494 72	Saint Gall
—494 73	Graubünden (Grisons)
	Including Graubünden National Park
—494 74	Glarus
—494 75	Schwyz and Zug
—494 752	Schwyz
—494 756	Zug
—494 76	Nidwalden and Obwalden
	Class here former Unterwalden canton
—494 762	Nidwalden
—494 764	Obwalden
—494 77	Uri
—494 78	Ticino
	Including *Lake of Lugano
—494 79	Valais (Wallis)

*Class parts of this physiographic region or feature as instructed under —4–9

—495   Greece

> (Option: Class here ancient Greece; prefer —38)

> *For Aegean Islands, see —499*

> *See also —16388 for Aegean Sea*

—495 1   Central Greece and Euboea

Contains Aetolia and Acarnania, Attica, Boeotia, Euboea, Eurytania, Phocis, Phthiotis, Piraeus nomes (provinces)

(Option: Class here ancient Aetolia, Acarnania, Doris, Locris, Malis, Phocis, Amphissa, Delphi, Boeotia, Euboea Island, Chalcis, Thebes, Attica, Marathon; prefer —383 for Aetolia, Acarnania, Doris, Locris, Malis, Phocis, Amphissa, Delphi; 384 for Boeotia, Euboea Island, Chalcis, Thebes; —385 for Attica, Marathon)

> *For Kythera island, see —4952*

—495 12   Athens

> (Option: Class here ancient Athens; prefer —385)

—495 2   Peloponnesus

Contains Achaea, Arcadia, Argolis, Corinth, Elis, Laconia, Messenia nomes (provinces)

Including Kythera island

(Option: Class here ancient Megaris, Peloponnessus, Achaea, Corinth, Arcadia, Argolis, Elis, Mycenae, Olympia, Phigalia, Tiryns, Laconia, Messenia, Sparta; prefer —384 for Megaris, —386 for Peloponnessus, —387 for Achaea, Corinth, —388 for Arcadia, Argolis, Elis, Mycenae, Olympia, Phigalia, Tiryns, —389 for Laconia, Messenia, Sparta)

> *See also —16386 for Gulf of Corinth*

—495 3   Epirus

Contains Arta, Ioannina, Preveza, Thesprotia nomes (provinces)

Class here comprehensive works on Epirus; *Pindus Mountains

(Option: Class here ancient Epirus; prefer —382)

Class Albanian Epirus in —4965

—495 4   Thessaly

Contains Karditsa, Larissa, Magnesia, Trikkala nomes (provinces)

(Option: Class here ancient Thessaly; prefer —382)

*Class parts of this physiographic region or feature as instructed under —4–9

—495 5   Ionian Islands

> Contains Cephalonia, Corfu, Leukas, Zante nomes (provinces)
>
> Including Ithaca Island
>
> (Option: Class here ancient Ionian Islands; prefer —382 for Ionian Islands, northern Ionian Islands, —383 for Ithaca Island, —386 for southern Ionian Islands)

—495 6   Macedonia

> Contains Chalcidice, Drama, Florina, Grevená, Hematheia, Kastoria, Kavalla, Kilkis, Kozáne, Pella, Pieria, Serrai, Thessalonike nomes (provinces)
>
> Including Mount Athos
>
> Class here comprehensive works on Macedonia
>
> (Option: Class here ancient Macedonia; prefer —381)
>
> Class Macedonia in Yugosavia in —4976, in Bulgaria in —49774

—495 7   Thrace

> Contains Evros, Rhodope, Xanthe nomes (provinces)
>
> Class here comprehensive works on Thrace
>
> (Option: Class here ancient Thracia; prefer —398)
>
> > *For Bulgarian Thrace, see —49778; Turkish Thrace, —4961*

—496   Balkan Peninsula

> Class here *Danube River
>
> (Option: Class here ancient southeastern Europe; prefer —398)
>
> Class each specific country of Balkan Peninsula not provided for here with the country, e.g., Greece —495
>
> > *See also —56 for Ottoman Empire*

—496 1   Turkey in Europe (Turkish Thrace) [*formerly* —563]

> Contains Edirne (Adrianople), Kirklareli, Tekirdag ilis; European portion of Canakkale ili
>
> > *See also —16389 for Dardanelles, Sea of Marmara*

—496 18   Istanbul Ili

> Class here Istanbul (Constantinople)
>
> (Option: Class here ancient Constantinople; prefer —398)
>
> > *For Asian portion of Istanbul ili, see —563*
> >
> > *See also —16389 for Bosporus*

—496 5   Albania

*Class parts of this physiographic region or feature as instructed under —4–9

—497   Yugoslavia and Bulgaria

                 (Option: Class here ancient Illyria; prefer —398)

\>   —497 1–497 6   Yugoslavia

                 Class comprehensive works in —497

—497 1   Serbia

                 Contains Belgrade, Kosovo-Metohija, Vojvodina, Yugoslav Banat

—497 2   Croatia

                 Contains Dalmatia, Istria, Slavonia

                 (Option: Class here ancient Istria; prefer —373)

—497 3   Slovenia

—497 4   Central republics of Yugoslavia

—497 42   Bosnia and Herzegovina

—497 45   Montenegro

—497 6   Macedonia (Vardar Macedonia)

                 Class here Vardar River

—497 7   Bulgaria

                 Class here *Balkan Mountains

                 (Option: Class here ancient Moesia; prefer —398)

—497 72   Northwestern Bulgaria

                 Contains Mikhaylovgrad, Vidin, Vratsa okruzi (provinces)

—497 73   West central Bulgaria

                 Contains Kyustendil, Pernik (Dimitrovo), Sofia okruzi (provinces); city commune of Sofia

—497 74   Southwestern Bulgaria

                 Contains Blagoevgrad, Pazardzhik okruzi (provinces)

                 Including Bulgarian Macedonia

—497 75   South central Bulgaria

                 Contains Khaskovo, Kurdzhali, Plovdiv, Smolyan, Stara Zagora okruzi (provinces)

                 Class here *Rhodope Mountains

—497 76   North central Bulgaria

                 Contains Gabrovo, Lovech, Pleven, Ruse, Veliko Turnovo okruzi (provinces)

*Class parts of this physiographic region or feature as instructed under —4–9

—497 77   Northeastern Bulgaria

> Contains Razgrad, Shumen (Kolarovgrad), Silistra, Tolbukhin, Turgovishte, Varna okruzi (provinces)
>
> Including South Dobruja

—497 78   Southeastern Bulgaria

> Contains Burgas, Sliven, Yambol okruzi (provinces)
>
> Including Bulgarian Thrace

—498   **Romania**

> (Option: Class here ancient Dacia; prefer —398)

—498 1   Northeast Romania

> Contains Bacau, Botosani, Braila, Galati, Iasi, Neamt, Suceava, Vaslui, Vrancea judete (districts)
>
> Class here *Moldavia
>
> *For Moldavian Soviet Socialist Republic, see —4775*

—498 2   Southeast Romania (Walachia)

> Contains Arges, Bucuresti, Buzau, Dimbovita, Ialomita, Olt, Prahova, Teleorman, Vilcea judete (districts)
>
> Including Ploiesti
>
> *For Black Sea area, see —4983*

—498 3   Black Sea area

> Contains Constanta, Dulcea judete (districts)
>
> Class here *Dobruja
>
> (Option: Class here ancient Scythia; prefer —3951)
>
> *For South Dobruja, see —49777*
>
> *See also —16389 for Black Sea*

—498 4   Central and west Romania

> Contains Alba, Arad, Bihor, Bistrita-Nasaud, Brasov, Caras-Severin, Cluj, Covasna, Dolj, Gorj, Harghita, Hunedoara, Maramures, Mehedinti, Mures, Salaj, Satu Mare, Sibiu, Timis judete (districts)
>
> Including Oltenia, Transylvania
>
> Class here *Bukovina, comprehensive works on *Banat
>
> *For North Bukovina, see —47718; Yugoslav Banat, —4971*

*Class parts of this physiographic region or feature as instructed under —4–9

—499   Aegean Islands

     Contains Northern Sporades, Samothrace, Thasos islands of Greece

     Chios, Cyclades, Lesbos, Samos nomes (provinces) of Greece

     (Option: Class here ancient Aegean Islands; prefer —391)

     For Euboea, see —4951; Kythera islands, —4952; Imbros (Imroz) and Tenedos (Bozcaada) islands of Turkey, see —562

     See also —16388 for Aegean Sea

—499 6   Dodecanese (Southern Sporades)

     Nome (Province) of Greece

     (Option: Class here ancient Rhodes, Southern Sporades, Karpathos; prefer —3916 for Rhodes, Southern Sporades, —3917 for Karpathos)

—499 8   Crete

     Contains Canea, Herakleion, Lasithion, Rethymnē nomes (provinces) of Greece

     (Option: Class here ancient Crete; prefer —3918)

—5   Asia   Orient   Far East

     Class here Eurasia

     For Europe, see —4

SUMMARY

—509 1	**Regional treatment**
—51	**China and adjacent areas**
—52	**Japan**
—53	**Arabian Peninsula and adjacent areas**
—54	**South Asia India**
—55	**Iran**
—56	**Middle East (Near East)**
—57	**Siberia (Asiatic Russia)**
—58	**Central Asia**
—59	**Southeast Asia**

—[500 9]   Regional treatment

     Relocated to —5091

—509 1   Regional treatment [*formerly* —5009]

     Add to base number —5091 the numbers following —1 in —11–18 of this table, e.g., Islamic Asia —50917671

—51   China and adjacent areas

     Class here People's Republic of China

     (Option: Class here ancient China; prefer —31)

SUMMARY

—511	Northeastern China
—512	Southeastern China and adjacent areas
—513	Southwestern China (South-Western Region)
—514	Northwestern China (North-Western Region)
—515	Tibet Autonomous Region (Xizang Zizhiqu)
—516	Sinkiang Uighur Autonomous Region (Xinjiang Weiwuer Zizhiqu)
—517	Mongolia
—518	Manchuria
—519	Korea

—511   Northeastern China

Class here Northern Region; *Hwang Ho (Yellow River)

> *For Manchuria, see —518; Inner Mongolia Autonomous Region, —5177*

> *See also —16456 for Yellow Sea*

—511 3   Shanghai Municipality and Kiangsu Province

—511 32   Shanghai Municipality (Shanghai Shih)

—511 36   Kiangsu Province (Jiangsu Sheng)

Including Nanking (Nanjing)

—511 4   Shantung Province (Shandong Sheng)

—511 5   Hopeh Province and Peking and Tientsin municipalities

—511 52   Hopeh Province (Hebei Sheng)

—511 54   Tientsin Municipality (Tianjin Shih)

—511 56   Peking Municipality (Beijing Shih)

—511 7   Shansi Province (Shanxi Sheng)

—511 8   Honan Province (Henan Sheng)

—512   Southeastern China and adjacent areas

Class here Eastern and Central-Southern Regions; *Yangtze River

> *For Shanghai Municipality, see —51132; Kiangsu Province, —51136; Shantung Province, —5114; Honan Province, —5118*

—512 1   Hupeh and Hunan provinces

—512 12   Hupeh Province (Hubei Sheng)

—512 15   Hunan Province (Hunan Sheng)

—512 2   Kiangsi and Anhwei provinces

—512 22   Kiangsi Province (Jiangxi Sheng)

—512 25   Anhwei Province (Anhui Sheng)

*Class parts of this physiographic region or feature as instructed under —4–9

—512 4	East China Sea area
	See also —16457 for East China Sea
—512 42	Chekiang Province (Zhejiang Sheng)
—512 45	Fukien Province (Fujian Sheng)
	See also —16457 for Formosa Strait
—512 49	Taiwan (Formosa) and adjacent islands
	Republic of China (Nationalist China)
	See also —16457 for Formosa Strait
—512 5	Hong Kong
	British crown colony
—512 6	Macao
	Overseas territory of Portugal
—512 7	Kwangtung Province (Guangdong Sheng)
—512 75	Canton
—512 8	Kwangsi Chuang Autonomous Region (Guangxi Zhuangzu Zizhiqu)
	See also —16472 for Gulf of Tonkin
—513	Southwestern China (South-Western Region)
	For Tibet, see —515
—513 4	Kweichow Province (Guizhou Sheng)
—513 5	Yunnan Province (Yunnan Sheng)
—513 8	Szechwan Province (Sichuan Sheng)
	Including Chungking (Chongqing)
—514	Northwestern China (North-Western Region)
	For Ningsia Hui Autonomous Region, see —5175; Sinkiang Uighur Autonomous Region, —516
—514 3	Shensi Province (Shaanxi Sheng)
—514 5	Kansu Province (Gansu Sheng)
—514 7	Tsinghai Province (Qinghai Sheng)
—515	Tibet Autonomous Region (Xizang Zizhiqu)
—516	Sinkiang Uighur Autonomous Region (Xinjiang Weiwuer Zizhiqu)
	Including *Kunlun Mountains, *Tien Shan

*Class parts of this physiographic region or feature as instructed under —4–9

—517	Mongolia
—517 3	Outer Mongolia (Mongolian People's Republic)
	Independent state
	Including *Gobi Desert; *Altai Mountains
—517 5	Ningsia Hui Autonomous Region (Ningxia Huizu Zizhiqu)
—517 7	Inner Mongolia Autonomous Region (Nei Monggol Zizhiqu)
—518	Manchuria
	Class here North-Eastern Region
—518 2	Liaoning Province (Liaoning Sheng)
—518 4	Heilungkiang Province (Heilongjiang Sheng)
—518 8	Kirin Province (Jilin Sheng)
—519	Korea
	See also —16456 for Yellow Sea
—519 3	North Korea (People's Democratic Republic of Korea)
—519 5	South Korea (Republic of Korea)
—52	**Japan**
—521	Honshū (Honsyu) island

SUMMARY

—521 1	**Tōhoku district**
—521 3	**Kantō district**
—521 5	**Hokuriku region**
—521 6	**Chūbu (Tyubu) district**
—521 8	**Kinki district**
—521 9	**Chūgoku (Tyugoku) district)**

—521 1	Tōhoku district
	Former heading: Northern Honshu prefectures
	See also —16454 for Tsugaru Strait
—521 12	Aomori-ken (Aomori prefecture)
	Including *Towada Lake
—521 13	Akita-ken (Akita prefecture)
—521 14	Iwate-ken (Iwate prefecture)
—521 15	Miyagi-ken (Miyagi prefecture)
—521 16	Yamagata-ken (Yamagata prefecture)
—521 17	Fukusima-ken (Fukushima prefecture)

*Class parts of this physiographic region or feature as instructed under —4—9

—521 3   Kantō district

         Former heading: East central Honshu prefectures

         Including *Kantō Mountains; *Tone River

—521 31   Ibaraki-ken (Ibaraki prefecture)

—521 32   Tochigi-ken (Tochigi prefecture)

—521 33   Gumma-ken (Gumma prefecture)

—521 34   Saitama-ken (Saitama prefecture)

—521 35   Tokyo-ken (Tokyo prefecture)

         Class here Tokyo

         For Ogasawara Islands, see —528

—521 36   Kanagawa-ken (Kanagawa prefecture)

—521 364   Yokohama

—521 37   Chiba-ken (Chiba prefecture)

—521 5   Hokuriku region

         Former heading: Northwest central Honshu prefectures

—521 52   Niigata-ken (Niigata prefecture)

         Class here *Shinano River

—521 53   Toyama-ken (Toyama prefecture)

—521 54   Ishikawa-ken (Ishikawa prefecture)

—521 55   Fukui-ken (Fukui prefecture)

—521 6   Chūbu (Tyubu) district

         Former heading: Southwest central Honshu prefectures

         Including *Akaishi, *Hida Mountains

         For Hokuriku region, see —5215

—521 62   Gifu-ken (Gifu prefecture)

—521 63   Nagano-ken (Nagano prefecture)

         Including *Kiso Mountains

—521 64   Yamanashi-ken (Yamanashi prefecture)

—521 65   Shizuoka-ken (Shizuoka prefecture)

         For Mount Fuji, see —52166

—521 66   Mount Fuji (Fujisan, Fujiyama)

—521 67   Aichi-ken (Aichi prefecture)

—521 674   Nagoya

*Class parts of this physiographic region or feature as instructed under —4–9

—521 8	Kinki district
	Former heading: Southern Honshu prefectures
—521 81	Mie-ken (Mie prefecture)
—521 82	Wakayama-ken (Wakayama prefecture)
—521 83	Ōsaka-ken (Ōsaka prefecture)
	Class here *Yodo River
—521 834	Ōsaka
—521 84	Nara-ken (Nara prefecture)
—521 85	Shiga-ken (Shiga prefecture)
—521 86	Kyōto-ken (Kyōto prefecture) [*formerly* —52191]
—521 864	Kyōto
—521 87	Hyōgo-ken (Hyōgo prefecture) [*formerly* —5219]
—521 874	Kōbe
—521 9	Chūgoku (Tyugoku) district
	Former heading: Western Honshu prefectures
	Hyōgo-ken (Hyōgo prefecture) relocated to —52187
	See also —16455 for Inland Sea (Seto-naikai)
—[521 91]	Kyōto-ken (Kyōto prefecture)
	Relocated to —52186
—521 93	Tottori-ken (Tottori prefecture)
—521 94	Okayama-ken (Okayama prefecture)
—521 95	Hiroshima-ken (Hiroshima prefecture)
—521 954	Hiroshima
—521 96	Shimane-ken (Shimane prefecture)
—521 97	Yamaguchi-ken (Yamaguchi prefecture)
—522	Kyūshū (Kyusyu) district

>	—522 2–522 8 Kyūshū (Kyusyu) island
	Class comprehensive works in —522
—522 2	Fukuoka-ken (Fukuoka prefecture)
—522 3	Saga-ken (Saga prefecture)
—522 4	Nagasaki-ken (Nagasaki prefecture)
—522 44	Nagasaki

*Class parts of this physiographic region or feature as instructed under —4–9

—522 5	Kumamoto-ken (Kumamoto prefecture)
—522 6	Kagoshima-ken (Kagoshima prefecture)
—522 7	Miyazaki-ken (Miyazaki prefecture)
—522 8	Ōita-ken (Ōita prefecture)
—522 9	Okinawa-ken (Okinawa prefecture)

> Class here Ryukyu Islands (Luchu) [*formerly* —5281]

—522 94	Okinawa island
—523	Shikoku (Sikoku) island and district
—523 2	Ehime-ken (Ehime prefecture)
—523 3	Kōchi-ken (Kōchi prefecture)
—523 4	Tokushima-ken (Tokushima prefecture)
—523 5	Kagawa-ken (Kagawa prefecture)
—524	Hokkaidō-ken (Hokkaidō prefecture)

> Including Etorofu, Kunashiri (islands claimed by both Japan and the Union of Soviet Socialist Republics)

> Class here Hokkaidō (Ezo) Island

> *See also* —16453 *for La Pérouse Strait,* —16454 *for Tsugaru Strait*

—528	Ogasawara Islands (Bonin Islands)

> Former heading: Southern islands

—[528 1]	Ryukyu Islands (Luchu)

> Relocated to —5229

—[528 5]	Bonin Islands

> Number discontinued; class in —528

—53	**Arabian Peninsula and adjacent areas**

> (Option: Class here ancient Arabia, Arabia Felix, Arabia Petraea; prefer —3949 for ancient Arabia, Arabia Felix, —3948 for Arabia Petraea)

> Comprehensive works on Syrian Desert relocated to —569

> *See also* —16532 *for Red Sea,* —16535 *for Persian Gulf*

—531	Sinai (Sinai Peninsula)

> Governorate of Egypt

> Including Gaza Strip

> (Option: Class here ancient Sinai Peninsula; prefer —3948)

—533	Southwestern coast of Arabia
—533 2	Yemen (Yemen Arab Republic)

—533 5   Southern Yemen (People's Democratic Republic of Yemen)

                 Former name: Federation of South Arabia

—535   Oman and United Arab Emirates

—535 3   Oman

                 See also —16536 for Gulf of Oman

—535 7   United Arab Emirates

                 Former name: Trucial States

                 Contains Abu Dhabi, Ajman, Dubai, Fujairah, Ras al Khaimah, Sharjah, Umm al-Qaiwain

—536   Persian Gulf States

                 For Oman and United Arab Emirates, see —535

—536 3   Qatar

—536 5   Bahrain

—536 7   Kuwait

—538   Saudi Arabia

                 Including Hasa, Hejaz, Nejd; Mecca; *Rub al Khali, Syrian Desert in Saudi Arabia

—54   **South Asia**   **India**

                 (Option: Class here ancient India; prefer —34)

                 For southeast Asia, see —59

SUMMARY

—541	**Northeastern India**
—542	**Uttar Pradesh**
—543	**Madhya Pradesh**
—544	**Rajasthan**
—545	**Punjab region of India**
—546	**Jammu and Kashmir**
—547	**Western India**
—548	**Southern India**
—549	**Other jurisdictions**

>   —541–548   India

                 Class comprehensive works in —54

—541   Northeastern India

                 Including *Ganges River

—541 2   Bihar

*Class parts of this physiographic region or feature as instructed under —4–9

—541 3	Orissa
—541 4	West Bengal

> Class here former province of Bengal
>
> *For former East Bengal, see* —5492

—541 47	Calcutta
—541 5	Tripura
—541 6	Far northeast

> Class here *Brahmaputra River in India
>
> *For Manipur, see* —5417

—541 62	Assam
—541 63	Arunachal Pradesh

> Former name: North East Frontier Agency

—541 64	Meghalaya
—541 65	Nāgāland
—541 66	Mizoram
—541 67	Sikkim
—541 7	Manipur
—542	Uttar Pradesh
—543	Madhya Pradesh

> Including former Madhya Bharat, former Vindhya Pradesh; Bhopal

—544	Rajasthan

> Class here *Thar (Great Indian) Desert

—545	Punjab region of India

> Class here former province of Punjab
>
> Class Punjab Province of Pakistan in —54914

—545 2	Himachal Pradesh
—545 5	Punjab and Haryana

> Class here former Punjab state

—545 52	Punjab

> Including Chandīgarh

—545 58	Haryana
—545 6	Delhi

> Class here Delhi, New Delhi

*Class parts of this physiographic region or feature as instructed under —4–9

—546	Jammu and Kashmir
	Kashmir is claimed by both India and Pakistan
	Including *Karakoram Range
—547	Western India
—547 5	Gujarat
—547 9	Maharashtra and adjacent territories
—547 92	Maharashtra
—547 923	Bombay
—547 96	Dādra and Nagar Haveli
—547 99	Goa, Daman and Diu
—548	Southern India
	Class here *Deccan
—548 1	Lakshadweep
	Contains Laccadive, Minicoy, Amindivi Islands
—548 2	Tamil Nadu
	Former name: Madras
	Including Madras
—548 3	Kerala
—548 4	Andhra Pradesh
	Including Hyderabad
	Class here former state of Hyderabad
	For Maharashtra, see —54792; *Karnataka,* —5487
—548 6	Pondicherry
—548 7	Karnataka
	Former name: Mysore
—548 8	Andaman and Nicobar Islands
—549	Other jurisdictions
	Class here Pakistan (West and East, 1947–1971)
—549 1	Pakistan
	Former name: West Pakistan
	Class here *Indus River
—549 12	North-West Frontier

*Class parts of this physiographic region or feature as instructed under —4–9

—549 122	Districts and agencies north of Peshawar
	Including Chitrāl, Dīr, Kalam, Swat
—549 123	Peshawar District
	Class here Peshawar
—549 124	Districts south of Peshawar
	Including Dera Ismāīl Khān District
—549 13	Kashmir
	Claimed by both Pakistan and India
—549 14	Punjab Province
	Including Multān, Sargodha Districts
	For Bahawalpur District, see —54916
—549 142	Rawalpindi District
	Including Islāmābād
—549 143	Lahore District
	Class here Lahore
—[549 144]	Sargodha District
	Number discontinued; class in —54914
—[549 145]	Multān District
	Number discontinued; class in —54914
—549 15	Baluchistan Province
	Class here comprehensive works on Baluchistan
	Class Iranian Baluchistan in —5583
—549 152	Quetta District
—549 153	Kalāt District
—549 16	Bahāwalpur District
—549 17	Khairpūr District
—549 18	Sind Province
	For Khairpūr District, see —54917
—549 182	Hyderabad District
	Class here Hyderabad
—549 183	Karachi District
	Class here Karachi

—549 2	**Bangladesh**
	Former names: East Bengal, East Pakistan
	Class here comprehensive works on Brahmaputra River
	For Brahmaputra River in India, see —5416
—549 22	Dacca District
	Class here Dacca
—549 23	Chittagong District
	Class here Chittagong
—549 24	Rājshāhi District
—549 25	Khulna District
—549 3	Sri Lanka
	Former name: Ceylon
	Including Colombo
—549 5	Maldives
—549 6	Nepal
	Class here *Himalaya Mountains
—549 8	Bhutan
—55	**Iran**
	Former name: Persia
	(Option: Class here ancient Iranian Plateau; prefer —35)
—551	Gilan and Zanjan (Zenjan) provinces
—552	Mazandaran, Semnan, Markazi provinces
—552 3	Mazandaran and Semnan (Samnan) provinces
	(Option: Class here ancient Hyrcania; prefer —396)
—552 5	Markazi (Central) province
	Including Tehran
—553	Azarbayjan-i Khavari (East Azerbaijan) province
	Class here Azerbaijan
	For West Azerbaijan of Iran, see —554; Azerbaijan Soviet Socialist Republic, —4791
—554	Azarbayjan-i Bakhtari (West Azerbaijan) province
—555	Hamadan, Ilam, Kermanshahan, Kordestan provinces
	(Option: Class here ancient Media, Ecbatana; prefer —35)

*Class parts of this physiographic region or feature as instructed under —4–9

—555 2	Hamadan, Ilam, Kermanshahan provinces
—555 4	Kordestan province

> Class comprehensive works on Kurdistan in —5667

—556	Boyer Ahmadi-ye Sardir va Kohkiluyeh, Khuzestan, Lorestan (Luristan) provinces

> (Option: Class here ancient Elam [Susiana], Susa; prefer —35)

—557	Bushehr, Fars, Persian Gulf provinces
—557 2	Fars province

> (Option: Class here ancient Persia, Pasargadae, Persepolis; prefer —35)

—557 5	Bushehr and Persian Gulf (Ports and Islands) provinces
—558	Kirman and Baluchistan va Sistan provinces
—558 2	Kirman (Kerman) province
—558 3	Baluchistan va Sistan (Seistan and Baluchistan) province

> Class comprehensive works on Baluchistan in —54915

—559	Bakhtiari va Chahar Mahall, Esfahan, Khorasan, Yazd provinces
—559 2	Khorasan (Khurasan) province
—559 5	Bakhtiari va Chahar Mahall, Esfahan (Isfahan), Yazd provinces
—56	**Middle East (Near East)**

Class here Ottoman Empire

(Option: Class here ancient Middle East; prefer —394)

Class each specific country of Middle East, of Ottoman Empire, not provided for here with the country, e.g., Saudi Arabia —538

SUMMARY

—561	**Turkey and Cyprus**
—562	**Western Turkey**
—563	**North central Turkey**
—564	**South central Turkey and Cyprus**
—565	**East central Turkey**
—566	**Eastern Turkey**
—567	**Iraq**
—569	**Eastern Mediterranean Region**

—561	Turkey and Cyprus

Class here Asia Minor

(Option: Class here ancient Asia Minor, western Asia Minor, eastern Asia Minor; prefer —392 for Asia Minor, western Asia Minor, —393 for eastern Asia Minor)

For divisions of Turkey and Cyprus, see —562–566

>   —562–566   Divisions of Turkey and Cyprus

         Class comprehensive works in —561

         For Turkey in Europe, see —4961

—562   Western Turkey

         Contains Afyon-Karahisar, Aydin, Balikesir, Burdur, Canakkale, Denizli, Izmir (Smyrna), Kutahya, Manisa, Mugla, Usak illeri (provinces)

         Including Imbros (Imroz) and Tenedos (Bozcaada) islands

         (Option: Class here ancient Imbros and Tenedos islands, Mysia, Troas, Lydia, Ionia, Caria, Phrygia; prefer —3911 for Imbros and Tenedos islands, —3921 for Mysia and Troas, —3922 for Lydia, —3923 for Ionia, —3924 for Caria, —3926 for Phrygia)

         For European portion of Canakkale Ili, see —4961

         See also —16389 for Dardanelles

—563   North central Turkey

         Contains Amasya, Ankara, Bilecik, Bolu, Bursa, Cankiri, Corum, Eskisehir, Kastamonu, Kocaeli, Sakarya, Samsun, Sinop, Yozgat, Zonguldak illeri (provinces); Asian portion of Istanbul Ili

         (Option: Class here ancient Bithynia, Paphlagonia, Galatia; prefer —3925 for Bithynia, —3931 for Paphlagonia, —3932 for Galatia)

         Turkey in Europe (Turkish Thrace) relocated to —4961

         See also —16389 for Bosporus, Sea of Marmara

—564   South central Turkey and Cyprus

         Contains Adana (Seyhan), Antalya, Gaziantep, Hatay (Antakya), Icel, Isparta, Kayseri, Kirsehir, Konya, Nevsehir, Nigde illeri (provinces) of Turkey

         Including Taurus Mountains

         (Option: Class here ancient Pisidia, Lycia, Pamphylia, Cappadocia, Cilicia, Commagene, Antioch; prefer —3927 for Pisidia, —3928 for Lycia, —3929 for Pamphylia, —3934 for Cappadocia, —3935 for Cilicia, —3936 for Commagene, —3943 for Antioch)

—564 5   Cyprus

         Independent island state

         (Option: Class here ancient Cyprus; prefer —3937)

—565   East central Turkey

         Contains Adiyaman, Giresun, Gumusane, Malatya, Maras, Ordu, Sivas, Tokat, Trabzon (Trebizond), Urfa illeri (provinces)

         (Option: Class here ancient Pontus; prefer —3933)

—566   Eastern Turkey

—566 2   Northeastern Turkey

>Contains Agri, Artvin (Coruh), Erzurum, Hakkari, Kars, Rize, Van illeri (provinces)
>
>Class here comprehensive works on Armenia
>
>(Option: Class here ancient Armenia; prefer —3955)
>
>> *For Armenian Soviet Socialist Republic, see* —4792

—566 7   Southeast central Turkey

>Contains Bingol, Bitlis, Diyarbakir, Elazig, Erzincan, Mardin, Mus, Siirt, Tunceli illeri (provinces)
>
>Class here comprehensive works on Kurdistan
>
>Class Iranian Kurdistan in —5554, Iraqi Kurdistan in —5672

—567   Iraq

>Class here Mesopotamia
>
>(Option: Class here ancient Mesopotamia, Seleucid Empire, Arabia Deserta; prefer —35 for Mesopotamia, Seleucid Empire; —3947 for Arabia Deserta)

—567 2   Kurdish Autonomous Region

>Contains Dahuk (Dohuk) [*formerly* —5674], As-Sulaymaniyah, Irbil (Arbil, Erbil) provinces
>
>Class comprehensive works on Kurdistan in —5667

—[567 3]   Desert

>Number discontinued; class in —567

—567 4   Upper Mesopotamia

>Contains Al-Anbar, Diyala, Ninawa (Nineveh), Salah ad-Din (Salahuddin), Tamin provinces
>
>Including Mosul; Syrian Desert in Iraq
>
>(Option: Class here ancient Assyria, Ashur, Nineveh; prefer —35)
>
>Use of this number for comprehensive works on modern Mesopotamia discontinued; class in —567
>
>Dahuk province relocated to —5672

—567 47   Baghdad Province

>>Class here Baghdad

—567 5   Lower Mesopotamia

>Contains Al-Basrah, Al-Muthanna, Al-Qadisiyah, An-Najaf, Babil, Dhi Qar, Karbala, Maysan, Wasit (Kut) provinces
>
>(Option: Class here ancient Babylonia, Sumer, Babylon, Ur; prefer —35)

—569   Eastern Mediterranean Region

>Class here comprehensive works on *Syrian Desert [*formerly* —53]

*Class parts of this physiographic region or feature as instructed under —4–9

—569 1	Syria
	(Option: Class here ancient Syria; prefer —3943)
—569 12	Desert provinces
	Contains Deir ez Zor, Haseke, Homs, Raqqa
	Class here Syrian Desert in Syria
	(Option: Class here ancient Palmyra; prefer —3943)
—569 13	Northwest provinces
	Contains Aleppo, Hama, Idlib, Latakia, Tartous
	(Option: Class here ancient Ebla, Ugarit; prefer —3943)
—569 14	Southwest provinces and city of Damascus
	Contains Damascus, Dera (Dara), El Quneitra, Es Suweida (Jebel Druze) provinces
	Including *Anti-Lebanon
—569 144	City of Damascus
	(Option: Class here ancient Damascus; prefer —3943)
—569 2	Lebanon
	(Option: Class here ancient Phoenicia, Coelesyria, Baalbek, Byblos, Sidon, Tyre; prefer —3944)
—569 25	Beirut
—569 4	Palestine Israel
	Palestine: area covering Israel, Gaza Strip, and West Bank of Jordan
	Including *Jordan River; *Dead Sea
	(Option: Class here ancient Palestine, Israel; prefer —33)
	For West Bank, see —56951–56953; Gaza Strip, —531
—569 44	Jerusalem district
—569 442	Jerusalem
	(Option: Class here ancient Jerusalem; prefer —33)
—569 45	Tsafon (Northern) district
	Class here Galilee
	(Option: Class here ancient Galilee; prefer —33)
—569 46	Haifa district
—569 47	Merkaz (Central) district
—569 48	Tel Aviv district
	Class here Tel Aviv

*Class parts of this physiographic region or feature as instructed under —4–9

—569 49	Darom (Southern) district
	Class here Negev
	(Option: Class here ancient Judah, Judaea, Edom; prefer —33 for Judah, Judaea, —3946 for Edom)
—569 5	Jordan
	(Option: Class here the Jordanian part of ancient Palestine; prefer —33)

>	—569 51–569 53 West Bank
	Class comprehensive works in —56953
—569 51	Hebron district
—569 52	Jerusalem district
	Class city of Jerusalem in —569442
—569 53	Nablus district
	Class here comprehensive works on West Bank
	(Option: Class here ancient Samaria; prefer —33)
	For Hebron district, see —56951; Jerusalem district, —56952
—569 54	Irbid district
	Including *Syrian Desert in Jordan
—569 55	Balqa district
—569 56	Karak district
	(Option: Class here ancient Moab; prefer —3946)
—569 57	Maan district
	(Option: Class here ancient Petra; prefer —3948)
—569 58	Amman district
	Class here Amman
—57	**Siberia (Asiatic Russia)**
	Class here Soviet Union in Asia
	For Soviet Central Asia, see —584
—573	Western Siberia
	Contains Kemerovo, Kurgan, Novosibirsk, Omsk, Tomsk, Tyumen oblasts (provinces); Altai Kray (Territory)
	Including Gorno-Altai Autonomous Oblast (Province), Khanty-Mansi and Yamal-Nenets national okrugs (regions)
	For Chelyabinsk and Sverdlovsk oblasts, see —4787

*Class parts of this physiographic region or feature as instructed under —4–9

—575   Eastern Siberia

> Contains Chita and Irkutsk oblasts (provinces); Krasnoyarsk Kray (Territory); Buryat, Tuva, Yakut Autonomous Soviet Socialist Republics

> Including Khakass Autonomous Oblast (Province); Agin Buryat, Evenki, Taimyr, Ust-Orda Buryat National okrugs (regions); *Sayan Mountains

>> *For Far Eastern Siberia, see —577; Severnaya Zemlya, —987; New Siberian Islands, —988*

—577   Far Eastern Siberia

> Contains Amur, Kamchatka, Magadan, Sakhalin oblasts (provinces); Khabarovsk and Primorski (Maritime) krays (territories)

> Including Jewish Autonomous Oblast (Province); Chukchi and Koryak National okrugs (regions); Kurile and Komandorski Islands, Wrangel Island; *Amur River

>> *See also —16451 for Bering Strait, —16453 for Sea of Okhotsk, —16454 for Tartar Strait*

—58   **Central Asia**

> (Option: Class here ancient Central Asia; prefer —396)

—581   Afghanistan

> Class here *Hindu Kush

> (Option: Class here ancient Bactria, Ariana, Parthia; prefer —396)

—584   Turkestan   Soviet Central Asia

> Class Sinkiang in —516

>> *For Turkmenistan, see —585; Tadzhikistan, —586; Uzbekistan, —587*

—584 3   Kirghizistan (Kirghiz Soviet Socialist Republic)

> Including *Tien Shan in Soviet Union

—584 5   Kazakhstan (Kazakh Soviet Socialist Republic)

—585   Turkmenistan (Turkmen Soviet Socialist Republic)

> (Option: Class here ancient Margiana; prefer —396)

—586   Tadzhikistan (Tadzhik Soviet Socialist Republic)

> Including Gorno-Badakhshan Autonomous Oblast (Province)

> Class here *Pamirs

—587   Uzbekistan (Uzbek Soviet Socialist Republic)

> Including Kara-Kalpak Autonomous Soviet Socialist Republic; *Aral Sea

> (Option: Class here ancient Sogdiana; prefer —396)

---

*Class parts of this physiographic region or feature as instructed under —4–9

—59   **Southeast Asia**

SUMMARY

—591	**Burma**
—593	**Thailand**
—594	**Laos**
—595	**Commonwealth of Nations territories** **Malaysia**
—596	**Cambodia (Khmer Republic, Kampuchea)**
—597	**Vietnam**
—598	**Indonesia**
—599	**Philippines**

—591   Burma

—593   Thailand

         Former name: Siam

           See also —16472 for Gulf of Siam

—594   Laos

—595   Commonwealth of Nations territories   Malaysia

—595 1   Peninsular Malaysia (Malaya, West Malaysia)

         States of Johore, Kedah, Kelantan, Malacca (Melaka), Negeri Sembilan, Pahang, Penang (Pinang), Perak, Perlis, Selangor, Trengganu

         Class here Malay Peninsula

           For Burma, see —591; Thailand, —593

—595 3   Sabah

         State of Malaysia

         Class here northern Borneo, East Malaysia

           For Sarawak, see —5954; Brunei, —5955

—595 4   Sarawak

         State of Malaysia

—595 5   Brunei

—595 7   Singapore

         Independent republic

           See also —16472 for Singapore Strait

—596   Cambodia (Khmer Republic, Kampuchea)

—597   Vietnam

         Including *Mekong River

*Class parts of this physiographic region or feature as instructed under —4–9

—598	Indonesia

Class here Malay Archipelago, Sunda Islands

> For Philippines, see —599; Irian Jaya, —951
>
> See also —16473 for inner sea of Malay Archipelago, —16474 for seas adjoining Sunda Islands

—598 1	Sumatra
—598 2	Java and Madura
—598 22	Jakarta (Djakarta)
—598 3	Kalimantan

Class here Borneo

> For northern Borneo, see —5953

—598 4	Celebes (Sulawesi)
—598 5	Maluku (Moluccas)
—598 6	Lesser Sunda Islands (Nusa Tenggara)

Including Bali, Flores, Lombok, Sumba, Sumbawa, Timor, Wetar; former Portuguese Timor

—599	Philippines

> See also —16471 for inner seas of Philippines

—599 1	Luzon and adjacent islands

Contains Abra, Albay, Bataan, Batanes, Batangas, Benguet, Bulacan, Cagayan, Camarines Norte, Camarines Sur, Catanduanes, Cavite, Ifugao, Ilocos Norte, Ilocos Sur, Isabela, Kalinga-Apayao, Laguna, La Union, Marinduque, Mountain, Nueva Ecija, Nueva Vizcaya, Pampanga, Pangasinan, Quezon, Rizal, Sorsogon, Tarlac, Zambales provinces

Including Batan, Catanduanes islands

> See also —16458 for Luzon Strait

—599 16	Manila
—599 3	Mindoro and adjacent islands

Contains Occidental Mindoro, Oriental Mindoro provinces

Including Lubang Islands

—599 4	Palawan and adjacent islands (Palawan province)

Including Calamian, Cuyo Islands

—599 5	Visayan Islands

Contains Aklan, Antique, Bohol, Capiz, Cebu, Eastern Samar, Iloilo, Leyte, Masbate, Negros Occidental, Negros Oriental, Northern Samar, Romblon, Southern Leyte, Western Samar provinces

Including Bohol, Cebu, Leyte, Masbate, Negros, Panay, Samar Islands

—599 7   Mindanao and adjacent islands

> Contains Agusan del Norte, Agusan del Sur, Basilan, Bukidnon, Camiguin, Davao del Norte, Davao del Sur, Davao Oriental, Lanao del Norte, Lanao del Sur, Maguindanao, Misamis Occidental, Misamis Oriental, North Cotabato, South Cotabato, Sultan Kudarat, Surigao del Norte, Surigao del Sur, Zamboanga del Norte, Zamboanga del Sur provinces

> Including Basilan, Dinagat Islands

—599 9   Sulu Archipelago

> Contains Sulu and Tawitawi provinces

> *See also —16473 for Sulu Sea*

—6   Africa

SUMMARY

—609 1	**Regional treatment**
—61	**Tunisia and Libya**
—62	**Egypt and Sudan**
—63	**Ethiopia**
—64	**Northwest African coast and offshore islands** **Morocco**
—65	**Algeria**
—66	**West Africa and offshore islands**
—67	**Central Africa and offshore islands**
—68	**Southern Africa** **Republic of South Africa**
—69	**South Indian Ocean islands**

—[600 9]   Regional treatment

> Relocated to —6091

—609 1   Regional treatment [*formerly* —6009]

> Add to base number —6091 the numbers following —1 in —11–18 of this table, e.g., Anglophone Africa —60917521

—61   Tunisia and Libya

> Class here Barbary States, comprehensive works on North Africa

> (Option: Class here ancient North Africa; prefer —397)

> Class each specific part of North Africa, of Barbary States, not provided for here with the part, e.g., Algeria —65

—611   Tunisia

> Including Bizerte, Tunis

> (Option: Class here ancient Carthage; prefer —3973)

—612   Libya

> Including Banghazi, Tripoli; *Libyan Desert

> (Option: Class here ancient Tripolis, Leptis Magna, Oea, Sabrata, Cyrenaica, Marmarica; prefer —3974 for Tripolis, Leptis Magna, Oea, Sabrata, —3975 for Cyrenaica, —3976 for Marmarica)

*Class parts of this physiographic region or feature as instructed under —4–9

—62   **Egypt and Sudan**

Class here Federation of Arab Republics, *Nile River

(Option: Class here ancient Egypt; prefer —32)

For Libya, see —612; Syria, —5691

>   **—621–623 Egypt**

Class comprehensive works in —62

For Sinai, see —531

—621   Lower Egypt

Contains Alexandria, Buhayrah (Beheira), Damietta (Dumyati), Daqahliya, Gharbiya, Kafr al-Shaykh (Kafr el Sheikh), Matruh, Minufiya, Qalyubiya, Sharqiya governorates

Class here Nile Delta

(Option: Class here ancient Alexandria; prefer —32)

—621 5   Isthmus of Suez

Contains Ismailia, Port Said, Suez governorates

See also —16533 for Gulf of Suez, Suez Canal

—621 6   Cairo

—622   Middle Egypt

Contains Asyut, Beni Suef, Faiyum, Giza, Minya, New Valley governorates

Including *Western Desert, *Qattara Depression

(Option: Class here ancient Giza, Memphis; prefer —32)

—623   Upper Egypt

Contains Al-Bahr al-Ahmar (Red Sea), Aswan, Qina (Qena), Suhaj (Soha) governorates

Including *Eastern (Arabian) Desert; *Lake Nasser

(Option: Class here ancient Abydos, Karnak, Luxor, Thebes; prefer —32)

—624   Sudan

For provinces of Sudan, see —625–629

>   **—625–629 Provinces of Sudan**

Class comprehensive works in —624

*Class parts of this physiographic region or feature as instructed under —4–9

—625   Eastern [*formerly* —6292] and Northern regions of Sudan

Contains Al-Bahr al-Ahmar (Red Sea), Nil, Ash-Shamaliyah (Northern), Kassala provinces

Including Nubian Desert, Port Sudan

(Option: Class here ancient Ethiopia, Cush, Nubia; prefer —3978)

See also —16533 for Red Sea

—626   Khartoum province and Central region of Sudan

—626 2   Khartoum province

Class here Khartoum

—626 4   Central region

Contains Al-Jazirah (Gezira), An-Nil al-Abyad (White Nile), An-Nil al-Azraq (Blue Nile) provinces

Class here *Blue Nile River

—627   Darfur region of Sudan

Contains Dafur al-Janubiyah (Southern Darfur) and Dafur al-Shamaliyah (Northern Darfur) provinces

—628   Kordofan region of Sudan

Contains Kurdufn al Janubiyah (Southern Kordofan) and Kurdufn al-Shamaliyah (Northern Kordofan) provinces

—629   Southern regions of Sudan

—[629 2]   Eastern region

Relocated to —625

—629 3   Upper Nile region

Contains Ali an-Nil (Upper Nile) and Junqali (Jongley) provinces

Class here *White Nile River

—629 4   Bahr al Ghazal and Buhayrah regions

—629 5   Equatoria region

Contains Mudiriyah al-Istiwaiyah al-Gharbiyah (Western Equatoria) and Mudiriyah al-Istiwaiyah al-Sharqiyah (Eastern Equatoria) provinces

—63   **Ethiopia**

Former name: Abyssinia

Class here Horn of Africa

For Djibouti and Somalia, see —677

—632   Provinces east of Great Rift Valley

Contains Arusi, Balē, Hārer, Sīdamo

*Class parts of this physiographic region or feature as instructed under —4–9

—633   Provinces west of Great Rift Valley

        Contains Gamu Gofa, Gojjam, Ilubabor, Keffa, Shewa (Shoa), Wallaga

        Including Addis Ababa

—634   Northern provinces

        Contains Bagēmder (Begēmdir), Tigre, Wallo

        For Eritrea, see —635

—635   Eritrea province

        Including Dahlak Archipelago; Āsmera, Massawa

—64   Northwest African coast and offshore islands   Morocco

        Class here *Atlas Mountains

        (Option: Class here ancient Mauretania Tingitana; prefer —3971)

>   —642–648 Morocco

        Class comprehensive works in —64

—642   Mediterranean provinces of Morocco

        Contains Chaouen (Chechaouen), Hoceima, Nador, Tangier, Tetouan

        Including Spanish cities of Ceuta and Melilla

        Class here former Spanish Morocco; *Rif Mountains

—643   Northern provinces of Morocco

        Contains Ben Slimane, Boulemane, Fez, Figuig, Ifrane, Jadida, Kenitra, Khemisset, Khenifra, Khouribga, Meknes, Oujda, Settat, Sidi Kacem, Tauounate, Taza provinces; Ain Chok-Hay Hassani, Ben Msik-Sidi Othmane, Casablanca-Anfa, Hay Mohamed-Ain Sebaa, Mohamedia-Znata, Rabat-Sale prefectures

        Including Casablanca, Rabat

        For Mediterranean provinces, see —642

—644   Azilal and Beni Mellal provinces

        Use of this number for comprehensive works on Atlas Mountains discontinued; class in —64

—645   Errachidia province

        Former name: Ksar-es-Souk province

—646   Southwestern provinces of Morocco

        Contains Agadir, Essaouira, Guelmim, Kelaa-Srarhna, Marrakesh, Ouarzazate, Safi, Tan-Tan, Taroudant, Tiznit

        For provinces of former Western Sahara, see —648

*Class parts of this physiographic region or feature as instructed under —4–9

—648   Provinces of former Western Sahara

> Former names: Spanish West Africa, Spanish Sahara (Saguia el Hamra, Rio de Oro)
>
> Contains Ad-Dakhla, Boujdour, Es Semara (Smara), Laayoune provinces

—649   Canary Islands

> Contains Santa Cruz de Tenerife and Las Palmas provinces of Spain

—65   Algeria

> (Option: Class here ancient Mauretania Caesariensis, comprehensive works on Mauretania; prefer —3971)

—651   Northwestern departments

> Contains Mascara, Mostaganem, Ouahran (Oran), Saida, Sidi-Bel-Abbes, Tiaret, Tlemcen

—653   North central departments

> Contains Al-Asnam (Orléansville), Al-Boulaida (Blida), Al-Jazair, Bouira, Djelfa, Médéa, Tizi-Ouzou
>
> Including Algiers

—655   Northeastern departments

> Contains Annaba (Bône), Batna, Bejaia (Bougie), Biskra, Guelma, Jijel, M'Sila, Oum el Bouaghi, Qacentina (Constantine), Sétif, Skikda, Tébessa
>
> (Option: Class here ancient Numidia; prefer —3972)

—657   Sahara departments

> Contains Adrar, Béchar, Laghouat, Ouargla, Tamanrasset
>
> (Option: Class here ancient Gaetulia; prefer —3977)

—66   West Africa and offshore islands

> Class here *Sahara Desert

SUMMARY

—660 917 521	**English-speaking West Africa**
—660 917 541	**French-speaking West Africa**
—661	**Mauritania**
—662	**Mali, Burkina Faso, Niger**
—663	**Senegal**
—664	**Sierra Leone**
—665	**Gambia, Guinea, Guinea-Bissau, Cape Verde**
—666	**Liberia and Ivory Coast**
—667	**Ghana**
—668	**Togo and Benin**
—669	**Nigeria**

—[660 097 521]   English-speaking West Africa

> Relocated to —660917521

*Class parts of this physiographic region or feature as instructed under —4–9

—[660 097 541]	French-speaking West Africa
	Relocated to —660917541
—660 917 521	English-speaking West Africa [*formerly* —660097521]
—660 917 541	French-speaking West Africa [*formerly* —660097541]

—661   Mauritania

        Including Nouakchott

—662   Mali, Burkina Faso, Niger

        Class here *Niger River

—662 3   Mali

        Former name: French Sudan

        Including Bamako

—662 5   Burkina Faso

        Former name: Upper Volta

        Including Bobo-Dioulasso, Ouagadougou

—662 6   Niger

        Including Niamey

—663   Senegal

        Contains Cap Vert, Casamance, Diourbel, Fleuve, Louga, Sénégal-Oriental, Sine-Saloum, Thiès regions

        Including Dakar, Saint-Louis

        Class here Senegambia

          For Gambia, see —6651

—664   Sierra Leone

        Including Freetown

—665   Gambia, Guinea, Guinea-Bissau, Cape Verde

        Class here Upper Guinea area

        Class each specific country of Upper Guinea not provided for here with the country, e.g., Sierra Leone —664

—665 1   Gambia

        Including Banjul

        Class here *Gambia River

—665 2   Guinea

        Former name: French Guinea

        Including Conakry, Kankan

*Class parts of this physiographic region or feature as instructed under —4–9

—665 7   **Guinea-Bissau**

> Former name: Portuguese Guinea
>
> Including Bissau

—665 8   **Cape Verde**

> Including Praia
>
> Class here Cape Verde Islands

—666   **Liberia and Ivory Coast**

—666 2   **Liberia**

> Including Monrovia

—666 8   **Ivory Coast**

> Including Abidjan, Bouaké, Yamoussoukro

—667   **Ghana**

> Former name: Gold Coast
>
> Including Accra, Kumasi
>
> Class here *Volta River

—668   **Togo and Benin**

—668 1   **Togo**

> Including Lomé

—668 3   **Benin**

> Former name: Dahomey
>
> Including Cotonou, Porto-Novo

—669   **Nigeria**

—669 1   **Lagos State**

> Class here Lagos

—669 2   **Western states**

> Class here former Western State, former Western Region
>
> Class each specific state of former Western State, of former Western Region not provided for here with the state, e.g., Lagos State —6691

—669 23   Ogun State

—669 25   Oyo State

—669 28   Ondo State

*Class parts of this physiographic region or feature as instructed under —4–9

—669 3   Bendel State

         Former names: Benin State, Mid-Western State

         Including Benin City

—669 4   Eastern states

         Class here former Eastern Region

—669 42   Rivers State

         Including Port Harcourt

—669 44   Cross River State

         Former name: South-Eastern State

         Including Calabar

—669 46   Imo State

         Class here former East-Central State

         For Anambra State, see —66948

—669 48   Anambra State

         Including Enugu

—669 5   Plateau, Benue, Kwara states

         Class here former Northern Region

         Sokoto and Niger states and Federal Capital Territory relocated to —6696; Kaduna and Kano states relocated to —6697; Bauchi, Borno, Gongola states relocated to —6698

         Class each specific part of former Northern Region not provided for here with the part, e.g., Niger State —66965

—669 52   Plateau State

         Including Jos

         Class here former Benue-Plateau State

         For Benue State, see —66954

—669 54   Benue State

         Including Makurdi

—669 57   Kwara State

         Including Ilorin

—669 6   Sokoto and Niger states and Federal Capital Territory [*formerly* —6695]

         Class here former North-Western State

—669 62   Sokoto State

         Including Sokoto

—669 65   Niger State

                          Including Minna

—669 68   Federal Capital Territory

                          Class here Abuja

—669 7   Kaduna and Kano states [*formerly* —6695]

—669 73   Kaduna State

                          Former name: North Central State

                          Including Kaduna

—669 78   Kano State

                          Including Kano

—669 8   Bauchi, Borno, Gongola states [*formerly* —6695]

                          Class here former North-Eastern State

—669 82   Bauchi State

—669 85   Borno State

                          Including Maiduguri

—669 88   Gongola State

—[669 9]   Islands of Gulf of Guinea

                          Relocated to —671

—67   **Central Africa and offshore islands**

                Class here Black Africa, Sub-Saharan Africa (Africa south of the Sahara)

                Class each specific part of Black Africa, of Sub-Saharan Africa not provided for here with the part, e.g., Nigeria —669

SUMMARY

—671	**Cameroon, Sao Tome and Principe, Equatorial Guinea**
—672	**Gabon and Republic of the Congo**
—673	**Angola**
—674	**Central African Republic and Chad**
—675	**Zaire, Rwanda, Burundi**
—676	**Uganda and Kenya**
—677	**Djibouti and Somalia**
—678	**Tanzania**
—679	**Mozambique**

—671   Cameroon, Sao Tome and Principe, Equatorial Guinea

                Class here Islands of Gulf of Guinea [*formerly* —6699], Lower Guinea area

                Class each specific country of Lower Guinea not provided for here with the country, e.g., Gabon —6721

                See also —16373 for Gulf of Guinea

—671 1	Cameroon
	Including Douala, Yaoundé
—[671 12]	West Cameroon
	Number discontinued; class in —6711
—[671 13]	East Cameroon
	Number discontinued; class in —6711
—671 5	Sao Tome and Principe
	Including São Tomé
—671 8	Equatorial Guinea
	Former name: Spanish Guinea
—671 83	Rio Muni
—671 86	Bioko (Fernando Po) and Pagalu (Annobón) islands
	Including Malabo
—672	Gabon and Republic of the Congo
—672 1	Gabon
	Including Libreville
—672 4	Republic of the Congo
	Former names: French Congo, Middle Congo
	Including Brazzaville
	See also —6751 for Democratic Republic of the Congo (Zaire)
—673	Angola
—673 1	Cabinda province
	Exclave of Angola
—673 2	Northern provinces
	Contains Bengo, Cuanza Norte, Cuanza Sul, Luanda, Uíge, Zaire
	Including Luanda (capital city)
	For Cabinda province, see —6731
—673 4	Central provinces
	Contains Benguela, Bié, Huambo, Lunda Norte, Lunda Sul, Malanje, Moxico
—673 5	Southern provinces
	Contains Cuando Cubango, Huíla, Kunene, Namibe (Moçâmedes)

—674	Central African Republic and Chad
—674 1	Central African Republic
	Former names: Central African Empire, Ubangi-Shari
	Including Bangui
—674 3	Chad
	Including Djamena
—675	Zaire, Rwanda, Burundi
—675 1	Zaire
	Former names: Democratic Republic of the Congo, Belgian Congo
	Class here *Congo (Zaire) River
	See also —6724 for Republic of the Congo
—675 11	Bas-Zaïre and Bandundu regions and Kinshasa
—675 112	Kinshasa
	Former name: Leopoldville
—675 114	Bas-Zaïre region
—675 116	Bandundu region
—675 12	Kasai-Occidental and Kasai-Oriental regions
—675 123	Kasai-Occidental region
—675 126	Kasai-Oriental region
—675 13	Equateur region
—675 15	Haute-Zaire region
	Including Kisangani
—675 17	Kivu region
	Including Lakes *Edward, *Kivu
—675 18	Shaba region
	Former name: Katanga province
	Including Lubumbashi; *Lake Mweru
—675 7	Rwanda and Burundi
	Class here former Ruanda-Urundi
—675 71	Rwanda
	Including Kigali
—675 72	Burundi
	Including Bujumbura

*Class parts of this physiographic region or feature as instructed under —4–9

—676 **Uganda and Kenya**

    Class here East Africa, *Great Rift Valley

    Class a specific part of East Africa not provided for here with the part, e.g., Tanzania —678

—676 1 **Uganda**

    Including Kampala; *Lake Albert

—676 2 **Kenya**

—676 22   North East Province

—676 23   Coast Province

    Including Mombasa

—676 24   Eastern Province

—676 25   Nairobi

—676 26   Central Province

—676 27   Rift Valley Province

    Including *Lake Turkana (Rudolf)

—676 28   Western Province

—676 29   Nyanza Province

—677 **Djibouti and Somalia**

    Class here Somaliland

—677 1 **Djibouti**

    Former names: French Somaliland, French Territory of the Afars and Issas

    Including Djibouti (capital city)

—677 3 **Somalia**

    Including Mogadishu

—678 **Tanzania**

—678 1 **Zanzibar and Pemba regions**

—678 2 **Tanganyika**

—678 22   Tanga Region

—678 23   Coast and Dar es Salaam regions

    Including Mafia Island

—678 232   Dar es Salaam Region

    Class here Dar es Salaam

—678 24   Lindi and Mtwara regions

*Class parts of this physiographic region or feature as instructed under —4–9

—678 25	South central regions
	Contains Iringa, Morogoro, Ruvuma
	Comprehensive works on Lake Nyasa (Lake Malawi) relocated to —6897
—678 26	North central regions
	Contains Arusha, Dodoma, Kilimanjaro, Singida
	Including *Mount Kilimanjaro; Kilimanjaro National Park
—678 27	Regions adjacent to Lake Victoria
	Contains Mara, Mwanza, West Lake
	Including Serengeti National Park
	Class here *Lake Victoria
—678 28	Western regions
	Contains Kigoma, Mbeya, Rukwa, Shinyanga, Tabora
	Including *Lake Tanganyika
—679	Mozambique
	Including *Zambezi River
—679 1	Maputo district
	Former name: Lourenço Marques district
	Class here Maputo; *Komati River; Pongola River (Rio Maputo) in Mozambique
—679 2	Gaza district
	Class here *Limpopo River
—679 3	Inhambane district
—679 4	Manica and Sofala districts
—679 5	Tete district
—679 6	Zambézia district
—679 7	Nampula district
	Former heading: Moçambique district
—679 8	Cabo Delgado district
—679 9	Niassa district
—68	**Southern Africa Republic of South Africa**

*Class parts of this physiographic region or feature as instructed under —4–9

SUMMARY

—682	Transvaal
—684	Natal
—685	Orange Free State
—687	Cape of Good Hope
—688	Botswana, Swaziland, Lesotho, Namibia
—689	Zimbabwe, Zambia, Malawi

—[681]   Botswana, Lesotho, Swaziland

     Relocated to —688

\>   —682–687   Republic of South Africa

     Class comprehensive works on Republic of South Africa in —68; on Orange River, Orange River Scheme in —687

—682   Transvaal

     Province of Republic of South Africa

     Class here *Highveld regions of South Africa; *Vaal River

---

\>   —682 1–682 7   Magisterial districts of Transvaal

     Class comprehensive works in —682

—682 1   Southern districts

     Contains Heidelberg, Vanderbijlpark, Vereeniging

     Including Meyerton

     Class here *Southern Transvaal, *Vaal Triangle

     Class comprehensive works on Pretoria-Witwatersrand-Vereeniging area (PWV area) in —6822

—682 2   Witwatersrand

     Contains Alberton, Benoni, Boksburg, Brakpan, Delmas, Germiston, Kempton Park, Krugersdorp, Nigel, Oberholzer, Randburg, Randfontein, Roodepoort, Springs, Westonaria

     Including Carletonville

     Class here East Rand, West Rand, Far Western Rand; *Pretoria-Witwatersrand-Vereeniging area (PWV area); goldfields of South Africa

     Class Vaal Triangle in —6821

—682 21   Johannesburg

     Including Soweto

     Class here Johannesburg

*Class parts of this physiographic region or feature as instructed under —4–9

—682 3   Central districts

Contains Brits, Bronkhorstspruit, Cullinan, Groblersdal, Marico, Rustenburg, Soshanguve, Swartruggens, Warmbaths

Including Zeerust; Marico, Pienaars Rivers; Hartbeespoort Dam

Class here *Magaliesberg Range; *Crocodile, *Elands Rivers

Moutse relocated to —68295

Class Pretoria-Witwatersrand-Vereeniging area (PWV area) in —6822, Vaal Triangle in —6821

—682 35   Pretoria and Wonderboom

Class here Pretoria

—682 4   Western districts

Contains Bloemhof, Christiana, Coligny, Delareyville, Klerksdorp, Koster, Lichtenburg, Potchefstroom, Schweizer-Reneke, Ventersdorp, Wolmaransstad

Including Fochville, Orkney, Stilfontein; Mooi River

Class here *Western Transvaal

—682 5   Northern districts

Contains Ellisras, Messina, Pietersburg, Potgietersrus, Soutpansberg, Thabazimbi, Waterberg

Including Haenertsburg, Louis Trichardt, Naboomspruit, Nylstroom; *Soutpansberg Range; *Shingwidzi River

Class here *Northern Transvaal; *Bushveld regions of Transvaal; *Limpopo River in South Africa

Class comprehensive works on Kruger National Park in —6826

—682 6   Eastern districts

Contains Barberton, Letaba, Lydenburg, Nelspruit, Phalaborwa, Pilgrim's Rest, White River

Including Graskop, Komatipoort, Sabie, Tzaneen; *Kruger National Park; *Lebombo Range; Blyde River Canyon; *Great Letaba, *Olifants, *Steelpoort Rivers, *Komati River in South Africa

Class here *Eastern Transvaal; *Lowveld regions of South Africa, *Transvaal Drakensberg Range; *Crocodile River (tributary of Komati River), *Sabie River

—682 7   Southeastern districts

Contains Amersfoort, Balfour, Belfast, Bethal, Carolina, Ermelo, Hoëveldrif, Middelburg, Piet Retief, Standerton, Volksrust, Wakkerstroom, Waterval-Boven, Witbank

Including Breyten, Evander, Secunda; Loskop Dam

*Class parts of this physiographic region or area as instructed under —4–9

—682 9   Homelands (National states [South African])

Class here comprehensive works on South African homelands

> *For KwaZulu, see —68491; Qwaqwa, —68591; Transkei, —68791; Ciskei, —68792*

—682 91   Venda

Contains Dzanani, Sibasa, Mutale, Vuwani

Including Makhado, Thohoyandou; Lake Fundudzi

Class here *Luvuvhu, *Nwanedzi Rivers

—682 92   Gazankulu

Contains Giyani, Malamulele, Mhala, Ritavi

—682 93   Lebowa

Contains Bochum, Bolobedu, Mapulaneng, Mokerong, Namakgale, Naphuno, Nebo, Sekgosese, Sekhukhuneland, Seshego, Thabamoopo

Including Lebowa-Kgomo; Sekhukhuneberg Range

Class here *Mogalakwena River

—682 94   Bophuthatswana

Contains Ditsobotla, Ganyesa, Lehurutshe, Madikwe, Mankwe, Molopo, Moretele, Odi, Selosesha, Taung, Thlaping Tlaro

Including Ga-Rankuwa, Mafikeng, Mmabatho, Thaba Nchu; Pilanesberg Game Reserve

—682 95   KwaNdebele

Former name: South Ndebele

Contains Moutse [*formerly* —6823], Mdutjana, Mkobola

Including Siyabuswa

—682 96   KaNgwane

Contains Eerstehoek, Kamhlushwa, Nsikazi

—684   Natal

Province of Republic of South Africa

Class here *Tugela River

>   —684 1–684 7   Magisterial districts of Natal

Class comprehensive works in —684

*Class parts of this physiographic region or feature as instructed under —4–9

—684 1   **Northwestern districts**

           Contains Dannhauser, Dundee, Glencoe, Newcastle, Utrecht

           Including Balelesberg Range

           Class here *Blood, *Buffalo Rivers

—684 2   **North central districts**

           Contains Babanango, Ngotshe, Paulpietersburg, Vryheid

           Including Louwsburg; *Pongola River; J. G. Strijdom Dam

           Class Pongola River (Rio Maputo) in Mozambique in —6791

—684 3   **Northeastern districts**

           Contains Hlabisa, Lower Umfolozi, Mtonjaneni

           Including Empangeni, Melmoth, Mtubatuba, Richard's Bay; Saint Lucia Game Reserve; St. Lucia Lake and Estuary

           Class here *Mfolozi, *Mhlatuze, *Mkuze Rivers

           Ubombo relocated to —68491

           Class Maputaland, Tongaland, Ulundi, Zululand in —68491

—684 4   **Northern coastal districts**

           Contains Eshowe, Inanda, Lower Tugela, Mtunzini

           Including Mandini, Stanger, Tongaat, Tugela, Umhlanga

           Class here *North Coast (area from north of Durban to Richard's Bay); *Mvoti River

—684 5   **Southern coastal districts**

           Contains Chatsworth, Pinetown, Port Shepstone, Umzinto

           Including Margate, Scottburgh, Uvongo; Oribi Gorge Nature Reserve

           Class here *South Coast (area south of Durban to Port Edward); *Mkomazi, *Mzimkulu Rivers

           Umlazi relocated to —68491

—684 55   **Durban**

           Including Amanzimtoti, Isipingo, Kingsburgh

           Class here Durban; *Durban-Pinetown industrial area

—684 6   **Southern interior districts**

           Contains Alfred, Mount Currie

           Including Harding, Kokstad, Matatiele; Ngeleberg Range

           Class here Griqualand East

           Class Mzimvubu River in —68791

*Class parts of this physiographic region or feature as instructed under —4–9

—684 7   Natal Midlands districts

Contains Bergville, Camperdown, Estcourt, Impendle, Ixopo, Klip River, Kranskop, Lion's River, Mooi River, New Hanover, Polela, Richmond, Umvoti, Underberg, Weenen

Including Colenso, Greytown, Howick, Ladysmith; Royal Natal National Park; Giant's Castle Game Reserve; Bushman's, *Mgeni, Mooi, Sundays Rivers; Howick Falls; Midmar, Spioenkop Dams

Class here comprehensive works on *Drakensberg Range in South Africa

—684 75   Pietermaritzburg

Including Albert Falls and Nature Reserve

—684 9   Homelands (National states [South African])

—684 91   KwaZulu

Contains Ubombo [*formerly* —6843], Umlazi [*formerly* —6845], Embumbulu, Emnambithi, Empumalanga, Emzumbe, Enseleni, Ezingolweni, Hlanganani, Ingwavuma, Inkanyezi, KwaMapumulu, Madadeni, Mahlabathini, Msinga, Ndwedwe, Nkandla, Nongoma, Nqutu, Ntuzuma, Okhahlamba, Ongoye, Simdlangentsha, Vulamehlo, Vulindlela

Including Ulundi; Maputaland, Tongaland, Zululand; Hluhluwe, Mkuze, Ndumu, Umfolozi Game Reserves; Kosi Lake, Lake Sibaya

Class here Zululand

Class cities and towns in districts partly KwaZulu and partly Natal in —6841–6847, e.g., Eshowe —6844

—685   Orange Free State

Province of Republic of South Africa

Class Bophuthatswana in —68294

>   —685 1–685 8   Magisterial districts of Orange Free State

Class comprehensive works in —685

—685 1   Northeastern districts

Contains Bethlehem, Ficksburg, Fouriesburg, Frankfort, Harrismith, Lindley, Reitz, Senekal, Vrede

Including Golden Gate Highlands National Park; Wilge River; Sterkfontein, *Vaal Dam

Class here *Northeastern Orange Free State

—685 2   Northern districts

Contains Bothaville, Heilbron, Koppies, Kroonstad, Parys, Viljoenskroon, Verdefort

Class here *Northern Orange Free State; *Vals River

*Class parts of this physiographic region or feature as instructed under —4–9

—685 25   Sasolburg

—685 3   North central districts

         Contains Brandfort, Bultfontein, Hennenman, Hoopstad, Odendaalsrus, Theunissen, Ventersburg, Virginia, Wesselsbron, Winburg

         Including Allanridge; Willem Pretorius Game Reserve; Sand River; Allemanskraal, Bloemhof, Erfenis Dams

         Class here *Vet River

—685 35   Welkom

—685 4   Bloemfontein

         Class here *Modder River

—685 5   Eastern districts

         Contains Clocolan, Excelsior, Ladybrand, Marquard

—685 6   Southeastern districts

         Contains Botshabelo, Dewetsdorp, Reddersburg, Rouxville, Smithfield, Wepener, Zastron

         Class here *Caledon River

         Class Caledon River in Lesotho in —6885

—685 7   Southwestern districts

         Contains Bethulie, Edenburg, Fauresmith, Jagersfontein, Petrusburg, Philippolis, Trompsburg

         Including Kalkfontein Dam

         Class here *Riet River

—685 8   Western districts

         Contains Boshof, Jacobsdal, Koffiefontein

—685 9   Homelands (National states [South African])

—685 91   Qwaqwa

         Contains Witsieshoek

         Including Phuthaditjhaba

—687   Cape of Good Hope

         Province of Republic of South Africa

         Class here *Orange River, *Orange River Scheme

         Class comprehensive works on Bophuthatswana in —68294

         For Walvis Bay exclave, see —6881

*Class parts of this physiographic region or feature as instructed under —4–9

>	—687 1–687 6 Magisterial districts of Cape of Good Hope

Class comprehensive works in —687

—687 1   Interior arid regions

—687 11   Northern districts

Contains Barkly West, Hartswater, Hay, Herbert, Kimberley, Kuruman, Postmasburg, Vryburg, Warrenton

Including Douglas, Griquatown; Vaalharts Irrigation Scheme; Asbesberg, Langberg Ranges; Ghaap Plateau

Class here *Northern Cape; *Kalahari Desert in South Africa; *Harts River

Class comprehensive works on Kalahari Desert in —6883

For Gordonia, Kenhardt, Prieska, see —68712

—687 12   Gordonia, Kenhardt, Prieska

Including Kakamas, Keimoes, Upington; Aughrabies, Kalahari Gemsbok National Parks; Aughrabies Falls

Class here *Hartbees River

—687 13   Eastern Upper Karoo districts

Contains Albert, Britstown, Colesberg, De Aar, Hanover, Hopetown, Noupoort, Philipstown, Richmond, Steynsburg, Venterstad

Including Burgersdorp; Orange-Fish Tunnel; *H. F. Verwoerd, *P. K. le Roux Dams

Class here *Upper Karoo

For western Upper Karoo districts, see —68717

—687 14   Cape Midlands districts

Contains Cradock, Graaff-Reinet, Hofmeyr, Jansenville, Middelburg, Pearston, Somerset East, Steytlerville, Tarka

Including Mountain Zebra National Park; Sneeuberg Range; *Sundays River

—687 15   Great Karoo districts

Contains Aberdeen, Beaufort West, Laingsburg, Murraysburg, Prince Albert, Willowmore

Including Karoo National Park; *Buffels River

Class here the *Karoo

*Class parts of this physiographic region or feature as instructed under —4–9

—687 16   Little Karoo districts

                 Contains Calitzdorp, Ladismith, Oudtshoorn

                 Including Cango Caves

                 Class here *Swartberg Range; *Gamka, *Groot, *Olifants Rivers (tributaries of Gourits River)

—687 17   Western Upper Karoo districts

                 Contains Calvinia, Carnarvon, Fraserburg, Sutherland, Victoria West, Williston

                 Including *Bokkeveld, *Nuweveld, Roggeveld Ranges; Sak River

—687 2   Northwestern districts

                 Contains Clanwilliam, Namaqualand, Vanrhynsdorp, Vredendal

                 Including Citrusdal, Lambert's Bay, Port Nolloth, Springbok; Kamiesberg Range

                 Class here *Northwestern Cape; *Bushmanland; *Cedarberg, *Olifants River Ranges; *Olifants River of the northwestern Cape

                 Class Walvis Bay exclave in —6881

—687 3   Western and southwestern districts

                 Contains Bredasdorp, Caledon, Ceres, Heidelberg, Hermanus, Hopefield, Malmesbury, Montagu, Moorresburg, Paarl, Piketberg, Riversdale, Robertson, Somerset West, Stellenbosch, Strand, Swellendam, Tulbagh, Vredenburg, Wellington, Worcester

                 Including Touws River, Vredenburg/Saldanha; Cape Agulhas; Drakenstein, Hex River, Langeberg, Sonderend Ranges; Berg, Breë Rivers

                 Class here *Western Province; Boland, Overberg regions

—687 35   Cape Peninsula districts

                 Contains Bellville, Goodwood, Kuils River, Simonstown, Wynberg

                 Including Crossroads, Hout Bay; Cape of Good Hope Nature Reserve; Cape Flats; Cape of Good Hope; Robben Island

—687 355   Cape district

                 Including Kirstenbosch Botanic Gardens; Table Mountain

                 Class here Cape Town

—687 4   Southern districts

                 Contains George, Hankey, Humansdorp, Joubertina, Knysna, Mossel Bay, Uniondale

                 Including Plettenberg Bay, Wilderness; Tsitsikamma Forest and Coastal National Park; *Kougaberg, Outeniqua, Tsitsikamma Ranges; *Gamtoos, *Gourits Rivers

                 Class here *Southern Cape; Long Kloof region; Garden Route

*Class parts of this physiographic region or feature as instructed under —4–9

—687 5   Eastern districts

        Contains Adelaide, Albany, Alexandria, Bathurst, Bedford, Cathcart, Fort Beaufort, King William's Town, Kirkwood, Komga, Queenstown, Sterkstroom, Stutterheim, Uitenhage

        Including Despatch, Grahamstown, Port Alfred; Addo Elephant National Park; Suurberg Range

        Class here *Eastern Province; Border region; British Kaffraria; *Winterberg Range; *Great Fish River

        Class Great Kei River in —68791, Keiskamma River in —68792

—687 52   Port Elizabeth

        Class here Port Elizabeth-Uitenhage-Despatch industrial area

—687 55   East London

—687 6   Northeastern districts

        Contains Aliwal North, Barkly East, Elliot, Indwe, Lady Grey, Maclear, Molteno, Wodehouse

        Including Dordrecht; Kraai River

        Class here *Stormberg Range

—687 9   Homelands (National states [South African])

—687 91   Transkei

        Contains Butterworth, Cala, Cofimvaba, Elliotdale, Engcobo, Flagstaff, Herschel, Idutywa, Kentani, Lady Frere, Libode, Lusikisiki, Mount Ayliff, Mount Fletcher, Mount Frere, Mqanduli, Ngqeleni, Nqamakwe, Port St. Johns, Qumbu, Thabankulu, Tsolo, Tsomo, Umtata, Umzimkulu, Willowvale

        Including Coffee Bay; Indwe, Mtata Rivers; Lubisi Dam

        Class here Pondoland, Wild Coast; Great Kei, *Mbashe, *Mzimvubu, *Tsomo Rivers

—687 92   Ciskei

        Contains Alice, Hewu, Keiskammahoek, Mdantsane, Middledrift, Peddie, Zwelitsha

        Including Braunschweig, Potsdam, Wittlesea

        Class here *Amatole Range; *Keiskamma River

—688   Botswana, Swaziland, Lesotho [*all formerly* —681], Namibia

—688 1   Namibia

        Former name: South-West Africa

        Including Walvis Bay exclave of Cape of Good Hope, Windhoek

*Class parts of this physiographic region or feature as instructed under —4–9

—688 3   Botswana

    Former name: Bechuanaland

    Including Gaborone

    Class here *Kalahari Desert

—688 5   Lesotho

    Former name: Basutoland

    Including Maseru

—688 7   Swaziland

    Including Mbabane

—689   Zimbabwe, Zambia, Malawi

    Former name: Rhodesia and Nyasaland

—689 1   Zimbabwe

    Former names: Southern Rhodesia, Zimbabwe-Rhodesia

    Including Matabeleland, Mashonaland; Bulawayo, Harare; *Victoria Falls

—689 4   Zambia

    Former name: Northern Rhodesia

    Contains Central, Copperbelt, Eastern, Luapala, North-Western, Northern, Southern, Western provinces

    Including Lusaka

—689 7   Malawi

    Former name: Nyasaland

    Including Blantyre, Lilongwe

    Class here comprehensive works on Lake Nyasa (Lake Malawi) [*formerly* —67825]

—69   South Indian Ocean islands

—691   Madagascar

    Former name: Malagasy Republic

    Contains Antananarivo, Antsiranana, Fianarantsoa, Mahajanga, Toamasina, Toliary provinces

    Including Glorioso Islands [*formerly* —694]; Antananarivo (capital city)

*Class parts of this physiographic region or feature as instructed under —4–9

—694　　　　　Comoro Islands

> Former heading: Islands north of Madagascar
>
> Class here Comoros (Federal and Islamic Republic of the Comoros)
>
> Including Mayotte; Moroni
>
> Glorioso Islands relocated to —691; Aldabra, Cosmoledo, Farquhar, Providence islands relocated to —696; Agalega Island relocated to —6982

—[695]　　　Amirante Islands

> Relocated to —696

—696　　　　　Seychelles

> Including Aldabra, Cosmoledo, Farquhar, Providence islands [*all formerly also* —694]; Amirante Islands [*formerly also* —695]; Mahé Island; Victoria

—697　　　　　Chagos Islands

—698　　　　　Réunion and Mauritius

> Class here Mascarene Islands

—698 1　　　Réunion

> Overseas department of France
>
> Including Saint-Denis

—698 2　　　Mauritius

> Including Agalega Island [*formerly* —694], Cargados Carajos Shoals, Rodrigues Island; Port Louis

—699　　　　　Isolated islands

> Contains Amsterdam, Cocos (Keeling), Crozet, Kerguelen, Prince Edward, Saint Paul

—7　　North America

> Class Western Hemisphere in —1812

SUMMARY

—709 1	**Regional treatment**
—71	**Canada**
—711	**British Columbia**
—712	**Prairie Provinces**
—713	**Ontario**
—714	**Quebec**
—715	**Atlantic Provinces**　　**Maritime Provinces**
—716	**Nova Scotia**
—717	**Prince Edward Island**
—718	**Newfoundland and Labrador, Saint-Pierre and Miquelon**
—719	**Northern territories**

—72	**Middle America Mexico**
—721	Northern states of Mexico
—722	Lower California peninsula
—723	Central Pacific states of Mexico
—724	Central states of Mexico
—725	Valley of Mexico
—726	Southern Gulf states of Mexico
—727	Southern Pacific states of Mexico
—728	Central America
—729	West Indies (Antilles) and Bermuda
—73	**United States**
—74	**Northeastern United States (New England and Middle Atlantic states)**
—741	Maine
—742	New Hampshire
—743	Vermont
—744	Massachusetts
—745	Rhode Island
—746	Connecticut
—747	New York
—748	Pennsylvania
—749	New Jersey
—75	**Southeastern United States (South Atlantic states)**
—751	Delaware
—752	Maryland
—753	District of Columbia (Washington)
—754	West Virginia
—755	Virginia
—756	North Carolina
—757	South Carolina
—758	Georgia
—759	Florida
—76	**South central United States Gulf Coast states**
—761	Alabama
—762	Mississippi
—763	Louisiana
—764	Texas
—766	Oklahoma
—767	Arkansas
—768	Tennessee
—769	Kentucky
—77	**North central United States Lake states**
—771	Ohio
—772	Indiana
—773	Illinois
—774	Michigan
—775	Wisconsin
—776	Minnesota
—777	Iowa
—778	Missouri

—78	**Western United States**	
—781	**Kansas**	
—782	**Nebraska**	
—783	**South Dakota**	
—784	**North Dakota**	
—786	**Montana**	
—787	**Wyoming**	
—788	**Colorado**	
—789	**New Mexico**	
—79	**Great Basin and Pacific Slope region of United States states**	**Pacific Coast**
—791	**Arizona**	
—792	**Utah**	
—793	**Nevada**	
—794	**California**	
—795	**Oregon**	
—796	**Idaho**	
—797	**Washington**	
—798	**Alaska**	

—[700 09]   Regional treatment

> Relocated to —7091

—709 1   Regional treatment [*formerly* —70009]

> Add to base number —7091 the numbers following —1 in —11–18 of this table, e.g., urban regions of North America —7091732

—71   **Canada**

SUMMARY

—711	**British Columbia**	
—712	**Prairie Provinces**	
—713	**Ontario**	
—714	**Quebec**	
—715	**Atlantic Provinces**	**Maritime Provinces**
—716	**Nova Scotia**	
—717	**Prince Edward Island**	
—718	**Newfoundland and Labrador, Saint-Pierre and Miquelon**	
—719	**Northern territories**	

—711   British Columbia

> This table is new and has been prepared with little or no reference to previous editions. Most numbers have been reused with new meanings.
>
> A comparative table giving both old and new numbers for a substantial list of topics and equivalence tables showing the numbers in the old and new schedules appear in Volume 1 in this edition
>
> Class here *Rocky Mountains in Canada; *Rocky Mountain Trench

*Class parts of this physiographic region or feature as instructed under —4–9

—711 1   Northern coastal region

Coastal mainland and Coast Mountains from Alaska border to Powell River

Contains Central Coast, Skeena-Queen Charlotte Regional Districts; mainland parts of Comox-Strathcona, Mount Waddington Regional Districts; Kitimat-Stikine Regional District south of 54°30′ N

Including Bella Coola, Kitimat, Ocean Falls, Prince Rupert; Cortes, Hardwicke, Maurelle, Read, East and West Redonda, Sonora, East and West Thurlow Islands; Bella Coola River

Class here comprehensive works on Kitimat-Stikine Regional District; *Pacific Coast in Canada; *Coast Mountains

Class coasts of southwestern British Columbia in —7113

> For Kitimat-Stikine Regional District north of 54 °30′ N, see —71185

> See also —16433 for Dixon Entrance, Hecate Strait, Inside Passage, Queen Charlotte Sound

—711 12   Queen Charlotte Islands

—711 2   Vancouver Island

Contains Alberni-Clayoquot, Nanaimo, Cowichan Valley Regional Districts; parts of Comox-Strathcona, Mount Waddington Regional Districts on Vancouver Island

Including Nanaimo; comprehensive works on Comox-Strathcona, Mount Waddington Regional Districts; Pacific Rim National Park; Denman, Hope, Hornby, Malcolm, Nigei, Quadra Islands; Koksilah River; Shawnigan Lake

> For mainland parts of Comox-Strathcona, Mount Waddington Regional Districts, see —7111

> See also —16433 for Strait of Georgia, Queen Charlotte Strait

—711 28   Victoria region

Contains Capital Regional District (Vancouver Island south of San Juan and Koksilah Rivers and Shawnigan Lake)

Including Central Saanich, Esquimalt, Metchosin, North Saanich, Oak Bay, Port Renfrew, Saanich, Sidney, Sooke; Saanich Penisula; *Gulf Islands; San Juan River; Sooke Lake

> See also —16432 for Strait of Juan de Fuca

*Class parts of this physiographic region or feature as instructed under —4–9

—711 3   Southwestern region

> Class here *Fraser River, *Lillooet River

—711 31   Southern coastal region

> Mainland coast from Powell River to Howe Sound

> Contains Powell River, Squamish-Lillooet, Sunshine Coast Regional Districts

> Including Lillooet, Pemberton, Powell River, Squamish, Whistler; Garibaldi Provincial Park; Desolation Sound Provincial Marine Park; Anvil, Gambier, Hernando, Keats, Lasqueti, Texada Islands; Malaspina Peninsula; Bridge River; Carpenter, Lillooet Lakes

> Class a specific part of Garibaldi Provincial Park not provided for here with the part, e.g., Garibaldi Provincial Park in Dewdney-Alouette Regional District —71137

—711 33   Greater Vancouver Regional District

> Including Burnaby, Coquitlam, Delta, Lions Bay, New Westminster, North Vancouver, Port Coquitlam, Port Moody, Richmond, Surrey, West Vancouver, White Rock; Bowen Island

> Class here city of Vancouver

—711 37   Lower Fraser Valley

> Contains Central Fraser Valley, Dewdney-Alouette, Fraser-Cheam Regional Districts

> Including Abbotsford, Chilliwack, Hope, Langley, Maple Ridge, Mission, Pitt Meadows; Golden Ears Provincial Park; Fraser Canyon; Coquihalla, Nahatlatch, *Pitt Rivers; Harrison Lake

—711 5   Okanagan-Similkameen region

> Contains Central Okanagan, North Okanagan, Okanagan-Similkameen Regional Districts

> Including Armstrong, Enderby, Kelowna, Osoyoos, Penticton, Princeton, Vernon; Manning Provincial Park; Shuswap, Tulameen Rivers; Okanagan Lake

> Class here *Cascade Mountains in British Columbia

—711 6   Southeastern region

> Class here *Columbia River in British Columbia

—711 62   West Kootenay region

> Contains Central Kootenay, Kootenay Boundary Regional Districts

> Including Castlegar, Creston, Grand Forks, Greenwood, Nelson, Rossland, Trail; *Monashee Mountains; *Granby, *Kettle, *West Kettle Rivers; Upper and Lower Arrow, Slocan, Kootenay Lakes

*Class parts of this physiographic region or feature as instructed under —4–9

—711 65   East Kootenay Regional District

Approximately the area drained by the upper Columbia and Kootenay Rivers

Including Cranbrook, Invermere, Kimberley; Kootenay National Park

Class here *Purcell Mountains; *Kootenay River

—711 68   Columbia-Shuswap Regional District

Including Golden, Revelstoke, Salmon Arm; Glacier, Mount Revelstoke, Yoho National Parks; Hamber Provincial Park; Illecillewaet, Seymour, Spillimacheen Rivers; *Kinbasket (McNaughton), Shuswap Lakes

Class here *Selkirk Mountains

—711 7   Central interior region

Class here *Cariboo Mountains

—711 72   Thompson-Nicola Regional District

Approximately the area drained by the Thompson and Nicola Rivers

Including Cache Creek, Chase, Clinton, Kamloops, Lytton, Merritt; Wells Gray Provincial Park; Bonaparte, Clearwater, Coldwater, Nicola, North and South Thompson, Thompson Rivers; Adams Lake

—711 75   Cariboo Regional District

Approximately the central Fraser Valley and the area drained by the Chilcotin, Nazko, and Quesnel Rivers

Including Anahim Lake, Barkerville, 100 Mile House, Quesnel, Wells, Williams Lake; Bowron Lake Provincial Park; Adams, Chilcotin, Chilko, Horsefly, Nazko, Quesnel, Taseko, West Road Rivers; Quesnel Lake

Class here *Fraser Plateau

—711 8   Northern region

—711 82   North central region

Approximately the corridor formed by the Bulkley, Nechako, and upper Fraser valleys

Contains Bulkley-Nechako, Fraser-Fort George Regional Districts

Including Mackenzie, McBride, Prince George, Smithers, Valemount, Vanderhoof; Tweedsmuir, Mount Robson Provincial Parks; *Bulkley, Chilako, McGregor, Morice, Nation, *Omineca, Parsnip Rivers; Morice, Takla Lakes; Nechako Reservoir

Class here *Nechako Plateau; Nechako River

Class a specific part of Tweedsmuir Provincial Park not provided for here with the part, e.g., Atnarko —7111

*Class parts of this physiographic region or feature as instructed under —4–9

—711 85   Northwestern region

          Contains Stikine Regional District; parts of Kitimat-Stikine Regional District north of 54°30′ N

          Including Hazelton, Stewart, Terrace; *Hazelton, *Omineca Mountains; Gataga, Kechika, Nass, Osilinka, Skeena, Spatsizi, *Stikine, Sustut Rivers

          Class here *Cassiar, *Skeena Mountains

—711 87   Peace River-Liard Regional District

          Including Dawson Creek, Fort Nelson, Fort St. John, Tumbler Ridge; Finlay, Fort Nelson, Ingenika, Mesilinka, Murray, Pine, Sukunka Rivers; *Williston Lake

          Class here Peace River in British Columbia, *Liard River

—712   Prairie Provinces

          Class here western Canada

          Class a specific part of western Canada not provided for here with the part, e.g., British Columbia —711

SUMMARY

—712 3	Alberta
—712 4	Saskatchewan
—712 7	Manitoba

—712 3   Alberta

—712 31   Northwestern region

          Area north of 55° N, and west of 114° W

          Including Grande Prairie, Peace River; Lesser Slave Lake

          Class here northern Alberta; *Peace River

          Class a specific part of northern Alberta not provided for here with the part, e.g., Fort McMurray —71232

—712 32   Northeastern region

          Area north of 55° N, and east of 114° W

          Including Fort McMurray

          Class here Wood Buffalo National Park; *Athabaska River

          Class a specific part of Wood Buffalo National Park not provided for here with the part, e.g., Wood Buffalo National Park in Fort Smith Region —7193

*Class parts of this physiographic region or feature as instructed under —4–9

—712 33	Central region
	Area between 55° N and 51° N
	Including Drumheller, Red Deer; Elk Island National Park; Lac La Biche
	Class here *Rocky Mountains in Alberta; *Bow, *North Saskatchewan, *Red Deer Rivers
—712 332	Rocky Mountain parks region
	Including Banff; Banff, Jasper National Parks; Willmore Wilderness Provincial Park; Kananaskis Country

See also —71234 for Waterton Lakes National Park

—712 334	Edmonton
—712 338	Calgary
—712 34	Southern region
	Area south of 51° N to international boundary
	Including Crowsnest Pass, Fort Macleod, Medicine Hat; Waterton Lakes National Park
—712 345	Lethbridge
—712 4	Saskatchewan
—712 41	Northern region
	Area north of 55° N
	Class here *Lake Athabasca
—712 42	Central region
	Area between 55° N and 51° N
	Including Battlefords, Lloydminster, Prince Albert, Yorkton; *Lake Diefenbaker
	Class here *Saskatchewan, *South Saskatchewan Rivers
	Class parts of Lloydminster in Alberta in —71233
—712 425	Saskatoon
—712 43	Southwestern region
	Area south of 51° N, and west of 106° W
	Including Swift Current; *Cypress Hills
—712 44	Southeastern region
	Area south of 51° N, and east of 106° W
	Including Fort Qu'Appelle, Melville, Moose Jaw
—712 445	Regina

*Class parts of this physiographic region or feature as instructed under —4–9

—712 7   Manitoba

—712 71   Northern region

          Area north of 55° N

          Including Churchill, Port Nelson, Thompson

          Class here *Churchill, *Nelson Rivers

—712 72   Central region

          Area between 55° N and 50°30′N

          Including Dauphin, Flin Flon, The Pas; Interlake region; Lakes *Manitoba, Winnipegosis, *Winnipeg

          Class here *Canadian Shield in Manitoba

—712 73   Southwestern region

          Area south of 50°30′N, and west of 98° W

          Including Brandon, Minnedosa, Portage la Prairie

          Class here *Assiniboine River

—712 74   Southeastern region

          Area south of 50°30′N, and east of 98° W

          Including Selkirk; Whiteshell Provincial Park

          Class here *Red River of the North in Manitoba

—712 743   Winnipeg

—713   Ontario

          Class here eastern Canada; *Great Lakes in Canada

          Class a specific part of eastern Canada not provided for here with the part, e.g., Nova Scotia —716

—713 1   Northern Ontario

          Including Patricia portion of Kenora District

          Class here Canadian Shield in Ontario

              See also —16327 for Hudson, James Bays

—713 11   Northwestern Ontario

          Including *Lake of the Woods in Canada

              For Thunder Bay District, see —71312

—713 112   Kenora District

              Class Patricia portion in —7131

—713 117   Rainy River District

—713 12   Thunder Bay District

          Class here *Lake Superior in Ontario

*Class parts of this physiographic region or feature as instructed under —4–9

—713 13	Northeastern Ontario

For clay belt, see —71314; Parry Sound District, —71315; District municipality of Muskoka, —71316

—713 132	Algoma District

Including *North Channel

—713 133	Sudbury District
—713 135	Manitoulin District
—713 14	Clay belt
—713 142	Cochrane District

Including *Lake Abitibi

—713 144	Timiskaming District
—713 147	Nipissing District

Including Algonquin Provincial Park; *Lake Nipissing

—713 15	Parry Sound District

Class here *Georgian Bay

—713 16	District municipality of Muskoka

Class here former Muskoka District

—713 17	Simcoe County
—713 18	Grey County

>	—713 2–713 8 Southern Ontario

Class comprehensive works in —713

For Simcoe County, see —71317; Grey County, —71318

—713 2	Lake Huron counties

Class here southwestern Ontario; *Lake Huron in Ontario

Class a specific part of southwestern Ontario not provided for here with the part, e.g., Essex County —71331

—713 21	Bruce County
—713 22	Huron County
—713 23	Perth County
—713 25	Middlesex County

For London, see —71326

—713 26	London

*Class parts of this physiographic region or feature as instructed under —4–9

—713 27   Lambton County

       Including *Saint Clair River in Ontario

—713 3   **Lake Erie counties**

       Class here *Lake Erie in Ontario

—713 31   Essex County

       Including *Lake Saint Clair in Ontario

        For Windsor, see —71332

—713 32   Windsor

—713 33   Kent County

—713 34   Elgin County

        For St. Thomas, see —71335

—713 35   St. Thomas

—713 36   Regional municipality of Haldimand-Norfolk

       Class here former Norfolk County

        For former Haldimand County, see —71337

—713 37   Former Haldimand County

—713 38   Regional municipality of Niagara

       Including Niagara Falls (city); *Niagara River; Welland Canal

       Class here former Welland County

       Class Niagara Falls (physiographic feature) in —71339, Niagara River in New York in —74798

        For former Lincoln County, see —71351

—713 39   Niagara Falls

       Physiographic feature

       Class Niagara Falls in New York in —74799

—713 4   **West central counties**

—713 41   Dufferin County

—713 42   Wellington County

        For Guelph, see —71343

—713 43   Guelph

—713 44   Regional municipality of Waterloo

       Class here former Waterloo County

        For Kitchener, see —71345

—713 45   Kitchener

*Class parts of this physiographic region or feature as instructed under —4–9

—713 46	Oxford County
—713 47	Brant County
	For Brantford, see —71348
—713 48	Brantford
—713 5	Lake Ontario counties
	Class here *Lake Ontario in Ontario
—713 51	Former Lincoln County
—713 52	Regional municipality of Hamilton-Wentworth
	Class here former Wentworth County; Hamilton
—713 53	Halton and Peel Regional municipalities
—713 533	Regional municipality of Halton
	Class here former Halton County
—713 535	Regional municipality of Peel
	Class here former Peel County
—713 54	Toronto and York
	Class here former York County
—713 541	Metropolitan Toronto
	Including cities of Toronto, Etobicoke, North York, Scarborough, York; borough of East York
—713 547	Regional municipality of York
—713 55	Former Ontario County
—713 56	Regional municipality of Durham
	Class here former Durham County
	For former Ontario County, see —71355
—713 57	Northumberland County
	Including *Rice Lake
—713 58	Hastings and Prince Edward Counties
—713 585	Hastings County
—713 587	Prince Edward County
—713 59	Lennox and Addington County
—713 6	East central counties
—713 61	Haliburton County
—713 64	Victoria County

*Class parts of this physiographic region or feature as instructed under —4–9

—713 67	Peterborough County
	For Peterborough, see —71368
—713 68	Peterborough
—713 7	**Saint Lawrence River counties**
	Class here eastern Ontario; *Thousand Islands in Ontario; *Saint Lawrence River in Ontario; *Saint Lawrence Seaway in Ontario
	Class a specific part of eastern Ontario not provided for here with the part, e.g., Lanark County —71382
—713 71	Frontenac County
	For Kingston, see —71372
—713 72	Kingston
—713 73	United Counties of Leeds and Grenville
	Class here former Leeds County
	For former Grenville County, see —71374
—713 74	Former Grenville County
—713 75	United Counties of Stormont, Dundas and Glengarry
	Class here former Dundas County
	For former Stormont County, see —71376; former Glengarry County, —71377
—713 76	Former Stormont County
—713 77	Former Glengarry County
—713 8	**Ottawa River counties**
	Class here *Ottawa River
—713 81	Renfrew County
—713 82	Lanark County
—713 83	Regional municipality of Ottawa-Carleton (Former Carleton County)
	Class here National Capital Region
	For Ottawa, see —71384; Outaouais Regional Community, —714221
—713 84	Ottawa
—713 85	United Counties of Prescott and Russell
	Class here former Russell County
	For former Prescott County, see —71386
—713 86	Former Prescott County

*Class parts of this physiographic region or feature as instructed under —4–9

—714   Quebec

> Class here *Canadian Shield; *Saint Lawrence River; comprehensive works on Saint Lawrence Seaway
>
> Class a specific part of the Saint Lawrence Seaway not provided for here with the part, e.g., Saint Lawrence Seaway in Ontario —7137
>
> *See also* —16344 *for Gulf of Saint Lawrence*

—714 1   Northern region

—714 11   New Quebec (Nouveau-Québec) [*formerly* —71417]

> *See also* —7182 *for Labrador*

—714 111   Extreme northern region (Grand-nord québécois, Administration régionale Kativik)

> Area north of 55°
>
> Including Hudson Bay and Ungava Bay regions
>
> Class here Kativik Regional Administration
>
> *See also* —16327 *for Hudson, Ungava Bays*

—714 115   Mid-northern region (Moyen-nord québécois)

> Including former Abitibi Territory [*formerly* —71412], former Mistassini Territory; Caniapiscau (Regional County Municipality); James Bay region; Chibougamau, Gagnon, Lebel-sur-Quévillon, Matagami, Schefferville
>
> Class here Noveau-Québec Administrative Region
>
> Class a specific part of Noveau-Québec Administrative Region not provided for here with the part, e.g., Poste-de-la-Baleine —714111

—[714 12]   Abitibi Territory

> Relocated to —714115

—714 13   Abitibi-Témiscamingue region

> Former Témiscamingue County [*formerly* —714212] and former Abitibi County
>
> Including Abitibi, Abitibi-Ouest, Vallée-de-l'Or, Rouyn-Noranda, Témiscamingue Regional County Municipalities
>
> Class here Abitibi-Témiscamingue Administrative Region
>
> Class a specific part of Abitibi-Témiscamingue Administrative Region, La Vallée Regional County Municipality not provided for here with the part, e.g., Lebel-sur-Quévillon —714115

*Class parts of this physiographic region or feature as instructed under —4–9

—714 14   Lac-Saint-Jean region

Former Lac-Saint-Jean-Est and Lac-Saint-Jean-Ouest Counties

Including Le Domaine-du-Roy, Lac-Saint-Jean-Est, Maria-Chapdelaine Regional County Municipalities; Chibougamau Wildlife Reserve

Class here Saguenay-Lac-Saint-Jean Administrative Region

Class a specific part of Saguenay-Lac-Saint-Jean Administrative Region; of Le Domaine-du-Roy, Lac-Saint-Jean-Est, Maria-Chapdelaine Regional County Municipalities with the part, e.g., Métabetchouane Lake in Montmorency region —71448

—714 16   Chicoutimi region

Former Chicoutimi County

Including Le Fjord-du-Saguenay Regional County Municipality; *Saguenay River

—714 17   Côte-Nord region

Former Saguenay County

Including Le Haute-Côte-Nord, Manicouagan, Minganie, Sept-Rivières Regional County Municipalities; Anticosti Island

Class here Côte-Nord Administrative Region

New Quebec (Nouveau-Québec) relocated to —71411

Class a specific part of Côte-Nord Administrative Region not provided for here with the part, e.g., Gagnon —714115

See also —7182 for Labrador

—714 2   Western counties (Ottawa Valley counties)

Class here *Ottawa River in the province of Quebec

—714 21   Pontiac region

Former Pontiac County

Including La Vérendrye Provincial Park

Class here Pontiac Regional County Municipality

—[714 212]   Former Témiscamingue County

Relocated to —71413

—[714 215]   Pontiac County

Number discontinued; class in —71421

—714 22   Outaouais region

Class here Outaouais Administrative Region

Class a specific part of Outaouais Administrative Region not provided for here with the part, e.g., Rapide-des-Joachims —71421

*Class parts of this physiographic region or feature as instructed under —4–9

185

—714 221   Gatineau-Hull region

> Former Gatineau and Hull Counties
>
> Including Aylmer, Gatineau, Hull; National Capital Region in the province of Quebec; Gatineau Park
>
> Class here La Vallée-de-la-Gatineau Regional County Municipality, Outaouais Regional Community (Communauté régionale de l'Outaouais); *Gatineau River
>
> Class comprehensive works on National Capital Region in —71383; a specific part of La Vallée-de-la-Gatineau Regional County Municipality, of Outaouais Regional Community not provided for here with the part, e.g., Buckingham —714227; Gatineau Park in Pontiac region in —71421

—714 225   Labelle region

> Former Labelle County
>
> Class here Antonine-Labelle Regional County Municipality
>
> Class a specific part of Antonine-Labelle Regional County Municipality not provided for here with the part, e.g., Notawassi Lake —714415

—714 227   Papineau region

> Former Papineau County
>
> Class here Papineau Regional County Municipality

—714 23   Argenteuil region

> Former Argenteuil County
>
> Including Argenteuil Regional County Municipality

—714 24   Terrebonne region

> Former Terrebonne County
>
> Class here lower Laurentians region
>
> Including Les Laurentides, Les Moulins, Les Pays-d'en-Haut, La Rivière-du-Nord, Thérèse-de-Blainville Regional County Municipalities
>
> Class a specific part of Les Laurentides, Les Moulins, Les Pays-d'en-Haut, La Rivière-du-Nord, Thérèse-de-Blainville Regional County Municipalities not provided for here with the part, e.g., La Minerve —714225

—714 25   Deux-Montagnes region

> Former Deux-Montagnes County
>
> Including Deux-Montagnes, Mirabel Regional County Municipalities

*Class parts of this physiographic region or feature as instructed under —4–9

—714 26	Vaudreuil-Soulanges region
	Former Vaudreuil and Soulanges Counties
	Class here Vaudreuil-Soulanges Regional County Municipality
—[714 263]	Vaudreuil County
	Number discontinued; class in —71426
—[714 265]	Soulanges County
	Number discontinued; class in —71426
—714 27	Montreal Administrative Region
	Former Île-de-Montréal and Île-Jésus Counties
	Class a specific part of Montreal Administrative Region not provided for here with the part, e.g., Mirabel —71425, Longueuil —71437
	For Montreal Urban Community, see —71428
—714 271	Laval (Jésus island)
—714 28	Montreal Urban Community (Communauté urbaine de Montréal)
	Including Bizard, Dorval islands
	Class here Montréal island
—[714 281]	Greater Montreal
	Number discontinued; class in —71428
—714 3	Southwestern region
	Area south of Saint Lawrence River, and west of Richelieu River
	Including *Richelieu River
—714 31	Huntingdon region
	Former Huntingdon County
	Class here Le Haut-Saint-Laurent Regional County Municipality
	Class a specific part of Le Haut-Saint-Laurent Regional County Municipality not provided for here with the part, e.g., Ormstown —71433
—714 32	Beauharnois region
	Former Beauharnois County
	Class here Beauharnois-Salaberry Regional County Municipality
	Class a specific part of Beauharnois-Salaberry Regional County Municipality not provided for here with the part, e.g., Sainte-Martine —71433
—714 33	Châteauguay region
	Former Châteauguay County

*Class parts of this physiographic region or feature as instructed under —4–9

—714 34   Laprairie region

Former Laprairie County

Class here Roussillon Regional County Municipality

Class a specific part of Roussillon Regional County Municipality not provided for here with the part, e.g., Mercier —71433

—714 35   Napierville region

Former Napierville County

Class here Les Jardins-de-Napierville Regional County Municipality

Class a specific part of Les Jardins-de-Napierville Regional County Municipality not provided for here with the part, e.g., Hemmingford —71431

—714 36   Verchères region

Former Verchères County

Including Lajemmerais, La Vallée-du-Richelieu Regional County Municipalities

Class a specific part of Lajemmerais, La Vallée-du-Richelieu Regional County Municipalities not provided for here with the part, e.g., Boucherville —71437

—714 37   Chambly region

Former Chambly County

Class here Champlain Regional County Municipality

Class a specific part of Champlain Regional County Municipality not provided here with the part, e.g., Brossard —71434

—714 38   Saint-Jean region

Former Saint-Jean County

—714 4   North central region

Area north of Saint Lawrence River from Montreal to Saguenay River

Including Mont-Tremblant, Laurentides Provincial Parks

Class a specific part of Mont-Tremblant, of Laurentides Provincial Parks not provided for here with the part, e.g., Laurentides Park in Chicoutimi region —71416

See also —71424 for lower Laurentians region

—714 41   Lanaudière region

Including Matawini Regional County Municipality

Class a specific part of Matawini Regional County Municipality not provided for here with the part, e.g., Saint-Damien —71443

—714 415   Montcalm region

                              Former Montcalm County

                              Class here Montcalm Regional County Municipality

                              Class a specific part of Montcalm Regional County Municipality not provided for here with the part, e.g., Saint-Lin —714416

—714 416   L'Assomption region

                              Former L'Assomption County

                              Class here L'Assomption Regional County Municipality

—714 42   Joliette region

                              Former Joliette County

                              Including Joliette Regional County Municipality

—714 43   Berthier region

                              Former Berthier County

                              Class here D'Autray Regional County Municipality

                              Class a specific part of D'Autray Regional County Municipality not provided for here with the part, e.g., Sainte-Elizabeth —71442

—714 44   Maskinongé region

                              Former Maskinongé County

                              Class here Maskinongé Regional County Municipality

                              Class a specific part of Maskinongé Regional County Municipality not provided for here with the part, e.g., Saint-Barnabé —714451

—714 45   Mauricie region

                              Including Le-Haut-Saint-Maurice, Mékinac Regional County Municipalities; La Mauricie National Park

                              Class here Trois-Rivières Administrative Region

                              Class a specific part of Trois-Rivières Administrative Region; of Le-Haut-Saint-Maurice, Mékinac Regional County Municipalities not provided for here with the part, e.g., Lac-aux-Sables —71446

—714 451   Saint-Maurice region

                              Former Saint-Maurice County

                              Including Le Centre-de-la-Mauricie, Francheville Regional County Municipalities; Trois-Rivières

                              Class a specific part of Le Centre-de-la-Mauricie, Francheville Regional County Municipalities not provided for here with the part, e.g., Champlain —714455

—714 455   Champlain region

                              Former Champlain County [*formerly* —714465]

                              Including Cap-de-la-Madeleine

—714 46	Portneuf region
	Former Portneuf County
	Including Portneuf Wildlife Reserve
	Class here Portneuf Regional County Municipality
	Class a specific part of Portneuf Regional County Municipality, of Portneuf Wildlife Reserve not provided for here with the part, e.g., Portneuf Wildlife Reserve in Champlain region —714455
—[714 465]	Champlain County
	Relocated to —714455
—[714 466]	Portneuf County
	Number discontinued; class in —71446
—714 47	Québec region and Jacques-Cartier River Valley
	Former Québec County
	Including La Jacques-Cartier Regional County Municipality
	Class here Québec Administrative Region
	Class a specific part of Québec Administrative Region, of La Jacques-Cartier Regional County Municipality not provided for here with the part, e.g., Sainte-Brigitte-de-Laval —71448
—714 471	Quebec Urban Community (Communauté urbaine de Québec)
	Including Ancienne-Lorette, Beauport, Cap-Rouge, Charlesbourg, Lac-Saint-Charles, Loretteville, Saint-Augustin-de-Desmaures, Saint-Foy, Saint-Emile, Sillery, Val-Bélair, Vanier
	Class here Québec
—714 48	Montmorency region
	Former Montmorency no. 1 and no. 2 counties
	Including La Côte-de-Beaupré, L'Île-d'Orléans Regional County Municipalities; Isle of Orléans (Île d'Orléans)
—714 49	Charlevoix region
	Former Charlevoix-Est and Charlevoix-Ouest Counties
	Including Charlevoix, Charlevoix-Est Regional County Municipalities; Île aux Coudres

—714 5	South central region

    Area south of Saint Lawrence River, and east of Richelieu River to Quebec

    Class here *Saint-François River

      For southern border area, see —7146

—714 51	Richelieu region

    Former Richelieu County

    Class here Le Bas-Richelieu Regional County Municipality

    Class a specific part of Le Bas-Richelieu Regional County Municipality not provided for here with the part, e.g., Saint-David —71454

—714 52	Saint-Hyacinthe and Bagot regions
—714 523	Saint-Hyacinthe region

      Former Saint-Hyacinthe County

      Class here Les Maskoutains Regional County Municipality

      Class a specific part of Les Maskoutains Regional County Municipality not provided for here with the part, e.g., Saint-Pie —714525

—714 525	Bagot region

      Former Bagot County

      Class here Acton Regional County Municipality

      Class a specific part of Acton Regional County Municipality not provided for here with the part, e.g., Saint-Valérien-de-Milton —71463

—714 53	Rouville region

    Former Rouville County

    Class here Rouville Regional County Municipality

—714 54	Yamaska region

    Former Yamaska County

    Class here Nicolet-Yamaska Regional County Municipality

    Class a specific part of Nicolet-Yamaska Regional County Municipality not provided for here with the part, e.g., Nicolet —71455

—714 55	Nicolet region

    Former Nicolet County

    Class here Bécancour Regional County Municipality

    Class a part of Bécancour Regional County Municipality not provided for here with the part, e.g., Saint-Jacques-de-Parisville —71458

—714 56	Drummond and Arthabaska regions

*Class parts of this physiographic region or feature as instructed under —4–9

—714 563   Drummond region

> Former Drummond County
>
> Class here Drummond Regional County Municipality
>
> Class a specific part of Drummond Regional County Municipality not provided for here with the part, e.g., Saint-Bonaventure —71454

—714 565   Arthabaska region

> Former Arthabaska County
>
> Class here Bois-Francs region; Arthabaska Regional County Municipality
>
> Class a specific part of Arthabaska Regional County Municipality not provided for here with the part, e.g., Ham-Nord —714573

—714 57   Wolfe and Megantic regions

—714 573   Wolfe region

> Former Wolfe County
>
> Including L'Amiante, L'Or-Blanc Regional County Municipalities
>
> Class a specific part of L'Amiante, L'Or-Blanc Regional County Municipalities not provided for here with the part, e.g., Danville —71465

—714 575   Mégantic region

> Former Mégantic County
>
> Class here L'Érable Regional County Municipality
>
> Class a specific part of L'Érable Regional County Municipality not provided for here with the part, e.g., Princeville —714565

—714 58   Lotbinière region

> Former Lotbinière County
>
> Class here Lotbinière Regional County Municipality

—714 59   Lévis region

> Former Lévis County
>
> Including Les Chutes-de-la-Chaudière, Desjardins Regional County Municipalities

—714 6   Southern region

> Southern border area east of Richelieu River
>
> Class here Eastern Townships, Estrie Administrative Region
>
> Class a specific part of Eastern Townships, of Estrie Administrative Region not provided for here with the part, e.g., Wotton —71473

—714 61   Iberville region

         Former Iberville County

         Class here Le Haut-Richelieu Regional County Municipality

         Class a specific part of Le Haut-Richelieu Regional County Municipality not provided for here with the part, e.g., Lacolle —71438

—714 62   Missisquoi region

         Former Missisquoi County

         Class here Brome-Missisquoi Regional County Municipality

         Class a specific part of Brome-Missisquoi Regional County Municipality not provided for here with the part, e.g., Lac-Brome —71464

—714 63   Shefford region

         Former Shefford County

         Class here La Haute-Yamaska Regional County Municipality

         Class a specific part of La Haute-Yamaska Regional County Municipality not provided for here with the part, e.g., Bromont —71464

—714 64   Brome region

         Former Brome County

         Including Memphrémagog Regional County Municipality; *Lake Memphrémagog

         Class a specific part of Memphrémagog Regional County Municipality not provided for here with the part, e.g., Rock Island —71467

—714 65   Richmond region

         Former Richmond County

         Class here Le Val-Saint-François Regional County Municipality

         Class a specific part of Le Val-Saint-François Regional County Municipality not provided for here with the part, e.g., Bonsecours —71463

—714 66   Sherbrooke region

         Former Sherbrooke County

         Class here Sherbrooke Regional County Municipality

         Class a specific part of Sherbrooke Regional County Municipality not provided for here with the part, e.g., Waterville —71468

*Class parts of this physiographic region or feature as instructed under —4–9

—714 67   Stanstead region

          Former Stanstead County

          Class here Coaticook Regional County Municipality

          Class a specific part of Coaticook Regional County Municipality not provided for here with the part, e.g., Compton —71468

—714 68   Compton region

          Former Compton County

          Class here Le Haut-Saint-François Regional County Municipality

          Class a specific part of Le Haut-Saint-François Regional County Municipality not provided for here with the part, e.g., Weedon-Centre —714573

—714 69   Frontenac region

          Former Frontenac County

          Class here Le Granit Regional County Municipality

          Class a specific part of Le Granit Regional County Municipality not provided for here with the part, e.g., Stratford —714573

—714 7   Southeastern region

          Area south of Saint Lawrence River from Quebec to Gulf of Saint Lawrence

          Class here eastern Quebec; *Notre Dame Mountains

—714 71   Beauce region

          Former Beauce County

          Including Beauce-Sartigan, La Nouvelle-Beauce, Robert-Cliche Regional County Municipalities

          Class here *Chaudière River

          Class a specific part of Beauce-Sartigan, La Nouvelle-Beauce, Robert-Cliche Regional County Municipalities not provided for here with the part, e.g., La Guadeloupe —71469

—714 72   Dorchester region

          Former Dorchester County

          Class here Les Etchemins Regional County Municipality

          Class a specific part of Les Etchemins Regional County Municipality not provided for here with the part, e.g., Saint-Camille-de-Lellis —714733

*Class parts of this physiographic region or feature as instructed under —4–9

—714 73   Bellechasse and Montmagny regions

—714 733   Bellechasse region

           Former Bellechasse County

           Class here Bellechasse Regional County Municipality

           Class a specific part of Bellechasse Regional County Municipality not provided for here with the part, e.g., Saint-Nazaire-de-Dorchester —71472

—714 735   Montmagny region

           Former Montmagny County

           Including Île aux Grues, Grosse Île

           Class here Montmagny Regional County Municipality

—714 74   L'Islet region

           Former L'Islet County

           Class here L'Islet Regional County Municipality

—714 75   Kamouraska region

           Former Kamouraska County

           Class here Kamouraska Regional County Municipality

—714 76   Témiscouata and Rivière-du-Loup regions

           Former Témiscouata and Rivière-du-Loup counties

           Including Les Basques, Rivière-du-Loup, Témiscouata Regional County Municipalities; Île Verte

           Class a specific part of Les Basques, Témiscouata Regional County Municipalities not provided for here with the part, e.g., Saint-Simon —714771

—714 77   Gaspé Peninsula

           Class here Bas-Saint-Laurent-Gaspésie Administrative Region

           For Bonaventure region, see —71478; Gaspé region, —71479

—714 771   Rimouski region

           Former Rimouski County

           Including La Mitis, Rimouski-Neigette Regional County Municipalities

           Class a specific part of La Mitis Regional County Municipality not provided for here with the part, e.g., Saint-Octave-de-Métis —714775

—714 775   Matane and Matapédia regions

           Former Matane and Matapédia counties

           Including Matane, La Matapédia Regional County Municipalities

—714 78	Bonaventure region
	Former Bonaventure County
	Including Avignon, Bonaventure Regional County Municipalities
—714 79	Gaspé region
	Former Gaspé-Est and Gaspé-Ouest counties
	Including La Côte-de-Gaspé, Denis Riverin, Pabok Regional County Municipalities
—714 797	Magdalen Islands (Îles de la Madeleine)
	Class here Îles de la Madeleine Regional County Municipality
—715	Atlantic Provinces Maritime Provinces

> *For Nova Scotia, see —716; Prince Edward Island, —717; Newfoundland and Labrador, —718*
>
> *See also —16344 for Gulf of Saint Lawrence, Northumberland Strait*

—715 1	New Brunswick

> *For eastern counties, see —7152; southern counties, —7153; central counties, —7154; western counties, —7155*

>	—715 11–715 12 Northern counties
	Class comprehensive works in —7151
—715 11	Restigouche County
	Including *Restigouche River
—715 12	Gloucester County
	Including Bathurst
—715 2	Eastern counties
—715 21	Northumberland County
	Class here *Miramichi River
—715 22	Kent County
—715 23	Westmorland County
	Including Sackville
—715 235	Moncton
—715 3	Southern counties
	See also —16345 for Bay of Fundy
—715 31	Albert County
—715 32	Saint John County

*Class parts of this physiographic region or feature as instructed under —4–9

—715 33	Charlotte County
	Including Grand Manan Island; *Saint Croix River in New Brunswick
—715 4	Central counties
—715 41	Kings County
—715 42	Queens County
—715 43	Sunbury County
—715 5	Western counties
	Class here *Saint John River
—715 51	York County
—715 515	Fredericton
—715 52	Carleton County
—715 53	Victoria County
—715 54	Madawaska County
—716	Nova Scotia
—716 1	Northern counties
—716 11	Cumberland County
	Including Amherst
—716 12	Colchester County
	Including Truro
—716 13	Pictou County
	Including New Glasgow, Pictou
—716 14	Antigonish County
—716 2	Southern counties
—716 21	Guysborough County
—716 22	Halifax County
—716 225	Halifax-Dartmouth metropolitan area
	Class here Halifax
—716 23	Lunenburg County
—716 24	Queens County
	Including Liverpool
—716 25	Shelburne County
—716 3	Bay of Fundy counties
	See also —*16345 for Bay of Fundy*
—716 31	Yarmouth County

*Class parts of this physiographic region or feature as instructed under —4–9

—716 32	Digby County
—716 33	Annapolis County
	Including Kejimkujik National Park
	Class Kejimkujik National Park in Queens County in —71624
—716 34	Kings County
	Including Wolfville
—716 35	Hants County
	Including Windsor
—716 9	Cape Breton Island and Sable Island
	Class here *Bras d'Or Lake

>	—716 91–716 98 Cape Breton Island
	Class comprehensive works in —7169
—716 91	Inverness County
	Including Cape Breton Highlands National Park
	Class Cape Breton Highlands National Park in Victoria County in —71693
—716 93	Victoria County
—716 95	Cape Breton County
	Including Sydney [*formerly* —71696], North Sydney
—716 955	Louisbourg
	Class here Louisbourg National Historical Park
—[716 96]	Sydney
	Relocated to —71695
—716 98	Richmond County
—716 99	Sable Island
—717	Prince Edward Island
—717 1	Prince County
—717 4	Queens County
	For Charlottetown, see —7175
—717 5	Charlottetown
—717 7	Kings County

*Class parts of this physiographic region or feature as instructed under —4–9

—718   **Newfoundland and Labrador, Saint-Pierre and Miquelon**

> *See also —16344 for Grand Banks of Newfoundland*

—718 1   St. John's

—718 2   Labrador

—718 8   Saint-Pierre and Miquelon

> Overseas territory of France

—719   Northern territories

> Class here *Canadian Arctic
>
> *See also —16327 for Beaufort Sea, Canadian Arctic waters, Northwest Passage*

—719 1   Yukon Territory

> Including Dawson, Whitehorse

—719 2   Northwest Territories

> Class here Denendeh, Nunavut
>
> *For specific regions of Northwest Territories, see —7193–7197*

\>   —719 3–719 7   Specific regions of Northwest Territories

> Class comprehensive works in —7192
>
> *See Manual at T2—7193–T2—7197*

—719 3   Fort Smith Region

> Including Fort Simpson, Fort Smith, Hay River, Pine Point, Rae, Rae Lakes, Snowdrift, Wrigley, Yellowknife; Nahanni National Park; *Mackenzie Mountains; *Slave River; *Great Bear, Great Slave Lakes
>
> Class here former Mackenzie district
>
> Class a specific part of Mackenzie district not provided for here with the part, e.g., Inuvik —7196

—719 4   Keewatin Region

> Including Baker Lake, Chesterfield Inlet, Coral Harbour, Rankin Inlet, Repulse Bay; Thelon Game Sanctuary; Coats, Southampton Islands; *Thelon River
>
> Class here former Keewatin district
>
> Class a specific part of former Keewatin district not provided for here with the part, e.g., Adelaide Peninsula —7197

*Class parts of this physiographic region or feature as instructed under —4–9

—719 5   Baffin Region

Including Arctic Bay, Cape Dorset, Grise Fiord, Hall Beach, Igloolik, Iqaluit (Frobisher Bay), Pangnirtung, Pond Inlet, Resolute, Sanikiluaq; Auyuittuq National Park; Baffin, Bylot, Mansel, Nottingham, Salisbury, Somerset, Wales Islands; Melville Peninsula

Class here former Franklin district; *Canadian Arctic Archipelago

Class a specific part of former Franklin district not provided for here with the part, e.g., Victoria Island —7197

See also —16327 for Hudson, James, Ungava Bays

—719 6   Inuvik region

Including Aklavik, Fort Franklin, Fort Norman, Inuvik, Paulatuk, Sach Harbour, Tuktoyaktuk; Banks Island

Class here *MacKenzie River

—719 7   Kitikmeot Region (Central Arctic Region)

Including Bathurst Inlet, Cambridge Bay, Coppermine, Gjoa Haven, Holman, Pelly Bay, Spence Bay, Umingmaktok; King William, Prince of Wales, Victoria Islands; Boothia, Simpson Peninsulas; Contwoyto Lake

See also —7193 for Great Bear Lake, —7194 for Repulse Bay

—[719 9]   Canadian Arctic

Number discontinued; class in —719

—72   **Middle America   Mexico**

SUMMARY

—721	**Northern states of Mexico**
—722	**Lower California peninsula**
—723	**Central Pacific states of Mexico**
—724	**Central states of Mexico**
—725	**Valley of Mexico**
—726	**Southern Gulf states of Mexico**
—727	**Southern Pacific states of Mexico**
—728	**Central America**
—729	**West Indies (Antilles) and Bermuda**

> —721–727 Mexico

Class comprehensive works in —72

—721   Northern states of Mexico

—721 2   Tamaulipas

—721 3   Nuevo León

—721 4   Coahuila

—721 5   Durango

*Class parts of this physiographic region or feature as instructed under —4–9

—721 6	Chihuahua
—721 7	Sonora

See also —1641 for Gulf of California

—722	Lower California peninsula

See also —1641 for Gulf of California

—722 3	Baja California Norte
—722 4	Baja California Sur
—723	Central Pacific states of Mexico
—723 2	Sinaloa
—723 4	Nayarit
—723 5	Jalisco
—723 6	Colima
—723 7	Michoacán
—724	Central states of Mexico

For Valley of Mexico, see —725

—724 1	Guanajuato
—724 2	Aguascalientes
—724 3	Zacatecas
—724 4	San Luis Potosí
—724 5	Querétaro
—724 6	Hidalgo
—724 7	Tlaxcala
—724 8	Puebla
—724 9	Morelos
—725	Valley of Mexico
—725 2	Mexico state
—725 3	Distrito Federal

Class here Mexico City

—726	Southern Gulf states of Mexico
—726 2	Veracruz
—726 3	Tabasco
—726 4	Campeche

—726 5	Yucatán
—726 7	Quintana Roo
—727	Southern Pacific states of Mexico
—727 3	Guerrero
—727 4	Oaxaca
—727 5	Chiapas
—728	Central America

SUMMARY

—728 1	Guatemala
—728 2	Belize
—728 3	Honduras
—728 4	El Salvador
—728 5	Nicaragua
—728 6	Costa Rica
—728 7	Panama

—728 1	Guatemala

SUMMARY

—728 11	Central District (Guatemala department)
—728 12	Petén province and department
—728 13	Izabal province
—728 14	Oriente province
—728 15	Verapaz province
—728 16	Atitlán province
—728 17	Quiché province
—728 18	Los Altos province

—728 11	Central District (Guatemala department)
	Class here Guatemala City
—728 12	Petén province and department
—728 13	Izabal province
—728 131	Izabal department
—728 132	Zacapa department
—728 14	Oriente province
—728 141	Chiquimula department
—728 142	Jalapa department
—728 143	Jutiapa department
—728 144	Santa Rosa department
—728 15	Verapaz province
—728 151	Alta Verapaz department

—728 152	Baja Verapaz department
—728 153	El Progreso department
—728 16	Atitlán province
—728 161	Chimaltenango department
—728 162	Sacatepéquez department
—728 163	Escuintla department
—728 164	Sololá department
—728 165	Suchitepéquez department
—728 17	Quiché province
—728 171	Huehuetenango department
—728 172	Quiché department
—728 18	Los Altos province
—728 181	Totonicapán department
—728 182	Quezaltenango department
—728 183	Retalhuleu department
—728 184	San Marcos department
—728 2	Belize
	Former name: British Honduras
—728 21	Corozal district
—728 22	Belize district
—728 23	Stann Creek district
—728 24	Toledo district
—728 25	Cayo district
—728 26	Orange Walk district
—728 3	Honduras
—728 31	Northern departments
—728 311	Cortés
—728 312	Atlántida
—728 313	Colón
—728 314	Yoro
—728 315	Islas de la Bahía
—728 32	Gracias a Dios department
—728 33	Olancho department
—728 34	El Paraíso department

—728 35	Southern departments
—728 351	Choluteca
—728 352	Valle
—728 36	La Paz department
—728 37	Central departments
—728 371	Francisco Morazán
	Class here Tegucigalpa
—728 372	Comayagua
—728 38	Western departments
—728 381	Intibucá
—728 382	Lempira
—728 383	Ocotepeque
—728 384	Copán
—728 385	Santa Bárbara
—728 4	El Salvador
—728 41	Western departments
—728 411	Ahuachapán
—728 412	Santa Ana
—728 413	Sonsonate
—728 42	Central departments
—728 421	Chalatenango
—728 422	La Libertad
—728 423	San Salvador
	Class here San Salvador
—728 424	Cuscatlán
—728 425	La Paz
—728 426	Cabañas
—728 427	San Vicente
—728 43	Eastern departments
—728 431	Usulután
—728 432	San Miguel
—728 433	Morazán
—728 434	La Unión

—728 5	Nicaragua
—728 51	Pacific departments
—728 511	Chinandega
—728 512	León
—728 513	Managua
	Class here Managua
—728 514	Masaya
—728 515	Granada
—728 516	Carazo
—728 517	Rivas
—728 52	Central departments
—728 521	Nueva Segovia
—728 522	Jinotega
—728 523	Madriz
—728 524	Estelí
—728 525	Matagalpa
—728 526	Boaco
—728 527	Chontales
—728 53	Atlantic region
—728 531	Río San Juan department
—728 532	Zelaya department
	Including former Cabo Gracias a Dios territory [*formerly* —728533]
—[728 533]	Cabo Gracias a Dios territory
	Relocated to —728532
—728 6	Costa Rica
—728 61	Limón province
—728 62	Cartago province
—728 63	San José province
	Class here San José
—728 64	Heredia province
—728 65	Alajuela province
—728 66	Guanacaste province
—728 67	Puntarenas province

—728 7	Panama
	See also —1641 for Gulf of Panama
—728 71	Western provinces
—728 711	Chiriquí
—728 712	Bocas del Toro
—728 72	Central provinces
—728 721	Coclé
—728 722	Veraguas
—728 723	Los Santos
—728 724	Herrera
—728 73	Metropolitan provinces
	Class Panama Canal Zone in —72875
—728 731	Panama
	Class here Panama City
—728 732	Colón
—728 74	Darién province
—728 75	Panama Canal Zone
—729	West Indies (Antilles) and Bermuda
	Class here *Caribbean Area
	See also —16365 for Caribbean Sea

SUMMARY

—729 1	**Cuba**
—729 2	**Jamaica and Cayman Islands**
—729 3	**Dominican Republic**
—729 4	**Haiti**
—729 5	**Puerto Rico**
—729 6	**Bahama Islands**
—729 7	**Leeward Islands**
—729 8	**Windward and other southern islands**
—729 9	**Bermuda**

>	—729 1–729 5 Greater Antilles
	Class comprehensive works in —729
—729 1	Cuba
—729 11	Pinar del Río province

*Class parts of this physiographic region or feature as instructed under —4–9

—729 12	Havana and Isla de la Juventud
—729 123	Havana
—729 124	Havana province
—729 125	Isla de la Juventud
	Former name: Isle of Pines
—729 13	Matanzas province
—729 14	Villa Clara, Cienfuegos, Sancti Spíritus provinces
	Class here former Las Villas province
—729 142	Villa Clara province
—729 143	Cienfuegos province
—729 145	Sancti Spíritus province
—729 15	Ciego de Avila and Camagüey provinces
—729 153	Ciego de Avila province
—729 156	Camagüey province
—729 16	Eastern Cuba
	Class here former Oriente province
—729 162	Las Tunas province
—729 163	Granma province
—729 164	Holguín province
—729 165	Santiago de Cuba province
—729 167	Guantánamo province
—729 2	**Jamaica and Cayman Islands**
—729 21	Cayman Islands
—729 3	**Dominican Republic**
	Class here comprehensive works on Hispaniola
	For Haiti, see —7294
—729 32	Southwestern provinces
—729 323	Pedernales
—729 324	Barahona
—729 325	Independencia
—729 326	Bahoruco
—729 34	Western provinces
—729 342	San Juan
—729 343	La Estrelleta
—729 345	Dajabón

—729 35	Northwestern provinces
—729 352	Montecristi
—729 353	Santiago Rodríguez
—729 356	Santiago
—729 357	Valverde
—729 358	Puerto Plata
—729 36	North central provinces
—729 362	Espaillat
—729 363	Salcedo
—729 364	María Trinidad Sánchez
—729 365	Samaná
—729 367	Duarte
—729 368	Sánchez Ramírez
—729 369	La Vega
—729 37	South central provinces
—729 372	Azua
—729 373	Peravia
—729 374	San Cristóbal
—729 375	Distrito Nacional
	Class here Santo Domingo
—729 38	Eastern provinces
—729 382	San Pedro de Macorís
—729 383	La Romana
—729 384	El Seibo
—729 385	La Altagracia
—729 4	Haiti
—729 42	Nord-Ouest department
	Including Île de la Tortue
—729 43	Nord department
—729 44	Artibonite department
—729 45	Ouest department
	Including Île de la Gonâve
	Class here Port-au-Prince
—729 46	Sud department

—729 5	Puerto Rico
—729 51	San Juan district
	Class here San Juan
—729 52	Bayamón district
—729 53	Arecibo district
—729 54	Aguadilla district
—729 56	Mayagüez district
—729 57	Ponce district
—729 58	Guayama district
—729 59	Humacao district
	Including Vieques, Culebra islands
—729 6	Bahama Islands
—729 61	Turks and Caicos Islands

>	—729 7–729 8 Lesser Antilles (Caribbees)
	Class comprehensive works in —729
—729 7	Leeward Islands
	For Dominica, see —729841
—729 72	Virgin Islands
—729 722	Virgin Islands of the United States
	Including Saint Croix, Saint John, Saint Thomas islands; Virgin Islands National Park
—729 725	British Virgin Islands
	Including Anegada, Jost Van Dyke, Tortola, Virgin Gorda islands
—729 73	Anguilla and Saint Christopher-Nevis
	Former name: Saint Christopher-Nevis-Anguilla
	Including Sombrero island
	Class here West Indies Associated States
	For Antigua, see —72974; Windward Islands, —72984
—729 74	Antigua and Barbuda
—729 75	Montserrat

—729 76	Guadeloupe

Overseas department of France

Contains islands of Désirade, Guadeloupe, Les Saintes, Marie Galante, Saint Barthélemy, part of Saint Martin

Class here French West Indies, comprehensive works on Saint Martin

For Martinique, see —72982; Netherlands part of Saint Martin, —72977

—729 77	Leeward Netherlands islands

Contains Saba, Saint Eustatius, part of Saint Martin

Class comprehensive works on Netherlands Antilles in —72986

—729 8	Windward and other southern islands

For Nueva Esparta, Venezuela, see —8754

—729 81	Barbados
—729 82	Martinique

Overseas department of France

—729 83	Trinidad and Tobago
—729 84	Windward Islands
—729 841	Dominica
—729 843	Saint Lucia
—729 844	Saint Vincent and the Grenadines

For Carriacou, see —729845

—729 845	Grenada and Carriacou
—729 86	Netherlands islands

Examples: Aruba, Bonaire, Curaçao

Class here Netherlands Antilles

For Leeward Netherlands islands, see —72977

—729 9	Bermuda
—73	**United States**

For specific states, see —74–79

—(734–739)	Specific states

(Optional numbers; prefer —74–79)

Add to base number —73 the numbers following —7 in notation 74–79 of this table, e.g., Pennsylvania —7348

>   **—74–79 Specific states of United States**

     (Option: Class in —734–739

     Class comprehensive works in —73

     For Hawaii, see —969

—74   **Northeastern United States (New England and Middle Atlantic states)**

Class here United States east of Allegheny Mountains, east of Mississippi River; *Appalachian Mountains; *Connecticut River

For southeastern United States, see —75; south central United States, —76; north central United States, —77

SUMMARY

—741	**Maine**
—742	**New Hampshire**
—743	**Vermont**
—744	**Massachusetts**
—745	**Rhode Island**
—746	**Connecticut**
—747	**New York**
—748	**Pennsylvania**
—749	**New Jersey**

>   **—741–746 New England**

     Class comprehensive works in —74

—741   Maine

—741 1   Aroostook County

     Class here Aroostook River

—741 2   Northwestern counties

     Including Moosehead Lake

     Class here *Longfellow Mountains

—741 22   Somerset County

     Class here *Kennebec River

—741 25   Piscataquis County

—741 3   Penobscot County

     Including Bangor

     Class here *Penobscot River

—741 4   Southeastern counties

*Class parts of this physiographic region or feature as instructed under —4–9

—741 42	Washington County
	Class here Machias, *Saint Croix Rivers
—741 45	Hancock County
	Including Mount Desert Island
	Class here Acadia National Park
	Class Acadia National Park in Knox County in —74153
—741 5	South central counties
—741 52	Waldo County
—741 53	Knox County
	Including Isle au Haut, Monhegan, Vinalhaven Islands
—741 57	Lincoln County
—741 6	Kennebec County
	Including Augusta
—741 7	West central counties
	Class here *Rangeley Lakes
—741 72	Franklin County
—741 75	Oxford County
—741 8	Southwest central counties
	Class here *Androscoggin River
—741 82	Androscoggin County
—741 85	Sagadahoc County
—741 9	Southwestern counties
—741 91	Cumberland County
	Class here Portland
—741 95	York County
—742	New Hampshire
—742 1	Coos County
	Including Connecticut Lakes, *Umbagog Lake
—742 2	*White Mountains
—742 3	Grafton County
	Including *Squam Lake
—742 4	Counties bordering *Lake Winnipesaukee
—742 42	Carroll County

*Class parts of this physiographic region or feature as instructed under —4–9

—742 45	Belknap County
—742 5	Strafford County
—742 6	Rockingham County
	Including Portsmouth
—742 7	West central counties
—742 72	Merrimack County
	Including Concord
	Class here *Merrimack River
—742 75	Sullivan County
—742 8	Hillsboro County
	Including Manchester
—742 9	Cheshire County
—743	Vermont
	Class here *Green Mountains
—743 1	Northwestern counties
	Class here *Lake Champlain in Vermont
—743 12	Grand Isle County
—743 13	Franklin County
	Class here *Missisquoi River
—743 17	Chittenden County
	Including Burlington
	Class here *Winooski River
—743 2	Northeastern counties
—743 23	Orleans County
—743 25	Essex County
—743 3	North central counties
—743 34	Caledonia County
—743 35	Lamoille County
	Class here *Lamoille River
—743 4	Washington County
	Including Montpelier
—743 5	Addison County
—743 6	East central counties

*Class parts of this physiographic region or feature as instructed under —4–9

—743 63	Orange County
—743 65	Windsor County
	Including *White River
—743 7	Rutland County
—743 8	Bennington County
—743 9	Windham County
—744	Massachusetts
—744 1	Berkshire County
	Class here *Berkshire Hills; *Hoosic River
—744 2	Connecticut River counties
—744 22	Franklin County
—744 23	Hampshire County
—744 26	Hampden County
	Including Springfield
—744 3	Worcester County
—744 4	Middlesex County
	Including Cambridge, Lexington, Lowell; *Charles River
—744 5	Essex County
—744 6	Suffolk County
—744 61	Boston
—744 7	Norfolk County
—744 8	Southeastern counties
	For counties bordering Nantucket Sound, see —7449
	See also —16345 for Cape Cod Bay
—744 82	Plymouth County
—744 85	Bristol County
—744 9	Counties bordering Nantucket Sound
	See also —16346 for Nantucket Sound
—744 92	Barnstable County (Cape Cod)
	See also —16345 for Cape Cod Bay
—744 94	Dukes County
	Contains Martha's Vineyard, Elizabeth Islands

*Class parts of this physiographic region or feature as instructed under —4–9

—744 97   Nantucket County

        Class here Nantucket Island

—745   Rhode Island

        See also —16346 for Rhode Island Sound, Narragansett Bay

—745 1   Providence County

        Including Pawtucket [*formerly —7453*]

        For Providence, see —7452

—745 2   Providence

—[745 3]   Pawtucket

        Relocated to —7451

—745 4   Kent County

—745 5   Bristol County

—745 6   Newport County

        For Newport, see —7457

—745 7   Newport

—745 8   Block Island

—745 9   Washington County

        For Block Island, see —7458

—746   Connecticut

        See also —16346 for Long Island Sound

—746 1   Litchfield County

—746 2   Hartford County

        For Hartford, see —7463

—746 3   Hartford

—746 4   Northeastern counties

—746 43   Tolland County

—746 45   Windham County

—746 5   New London County

—746 6   Middlesex County

—746 7   New Haven County

        For New Haven, see —7468

—746 8   New Haven

—746 9   Fairfield County

                         Including Stamford

>   —747–749 Middle Atlantic states

                         Class comprehensive works in —74

—747   New York

—747 1   New York   Borough of Manhattan (Manhattan Island, New York
                         County)

                              *For borough of Brooklyn, see —74723; of Queens, —747243; of
                              Richmond, —74726; of the Bronx, —747275*

                              See also —16346 for New York Bay

—747 2   Other parts of New York metropolitan area

                              *For Fairfield County, Connecticut, see —7469; New Jersey counties
                              of metropolitan area, —7493*

—747 21   Long Island

                              For specific parts of Long Island, see —74723–74725

                              See also —16346 for Long Island Sound

---

>   —747 23–747 25 Specific parts of Long Island

                         Class comprehensive works in —74721

—747 23   Borough of Brooklyn (Kings County)

—747 24   Queens and Nassau Counties

—747 243   Borough of Queens (Queens County)

—747 245   Nassau County

—747 25   Suffolk County

—747 26   Staten Island (Borough of Richmond, Richmond County)

—747 27   Mainland east of Hudson River

—747 275   Borough of the Bronx (Bronx County)

—747 277   Westchester County

—747 28   Rockland County

—747 3   Other southeastern counties

                         Class here *Hudson River

—747 31   Orange County

—747 32   Putnam County

*Class parts of this physiographic region or feature as instructed under —4–9

—747 33	Dutchess County
—747 34	Ulster County
—747 35	Sullivan County
—747 36	Delaware County
—747 37	Greene County
—747 38	*Catskill Mountains
—747 39	Columbia County
—747 4	Middle eastern counties
—747 41	Rensselaer County
—747 42	Albany County
	For Albany, see —74743
—747 43	Albany
—747 44	Schenectady County
—747 45	Schoharie County
—747 46	Montgomery County
—747 47	Fulton County
—747 48	Saratoga County
—747 49	Washington County
—747 5	Northern counties
	Class here *Adirondack Mountains
—747 51	Warren County
	Including *Lake George
—747 52	Hamilton County
—747 53	Essex County
	Use of this number for comprehensive works on Adirondack Mountains discontinued; class in —7475
—747 54	Clinton County
	Class here *Lake Champlain
—747 55	Franklin County
—747 56	Saint Lawrence County
	Including *Saint Lawrence River in New York
—747 57	Jefferson County
—747 58	*Thousand Islands
—747 59	Lewis County

*Class parts of this physiographic region or feature as instructed under —4–9

—747 6	North central counties
	Class here *Mohawk River
—747 61	Herkimer County
—747 62	Oneida County
	Including Utica [*formerly* —74763]; *Oneida Lake
—[747 63]	Utica
	Relocated to —74762
—747 64	Madison County
—747 65	Onondaga County
	Including *Skaneatales Lake
	For Syracuse, see —74766
—747 66	Syracuse
—747 67	Oswego County
—747 68	Cayuga County
	Including *Cayuga Lake
—747 69	Seneca County
	Class here *Seneca Lake
—747 7	South central counties
—747 71	Tompkins County
	Class here Ithaca
—747 72	Cortland County
—747 73	Chenango County
	Class here *Chenango River
—747 74	Otsego County
—747 75	Broome County
	Including Binghamton [*formerly* —74776]
—[747 76]	Binghamton
	Relocated to —74775
—747 77	Tioga County
—747 78	Chemung County
	Including Elmira [*formerly* —74779]
—[747 79]	Elmira
	Relocated to —74778

*Class parts of this physiographic region or feature as instructed under —4–9

—747 8	West central counties
	Class here *Finger Lakes
—747 81	Schuyler County
—747 82	Yates County
	Class here *Keuka Lake
—747 83	Steuben County
—747 84	Allegany County
—747 85	Livingston County
—747 86	Ontario County
	Including *Canandaigua Lake
—747 87	Wayne County
—747 88	Monroe County
	Class here *Genesee River
	For Rochester, see —74789
—747 89	Rochester
—747 9	Western counties
	Class here *Lake Ontario
—747 91	Orleans County
—747 92	Genesee County
—747 93	Wyoming County
—747 94	Cattaraugus County
—747 95	Chautauqua County
—747 96	Erie County
	For Buffalo, see —74797
—747 97	Buffalo
—747 98	Niagara County
	Including Niagara Falls (city)
	Class Niagara Falls (physiographic feature) in —74799
—747 99	Niagara Falls in New York
	Physiographic feature
—748	Pennsylvania
	Class here *Susquehanna River

*Class parts of this physiographic region or feature as instructed under —4–9

—748 1	Southeastern counties
	Class here *Schuylkill River
—748 11	Philadelphia County (Philadelphia)
—748 12	Montgomery County
—748 13	Chester County
—748 14	Delaware County
—748 15	Lancaster County
—748 16	Berks County
—748 17	Schuylkill County
—748 18	Dauphin County
	Including Harrisburg
—748 19	Lebanon County
—748 2	Eastern counties
	Class here *Pocono Mountains
—748 21	Bucks County
—748 22	Northampton County
—748 23	Wayne County
	Including *Lake Wallenpaupack
—748 24	Pike County
—748 25	Monroe County
	Including *Delaware Water Gap
—748 26	Carbon County
—748 27	Lehigh County
—748 3	Northeastern counties
	Class here *East Branch of Susquehanna River
—748 31	Northumberland County
—748 32	Luzerne County
	Including Wilkes-Barre [*formerly* —74833]
—[748 33]	Wilkes-Barre
	Relocated to —74832
—748 34	Susquehanna County
—748 35	Wyoming County
—748 36	Lackawanna County
	For Scranton, see —74837

*Class parts of this physiographic region or feature as instructed under —4–9

—748 37	Scranton
—748 38	Columbia County
—748 39	Montour County
—748 4	**Southeast central counties**
—748 41	York County
—748 42	Adams County
—748 43	Cumberland County
—748 44	Franklin County
	Including *Tuscarora Mountain
—748 45	Perry County
	Class here *Juniata River
—748 46	Mifflin County
—748 47	Juniata County
—748 48	Union County
—748 49	Snyder County
—748 5	**Northeast central counties**
	Class here *West Branch of Susquehanna River
—748 51	Lycoming County
—748 53	Centre County
—748 54	Clinton County
—748 55	Potter County
—748 56	Tioga County
—748 57	Bradford County
—748 59	Sullivan County
—748 6	**Northwest central counties**
	Class here *Allegheny River
—748 61	Clearfield County
—748 62	Jefferson County
—748 63	McKean County
—748 65	Elk County
—748 66	Cameron County
—748 67	Warren County
—748 68	Forest County
—748 69	Clarion County

*Class parts of this physiographic region or feature as instructed under —4–9

—748 7	Southwest central counties
	Class here *Allegheny Mountains
—748 71	Bedford County
—748 72	Fulton County
—748 73	Huntingdon County
—748 75	Blair County
	Including Altoona [*formerly* —74876]
—[748 76]	Altoona
	Relocated to —74875
—748 77	Cambria County
—748 79	Somerset County
—748 8	Southwestern counties
	Class here *Monongahela River
—748 81	Westmoreland County
	Including *Laurel Hill
—748 82	Washington County
—748 83	Greene County
—748 84	Fayette County
	Including *Chestnut Ridge
—748 85	Allegheny County
	For Pittsburgh, see —74886
—748 86	Pittsburgh
—748 88	Armstrong County
—748 89	Indiana County
—748 9	Northwestern counties
—748 91	Butler County
—748 92	Beaver County
—748 93	Lawrence County
—748 95	Mercer County
—748 96	Venango County
—748 97	Crawford County
—748 99	Erie County

*Class parts of this physiographic region or feature as instructed under —4–9

—749   New Jersey
                Class here *Delaware River

—749 2   Northeastern counties

—749 21   Bergen County
                    Class here *Hackensack River

—749 23   Passaic County
                    Including Paterson [formerly —74924]

—[749 24]   Paterson
                    Relocated to —74923

—749 26   Hudson County
                    Including Hoboken [formerly —74928]
                    For Jersey City, see —74927

—749 27   Jersey City

—[749 28]   Hoboken
                    Relocated to —74926

—749 3   Counties of New York metropolitan area
                Class here *Passaic River
                Class each specific metropolitan county not provided for here with the
                county, e.g., Hudson County —74926

—749 31   Essex County
                    For Newark, see —74932; The Oranges, —74933

—749 32   Newark

—749 33   The Oranges
                    Contains East Orange, Maplewood, Orange, South Orange, West
                    Orange

—749 36   Union County
                    Including Elizabeth [formerly —74937], Rahway [formerly —74938]

—[749 37]   Elizabeth
                    Relocated to —74936

—[749 38]   Rahway
                    Relocated to —74936

—749 4   East central counties
                See also —16346 for New York Bay

*Class parts of this physiographic region or feature as instructed under —4–9

—749 41	Middlesex County
	For New Brunswick, see —74942
—749 42	New Brunswick
—749 44	Somerset County
	Class here *Raritan River
—749 46	Monmouth County
—749 48	Ocean County
—749 6	West central counties
—749 61	Burlington County
	Including *Mullica River
—749 65	Mercer County
	Including Princeton [formerly —74967]
	For Trenton, see —74966
—749 66	Trenton
—[749 67]	Princeton
	Relocated to —74965
—749 7	Northwestern counties
—749 71	Hunterdon County
—749 74	Morris County
—749 76	Sussex County
	Class here *Kittatinny Mountain
—749 78	Warren County
—749 8	South central counties
—749 81	Gloucester County
—749 84	Atlantic County
	For Atlantic City, see —74985
—749 85	Atlantic City
—749 87	Camden County
	Including Camden [formerly —74988]
—[749 88]	Camden
	Relocated to —74987
—749 9	Southern counties
	See also —16346 for Delaware Bay

*Class parts of this physiographic region or feature as instructed under —4–9

—749 91   Salem County

                  Including Salem [*formerly* —74992]

—[749 92]   Salem

                  Relocated to —74991

—749 94   Cumberland County

                  Including Bridgeton [*formerly* —74995]

—[749 95]   Bridgeton

                  Relocated to —74994

—749 98   Cape May County

—75   **Southeastern United States (South Atlantic states)**

        Class here southern states, *Piedmont, *Atlantic Coastal Plain

          For south central United States, see —76

SUMMARY

—751	**Delaware**
—752	**Maryland**
—753	**District of Columbia (Washington)**
—754	**West Virginia**
—755	**Virginia**
—756	**North Carolina**
—757	**South Carolina**
—758	**Georgia**
—759	**Florida**

—751   Delaware

          See also —16346 *for Delaware Bay*

—751 1   New Castle County

          For Wilmington, see —7512

—751 2   Wilmington

—751 4   Kent County

          Including Dover [*formerly* —7515]

—[751 5]   Dover

          Relocated to —7514

—751 7   Sussex County

—752   Maryland

        Class here *Potomac River

         See also —16347 *for Chesapeake Bay*

*Class parts of this physiographic region or feature as instructed under —4–9

—752 1	Eastern Shore

Class here *Delmarva Peninsula; *Tidewater Maryland

For southern counties of Eastern Shore, see —7522; northern counties of Eastern Shore, —7523

—752 2	Southern counties of Eastern Shore
—752 21	Worcester County

Including *Assateague Island

—752 23	Somerset County
—752 25	Wicomico County
—752 27	Dorchester County
—752 3	Northern counties of Eastern Shore
—752 31	Caroline County

Class here *Choptank River

—752 32	Talbot County
—752 34	Queen Annes County

Class here *Chester River

—752 36	Kent County
—752 38	Cecil County

>	—752 4–752 9 Maryland west of Chesapeake Bay

Class comprehensive works in —752

—752 4	Southern counties

Class here *Patuxent River

—752 41	Saint Marys County

Use of this number for comprehensive works on Patuxent River discontinued; class in —7524

—752 44	Calvert County
—752 47	Charles County
—752 5	South central counties
—752 51	Prince George's County
—752 55	Anne Arundel County

For Annapolis, see —75256

—752 56	Annapolis
—752 6	Independent city of Baltimore

*Class parts of this physiographic region or feature as instructed under —4–9

—752 7	North central counties
	Class here *Piedmont in Maryland
—752 71	Baltimore County
—752 74	Harford County
	Including *Susquehanna River in Maryland
—752 77	Carroll County
—752 8	West central counties
—752 81	Howard County
—752 84	Montgomery County
—752 87	Frederick County
	Including Frederick [*formerly* —75288]
—[752 88]	Frederick
	Relocated to —75287
—752 9	Western counties
—752 91	Washington County
	Including Hagerstown [*formerly* —75292]
—[752 92]	Hagerstown
	Relocated to —75291
—752 94	Allegany County
	Including Cumberland [*formerly* —75295]
—[752 95]	Cumberland
	Relocated to —75294
—752 97	Garrett County
—753	District of Columbia (Washington)
—754	West Virginia
—754 1	Northern Panhandle counties
	Class here *Ohio River in West Virginia
—754 12	Hancock County
—754 13	Brooke County
—754 14	Ohio County
	Class here Wheeling [*formerly* —75415]
—[754 15]	Wheeling
	Relocated to —75414

*Class parts of this physiographic region or feature as instructed under —4–9

—754 16	Marshall County
—754 18	Wetzel County
—754 19	Tyler County
—754 2	Little Kanawha Valley counties
	Class here *Little Kanawha River
—754 21	Pleasants County
—754 22	Wood County
	Including Parkersburg [*formerly* —75423]
—[754 23]	Parkersburg
	Relocated to —75422
—754 24	Ritchie County
—754 26	Wirt County
—754 27	Gilmer County
—754 29	Calhoun County
—754 3	Kanawha Valley counties
	Class here *Kanawha River
—754 31	Jackson County
—754 33	Mason County
—754 35	Putnam County
—754 36	Roane County
—754 37	Kanawha County
	Including Charleston [*formerly* —75438]
—[754 38]	Charleston
	Relocated to —75437
—754 39	Boone County
—754 4	Southwestern border counties
	Including *Tug Fork
	Class here *Guyandotte River
—754 42	Cabell County
—754 43	Lincoln County
—754 44	Logan County
—754 45	Wyoming County
—754 47	Wayne County
	Including *Big Sandy River

*Class parts of this physiographic region or feature as instructed under —4–9

—754 48	Mingo County
—754 49	McDowell County
—754 5	Monongahela Valley counties
	Class here *Monongahela River in West Virginia
—754 52	Monongalia County
	Including Morgantown [*formerly* —75453]
—[754 53]	Morgantown
	Relocated to —75452
—754 54	Marion County
—754 55	Taylor County
—754 56	Doddridge County
—754 57	Harrison County
	Including Clarksburg [*formerly* —75458]
—[754 58]	Clarksburg
	Relocated to —75457
—754 59	Barbour County
—754 6	Central counties
	Class here *Elk River
—754 61	Lewis County
—754 62	Upshur County
—754 65	Webster County
—754 66	Braxton County
—754 67	Clay County
—754 69	Nicholas County
	Class here *Gauley River
—754 7	New River Valley counties
	Class here *New River
—754 71	Fayette County
—754 73	Raleigh County
—754 74	Mercer County
—754 76	Summers County
—754 78	Monroe County

*Class parts of this physiographic region or feature as instructed under —4–9

—754 8	Allegheny Crest counties	

Class here *Allegheny Mountains in West Virginia; *Cheat River

—754 82	Preston County	
—754 83	Tucker County	
—754 85	Randolph County	
—754 87	Pocahontas County	
—754 88	Greenbrier County	

Including White Sulphur Springs [*formerly* —75489]

Class here *Greenbrier River

—[754 89]	White Sulphur Springs	

Relocated to —75488

—754 9	Eastern Panhandle counties	

Class here *Potomac Valley of West Virginia

—754 91	Pendleton County	
—754 92	Grant County	
—754 93	Hardy County	
—754 94	Mineral County	
—754 95	Hampshire County	
—754 96	Morgan County	
—754 97	Berkeley County	
—754 99	Jefferson County	
—755	Virginia	

Class here *Blue Ridge

—755 1	Eastern Peninsula and Chesapeake Bay Region	

Class here *Tidewater Virginia

—755 15	Northampton County	
—755 16	Accomack County	
—755 18	*Chesapeake Bay Region	

See also —16347 for Chesapeake Bay

—755 2	Northern Neck	

Class here *Rappahannock River

—755 21	Northumberland County	
—755 22	Lancaster County	

*Class parts of this physiographic region or feature as instructed under —4–9

—755 23	Richmond County
—755 24	Westmoreland County
—755 25	King George County
—755 26	Stafford County
—755 27	Prince William and Fauquier Counties and environs
—755 273	Prince William County, Manassas, Manassas Park
—755 273 2	Prince William County
—755 273 4	Independent city of Manassas
—755 273 6	Independent city of Manassas Park
—755 275	Fauquier County
—755 28	Loudoun County
—755 29	Washington metropolitan area of Virginia
—755 291	Fairfax County
—755 292	Independent city of Fairfax
—755 293	Independent city of Falls Church
—755 295	Arlington County
—755 296	Independent city of Alexandria
—755 3	**Rappahannock-York region**
	York River relocated to —16347
—755 31	Mathews County
—755 32	Gloucester County
—755 33	Middlesex County
—755 34	Essex County
—755 35	King and Queen and King William Counties
—755 352	King and Queen County
—755 355	King William County
—755 36	Caroline and Spotsylvania Counties and environs
—755 362	Caroline County
—755 365	Spotsylvania County
—755 366	Independent city of Fredericksburg
—755 37	Orange and Greene Counties
—755 372	Orange County
—755 375	Greene County
—755 38	Madison County

—755 39	Culpeper and Rappahannock Counties
—755 392	Culpeper County
—755 395	Rappahannock County
—755 4	York-James region
	Class here *James River
—755 41	Southern end of peninsula
—755 412	Independent city of Hampton
—755 416	Independent city of Newport News
—755 42	York and James City Counties and environs
—755 422	Independent city of Poquoson [*formerly* —755423]
—755 423	York County
	Independent city of Poquoson relocated to —755422
—755 425	James City County and Williamsburg
—755 425 1	James City County
—755 425 2	Independent city of Williamsburg
—755 43	New Kent County
—755 44	Charles City County
—755 45	Henrico and Goochland Counties and environs
—755 451	Independent city of Richmond
—755 453	Henrico County
—755 455	Goochland County
—755 46	Hanover and Louisa Counties
—755 462	Hanover County
—755 465	Louisa County
—755 47	Fluvanna County
—755 48	Albermarle County and environs
—755 481	Independent city of Charlottesville
—755 482	Albemarle County
—755 49	Nelson and Amherst Counties
—755 493	Nelson County
—755 496	Amherst County
—755 5	Southeastern region
—755 51	Independent city of Virginia Beach
—755 52	Independent cities of Norfolk, Portsmouth, Chesapeake

*Class parts of this physiographic region or feature as instructed under —4–9

—755 521	Independent city of Norfolk
—755 522	Independent city of Portsmouth
—755 523	Independent city of Chesapeake
	Class here *Dismal Swamp
—755 53	Independent city of Suffolk
—755 54	Isle of Wight County
—755 55	Southampton County and environs
—755 552	Southampton County
—755 553	Independent city of Franklin
—755 56	Surry and Sussex Counties
—755 562	Surry County
—755 565	Sussex County
—755 57	Greensville and Brunswick Counties and environs
—755 572	Greensville County
—755 573	Independent city of Emporia
—755 575	Brunswick County
—755 58	Dinwiddie and Prince George Counties and environs
—755 581	Independent city of Petersburg
—755 582	Dinwiddie County
—755 585	Prince George County
—755 586	Independent city of Hopewell
—755 59	Chesterfield County and environs
—755 594	Chesterfield County
—755 595	Independent city of Colonial Heights
—755 6	South central region
	Class here *Piedmont in Virginia; *Roanoke River in Virginia
—755 61	Powhatan and Cumberland Counties
—755 612	Powhatan County
—755 615	Cumberland County
—755 62	Buckingham and Appomattox Counties
—755 623	Buckingham County
—755 625	Appomattox County
—755 63	Prince Edward, Amelia, Nottoway Counties
—755 632	Prince Edward County

*Class parts of this physiographic region or feature as instructed under —4–9

—755 634	Amelia County
—755 637	Nottoway County
—755 64	Lunenburg and Mecklenburg Counties
—755 643	Lunenburg County
—755 645	Mecklenburg County
—755 65	Charlotte County
—755 66	Halifax and Pittsylvania Counties and environs
—755 661	Halifax County
—755 662	Independent city of South Boston
—755 665	Pittsylvania County
—755 666	Independent city of Danville
—755 67	Campbell and Bedford Counties and environs
—755 671	Independent city of Lynchburg
—755 672	Campbell County
—755 675	Bedford County
—755 676	Independent city of Bedford
—755 68	Franklin County
—755 69	Henry and Patrick Counties and environs
—755 692	Henry County
—755 693	Independent city of Martinsville
—755 695	Patrick County
—755 7	Southwestern region
—755 71	Floyd, Carroll, Grayson Counties and environs
—755 712	Floyd County
—755 714	Carroll County
—755 715	Independent city of Galax
—755 717	Grayson County
—755 72	Smyth and Washington Counties and environs
—755 723	Smyth County
—755 725	Washington County
—755 726	Independent city of Bristol
—755 73	Scott and Lee Counties
—755 732	Scott County
—755 735	Lee County

—755 74	Wise and Dickenson Counties and environs
—755 743	Wise County
—755 744	Independent city of Norton
—755 745	Dickenson County
—755 75	Buchanan and Russell Counties
—755 752	Buchanan County
—755 755	Russell County
—755 76	Tazewell and Bland Counties
—755 763	Tazewell County
—755 765	Bland County
—755 77	Wythe and Pulaski Counties
—755 773	Wythe County
—755 775	Pulaski County
—755 78	Giles and Montgomery Counties and environs
—755 782	Giles County
—755 785	Montgomery County
—755 786	Independent city of Radford
—755 79	Roanoke and Craig Counties and environs
—755 791	Independent city of Roanoke
—755 792	Roanoke County
—755 793	Independent city of Salem
—755 795	Craig County
—755 8	Central western region
—755 81	Alleghany County and environs
—755 811	Independent city of Clifton Forge
—755 812	Independent city of Covington
—755 816	Alleghany County
—755 83	Botetourt County
—755 85	Rockbridge County and environs
—755 851	Independent city of Buena Vista
—755 852	Rockbridge County
—755 853	Independent city of Lexington
—755 87	Bath County
—755 89	Highland County

—755 9	Northwestern region
	Class here *Shenandoah National Park; *Shenandoah Valley
—755 91	Augusta County and environs
—755 911	Independent city of Staunton
—755 912	Independent city of Waynesboro
—755 916	Augusta County
—755 92	Rockingham County and environs
—755 921	Independent city of Harrisonburg
—755 922	Rockingham County
—755 94	Page County
—755 95	Shenandoah County
—755 97	Warren County
—755 98	Clarke County
—755 99	Frederick County and environs
—755 991	Independent city of Winchester
—755 992	Frederick County
—756	North Carolina
—756 1	Northeast coastal plain counties
	Class here *Coastal Plain in North Carolina; *Outer Banks
	See also —16348 for Albemarle, Pamlico Sounds
—756 13	Currituck and Camden Counties
—756 132	Currituck County
—756 135	Camden County
	Including *Dismal Swamp in North Carolina
—756 14	Pasquotank, Perquimans, Chowan Counties
—756 142	Pasquotank County
—756 144	Perquimans County
—756 147	Chowan County
—756 15	Gates and Hertford Counties
	Class here Chowan River
—756 153	Gates County
—756 155	Hertford County
—756 16	Bertie and Washington Counties
	Class here *Roanoke River

*Class parts of this physiographic region or feature as instructed under —4–9

—756 163	Bertie County
—756 165	Washington County
—756 17	Tyrrell and Dare Counties
—756 172	Tyrrell County
—756 175	Dare County
	Including Roanoke Island; Cape Hatteras
—756 18	Hyde and Beaufort Counties
—756 184	Hyde County
—756 186	Beaufort County
—756 19	Craven, Pamlico, Carteret Counties
	Class here *Neuse River
—756 192	Craven County
—756 194	Pamlico County
—756 197	Carteret County
—756 2	Southeast Coastal Plain counties
	Class here *Cape Fear River
—756 21	Jones County
—756 23	Onslow County
—756 25	Pender County
—756 27	New Hanover County
	Class here Wilmington
—756 29	Brunswick County
—756 3	Southwest Coastal Plain counties
—756 31	Columbus County
—756 32	Bladen County
—756 33	Robeson and Scotland Counties
—756 332	Robeson County
—756 335	Scotland County
—756 34	Richmond County
—756 35	Moore and Lee Counties
—756 352	Moore County
—756 355	Lee County
—756 36	Harnett and Hoke Counties
—756 362	Harnett County

*Class parts of this physiographic region or feature as instructed under —4–9

—756 365	Hoke County
—756 37	Cumberland and Sampson Counties
—756 373	Cumberland County
—756 375	Sampson County
—756 38	Duplin and Lenoir Counties
—756 382	Duplin County
—756 385	Lenoir County
	Including Kinston [*formerly* —756386]
—[756 386]	Kinston
	Relocated to —756385
—756 39	Greene and Wayne Counties
—756 393	Greene County
—756 395	Wayne County
	Including Goldsboro [*formerly* —756396]
—[756 396]	Goldsboro
	Relocated to —756395
—756 4	Northwest Coastal Plain counties
—756 41	Johnston County
—756 43	Wilson County
—756 44	Pitt County
—756 45	Martin County
—756 46	Edgecombe County
—756 47	Nash County
—756 48	Halifax County
—756 49	Northampton County
—756 5	Northeast Piedmont counties
	Class here *Piedmont in North Carolina
—756 52	Warren County
—756 53	Vance and Granville Counties
—756 532	Vance County
—756 535	Granville County
—756 54	Franklin County
—756 55	Wake County
	Class here Raleigh

*Class parts of this physiographic region or feature as instructed under —4–9

—756 56	Durham and Orange Counties
—756 563	Durham County
—756 565	Orange County
—756 57	Person and Caswell Counties
—756 573	Person County
—756 575	Caswell County
—756 58	Alamance County
—756 59	Chatham County
—756 6	Northwest Piedmont counties
—756 61	Randolph County
—756 62	Guilford County
—756 63	Rockingham County
—756 64	Stokes County
—756 65	Surry County
—756 66	Yadkin County
—756 67	Forsyth County
—756 68	Davidson County
	Class here *Yadkin River
—756 69	Davie County
—756 7	Southern Piedmont counties
—756 71	Rowan County
—756 72	Cabarrus County
—756 73	Stanly County
—756 74	Montgomery County
—756 75	Anson and Union Counties
—756 753	Anson County
—756 755	Union County
—756 76	Mecklenburg County
	Class here Charlotte
—756 77	Gaston and Cleveland Counties
—756 773	Gaston County
—756 775	Cleveland County
—756 78	Lincoln and Catawba Counties
—756 782	Lincoln County

*Class parts of this physiographic region or feature as instructed under —4–9

—756 785	Catawba County
—756 79	Iredell and Alexander Counties
—756 793	Iredell County
—756 795	Alexander County
—756 8	**Northern Appalachian region counties**

Class here *Blue Ridge in North Carolina, *Appalachian region in North Carolina

—756 82	Wilkes County
—756 83	Alleghany and Ashe Counties
—756 832	Alleghany County
—756 835	Ashe County
—756 84	Watauga and Caldwell Counties
—756 843	Watauga County
—756 845	Caldwell County
—756 85	Burke County
—756 86	Avery and Mitchell Counties
—756 862	Avery County
—756 865	Mitchell County
—756 87	Yancey and Madison Counties
—756 873	Yancey County
—756 875	Madison County
—756 88	Buncombe County

Including Asheville

—756 89	McDowell County
—756 9	**Southern Appalachian region counties**
—756 91	Rutherford and Polk Counties
—756 913	Rutherford County
—756 915	Polk County
—756 92	Henderson County
—756 93	Transylvania County
—756 94	Haywood County
—756 95	Jackson County
—756 96	Swain County

Class here *Great Smoky Mountains in North Carolina

*Class parts of this physiographic region or feature as instructed under —4–9

—756 97	Graham County
—756 98	Macon and Clay Counties
—756 982	Macon County
—756 985	Clay County
—756 99	Cherokee County
—757	South Carolina
—757 2	Mountain counties

Class here *Blue Ridge in South Carolina; *Saluda River

—757 21	Oconee County
—757 23	Pickens County
—757 25	Anderson County
—757 27	Greenville County
—757 29	Spartanburg County
—757 3	Southwest Piedmont counties

Class here *Piedmont in South Carolina

—757 31	Laurens County

Including *Enoree River

—757 33	Greenwood County
—757 35	Abbeville County
—757 36	McCormick County
—757 37	Edgefield County
—757 38	Saluda County
—757 39	Newberry County
—757 4	Northeast Piedmont counties

Class here *Broad River

—757 41	Union County

Use of this number for comprehensive works on Broad River discontinued; class in —7574

—757 42	Cherokee County
—757 43	York County
—757 45	Lancaster County

Class here *Catawba River

—757 47	Chester County
—757 49	Fairfield County

*Class parts of this physiographic region or feature as instructed under —4–9

—757 6	Northeast counties of sand hills and upper pine belt
	Including *Lynches River
	Class here *Coastal Plain in South Carolina
	Comprehensive works on Pee Dee River relocated to —7578
—757 61	Kershaw County
—757 63	Chesterfield County
—757 64	Marlboro County
—757 66	Darlington County
—757 67	Lee County
—757 69	Sumter County
	Including *Wateree River
—757 7	Southwest counties of sand hills and upper pine belt
—757 71	Richland County
	Class here Columbia
—757 72	Calhoun County
—757 73	Lexington County
—757 75	Aiken County
—757 76	Barnwell County
—757 77	Allendale County
—757 78	Bamberg County
—757 79	Orangeburg County
—757 8	Northeast counties of lower pine belt
	Including *Black, *Santee Rivers
	Class here comprehensive works on *Pee Dee River [*formerly* —7576]
—757 81	Clarendon County
	Class here *Lake Marion
—757 83	Williamsburg County
	Use of this number for comprehensive works on Black River discontinued; class in —7578
—757 84	Florence County
—757 85	Dillon County
—757 86	Marion County
—757 87	Horry County
—757 89	Georgetown County

*Class parts of this physiographic region or feature as instructed under —4–9

—757 9	Southwest counties of lower pine belt
	Including *Edisto River; *Savannah River in South Carolina
—757 91	Charleston County
—757 915	Charleston
—757 93	Berkeley County
—757 94	Dorchester County
—757 95	Colleton County
—757 97	Hampton County
—757 98	Jasper County
—757 99	Beaufort County
	Class here *Sea Islands
—758	Georgia
	Class here *Chattahoochee River
—758 1	Northeastern counties
	Class here *Savannah River
—758 12	Rabun and Habersham Counties
—758 123	Rabun County
—758 125	Habersham County
—758 13	Stephens and Franklin Counties
—758 132	Stephens County
—758 135	Franklin County
—758 14	Banks and Jackson Counties
—758 143	Banks County
—758 145	Jackson County
—758 15	Madison and Hart Counties
—758 152	Madison County
—758 155	Hart County
—758 16	Elbert and Lincoln Counties
—758 163	Elbert County
—758 165	Lincoln County
—758 17	Wilkes and Oglethorpe Counties
—758 172	Wilkes County
—758 175	Oglethorpe County

*Class parts of this physiographic region or feature as instructed under —4–9

—758 18	Clarke County
	Class here Athens
—758 19	Oconee and Barrow Counties
—758 193	Oconee County
—758 195	Barrow County
—758 2	**North central counties**
	Class here *Blue Ridge in Georgia
—758 21	Walton and Rockdale Counties
—758 212	Walton County
—758 215	Rockdale County
—758 22	Gwinnett and De Kalb Counties
—758 223	Gwinnett County
—758 225	De Kalb County
—758 23	Fulton County
—758 231	Atlanta
—758 24	Douglas and Cobb Counties
—758 243	Douglas County
—758 245	Cobb County
—758 25	Cherokee and Pickens Counties
—758 253	Cherokee County
—758 255	Pickens County
—758 26	Dawson and Forsyth Counties
—758 263	Dawson County
—758 265	Forsyth County
—758 27	Hall, Lumpkin, White Counties
—758 272	Hall County
—758 273	Lumpkin County
	Use of this number for comprehensive works on Blue Ridge in Georgia discontinued; class in —7582
—758 277	White County
—758 28	Towns and Union Counties
—758 282	Towns County
—758 285	Union County
—758 29	Fannin and Gilmer Counties

*Class parts of this physiographic region or feature as instructed under —4–9

—758 293　　　　　　　Fannin County

—758 295　　　　　　　Gilmer County

—758 3　　　　　Northwestern counties

—758 31　　　　　　Murray County

—758 32　　　　　　Whitfield and Catoosa Counties

—758 324　　　　　　　Whitfield County

—758 326　　　　　　　Catoosa County

—758 33　　　　　　Walker County

—758 34　　　　　　Dade and Chattooga Counties

—758 342　　　　　　　Dade County

　　　　　　　　　Class here *Lookout Mountain in Georgia

—758 344　　　　　　　Chattooga County

—758 35　　　　　　Floyd County

—758 36　　　　　　Gordon and Bartow Counties

—758 362　　　　　　　Gordon County

—758 365　　　　　　　Bartow County

—758 37　　　　　　Paulding and Polk Counties

—758 373　　　　　　　Paulding County

—758 375　　　　　　　Polk County

—758 38　　　　　　Haralson County

—758 39　　　　　　Carroll County

—758 4　　　　　West central counties

　　　　　　　Class here *Piedmont in Georgia

—758 42　　　　　　Heard, Coweta, Fayette Counties

—758 422　　　　　　　Heard County

—758 423　　　　　　　Coweta County

—758 426　　　　　　　Fayette County

—758 43　　　　　　Clayton and Henry Counties

—758 432　　　　　　　Clayton County

—758 435　　　　　　　Henry County

—758 44　　　　　　Spalding and Lamar Counties

—758 443　　　　　　　Spalding County

—758 446　　　　　　　Lamar County

—758 45　　　　　　Pike and Meriwether Counties

*Class parts of this physiographic region or feature as instructed under —4–9

—758 453	Pike County
—758 455	Meriwether County
—758 46	Troup and Harris Counties
—758 463	Troup County
—758 466	Harris County
—758 47	Muscogee and Chattahoochee Counties
—758 473	Muscogee County
—758 476	Chattahoochee County
—758 48	Marion, Talbot, Upson Counties
—758 482	Marion County
—758 483	Talbot County
—758 486	Upson County
—758 49	Taylor and Schley Counties
—758 493	Taylor County
—758 495	Schley County
—758 5	Central counties
	Class here *Ocmulgee River
—758 51	Macon and Houston Counties
—758 513	Macon County
—758 515	Houston County
—758 52	Pulaski and Bleckley Counties
—758 523	Pulaski County
—758 525	Bleckley County
—758 53	Dodge and Laurens Counties
—758 532	Dodge County
—758 535	Laurens County
—758 54	Wilkinson and Twiggs Counties
—758 543	Wilkinson County
—758 545	Twiggs County
—758 55	Bibb and Peach Counties
—758 552	Bibb County
	Class here Macon
—758 556	Peach County
—758 56	Crawford, Monroe, Jones Counties

*Class parts of this physiographic region or feature as instructed under —4–9

—758 562	Crawford County
—758 563	Monroe County
—758 567	Jones County
—758 57	Baldwin and Putnam Counties
—758 573	Baldwin County
—758 576	Putnam County
—758 58	Jasper and Butts Counties
—758 583	Jasper County
—758 585	Butts County
—758 59	Newton and Morgan Counties
—758 593	Newton County
—758 595	Morgan County
—758 6	East central counties
	Including *Oconee River
	Class here *Ogeechee River
—758 61	Greene and Taliaferro Counties
—758 612	Greene County
—758 616	Taliaferro County
—758 62	Hancock and Warren Counties
—758 623	Hancock County
—758 625	Warren County
—758 63	McDuffie and Columbia Counties
—758 632	McDuffie County
—758 635	Columbia County
—758 64	Richmond County
	Class here Augusta
—758 65	Burke County
—758 66	Jefferson and Glascock Counties
	Use of this number for comprehensive works on Ogeechee River discontinued; class in —7586
—758 663	Jefferson County
—758 666	Glascock County
—758 67	Washington and Johnson Counties
—758 672	Washington County

*Class parts of this physiographic region or feature as instructed under —4–9

—758 676	Johnson County
—758 68	Treutlen and Emanuel Counties
—758 682	Treutlen County
—758 684	Emanuel County
—758 69	Jenkins and Screven Counties
—758 693	Jenkins County
—758 695	Screven County
—758 7	Southeastern counties

Including *Sea Islands of Georgia; *Altamaha River

—758 72	Effingham and Chatham Counties
—758 722	Effingham County
—758 724	Chatham County

Class here Savannah

—758 73	Bryan, Liberty, McIntosh Counties
—758 732	Bryan County
—758 733	Liberty County
—758 737	McIntosh County
—758 74	Glynn and Camden Counties
—758 742	Glynn County
—758 746	Camden County
—758 75	Charlton, Brantley, Wayne Counties
—758 752	Charlton County

Class here *Okefenokee Swamp

—758 753	Brantley County
—758 756	Wayne County

Use of this number for comprehensive works on Altamaha River discontinued; class in —7587

—758 76	Long, Evans, Bulloch Counties
—758 762	Long County
—758 763	Evans County
—758 766	Bulloch County
—758 77	Candler and Tattnall Counties
—758 773	Candler County
—758 775	Tattnall County

*Class parts of this physiographic region or feature as instructed under —4–9

—758 78	Toombs, Appling, Bacon Counties
—758 782	Toombs County
—758 784	Appling County
—758 787	Bacon County
—758 79	Pierce and Ware Counties
—758 792	Pierce County
—758 794	Ware County
	Including Waycross [*formerly* —758795]
—[758 795]	Waycross
	Relocated to —758794
—758 8	**South central counties**
—758 81	Clinch, Echols, Lanier Counties
—758 812	Clinch County
—758 814	Echols County
—758 817	Lanier County
—758 82	Atkinson, Coffee, Jeff Davis Counties
—758 822	Atkinson County
—758 823	Coffee County
—758 827	Jeff Davis County
—758 83	Montgomery and Wheeler Counties
—758 832	Montgomery County
—758 835	Wheeler County
—758 84	Telfair and Wilcox Counties
—758 843	Telfair County
—758 845	Wilcox County
—758 85	Ben Hill and Irwin Counties
—758 852	Ben Hill County
—758 855	Irwin County
—758 86	Berrien and Lowndes Counties
—758 862	Berrien County
—758 864	Lowndes County
	Including Valdosta [*formerly* —758865]
—[758 865]	Valdosta
	Relocated to —758864

—758 87	Brooks and Cook Counties
—758 874	Brooks County
—758 876	Cook County
—758 88	Tift and Turner Counties
—758 882	Tift County
—758 885	Turner County
—758 89	Crisp and Dooly Counties
—758 893	Crisp County
—758 895	Dooly County
—758 9	Southwestern counties
	Class here *Flint River
—758 91	Sumter and Webster Counties
—758 913	Sumter County
—758 916	Webster County
—758 92	Stewart, Quitman, Clay Counties
—758 922	Stewart County
—758 924	Quitman County
—758 927	Clay County
—758 93	Randolph and Terrell Counties
—758 932	Randolph County
—758 935	Terrell County
—758 94	Lee and Worth Counties
—758 943	Lee County
—758 945	Worth County
—758 95	Dougherty and Calhoun Counties
—758 953	Dougherty County
—758 956	Calhoun County
—758 96	Early, Miller, Baker Counties
—758 962	Early County
—758 964	Miller County
—758 967	Baker County
—758 97	Mitchell and Colquitt Counties
—758 973	Mitchell County
—758 975	Colquitt County

*Class parts of this physiographic region or feature as instructed under —4–9

—758 98	Thomas and Grady Counties
—758 984	Thomas County
—758 986	Grady County
—758 99	Decatur and Seminole Counties
—758 993	Decatur County
—758 996	Seminole County
—759	Florida
—759 1	Northeastern counties
	Class here *Saint Johns River
—759 11	Nassau County
	Class here *Saint Marys River
—759 12	Duval County
	Class here Jacksonville
—[759 121]	Jacksonville
	Number discontinued; class in —75912
—759 13	Baker County
—759 14	Union County
—759 15	Bradford County
—759 16	Clay County
—759 17	Putnam County
—759 18	Saint Johns County
—759 19	Flagler County
—759 2	East central counties
—759 21	Volusia County
—759 22	Lake County
—759 23	Seminole County
—759 24	Orange County
—759 25	Osceola County
—759 27	Brevard County
—759 28	Indian River County
—759 29	Saint Lucie County
—759 3	Southeastern counties
—759 31	Martin County
—759 32	Palm Beach County

*Class parts of this physiographic region or feature as instructed under —4–9

—759 35	Broward County
	Including Fort Lauderdale
—759 38	Dade County
—759 381	Miami and Miami Beach
—759 39	*The Everglades and *Lake Okeechobee
	Class here *Everglades National Park
—759 4	Southwestern counties
—759 41	Monroe County
	Including Key West
	Class here *Florida Keys
—759 44	Collier County
	Including *Ten Thousand Islands
	Class here *Big Cypress Swamp
—759 46	Hendry County
	Including *Okaloacoochee Slough
—759 48	Lee County
	Class here *Caloosahatchee River
—759 49	Charlotte County
—759 5	South central counties
—759 51	Glades County
—759 53	Okeechobee County
	Class here *Kissimmee River
—759 55	Highlands County
—759 57	Hardee County
	Class here *Peace River
—759 59	De Soto County
—759 6	Southern west central counties
—759 61	Sarasota County
—759 62	Manatee County
—759 63	Pinellas County
—759 65	Hillsborough County
	Class here Tampa
—759 67	Polk County
—759 69	Pasco County

*Class parts of this physiographic region or feature as instructed under —4–9

—759 7	Northern west central counties
	Class here *Withlacoochee River
—759 71	Hernando County
—759 72	Citrus County
	Use of this number for comprehensive works on Withlacoochee River discontinued; class in —7597
—759 73	Sumter County
—759 75	Marion County
—759 77	Levy County
—759 78	Gilchrist County
—759 79	Alachua County
	Including *Santa Fe River
—759 8	North central counties
	Class here *Suwannee River
—759 81	Dixie and Lafayette Counties
—759 812	Dixie County
—759 816	Lafayette County
—759 82	Suwannee County
—759 83	Columbia County
—759 84	Hamilton County
—759 85	Madison County
—759 86	Taylor County
—759 87	Jefferson County
—759 88	Leon County
	Including Tallahassee
—759 89	Wakulla County
—759 9	Northwestern counties (Panhandle)
—759 91	Franklin County
—759 92	Liberty and Gadsden Counties
	Including *Apalachicola River
—759 923	Liberty County
—759 925	Gadsden County
—759 93	Jackson County
—759 94	Calhoun and Gulf Counties

*Class parts of this physiographic region or feature as instructed under —4–9

—759 943	Calhoun County
—759 947	Gulf County
—759 95	Bay County
—759 96	Washington and Holmes Counties
—759 963	Washington County
—759 965	Holmes County
—759 97	Walton County
—759 98	Okaloosa and Santa Rosa Counties
—759 982	Okaloosa County
—759 985	Santa Rosa County
—759 99	Escambia County
	Including Pensacola

—76   **South central United States   Gulf Coast states**

Class here Old Southwest

SUMMARY

—761	**Alabama**
—762	**Mississippi**
—763	**Louisiana**
—764	**Texas**
—766	**Oklahoma**
—767	**Arkansas**
—768	**Tennessee**
—769	**Kentucky**

\>   —761–764 Gulf Coast states

Class comprehensive works in —76

For Florida, see —759

—761	Alabama
—761 2	Gulf and Lower Coastal Plain counties
	Class here *Alabama, *Tombigbee Rivers
—761 21	Baldwin County
	Class here *Perdido River
—761 22	Mobile County
	Including *Mobile River
	Class here Mobile

*Class parts of this physiographic region or feature as instructed under —4–9

—761 23	Lime Hills counties
	Class specific counties in —76124–76127
—761 24	Washington and Clarke Counties
—761 243	Washington County
—761 245	Clarke County
—761 25	Monroe County
—761 26	Conecuh and Escambia Counties
—761 263	Conecuh County
—761 265	Escambia County
—761 27	Covington County
—761 29	Lime sink counties (Wire-grass region)
—761 292	Geneva County
—761 295	Houston County
—761 3	Southern red hills counties
—761 31	Henry County
—761 32	Barbour County
—761 33	Dale County
—761 34	Coffee County
—761 35	Pike County
—761 36	Crenshaw County
—761 37	Butler County
—761 38	Wilcox County
—761 39	Marengo and Choctaw Counties
—761 392	Marengo County
—761 395	Choctaw County
—761 4	Black Belt counties
—761 41	Sumter County
—761 42	Greene County
—761 43	Hale County
—761 44	Perry County
—761 45	Dallas County
—761 46	Autauga and Lowndes Counties
—761 463	Autauga County
—761 465	Lowndes County

—761 47	Montgomery County
	Class here Montgomery
—761 48	Bullock and Russell Counties
—761 483	Bullock County
—761 485	Russell County
—761 49	Macon County
—761 5	Counties of *Piedmont
	Class here *Tallapoosa River
—761 52	Elmore County
—761 53	Tallapoosa County
	Class here *Lake Martin
	Use of this number for comprehensive works on Tallapoosa River discontinued; class in —7615
—761 55	Lee County
—761 56	Chambers County
—761 57	Randolph County
—761 58	Clay County
—761 59	Coosa County
—761 6	Coosa Valley region counties
	Class here *Coosa River
—761 61	Talladega County
—761 63	Calhoun County
—761 64	Cleburne County
—761 65	Cherokee County
—761 66	De Kalb County
—761 67	Etowah County
—761 69	Saint Clair County
—761 7	Central Plateau and Basin counties
—761 72	Blount County
—761 73	Cullman County
—761 74	Winston County
—761 76	Walker County
—761 78	Jefferson County
—761 781	Birmingham

*Class parts of this physiographic region or feature as instructed under —4–9

—761 79	Shelby County
—761 8	**Central pine belt counties**
—761 81	Chilton County
—761 82	Bibb County
—761 84	Tuscaloosa County
—761 85	Pickens County
—761 86	Lamar County
—761 87	Fayette County
—761 89	Marion County
—761 9	**Tennessee Valley counties**
	Class here *Tennessee River in Alabama
—761 91	Franklin and Colbert Counties
—761 913	Franklin County
—761 915	Colbert County
—761 92	Lawrence County
—761 93	Morgan County
—761 94	Marshall County
	Class here *Guntersville Lake
—761 95	Jackson County
—761 97	Madison County
	Class here Huntsville
—761 98	Limestone County
	Class here *Wheeler Lake
—761 99	Lauderdale County
—762	**Mississippi**
—762 1	**Southeastern counties**
—762 12	Jackson County
	Class here *Pascagoula River
—762 13	Harrison County
—762 14	Hancock County
—762 15	Pearl River County
—762 16	Stone and George Counties
—762 162	Stone County
—762 165	George County

*Class parts of this physiographic region or feature as instructed under —4–9

—762 17	Greene and Perry Counties
—762 173	Greene County
—762 175	Perry County
—762 18	Forrest County
—762 19	Lamar County
—762 2	**Southwestern counties**
—762 21	Marion County
—762 22	Walthall County
—762 23	Pike County
—762 24	Amite County
—762 25	Wilkinson County
—762 26	Adams County
	Class here Natchez
—762 27	Franklin County
—762 28	Jefferson and Claiborne Counties
—762 283	Jefferson County
—762 285	Claiborne County
—762 29	Warren County
—762 4	**West central counties (Yazoo-Mississippi Delta)**
	Class here *Big Black, *Yazoo Rivers
—762 41	Issaquena and Sharkey Counties
—762 412	Issaquena County
—762 414	Sharkey County
—762 42	Washington County
—762 43	Bolivar County
—762 44	Coahoma County
—762 45	Quitman and Tallahatchie Counties
—762 453	Quitman County
—762 455	Tallahatchie County
—762 46	Leflore County
—762 47	Sunflower County
—762 48	Humphreys County
—762 49	Yazoo County

*Class parts of this physiographic region or feature as instructed under —4–9

—762 5	South central counties (Piney woods region)
	Class here *Pearl River
—762 51	Hinds County
	Class here Jackson
—762 52	Copiah County
—762 53	Lincoln and Lawrence Counties
—762 534	Lincoln County
—762 536	Lawrence County
—762 54	Jefferson Davis and Covington Counties
—762 543	Jefferson Davis County
—762 545	Covington County
—762 55	Jones County
—762 57	Wayne and Jasper Counties
—762 573	Wayne County
—762 575	Jasper County
—762 58	Smith and Simpson Counties
—762 582	Smith County
—762 585	Simpson County
—762 59	Rankin County
—762 6	Central and east central counties (Plateau region)
	For Northern Plateau region, see —7628
—762 62	Madison and Holmes Counties
—762 623	Madison County
—762 625	Holmes County
—762 63	Carroll and Grenada Counties
—762 633	Carroll County
—762 635	Grenada County
	Class here *Grenada Lake
—762 64	Montgomery and Attala Counties
—762 642	Montgomery County
—762 644	Attala County
—762 65	Leake and Scott Counties
—762 653	Leake County
—762 655	Scott County

*Class parts of this physiographic region or feature as instructed under —4–9

—762 67	Newton, Clarke, Lauderdale Counties
—762 672	Newton County
—762 673	Clarke County
—762 676	Lauderdale County
	For Meridian, see —762677
—762 677	Meridian
—762 68	Kemper and Neshoba Counties
—762 683	Kemper County
—762 685	Neshoba County
—762 69	Winston, Choctaw, Webster Counties
—762 692	Winston County
—762 694	Choctaw County
—762 697	Webster County
—762 8	Northwestern counties (Northern Plateau region)
—762 81	Calhoun County
—762 82	Yalobusha County
	Class here *Enid Lake
—762 83	Lafayette County
	Class here *Sardis Lake
—762 84	Panola County
—762 85	Tate County
	Class here *Arkabutla Lake
—762 86	Tunica County
—762 87	De Soto County
—762 88	Marshall County
—762 89	Benton County
—762 9	Northeastern counties
—762 92	Tippah and Union Counties
—762 923	Tippah County
—762 925	Union County
—762 93	Pontotoc and Lee Counties
—762 932	Pontotoc County
—762 935	Lee County
—762 94	Chickasaw and Clay Counties

*Class parts of this physiographic region or feature as instructed under —4–9

—762 942	Chickasaw County
—762 945	Clay County
—762 95	Oktibbeha and Noxubee Counties
—762 953	Oktibbeha County
—762 955	Noxubee County
—762 97	Lowndes and Monroe Counties
—762 973	Lowndes County
—762 975	Monroe County
—762 98	Itawamba and Prentiss Counties
—762 982	Itawamba County
—762 985	Prentiss County
—762 99	Alcorn and Tishomingo Counties
—762 993	Alcorn County
—762 995	Tishomingo County
—763	Louisiana
—763 1	Eastern parishes
—763 11	Washington Parish
—763 12	Saint Tammany Parish
—763 13	Tangipahoa Parish
—763 14	Livingston Parish
—763 15	Saint Helena Parish
—763 16	East Feliciana Parish
—763 17	West Feliciana Parish
—763 18	East Baton Rouge Parish
	Class here Baton Rouge
—763 19	Ascension Parish
—763 3	Southeastern parishes (Mississippi Delta)
—763 31	Saint James Parish
—763 32	Saint John the Baptist Parish
	Including *Lake Maurepas, *Lake Des Allemands
—763 33	Saint Charles Parish
	Class here *Lake Salvador
—763 34	*Lake Pontchartrain
—763 35	Orleans Parish (New Orleans)

*Class parts of this physiographic region or feature as instructed under —4–9

—763 36	Saint Bernard Parish
—763 37	Plaquemines Parish
—763 38	Jefferson Parish
—763 39	Lafourche Parish
—763 4	South central parishes
—763 41	Terrebonne Parish
—763 42	Saint Mary Parish
—763 43	Assumption Parish
—763 44	Iberville Parish
—763 45	West Baton Rouge and Pointe Coupee Parishes
—763 452	West Baton Rouge Parish
—763 454	Pointe Coupee Parish
—763 46	Saint Landry Parish
—763 47	Lafayette Parish
—763 48	Saint Martin Parish
—763 49	Iberia Parish
	Class here *Grand Lake
—763 5	Southwestern parishes
—763 51	Vermilion Parish
—763 52	Cameron Parish
	Including Calcasieu, Grand, *Sabine Lakes
—763 54	Calcasieu Parish
—763 55	Jefferson Davis Parish
—763 56	Acadia Parish
—763 57	Evangeline Parish
—763 58	Allen Parish
—763 59	Beauregard Parish
—763 6	West central parishes
	Class here *Red River in Louisiana
—763 61	Vernon Parish
—763 62	Sabine Parish
	Class here *Toledo Bend Reservoir
—763 63	De Soto Parish
—763 64	Red River Parish

*Class parts of this physiographic region or feature as instructed under —4–9

—763 65	Natchitoches Parish
—763 66	Winn Parish
—763 67	Grant Parish
—763 69	Rapides Parish
—763 7	East central parishes
	Class here *Ouachita River
—763 71	Avoyelles Parish
—763 73	Concordia Parish
—763 74	Catahoula Parish
—763 75	La Salle Parish
—763 76	Caldwell Parish
—763 77	Franklin Parish
—763 79	Tensas Parish
—763 8	Northeastern parishes
—763 81	Madison Parish
—763 82	East Carroll Parish
—763 83	West Carroll Parish
—763 84	Morehouse Parish
—763 86	Richland Parish
—763 87	Ouachita Parish
—763 89	Union Parish
—763 9	Northwestern parishes
—763 91	Lincoln Parish
—763 92	Jackson Parish
—763 93	Bienville Parish
—763 94	Claiborne Parish
—763 96	Webster Parish
—763 97	Bossier Parish
—763 99	Caddo Parish
	Including *Caddo Lake
	Class here Shreveport
—764	Texas
	Class here *Brazos, *Colorado Rivers

*Class parts of this physiographic region or feature as instructed under —4–9

—764 1	Coastal plains

Use of this number for comprehensive works on Brazos and Colorado Rivers discontinued; class in —764

For East Texas timber belt and blackland prairie, see —7642; Rio Grande Plain, —7644

—764 11	Nueces and neighboring counties

Class here *Nueces River

—764 113	Nueces County

Class here Corpus Christi

—764 115	San Patricio County
—764 117	Bee County
—764 119	Refugio County
—764 12	Calhoun and neighboring counties

Class here *Guadalupe, *San Antonio rivers

—764 121	Calhoun County
—764 122	Aransas County
—764 123	Goliad County
—764 125	Victoria County
—764 127	Jackson County
—764 13	Matagorda and neighboring counties
—764 132	Matagorda County
—764 133	Wharton County
—764 135	Fort Bend County
—764 137	Brazoria County
—764 139	Galveston County
—764 14	Harris and neighboring counties

Class here *East Texas; *Sabine, *Trinity rivers

—764 141	Harris County
—764 141 1	Houston
—764 143	Chambers County
—764 145	Jefferson County
—764 147	Orange County
—764 15	Montgomery and neighboring counties

Class here *Neches River

—764 153	Montgomery County

*Class parts of this physiographic region or feature as instructed under —4–9

—764 155	Liberty County
—764 157	Hardin County
—764 159	Jasper County
—764 16	Newton, Tyler, and neighboring counties
—764 162	Newton County
—764 163	Tyler County
—764 165	Polk County
—764 167	San Jacinto County
—764 169	Walker County
—764 17	Trinity and neighboring counties
—764 172	Trinity County
—764 173	Angelina County
—764 175	San Augustine County
—764 177	Sabine County
—764 179	Shelby County
—764 18	Nacogdoches and neighboring counties
—764 182	Nacogdoches County
—764 183	Cherokee County
—764 185	Rusk County
—764 187	Panola County
—764 189	Gregg County
—764 19	Harrison and neighboring counties
—764 192	Harrison County
—764 193	Marion County
—764 195	Cass County
—764 197	Bowie County
—764 2	**East Texas timber belt and blackland prairie**
	For Austin-San Antonio region, see —7643
—764 21	Red River and neighboring counties
—764 212	Red River County
—764 213	Franklin County
—764 215	Titus County
—764 217	Morris County
—764 219	Camp County

—764 22	Upshur and neighboring counties
—764 222	Upshur County
—764 223	Wood County
—764 225	Smith County
—764 227	Henderson County
—764 229	Anderson County
—764 23	Freestone and neighboring counties
—764 232	Freestone County
—764 233	Leon County
—764 235	Houston County
—764 237	Madison County
—764 239	Robertson County
—764 24	Burleson and neighboring counties
—764 241	Burleson County
—764 242	Brazos County
—764 243	Grimes County
—764 245	Washington County
—764 247	Lee County
—764 249	Waller County
—764 25	Fayette and neighboring counties
—764 251	Fayette County
—764 252	Austin County
—764 253	Colorado County
—764 255	Lavaca County
—764 257	Gonzales County
—764 259	De Witt County
—764 26	Lamar and Fannin Counties
	Class here *blackland prairie
—764 263	Lamar County
—764 265	Fannin County
—764 27	Hunt and neighboring counties
—764 272	Hunt County
—764 273	Delta County
—764 274	Hopkins County

*Class parts of this physiographic region or feature as instructed under —4–9

—764 275	Rains County
—764 276	Van Zandt County
—764 277	Kaufman County
—764 278	Rockwall County
—764 28	Dallas and neighboring counties
—764 281	Dallas and Ellis Counties
—764 281 1	Dallas County

For Dallas, see —7642812

—764 281 2	Dallas

Class here Dallas-Fort Worth metropolitan area

For Fort Worth, see —7645315

—764 281 5	Ellis County
—764 282	Navarro County
—764 283	Hill County
—764 284	McLennan County
—764 285	Limestone County
—764 286	Falls County
—764 287	Bell County
—764 288	Milam County
—764 289	Williamson County
—764 3	Austin-San Antonio region

For Hays County, see —764888; Comal County, —764887

—764 31	Travis County
	Class here Austin
—764 32	Bastrop County
—764 33	Caldwell County
—764 34	Guadalupe County
—764 35	Bexar County
—764 351	San Antonio
—764 4	Rio Grande Plain (Lower Rio Grande Valley)
	Class here *Rio Grande
—764 42	Medina County
—764 43	Uvalde and neighboring counties
—764 432	Uvalde County

*Class parts of this physiographic region or feature as instructed under —4–9

—764 433	Kinney County
—764 435	Maverick County
—764 437	Zavala County
—764 44	Frio and neighboring counties
—764 442	Frio County
—764 443	Atascosa County
—764 444	Karnes County
—764 445	Wilson County
—764 447	Live Oak County
—764 45	McMullen and neighboring counties
—764 452	McMullen County
—764 453	La Salle County
—764 455	Dimmit County
—764 46	Webb and neighboring counties
—764 462	Webb County
—764 463	Duval County
—764 465	Jim Wells County
—764 47	Kleberg and neighboring counties
	Class here *Padre Island
—764 472	Kleberg County
—764 473	Kenedy County
—764 475	Brooks County
—764 48	Jim Hogg and neighboring counties
—764 482	Jim Hogg County
—764 483	Zapata County
—764 485	Starr County
—764 49	Hidalgo and neighboring counties
—764 492	Hidalgo County
—764 493	Willacy County
—764 495	Cameron County
—764 5	**North central plains**
	For Burnet-Llano region, see —7646; *Northwestern lowland,* —7647
—764 51	Mills and neighboring counties
	Class here *Grand Prairie

*Class parts of this physiographic region or feature as instructed under —4–9

—764 512	Mills County
—764 513	Lampasas County
—764 515	Coryell County
—764 518	Bosque County
—764 52	Somervell and neighboring counties
—764 521	Somervell County
—764 522	Hood County
—764 524	Johnson County
—764 53	Tarrant and neighboring counties
—764 531	Tarrant County
—764 531 5	Fort Worth

                 Class comprehensive works on Dallas-Fort Worth metropolitan area in —7642812

—764 532	Wise County
—764 533	Cooke County
—764 54	Montague and neighboring counties
—764 541	Montague County
—764 542	Clay County
—764 543	Archer County
—764 544	Jack County
—764 545	Young County
—764 546	Stephens County
—764 547	Eastland County
—764 548	Brown County
—764 549	Hamilton County
—764 55	Erath and neighboring counties
—764 551	Erath County
—764 552	Palo Pinto County
—764 553	Parker County
—764 554	Comanche County
—764 555	Denton County
—764 556	Collin County
—764 557	Grayson County
—764 6	Burnet-Llano region
—764 62	Llano County

—764 63	Burnet County
—764 64	Blanco County
—764 65	Gillespie County
—764 66	Mason County
—764 67	McCulloch County
—764 68	San Saba County
—764 7	Northwestern lowland
—764 71	Concho County
—764 72	Tom Green and neighboring counties
—764 721	Tom Green County
—764 723	Coke County
—764 724	Runnels County
—764 725	Coleman County
—764 726	Callahan County
—764 727	Taylor County
—764 728	Nolan County
—764 729	Mitchell County
—764 73	Scurry and neighboring counties
—764 731	Scurry County
—764 732	Fisher County
—764 733	Jones County
—764 734	Shackelford County
—764 735	Throckmorton County
—764 736	Haskell County
—764 737	Stonewall County
—764 738	Kent County
—764 74	Dickens and neighboring counties
—764 741	Dickens County
—764 742	King County
—764 743	Knox County
—764 744	Baylor County
—764 745	Wichita County
—764 746	Wilbarger County
—764 747	Hardeman County

—764 748	Foard County
—764 75	Cottle and neighboring counties
—764 751	Cottle County
—764 752	Motley County
—764 753	Hall County
—764 754	Childress County
—764 8	Great Plains
	Class here *Llano Estacado
—764 81	Northern Panhandle counties
—764 812	Dallam County
—764 813	Sherman County
—764 814	Hansford County
—764 815	Ochiltree County
—764 816	Lipscomb County
—764 817	Hemphill County
—764 818	Roberts County
—764 82	Middle Panhandle counties
—764 821	Hutchinson County
—764 822	Moore County
—764 823	Hartley County
—764 824	Oldham County
—764 825	Potter County
—764 826	Carson County
—764 827	Gray County
—764 828	Wheeler County
—764 83	Southern Panhandle counties
—764 831	Collingsworth County
—764 832	Donley County
—764 833	Armstrong County
—764 834	Randall County
—764 835	Deaf Smith County
—764 836	Parmer County
—764 837	Castro County
—764 838	Swisher County

*Class parts of this physiographic region or feature as instructed under —4–9

—764 839	Briscoe County
—764 84	Floyd and neighboring counties
—764 841	Floyd County
—764 842	Hale County
—764 843	Lamb County
—764 844	Bailey County
—764 845	Cochran County
—764 846	Hockley County
—764 847	Lubbock County
—764 848	Crosby County
—764 849	Yoakum County
—764 85	Lynn and neighboring counties
—764 851	Lynn County
—764 852	Garza County
—764 853	Borden County
—764 854	Dawson County
—764 855	Gaines County
—764 856	Andrews County
—764 857	Martin County
—764 858	Howard County
—764 859	Terry County
—764 86	Midland and neighboring counties
—764 861	Midland County
—764 862	Ector County
—764 863	Upton County
—764 87	Counties of *Edwards Plateau
	Balcones Escarpment relocated to —76488
—764 871	Sterling County
—764 872	Glasscock County
—764 873	Reagan County
—764 874	Irion County
—764 875	Crockett County
—764 876	Schleicher County
—764 877	Menard County

*Class parts of this physiographic region or feature as instructed under —4–9

—764 878	Kimble County
—764 879	Sutton County
—764 88	Val Verde and neighboring counties
	Class here *Balcones Escarpment [*formerly* —76487]
—764 881	Val Verde County
—764 882	Edwards County
—764 883	Real County
—764 884	Kerr County
—764 885	Bandera County
—764 886	Kendall County
—764 887	Comal County
—764 888	Hays County
—764 9	**Western mountain and basin region**
	Class here *Pecos River
—764 91	Pecos Basin counties
—764 912	Loving County
—764 913	Winkler County
—764 914	Ward County
—764 915	Crane County
—764 92	Counties of Stockton Plateau
—764 922	Terrell County
—764 923	Pecos County
—764 924	Reeves County
—764 93	Counties of Big Bend region
—764 932	Brewster County
	Including Big Bend National Park
—764 933	Presidio County
—764 934	Jeff Davis County
—764 94	Culberson County
	Including Guadalupe Mountains National Park
	Class Guadalupe Mountains National Park in Hudspeth County in —76495
—764 95	Hudspeth County

*Class parts of this physiographic region or feature as instructed under —4–9

—764 96	El Paso County
	Class here El Paso; *upper Rio Grande of Texas
—766	Oklahoma
	Class here *Canadian River
—766 1	Northwestern counties
	Class here former Oklahoma Territory; *North Canadian River
	Use of this number for comprehensive works on Canadian River discontinued; class in —766
	Class a specific part of former Oklahoma Territory not provided for here with the part, e.g., Beckham County —76643
—766 13	Panhandle counties
	For Beaver County, see —76614
—766 132	Cimarron County
—766 135	Texas County
—766 14	Beaver County
—766 15	Harper and Ellis Counties
—766 153	Harper County
—766 155	Ellis County
—766 16	Roger Mills County
—766 17	Custer County
—766 18	Dewey County
—766 19	Woodward County
—766 2	North central counties
—766 21	Woods County
—766 22	Alfalfa County
—766 23	Grant County
—766 24	Kay County
—766 25	Osage County
—766 26	Pawnee County
—766 27	Noble County
—766 28	Garfield County
—766 29	Major County
—766 3	Central counties
	Class here *Cimarron River

*Class parts of this physiographic region or feature as instructed under —4–9

—766 31	Blaine County
—766 32	Kingfisher County
—766 33	Logan County
—766 34	Payne County
—766 35	Lincoln County
—766 36	Pottawatomie County
—766 37	Cleveland County
—766 38	Oklahoma County

> Class here Oklahoma City

| —766 39 | Canadian County |

—766 4   Southwestern counties

—766 41	Caddo County
—766 42	Washita County
—766 43	Beckham County
—766 44	Greer and Harmon Counties
—766 443	Greer County
—766 445	Harmon County
—766 45	Jackson County
—766 46	Tillman County
—766 47	Kiowa County
—766 48	Comanche County
—766 49	Cotton County

—766 5   South central counties

> Class here former Indian Territory; *Arbuckle Mountains; *Washita River

> Class a specific part of former Indian Territory not provided for here with the part, e.g., Choctaw County —76663

—766 52	Jefferson County
—766 53	Stephens County
—766 54	Grady County
—766 55	McClain County
—766 56	Garvin County
—766 57	Murray County

> Including Platt National Park

*Class parts of this physiographic region or feature as instructed under —4–9

—766 58	Carter County
—766 59	Love County
—766 6	**Southeastern counties**

        Class here *Ouachita Mountains; *Red River

—766 61	Marshall County

        Class here *Lake Texoma

—766 62	Bryan County
—766 63	Choctaw County
—766 64	McCurtain County
—766 65	Pushmataha County
—766 66	Atoka County
—766 67	Coal County
—766 68	Johnston County
—766 69	Pontotoc County
—766 7	**Southeast central counties**
—766 71	Seminole County
—766 72	Hughes County
—766 73	Okfuskee County
—766 74	McIntosh County
—766 75	Pittsburg County
—766 76	Latimer County
—766 77	Haskell County
—766 79	Le Flore County
—766 8	**Northeast central counties**

        Class here *Ozark Plateau in Oklahoma; *Boston Mountains in Oklahoma; *Arkansas River in Oklahoma

—766 81	Sequoyah County
—766 82	Muskogee County
—766 83	Okmulgee County
—766 84	Creek County
—766 86	Tulsa County

        Class here Tulsa

—766 87	Wagoner County

        Class here *Fort Gibson Reservoir

*Class parts of this physiographic region or feature as instructed under —4–9

—766 88   Cherokee County

                   Including *Tenkiller Ferry Reservoir

—766 89   Adair County

—766 9   Northeastern counties

—766 91   Delaware County

                   Class here *Lake of the Cherokees

—766 93   Mayes County

—766 94   Rogers County

—766 96   Washington County

—766 97   Nowata County

—766 98   Craig County

—766 99   Ottawa County

—767   Arkansas

—767 1   Northwestern counties

                   Class here *Ozark Plateau; *Boston Mountains

—767 13   Benton County

—767 14   Washington County

—767 15   Madison County

—767 16   Newton County

—767 17   Carroll County

—767 18   Boone County

—767 19   Marion and Searcy Counties

—767 193   Marion County

                   Class here *Bull Shoals Lake

—767 195   Searcy County

—767 2   North central counties

                   Class here *Black, *White Rivers

—767 21   Baxter County

                   Class here *Norfork Lake

—767 22   Fulton County

—767 23   Sharp County

—767 24   Randolph County

—767 25   Lawrence County

—767 26   Independence County

*Class parts of this physiographic region or feature as instructed under —4–9

—767 27	Izard County
—767 28	Stone and Cleburne Counties
—767 283	Stone County
—767 285	Cleburne County
—767 29	Van Buren County
—767 3	Northwest central counties
	Class here *Arkansas River
—767 31	Conway County
—767 32	Pope County
—767 33	Johnson County
—767 34	Franklin County
—767 35	Crawford County
—767 36	Sebastian County
—767 37	Logan County
—767 38	Yell County
—767 39	Perry County
—767 4	Southwest central counties
	Class here *Ouachita Mountains in Arkansas
—767 41	Garland County
	Including Hot Springs National Park
—767 42	Hot Spring County
—767 43	Montgomery County
—767 44	Scott County
—767 45	Polk County
—767 47	Sevier County
—767 48	Howard and Pike Counties
—767 483	Howard County
—767 485	Pike County
—767 49	Clark County
—767 5	Southwestern counties
—767 52	Nevada County
—767 54	Hempstead County
—767 55	Little River County
—767 56	Miller County

*Class parts of this physiographic region or feature as instructed under —4–9

—767 57	Lafayette County
—767 59	Columbia County
—767 6	**South central counties**
—767 61	Union County
—767 63	Bradley County
—767 64	Calhoun County
—767 66	Ouachita County
—767 67	Dallas County
—767 69	Cleveland County
—767 7	**Central counties**
—767 71	Grant County
—767 72	Saline County
—767 73	Pulaski County
	Class here Little Rock
—767 74	Faulkner County
—767 76	White County
—767 77	Prairie County
—767 78	Lonoke County
—767 79	Jefferson County
—767 8	**Southeastern counties**
	Class here *Mississippi River in Arkansas
—767 82	Lincoln and Drew Counties
—767 823	Lincoln County
—767 825	Drew County
—767 83	Ashley County
—767 84	Chicot County
—767 85	Desha County
—767 86	Arkansas County
—767 87	Monroe County
—767 88	Phillips County
—767 89	Lee County
—767 9	**Northeastern counties**
	Class here *Saint Francis River
—767 91	Saint Francis County

*Class parts of this physiographic region or feature as instructed under —4–9

—767 92	Woodruff County
—767 93	Cross County
—767 94	Crittenden County
—767 95	Mississippi County
—767 96	Poinsett County
—767 97	Jackson County
—767 98	Craighead County
—767 99	Greene and Clay Counties
—767 993	Greene County
—767 995	Clay County
—768	Tennessee

Class here *Tennessee River and Valley

—768 1	Mississippi Valley counties
—768 12	Lake County

Including *Reelfoot Lake

—768 13	Obion County
—768 15	Dyer County
—768 16	Lauderdale County
—768 17	Tipton County
—768 19	Shelby County

Class here Memphis

—768 2	West Tennessee Plain counties
—768 21	Fayette County
—768 22	Haywood and Crockett Counties
—768 223	Haywood County
—768 225	Crockett County
—768 23	Gibson County
—768 24	Weakley County
—768 25	Carroll County
—768 26	Henderson and Chester Counties
—768 263	Henderson County
—768 265	Chester County
—768 27	Madison County
—768 28	Hardeman County

*Class parts of this physiographic region or feature as instructed under —4–9

—768 29	McNairy County
—768 3	**Western Tennessee River Valley counties**
—768 31	Hardin County
—768 32	Decatur County
—768 33	Benton County
—768 34	Henry County
—768 35	Stewart County
—768 36	Houston County
—768 37	Humphreys County
—768 38	Perry County
—768 39	Wayne County
—768 4	**West Highland Rim counties**

> Class here comprehensive works on Highland Rim counties
>
> *For east Highland Rim counties, see —7686*

—768 42	Lawrence County
—768 43	Lewis and Hickman Counties
—768 432	Lewis County
—768 434	Hickman County

> Class here *Duck River

—768 44	Dickson County
—768 45	Montgomery County
—768 46	Cheatham and Robertson Counties
—768 462	Cheatham County
—768 464	Robertson County
—768 47	Sumner County
—768 48	Trousdale and Macon Counties
—768 482	Trousdale County
—768 484	Macon County
—768 49	Clay County

> Class here *Dale Hollow Lake

—768 5	**Central Basin counties**

> Class here *Cumberland River

—768 51	Jackson County
—768 52	Smith County

*Class parts of this physiographic region or feature as instructed under —4–9

—768 53	De Kalb and Cannon Counties
—768 532	De Kalb County
	Class here *Center Hill Lake
—768 535	Cannon County
—768 54	Wilson County
—768 55	Davidson County
	Class here Nashville
—768 56	Williamson County
—768 57	Rutherford County
—768 58	Bedford and Marshall Counties
—768 583	Bedford County
—768 585	Marshall County
—768 59	Maury County
—768 6	East Highland Rim counties
—768 61	Giles County
—768 62	Lincoln and Moore Counties
—768 624	Lincoln County
—768 627	Moore County
—768 63	Franklin County
—768 64	Coffee County
—768 65	Warren and Van Buren Counties
—768 653	Warren County
—768 657	Van Buren County
—768 66	White County
—768 67	Putnam County
—768 68	Overton and Pickett Counties
—768 684	Overton County
—768 687	Pickett County
—768 69	Fentress County
—768 7	Counties of *Cumberland Plateau
—768 71	Scott County
—768 72	Campbell County
—768 73	Anderson County
	Class here *Clinch River

*Class parts of this physiographic region or feature as instructed under —4–9

—768 74	Morgan County
—768 75	Cumberland County
—768 76	Bledsoe County
—768 77	Sequatchie County
	Class here *Sequatchie River
—768 78	Grundy County
—768 79	Marion County
—768 8	**Southeastern counties**
—768 82	Hamilton County
	Including *Lookout Mountain
	Class here Chattanooga; *Chickamauga Lake
—768 83	Rhea and Meigs Counties
—768 834	Rhea County
—768 836	Meigs County
—768 84	Roane County
—768 85	Knox County
	Including *Fort Loudoun Lake
	Class here Knoxville
—768 86	Loudon and McMinn Counties
—768 863	Loudon County
	Including *Little Tennessee River
—768 865	McMinn County
—768 87	Bradley and Polk Counties
—768 873	Bradley County
—768 875	Polk County
—768 88	Monroe and Blount Counties
—768 883	Monroe County
—768 885	Blount County
—768 89	*Great Smoky Mountains area
	Class here *Great Smoky Mountains National Park
—768 893	Sevier County
—768 895	Cocke County
	Class here *French Broad River

*Class parts of this physiographic region or feature as instructed under —4–9

—768 9   Northeastern counties

        Class here *Holston River

—768 91   Greene County

        Including *Bald Mountains

—768 92   Hamblen and Jefferson Counties

—768 923   Hamblen County

        Class here *Cherokee Lake

—768 924   Jefferson County

        Class here *Douglas Lake

—768 93   Grainger and Union Counties

—768 932   Grainger County

—768 935   Union County

        Class here *Norris Lake

—768 94   Claiborne and Hancock Counties

—768 944   Claiborne County

        Class here *Cumberland Mountains in Tennessee; *Cumberland Gap

—768 946   Hancock County

—768 95   Hawkins County

—768 96   Sullivan County

        Including *Boone, *South Holston Lakes

—768 97   Washington County

—768 98   Unicoi and Carter Counties

—768 982   Unicoi County

—768 984   Carter County

        Class here *Iron Mountains; *Watauga Lake

—768 99   Johnson County

        Including *Stone Mountains

—769   Kentucky

        Comprehensive works on Ohio River relocated to —77

—769 1   Southern mountain region counties

        Including *Cumberland Plateau in Kentucky

        Class here *Cumberland Mountains

—769 12   Bell and Knox Counties

*Class parts of this physiographic region or feature as instructed under —4–9

—769 123	Bell County
	Including *Pine Mountain
—769 125	Knox County
—769 13	Whitley and McCreary Counties
—769 132	Whitley County
—769 135	McCreary County
—769 14	Laurel and Clay Counties
—769 143	Laurel County
—769 145	Clay County
—769 15	Leslie and Harlan Counties
—769 152	Leslie County
—769 154	Harlan County
	Including *Big Black Mountains
—769 16	Letcher and Knott Counties
—769 163	Letcher County
—769 165	Knott County
—769 17	Perry and Owsley Counties
—769 173	Perry County
—769 176	Owsley County
—769 18	Jackson and Lee Counties
—769 183	Jackson County
—769 185	Lee County
—769 19	Breathitt County
—769 2	Northern mountain region counties
	Class here *Big Sandy River and *Tug Fork in Kentucky, *Levisa River
—769 21	Wolfe and Magoffin Counties
—769 213	Wolfe County
—769 215	Magoffin County
—769 22	Floyd County
—769 23	Pike County
—769 24	Martin and Johnson Counties
—769 243	Martin County
—769 245	Johnson County
—769 25	Morgan and Elliott Counties

*Class parts of this physiographic region or feature as instructed under —4–9

—769 253	Morgan County
—769 255	Elliott County
—769 26	Lawrence County
—769 27	Boyd County
—769 28	Carter County
—769 29	Greenup and Lewis Counties
—769 293	Greenup County
—769 295	Lewis County

—769 3   Northern Bluegrass counties

Class here *Licking, *Kentucky Rivers

—769 32	Mason and Bracken Counties
—769 323	Mason County
—769 325	Bracken County
—769 33	Pendleton County
—769 34	Campbell County
—769 35	Kenton County
—769 36	Boone and Gallatin Counties
—769 363	Boone County
—769 365	Gallatin County
—769 37	Carroll and Trimble Counties
—769 373	Carroll County
—769 375	Trimble County
—769 38	Oldham and Henry Counties
—769 383	Oldham County
—769 385	Henry County
—769 39	Owen and Grant Counties
—769 393	Owen County
—769 395	Grant County

—769 4   Southern Bluegrass counties

—769 41	Harrison, Robertson, Nicholas Counties
—769 413	Harrison County
—769 415	Robertson County
—769 417	Nicholas County
—769 42	Bourbon and Scott Counties

*Class parts of this physiographic region or feature as instructed under —4–9

—769 423	Bourbon County
—769 425	Scott County
—769 43	Franklin and Shelby Counties
—769 432	Franklin County
	Including Frankfort
—769 435	Shelby County
—769 44	Jefferson County
	Class here Louisville
—769 45	Bullitt and Spencer Counties
	Class here *Salt River
—769 453	Bullitt County
—769 455	Spencer County
—769 46	Anderson and Woodford Counties
—769 463	Anderson County
—769 465	Woodford County
—769 47	Lexington Fayette Urban County
—769 48	Jessamine and Mercer Counties
—769 483	Jessamine County
—769 485	Mercer County
—769 49	Washington and Nelson Counties
—769 493	Washington County
—769 495	Nelson County
—769 5	The Knobs counties
—769 51	Marion County
—769 52	Boyle and Garrard Counties
—769 523	Boyle County
—769 525	Garrard County
—769 53	Madison County
—769 54	Clark County
—769 55	Montgomery and Bath Counties
—769 553	Montgomery County
—769 555	Bath County
—769 56	Fleming County
—769 57	Rowan County

*Class parts of this physiographic region or feature as instructed under —4–9

—769 58	Menifee and Powell Counties
—769 583	Menifee County
—769 585	Powell County
—769 59	Estill County
—769 6	Eastern Pennyroyal counties

Class here *Highland Rim in Kentucky, comprehensive works on Pennyroyal counties

For western Pennyroyal counties, see —7697

—769 62	Rockcastle and Lincoln Counties
—769 623	Rockcastle County
—769 625	Lincoln County
—769 63	Pulaski County

Class here *Lake Cumberland

—769 64	Wayne County
—769 65	Clinton and Russell Counties
—769 653	Clinton County
—769 655	Russell County
—769 66	Casey County
—769 67	Taylor and Adair Counties
—769 673	Taylor County
—769 675	Adair County
—769 68	Cumberland and Monroe Counties
—769 683	Cumberland County
—769 685	Monroe County
—769 69	Metcalfe and Green Counties
—769 693	Metcalfe County
—769 695	Green County
—769 7	Western Pennyroyal counties
—769 71	Larue and Hart Counties
—769 713	Larue County
—769 715	Hart County
—769 72	Barren County
—769 73	Allen and Simpson Counties
—769 732	Allen County

*Class parts of this physiographic region or feature as instructed under —4–9

—769 735	Simpson County
—769 74	Warren County
—769 75	Edmonson and Butler Counties and environs
—769 752	Edmonson County
—769 754	*Mammoth Cave National Park
—769 755	Butler County
—769 76	Logan County
—769 77	Todd County
—769 78	Christian County
—769 79	Trigg County
	Class here *Land Between the Lakes; *Lake Barkley
—769 8	Western Basin counties
	Class here *Green River
—769 81	Lyon and Caldwell Counties
—769 813	Lyon County
—769 815	Caldwell County
—769 82	Hopkins and McLean Counties
—769 823	Hopkins County
—769 826	McLean County
—769 83	Muhlenberg and Ohio Counties
—769 832	Muhlenberg County
—769 835	Ohio County
—769 84	Grayson and Hardin Counties
—769 842	Grayson County
—769 845	Hardin County
—769 85	Meade and Breckinridge Counties
—769 852	Meade County
—769 854	Breckinridge County
—769 86	Hancock and Daviess Counties
—769 862	Hancock County
—769 864	Daviess County
	Class here Owensboro [*formerly* —769865]
—[769 865]	Owensboro
	Relocated to —769864

*Class parts of this physiographic region or feature as instructed under —4–9

—769 87	Henderson County
—769 88	Webster and Union Counties
—769 883	Webster County
—769 885	Union County
—769 89	Crittenden and Livingston Counties
—769 893	Crittenden County
—769 895	Livingston County
	Class here *Kentucky Lake
—769 9	**Counties west of Tennessee River**
—769 91	Marshall County
—769 92	Calloway County
—769 93	Graves County
—769 95	McCracken County
—769 96	Ballard County
—769 97	Carlisle County
—769 98	Hickman County
—769 99	Fulton County
—77	**North central United States Lake states**

Class here comprehensive works on *Ohio River [*formerly* —769] and Valley, Middle West, *Mississippi River and Valley, *Great Lakes

Class each specific state of Middle West not provided for here with the state, e.g., Kansas —781

SUMMARY

—771	**Ohio**
—772	**Indiana**
—773	**Illinois**
—774	**Michigan**
—775	**Wisconsin**
—776	**Minnesota**
—777	**Iowa**
—778	**Missouri**

>	—771–776 Lake states

Class comprehensive works in —77

For New York, see —747; Pennsylvania, —748

—771	Ohio

*Class parts of this physiographic region or feature as instructed under —4–9

—771 1	**Northwestern counties**
	Class here *Maumee River
—771 11	Williams and Fulton Counties
—771 113	Williams County
—771 115	Fulton County
—771 12	Lucas County
	For Toledo, see —77113
—771 13	Toledo
—771 14	Defiance County
—771 15	Henry County
—771 16	Wood County
—771 17	Paulding County
—771 18	Putnam County
—771 19	Hancock County
—771 2	**North central counties**
	Class here *Sandusky River; *Lake Erie
—771 21	Ottawa and Sandusky Counties
—771 212	Ottawa County
—771 214	Sandusky County
	Class here *Sandusky Bay
—771 22	Erie County
—771 23	Lorain County
—771 24	Seneca County
—771 25	Huron County
—771 26	Wyandot County
—771 27	Crawford County
—771 28	Richland County
—771 29	Ashland County
—771 3	**Northeastern counties**
—771 31	Cuyahoga County
	Class here *Cuyahoga River
	For Cleveland, see —77132
—771 32	Cleveland
—771 33	Lake and Geauga Counties

*Class parts of this physiographic region or feature as instructed under —4–9

—771 334	Lake County
—771 336	Geauga County
—771 34	Ashtabula County
—771 35	Medina County
—771 36	Summit County
	Class here Akron
—771 37	Portage County
	Including *Berlin Reservoir
—771 38	Trumbull County
—771 39	Mahoning County
	Class here Youngstown; *Mahoning River
—771 4	**West central counties**
—771 41	Van Wert and Mercer Counties
—771 413	Van Wert County
—771 415	Mercer County
	Class here *Lake Saint Marys
—771 42	Allen County
—771 43	Auglaize County
—771 44	Hardin County
—771 45	Shelby County
—771 46	Logan and Champaign Counties
—771 463	Logan County
—771 465	Champaign County
—771 47	Darke County
—771 48	Miami County
—771 49	Clark County
—771 5	**Central counties**
	Class here *Scioto River
—771 51	Marion and Morrow Counties
—771 514	Marion County
—771 516	Morrow County
—771 52	Knox County
—771 53	Union and Delaware Counties
—771 532	Union County

*Class parts of this physiographic region or feature as instructed under —4–9

—771 535	Delaware County
—771 54	Licking County
—771 55	Madison County
—771 56	Franklin County
	For Columbus, see —77157
—771 57	Columbus
—771 58	Fairfield County
—771 59	Perry County
—771 6	**East central counties**
—771 61	Wayne County
—771 62	Stark County
—771 63	Columbiana County
—771 64	Holmes County
—771 65	Coshocton County
—771 66	Tuscarawas County
	Class here *Tuscarawas River
—771 67	Carroll County
—771 68	Harrison County
—771 69	Jefferson County
—771 7	**Southwestern counties**
	Class here *Miami River
—771 71	Preble County
—771 72	Montgomery County
	For Dayton, see —77173
—771 73	Dayton
—771 74	Greene County
—771 75	Butler County
—771 76	Warren and Clinton Counties
—771 763	Warren County
—771 765	Clinton County
—771 77	Hamilton County
	For Cincinnati, see —77178
—771 78	Cincinnati
—771 79	Clermont and Brown Counties

*Class parts of this physiographic region or feature as instructed under —4–9

—771 794	Clermont County
—771 796	Brown County
—771 8	**South central counties**
—771 81	Fayette and Pickaway Counties
—771 813	Fayette County
—771 815	Pickaway County
—771 82	Ross County
—771 83	Hocking and Vinton Counties
—771 835	Hocking County
—771 837	Vinton County
—771 84	Highland and Pike Counties
—771 845	Highland County
—771 847	Pike County
—771 85	Jackson County
—771 86	Adams County
—771 87	Scioto County
—771 88	Lawrence County
—771 89	Gallia County
—771 9	**Southeastern counties**
—771 91	Muskingum County
	Class here *Muskingum River
—771 92	Guernsey County
—771 93	Belmont County
—771 94	Morgan County
—771 95	Noble County
—771 96	Monroe County
—771 97	Athens County
	Class here *Hocking River
—771 98	Washington County
—771 99	Meigs County
—772	**Indiana**
—772 1	**Southeastern counties**
—772 11	Dearborn County
—772 12	Ohio and Switzerland Counties

*Class parts of this physiographic region or feature as instructed under —4–9

—772 123	Ohio County
—772 125	Switzerland County
—772 13	Jefferson County
—772 14	Ripley County
—772 15	Franklin County
—772 16	Decatur County
—772 17	Jennings County
—772 18	Scott and Clark Counties
—772 183	Scott County
—772 185	Clark County
—772 19	Floyd County
—772 2	South central counties
—772 21	Harrison County
—772 22	Washington County
—772 23	Jackson County
—772 24	Bartholomew County
—772 25	Brown and Monroe Counties
—772 253	Brown County
—772 255	Monroe County
—772 26	Lawrence County
—772 27	Orange County
—772 28	Crawford County
—772 29	Perry County
—772 3	Southwestern counties
	Class here *White River
—772 31	Spencer County
—772 32	Warrick County
—772 33	Vanderburgh County
—772 34	Posey County
—772 35	Gibson County
—772 36	Pike County
—772 37	Dubois County
—772 38	Martin and Daviess Counties
—772 382	Martin County

*Class parts of this physiographic region or feature as instructed under —4–9

—772 385	Daviess County
—772 39	Knox County
—772 4	West central counties
	Class here *Wabash River
—772 41	Sullivan County
—772 42	Greene County
—772 43	Owen County
—772 44	Clay County
—772 45	Vigo County
—772 46	Vermillion and Parke Counties
—772 462	Vermillion County
—772 465	Parke County
—772 47	Fountain County
—772 48	Montgomery County
—772 49	Putnam County
—772 5	Central counties
—772 51	Morgan and Johnson Counties
—772 513	Morgan County
—772 515	Johnson County
—772 52	Marion County
	Class here Indianapolis
—772 53	Hendricks County
—772 54	Boone County
—772 55	Clinton and Tipton Counties
—772 553	Clinton County
—772 555	Tipton County
—772 56	Hamilton County
—772 57	Madison County
—772 58	Hancock County
—772 59	Shelby County
—772 6	East central counties
—772 61	Rush County
—772 62	Fayette and Union Counties
—772 623	Fayette County

*Class parts of this physiographic region or feature as instructed under —4–9

—772 625	Union County
—772 63	Wayne County
—772 64	Henry County
—772 65	Delaware County
	Including Muncie
—772 66	Randolph County
—772 67	Jay County
—772 68	Blackford County
—772 69	Grant County
—772 7	Northeastern counties
—772 71	Huntington County
—772 72	Wells County
—772 73	Adams County
—772 74	Allen County
	Class here Fort Wayne
—772 75	Whitley County
—772 76	Noble County
—772 77	De Kalb County
—772 78	Steuben County
—772 79	Lagrange County
—772 8	North central counties
—772 81	Elkhart County
—772 82	Kosciusko County
—772 83	Wabash County
—772 84	Miami County
—772 85	Howard County
—772 86	Cass County
—772 87	Fulton County
—772 88	Marshall County
—772 89	Saint Joseph County
	Class here South Bend
—772 9	Northwestern counties
—772 91	La Porte County
—772 92	Starke and Pulaski Counties

—772 923	Starke County
—772 925	Pulaski County
—772 93	White County
—772 94	Carroll County
—772 95	Tippecanoe County
—772 96	Warren County
—772 97	Benton, Newton, Jasper Counties
—772 972	Benton County
—772 974	Newton County
—772 977	Jasper County
—772 98	Porter County
—772 99	Lake County
	Including Gary
—773	**Illinois**
—773 1	**Cook County**
—773 11	Chicago
—773 2	**Northeastern counties**
	Class here *Des Plaines River
	For Cook County, see —7731
—773 21	Lake County
—773 22	McHenry County
—773 23	Kane County
—773 24	Du Page County
—773 25	Will County
—773 26	Kendall and Grundy Counties
—773 263	Kendall County
—773 265	Grundy County
—773 27	La Salle County
—773 28	De Kalb County
—773 29	Boone County
—773 3	**Northwestern counties**
	Class here *Rock River
—773 31	Winnebago County
—773 32	Ogle County

*Class parts of this physiographic region or feature as instructed under —4–9

—773 33	Stephenson County
—773 34	Jo Daviess and Carroll Counties
—773 343	Jo Daviess County
—773 345	Carroll County
—773 35	Whiteside County
—773 36	Lee County
—773 37	Bureau and Putnam Counties
—773 372	Bureau County
—773 375	Putnam County
—773 38	Henry County
—773 39	Rock Island and Mercer Counties
—773 393	Rock Island County

Class comprehensive works on Davenport-Rock Island-Moline tri-city area in —77769

—773 395	Mercer County
—773 4	West central counties
—773 41	Henderson and Warren Counties
—773 413	Henderson County
—773 415	Warren County
—773 42	McDonough County
—773 43	Hancock County
—773 44	Adams County
—773 45	Pike and Scott Counties
—773 453	Pike County
—773 455	Scott County
—773 46	Morgan and Cass Counties
—773 463	Morgan County
—773 465	Cass County
—773 47	Brown and Schuyler Counties
—773 473	Brown County
—773 475	Schuyler County
—773 48	Fulton County
—773 49	Knox County
—773 5	Central counties

Class here *Illinois River

*Class parts of this physiographic region or feature as instructed under —4–9

—773 51	Stark and Marshall Counties
—773 513	Stark County
—773 515	Marshall County
—773 52	Peoria County
—773 53	Woodford County
—773 54	Tazewell County
—773 55	Mason and Menard Counties
	Class here *Sangamon River
—773 553	Mason County
—773 555	Menard County
—773 56	Sangamon County
	Including Springfield
—773 57	Logan County
—773 58	Macon and De Witt Counties
—773 582	Macon County
—773 585	De Witt County
—773 59	McLean County
—773 6	East central counties
—773 61	Livingston County
—773 62	Ford County
—773 63	Kankakee County
—773 64	Iroquois County
—773 65	Vermilion County
—773 66	Champaign County
—773 67	Piatt and Moultrie Counties
—773 673	Piatt County
—773 675	Moultrie County
—773 68	Douglas County
—773 69	Edgar County
—773 7	Southeastern counties
—773 71	Clark County
—773 72	Coles County
—773 73	Cumberland County
—773 74	Jasper County

*Class parts of this physiographic region or feature as instructed under —4–9

—773 75	Crawford County
—773 76	Lawrence County
—773 77	Richland County
—773 78	Wabash County
—773 79	Counties south of Decatur
—773 791	Edwards County
—773 792	Wayne County
—773 793	Jefferson County
—773 794	Marion County
—773 795	Clay County
—773 796	Effingham County
—773 797	Fayette County
—773 798	Shelby County
—773 8	**Southwestern counties**
—773 81	Christian County
—773 82	Montgomery County
—773 83	Macoupin County
—773 84	Greene County
—773 85	Calhoun and Jersey Counties
—773 853	Calhoun County
—773 855	Jersey County
—773 86	Madison County
—773 87	Bond and Clinton Counties
—773 873	Bond County
—773 875	Clinton County
—773 88	Washington County
—773 89	Saint Clair County
—773 9	**Southern counties**
—773 91	Monroe County
—773 92	Randolph County
—773 93	Perry County
—773 94	Franklin County
—773 95	Hamilton County
—773 96	White County

—773 97	Gallatin County
—773 98	Hardin County
—773 99	Southernmost counties
—773 991	Pope County
—773 992	Saline County
—773 993	Williamson County
—773 994	Jackson County
—773 995	Union County
—773 996	Johnson County
—773 997	Massac County
—773 998	Pulaski County
—773 999	Alexander County
—774	**Michigan**

Class here Lakes *Huron, *Michigan

>	**—774 1–774 8 Lower Peninsula**

Class comprehensive works in —774

—774 1	**Southwestern counties of Lower Peninsula**

Class here *Kalamazoo River

—774 11	Berrien County
—774 12	Cass County
—774 13	Van Buren County
—774 14	Allegan County
—774 15	Ottawa County

Class here *Grand River

—774 16	Barry County
—774 17	Kalamazoo County

Including Kalamazoo [*formerly* —77418]

—[774 18]	Kalamazoo

Relocated to —77417

—774 19	Saint Joseph County
—774 2	**South central counties of Lower Peninsula**
—774 21	Branch County

*Class parts of this physiographic region or feature as instructed under —4–9

—774 22	Calhoun County
—774 23	Eaton County
—774 24	Clinton County
—774 25	Shiawassee County
—774 26	Ingham County
	For Lansing and East Lansing, see —77427
—774 27	Lansing and East Lansing
—774 28	Jackson County
—774 29	Hillsdale County
—774 3	**Southeastern counties of Lower Peninsula**
—774 31	Lenawee County
—774 32	Monroe County
—774 33	Wayne County
	Including Dearborn; *Detroit River
	For Detroit, see —77434
—774 34	Detroit
—774 35	Washtenaw County
	Including Ann Arbor
—774 36	Livingston County
—774 37	Genesee County
	Including Flint
	Class here *Flint River
—774 38	Oakland County
—774 39	Macomb County
	Including *Lake Saint Clair
—774 4	**Southeast central counties of Lower Peninsula**
—774 41	Saint Clair County
	Including *Saint Clair River
—774 42	Lapeer County
—774 43	Sanilac County
—774 44	Huron County
—774 45	Tuscola County
—774 46	Saginaw County

*Class parts of this physiographic region or feature as instructed under —4–9

—774 47	Bay County
	Class here *Saginaw River; *Saginaw Bay
—774 48	Midland County
—774 49	Gratiot County
—774 5	Southwest central counties of Lower Peninsula
	Class here *Muskegon River
—774 51	Isabella County
—774 52	Mecosta County
—774 53	Montcalm County
—774 54	Ionia County
—774 55	Kent County
	For Grand Rapids, see —77456
—774 56	Grand Rapids
—774 57	Muskegon County
—774 58	Newaygo County
—774 59	Oceana County
—774 6	Northwest central counties of Lower Peninsula
	Class here *Manistee River
—774 61	Mason County
—774 62	Manistee County
—774 63	Benzie and Leelanau Counties
—774 632	Benzie County
—774 635	Leelanau County
—774 64	Grand Traverse County
	Class here *Grand Traverse Bay
—774 65	Kalkaska County
—774 66	Missaukee County
—774 67	Wexford County
—774 68	Lake County
—774 69	Osceola County
—774 7	Northeast central counties of Lower Peninsula
	Class here *Au Sable River
—774 71	Clare County
—774 72	Gladwin County

*Class parts of this physiographic region or feature as instructed under —4–9

—774 73	Arenac County
—774 74	Iosco County
—774 75	Ogemaw County
—774 76	Roscommon County
—774 77	Crawford County
—774 78	Oscoda County
—774 79	Alcona County

—774 8   **Northern counties of Lower Peninsula**

> Comprehensive works on Straits of Mackinac relocated to —774923

—774 81	Alpena County
—774 82	Presque Isle County
—774 83	Montmorency County
—774 84	Otsego County
—774 85	Antrim County
—774 86	Charlevoix County
—774 87	Cheboygan County
—774 88	Emmet County

—774 9   **Upper Peninsula**

> Class here *Lake Superior

—774 91   Chippewa County

> Including *Saint Marys River; *Whitefish Bay

—774 92   Mackinac and Luce Counties

—774 923   Mackinac County

> Including comprehensive works on *Straits of Mackinac [*formerly* —7748]

—774 925   Luce County

—774 93   Alger and Schoolcraft Counties

—774 932   Alger County

—774 935   Schoolcraft County

—774 94   Delta County

—774 95   Menominee and Dickinson Counties

> Class here *Menominee River

—774 953   Menominee County

—774 955   Dickinson County

*Class parts of this physiographic region or feature as instructed under —4–9

—774 96	Marquette County
—774 97	Baraga and Iron Counties
—774 973	Baraga County
—774 975	Iron County
—774 98	Gogebic and Ontonagon Counties
—774 983	Gogebic County
—774 985	Ontonagon County
—774 99	Houghton and Keweenaw Counties
	Class here Keweenaw Peninsula
—774 993	Houghton County
—774 995	Keweenaw County
	For Isle Royale, see —774997
—774 997	Isle Royale (Isle Royale National Park)
—775	Wisconsin
	Class here *Wisconsin River
—775 1	Northwestern counties
	Class here *Saint Croix River
—775 11	Douglas County
	Including Superior [*formerly* —77512]
	Class comprehensive works on Duluth and Superior in —776771
—[775 12]	Superior
	Relocated to —77511
—775 13	Bayfield County
—775 14	Burnett County
—775 15	Washburn County
—775 16	Sawyer County
—775 17	Polk County
—775 18	Barron County
—775 19	Rusk County
—775 2	North central counties
—775 21	Ashland County
—775 22	Iron County
—775 23	Vilas County
—775 24	Price County

*Class parts of this physiographic region or feature as instructed under —4–9

—775 25	Oneida County
—775 26	Taylor County
—775 27	Lincoln County
—775 28	Clark County
—775 29	Marathon County
—775 3	Northeastern counties
	Comprehensive works on Green Bay relocated to —77563
—775 31	Forest County
—775 32	Florence County
—775 33	Marinette County
	Including Marinette [*formerly* —77534]
—[775 34]	Marinette
	Relocated to —77533
—775 35	Langlade and Menominee Counties
—775 354	Langlade County
—775 356	Menominee County
—775 36	Shawano County
—775 37	Oconto County
—775 38	Waupaca County
—775 39	Outagamie County
—775 4	West central counties
	Class here *Chippewa River
—775 41	Saint Croix County
—775 42	Pierce County
—775 43	Dunn County
—775 44	Chippewa County
—775 45	Eau Claire County
	Including Eau Claire [*formerly* —77546]
—[775 46]	Eau Claire
	Relocated to —77545
—775 47	Pepin County
—775 48	Buffalo County
—775 49	Trempealeau County
—775 5	Central counties

*Class parts of this physiographic region or feature as instructed under —4–9

—775 51	Jackson County
—775 52	Wood County
—775 53	Portage County
—775 54	Monroe County
—775 55	Juneau County
—775 56	Adams County
—775 57	Waushara County
—775 58	Marquette County
—775 59	Green Lake County
—775 6	**East central counties**
	Class here *Fox River
—775 61	Brown County
—775 62	Kewaunee County
—775 63	Door County
	Class here comprehensive works on *Green Bay [*formerly* —7753]
—775 64	Winnebago County
	Including Oshkosh [*formerly* —77565]
	Class here *Lake Winnebago
—[775 65]	Oshkosh
	Relocated to —77564
—775 66	Calumet County
—775 67	Manitowoc County
—775 68	Fond du Lac County
—775 69	Sheboygan County
—775 7	**Southwestern counties**
—775 71	La Crosse County
	Including La Crosse [*formerly* —77572]
—[775 72]	La Crosse
	Relocated to —77571
—775 73	Vernon County
—775 74	Crawford County
—775 75	Richland County
—775 76	Sauk County
—775 77	Grant County

*Class parts of this physiographic region or feature as instructed under —4–9

—775 78	Iowa County
—775 79	Lafayette County
—775 8	**South central counties**
—775 81	Columbia County
—775 82	Dodge County
—775 83	Dane County
	Class here Madison [*formerly* —77584]
—[775 84]	Madison
	Relocated to —77583
—775 85	Jefferson County
—775 86	Green County
—775 87	Rock County
	Including Beloit [*formerly* —77588]
—[775 88]	Beloit
	Relocated to —77587
—775 89	Walworth County
—775 9	**Southeastern counties**
—775 91	Washington County
—775 92	Ozaukee County
—775 93	Waukesha County
—775 94	Milwaukee County
	For Milwaukee, see —77595
—775 95	Milwaukee
—775 96	Racine County
	Including Racine [*formerly* —77597]
—[775 97]	Racine
	Relocated to —77596
—775 98	Kenosha County
	Including Kenosha [*formerly* —77599]
—[775 99]	Kenosha
	Relocated to —77598
—776	**Minnesota**
—776 1	**Southeastern counties**
—776 11	Houston County

—776 12	Winona County
—776 13	Wabasha County
	Including *Lake Pepin
—776 14	Goodhue County
—776 15	Dodge and Olmsted Counties
—776 153	Dodge County
—776 155	Olmsted County
—776 16	Fillmore County
—776 17	Mower County
—776 18	Freeborn County
—776 19	Steele and Waseca Counties
—776 193	Steele County
—776 195	Waseca County
—776 2	Southwestern counties
—776 21	Blue Earth County
—776 22	Faribault County
—776 23	Martin and Jackson Counties
—776 232	Martin County
—776 235	Jackson County
—776 24	Nobles County
—776 25	Rock County
—776 26	Pipestone County
—776 27	Murray County
—776 28	Cottonwood County
—776 29	Watonwan County
—776 3	Southwest central counties
	Class here *Minnesota River
—776 31	Brown County
—776 32	Nicollet County
—776 33	Sibley County
—776 34	Renville County
—776 35	Redwood County
—776 36	Lyon and Lincoln Counties
—776 363	Lyon County

*Class parts of this physiographic region or feature as instructed under —4–9

—776 365	Lincoln County
—776 37	Yellow Medicine County
—776 38	Lac qui Parle County
—776 39	Chippewa County
—776 4	West central counties
—776 41	Swift County
—776 42	Stevens County
—776 43	Big Stone and Traverse Counties
—776 432	Big Stone County
—776 435	Traverse County
—776 44	Grant County
—776 45	Douglas County
—776 46	Pope County
—776 47	Stearns County
—776 48	Kandiyohi County
—776 49	Meeker County
—776 5	Southeast central counties
—776 51	Wright County
—776 52	McLeod County
—776 53	Carver County
—776 54	Scott County
—776 55	Le Sueur and Rice Counties
—776 553	Le Sueur County
—776 555	Rice County
—776 56	Dakota County
—776 57	Hennepin County
—776 579	Minneapolis
	Class here Twin Cities
	For Saint Paul, see —776581
—776 58	Ramsey County
—776 581	Saint Paul
	Class Twin Cities in —776579
—776 59	Washington County
—776 6	East central counties

—776 61	Chisago County
—776 62	Pine County
—776 63	Kanabec County
—776 64	Isanti County
—776 65	Anoka County
—776 66	Sherburne County
—776 67	Benton County
—776 68	Mille Lacs County

           Including *Mille Lacs Lake

—776 69	Morrison County
—776 7	Northeastern counties
—776 71	Crow Wing County
—776 72	Aitkin County
—776 73	Carlton County
—776 75	Cook County
—776 76	Lake County
—776 77	Saint Louis County

           Including Voyageurs National Park; *Mesabi Range

           Class Voyageurs National Park in Koochiching County in —77679

—776 771	Duluth

           Class here comprehensive works on Duluth and Superior, Wisconsin

           For Superior, see —77511

—776 78	Itasca County

           Including *Lake Winnibigoshish

—776 79	Koochiching County

           Including *Rainy River; *Rainy Lake

—776 8	North central counties
—776 81	Lake of the Woods County

           Class here *Lake of the Woods

—776 82	Beltrami County
—776 83	Clearwater County
—776 84	Becker County
—776 85	Hubbard County

*Class parts of this physiographic region or feature as instructed under —4–9

—776 86	Cass County
—776 87	Wadena County
—776 88	Todd County
—776 89	Otter Tail County
—776 9	Northwestern counties
	Class here *Red River of the North in Minnesota
—776 91	Wilkin County
—776 92	Clay County
—776 93	Norman County
—776 94	Mahnomen County
—776 95	Polk County
—776 96	Red Lake and Pennington Counties
—776 963	Red Lake County
—776 965	Pennington County
—776 97	Marshall County
—776 98	Roseau County
—776 99	Kittson County
—777	Iowa
	Class here *Des Moines River
—777 1	Northwestern counties
	Including *Big Sioux River in Iowa
	Class here *Little Sioux River
—777 11	Lyon and Osceola Counties
—777 114	Lyon County
—777 116	Osceola County
—777 12	Dickinson and Emmet Counties
—777 123	Dickinson County
—777 125	Emmet County
—777 13	Sioux County
—777 14	O'Brien County
—777 15	Clay and Palo Alto Counties
—777 153	Clay County
—777 155	Palo Alto County
—777 16	Plymouth County

*Class parts of this physiographic region or feature as instructed under —4–9

—777 17	Cherokee County
—777 18	Buena Vista County
—777 19	Pocahontas County
—777 2	North central counties
—777 21	Kossuth County
—777 22	Winnebago County
—777 23	Worth and Mitchell Counties
—777 232	Worth County
—777 234	Mitchell County
—777 24	Hancock County
—777 25	Cerro Gordo County
—777 26	Floyd County
—777 27	Humboldt and Wright Counties
—777 272	Humboldt County
—777 274	Wright County
—777 28	Franklin County
—777 29	Butler County
—777 3	Northeastern counties
—777 31	Howard and Chickasaw Counties
—777 312	Howard County
—777 315	Chickasaw County
—777 32	Winneshiek County
—777 33	Allamakee County
—777 34	Bremer County
—777 35	Fayette County
—777 36	Clayton County
—777 37	Black Hawk County
—777 38	Buchanan and Delaware Counties
—777 382	Buchanan County
—777 385	Delaware County
—777 39	Dubuque County
—777 4	West central counties
	Class here *Boyer River

*Class parts of this physiographic region or feature as instructed under —4–9

—777 41	Woodbury County
	Including Sioux City
—777 42	Ida and Sac Counties
—777 422	Ida County
—777 424	Sac County
—777 43	Calhoun County
—777 44	Monona County
—777 45	Crawford County
—777 46	Carroll and Greene Counties
	Class here *Raccoon River
—777 465	Carroll County
—777 466	Greene County
—777 47	Harrison County
—777 48	Shelby and Audubon Counties
—777 484	Shelby County
—777 486	Audubon County
—777 49	Guthrie County
—777 5	Central counties
—777 51	Webster County
—777 52	Hamilton County
—777 53	Hardin and Grundy Counties
—777 535	Hardin County
—777 537	Grundy County
—777 54	Boone and Story Counties
—777 544	Boone County
—777 546	Story County
—777 55	Marshall County
—777 56	Tama County
—777 57	Dallas County
—777 58	Polk County
	Class here Des Moines
—777 59	Jasper and Poweshiek Counties
—777 594	Jasper County
—777 596	Poweshiek County

*Class parts of this physiographic region or feature as instructed under —4–9

—777 6	East central counties
	Class here *Cedar, *Iowa, *Wapsipinicon Rivers
—777 61	Benton County
—777 62	Linn County
—777 63	Jones County
—777 64	Jackson County
—777 65	Iowa and Johnson Counties
—777 653	Iowa County
—777 655	Johnson County
—777 66	Cedar County
—777 67	Clinton County
—777 68	Muscatine County
—777 69	Scott County
	Class here Davenport-Rock Island-Moline tri-city area
	For Rock Island County, Illinois, see —773393
—777 7	Southwestern counties
	Class here *Nishnabotna River
—777 71	Pottawattamie County
—777 72	Cass County
—777 73	Adair County
—777 74	Mills County
—777 75	Montgomery County
—777 76	Adams County
—777 77	Fremont County
—777 78	Page County
—777 79	Taylor County
—777 8	South central counties
—777 81	Madison County
—777 82	Warren County
—777 83	Marion County
—777 84	Mahaska County
—777 85	Union and Clarke Counties
—777 853	Union County
—777 856	Clarke County

*Class parts of this physiographic region or feature as instructed under —4–9

—777 86	Lucas and Monroe Counties
—777 863	Lucas County
—777 865	Monroe County
—777 87	Ringgold and Decatur Counties
—777 873	Ringgold County
—777 875	Decatur County
—777 88	Wayne County
—777 89	Appanoose County
—777 9	Southeastern counties
	Class here *Skunk River
—777 91	Keokuk County
—777 92	Washington and Louisa Counties
—777 923	Washington County
—777 926	Louisa County
—777 93	Wapello County
—777 94	Jefferson County
—777 95	Henry County
—777 96	Des Moines County
—777 97	Davis County
—777 98	Van Buren County
—777 99	Lee County
—778	Missouri
	Class here *Missouri River in Missouri
—778 1	Northwestern counties
—778 11	Atchison and Holt Counties
—778 113	Atchison County
—778 115	Holt County
—778 12	Nodaway and Andrew Counties
—778 124	Nodaway County
—778 126	Andrew County
—778 13	Buchanan and Platte Counties
—778 132	Buchanan County
—778 135	Platte County
—778 14	Worth and Gentry Counties

*Class parts of this physiographic region or feature as instructed under —4–9

—778 143	Worth County
—778 145	Gentry County
—778 15	De Kalb and Clinton Counties
—778 153	De Kalb County
—778 155	Clinton County
—778 16	Clay County
—778 17	Harrison County
—778 18	Daviess and Caldwell Counties
—778 183	Daviess County
—778 185	Caldwell County
—778 19	Ray County
—778 2	North central counties
	Class here *Chariton River
—778 21	Mercer and Grundy Counties
—778 213	Mercer County
—778 215	Grundy County
—778 22	Livingston and Carroll Counties
—778 223	Livingston County
—778 225	Carroll County
—778 23	Putnam and Sullivan Counties
—778 232	Putnam County
—778 235	Sullivan County
—778 24	Linn County
—778 25	Chariton County
—778 26	Schuyler and Adair Counties
—778 262	Schuyler County
—778 264	Adair County
—778 27	Macon County
—778 28	Randolph and Howard Counties
—778 283	Randolph County
—778 285	Howard County
—778 29	Boone County
—778 3	Northeastern counties
—778 31	Scotland and Knox Counties

*Class parts of this physiographic region or feature as instructed under —4–9

—778 312	Scotland County
—778 315	Knox County
—778 32	Shelby and Monroe Counties
—778 323	Shelby County
—778 325	Monroe County
—778 33	Audrain and Callaway Counties
—778 332	Audrain County
—778 335	Callaway County
—778 34	Clark and Lewis Counties
—778 343	Clark County
—778 345	Lewis County
—778 35	Marion and Ralls Counties
—778 353	Marion County
—778 355	Ralls County
—778 36	Pike County
—778 37	Lincoln County
—778 38	Montgomery and Warren Counties
—778 382	Montgomery County
—778 386	Warren County
—778 39	Saint Charles County
—778 4	West central counties
—778 41	Jackson County
—778 411	Kansas City

Class here Greater Kansas City

For Wyandotte County, Kansas, see —78139

—778 42	Cass County
—778 43	Bates County
—778 44	Vernon County
—778 45	Lafayette and Johnson Counties
—778 453	Lafayette County
—778 455	Johnson County
—778 46	Henry and Saint Clair Counties
—778 462	Henry County
—778 466	Saint Clair County

—778 47	Saline County
—778 48	Pettis County
—778 49	Benton and Hickory Counties
—778 493	Benton County
	Class here *Lake of the Ozarks
—778 496	Hickory County
—778 5	**Central counties**
—778 51	Cooper County
—778 52	Moniteau County
—778 53	Morgan County
—778 54	Camden County
—778 55	Cole County
	Including Jefferson City
—778 56	Miller County
—778 57	Pulaski County
—778 58	Osage County
—778 59	Maries and Phelps Counties
—778 592	Maries County
—778 594	Phelps County
—778 6	**East central counties**
—778 61	Gasconade County
—778 62	Crawford County
—778 63	Franklin County
—778 64	Washington County
—778 65	Saint Louis County
—778 66	Independent city of Saint Louis
—778 67	Jefferson County
—778 68	Saint Francois County
—778 69	Sainte Genevieve and Perry Counties
—778 692	Sainte Genevieve County
—778 694	Perry County
—778 7	**Southwestern counties**
—778 71	Barton County
—778 72	Jasper County

*Class parts of this physiographic region or feature as instructed under —4–9

—778 73	Newton and McDonald Counties
—778 732	Newton County
—778 736	McDonald County
—778 74	Cedar and Dade Counties
—778 743	Cedar County
—778 745	Dade County
—778 75	Lawrence County
—778 76	Barry County
—778 77	Polk County
—778 78	Greene County
—778 79	Christian, Stone, Taney Counties
—778 792	Christian County
—778 794	Stone County
—778 797	Taney County
—778 8	South central counties
	Class here *Ozark Plateau in Missouri
—778 81	Dallas and Laclede Counties
—778 813	Dallas County
—778 815	Laclede County
—778 82	Webster and Wright Counties
—778 823	Webster County
—778 825	Wright County
—778 83	Douglas and Ozark Counties
—778 832	Douglas County
—778 835	Ozark County
—778 84	Texas County
—778 85	Howell County
—778 86	Dent County
—778 87	Shannon and Oregon Counties
—778 873	Shannon County
—778 875	Oregon County
—778 88	Iron and Reynolds Counties
—778 883	Iron County
—778 885	Reynolds County

*Class parts of this physiographic region or feature as instructed under —4–9

—778 89	Carter and Ripley Counties
—778 892	Carter County
—778 894	Ripley County
—778 9	Southeastern counties
—778 91	Madison County
—778 92	Wayne County
—778 93	Butler County
—778 94	Bollinger County
—778 95	Stoddard County
—778 96	Cape Girardeau County
—778 97	Scott County
—778 98	Mississippi and New Madrid Counties
—778 983	Mississippi County
—778 985	New Madrid County
—778 99	Dunklin and Pemiscot Counties
—778 993	Dunklin County
—778 996	Pemiscot County

—78   **Western United States**

Class here the West; *Great Plains; *Rocky Mountains; *Missouri River

For Great Basin and Pacific Slope region, see —79

SUMMARY

—781	**Kansas**
—782	**Nebraska**
—783	**South Dakota**
—784	**North Dakota**
—786	**Montana**
—787	**Wyoming**
—788	**Colorado**
—789	**New Mexico**

—781	Kansas

Class here *Arkansas River in Kansas

—781 1	Northwestern counties
—781 11	Cheyenne and Sherman Counties
—781 112	Cheyenne County
—781 115	Sherman County
—781 12	Wallace and Rawlins Counties

*Class parts of this physiographic region or feature as instructed under —4–9

—781 123	Wallace County
—781 125	Rawlins County
—781 13	Thomas and Logan Counties
—781 132	Thomas County
—781 135	Logan County
—781 14	Decatur and Sheridan Counties
—781 143	Decatur County
—781 145	Sheridan County
—781 15	Gove and Norton Counties
—781 152	Gove County
—781 155	Norton County
—781 16	Graham and Trego Counties
—781 163	Graham County
—781 165	Trego County
—781 17	Phillips County
—781 18	Rooks County
—781 19	Ellis County
—781 2	**North central counties**
	Class here *Republican, *Solomon Rivers
—781 21	Smith and Osborne Counties
—781 213	Smith County
—781 215	Osborne County
—781 22	Jewell County
—781 23	Mitchell County
—781 24	Republic County
—781 25	Cloud County
—781 26	Ottawa County
—781 27	Washington and Clay Counties
—781 273	Washington County
—781 275	Clay County
—781 28	Riley County
	Including *Big Blue River
—781 29	Geary County

*Class parts of this physiographic region or feature as instructed under —4–9

—781 3 Northeastern counties

Class here *Kansas (Kaw) River

—781 31 Marshall County

—781 32 Pottawatomie County

—781 33 Nemaha and Jackson Counties

—781 332 Nemaha County

—781 335 Jackson County

—781 34 Brown County

—781 35 Doniphan County

—781 36 Atchison County

—781 37 Jefferson County

—781 38 Leavenworth County

—781 39 Wyandotte County

Class here Kansas City

Class comprehensive works on Greater Kansas City in —778411

—781 4 West central counties

Use of this number for comprehensive works on Arkansas River in Kansas discontinued; class in —781

—781 41 Greeley and Hamilton Counties

—781 413 Greeley County

—781 415 Hamilton County

—781 42 Wichita and Kearny Counties

—781 423 Wichita County

—781 425 Kearny County

—781 43 Scott County

—781 44 Finney County

—781 45 Lane County

—781 46 Ness County

—781 47 Hodgeman County

—781 48 Rush County

—781 49 Pawnee County

—781 5 Central counties

Class here *Smoky Hill River

—781 51 Russell County

*Class parts of this physiographic region or feature as instructed under —4–9

—781 52	Barton County
—781 53	Lincoln and Ellsworth Counties
—781 532	Lincoln County
—781 535	Ellsworth County
—781 54	Rice and Saline Counties
—781 543	Rice County
—781 545	Saline County
—781 55	McPherson County
—781 56	Dickinson County
—781 57	Marion County
—781 58	Morris County
—781 59	Chase County
—781 6	East central counties
—781 61	Wabaunsee County
—781 62	Lyon County
—781 63	Shawnee County
	Class here Topeka
—781 64	Osage and Coffey Counties
—781 643	Osage County
—781 645	Coffey County
—781 65	Douglas County
—781 66	Franklin County
—781 67	Anderson and Johnson Counties
—781 672	Anderson County
—781 675	Johnson County
—781 68	Miami County
—781 69	Linn County
—781 7	Southwestern counties
—781 71	Stanton and Morton Counties
—781 712	Stanton County
—781 715	Morton County
—781 72	Grant and Stevens Counties
—781 723	Grant County
—781 725	Stevens County

—781 73	Haskell and Seward Counties
—781 732	Haskell County
—781 735	Seward County
—781 74	Gray County
—781 75	Meade County
—781 76	Ford County
—781 77	Clark County
—781 78	Edwards and Kiowa Counties
—781 782	Edwards County
—781 785	Kiowa County
—781 79	Comanche County
—781 8	South central counties
—781 81	Stafford and Pratt Counties
—781 813	Stafford County
—781 815	Pratt County
—781 82	Barber County
—781 83	Reno County
—781 84	Kingman and Harper Counties
—781 843	Kingman County
—781 845	Harper County
—781 85	Harvey County
—781 86	Sedgwick County
	Class here Wichita
—781 87	Sumner County
—781 88	Butler County
—781 89	Cowley County
—781 9	Southeastern counties
—781 91	Greenwood, Elk, Chautauqua Counties
—781 913	Greenwood County
—781 915	Elk County
—781 918	Chautauqua County
—781 92	Woodson and Wilson Counties
—781 923	Woodson County
—781 925	Wilson County

—781 93	Montgomery County
—781 94	Allen County
—781 95	Neosho County
—781 96	Labette County
—781 97	Bourbon County
—781 98	Crawford County
—781 99	Cherokee County
—782	Nebraska
	Class here *Platte River
—782 2	Missouri River lowland counties
—782 22	Dixon, Dakota, Thurston Counties
—782 223	Dixon County
—782 224	Dakota County
—782 227	Thurston County
—782 23	Cuming and Dodge Counties
—782 232	Cuming County
—782 235	Dodge County
—782 24	Burt and Washington Counties
—782 243	Burt County
—782 245	Washington County
—782 25	Douglas and Sarpy Counties
—782 254	Douglas County
	Class here Omaha
—782 256	Sarpy County
—782 27	Cass and neighboring counties
—782 272	Cass County
—782 273	Otoe County
—782 276	Johnson County
—782 278	Nemaha County
—782 28	Richardson, Pawnee, Gage Counties
—782 282	Richardson County
—782 284	Pawnee County
—782 286	Gage County

Including Beatrice [*formerly* —782287]

*Class parts of this physiographic region or feature as instructed under —4–9

—[782 287]	Beatrice
	Relocated to —782286
—782 29	Lancaster and Saunders Counties
—782 293	Lancaster County
	Class here Lincoln
—782 296	Saunders County
—782 3	South central counties
—782 32	Butler, Seward, Saline Counties
—782 322	Butler County
—782 324	Seward County
—782 327	Saline County
—782 33	Jefferson and Thayer Counties
—782 332	Jefferson County
—782 335	Thayer County
—782 34	Fillmore and York Counties
—782 342	Fillmore County
—782 345	York County
—782 35	Polk, Hamilton, Clay Counties
—782 352	Polk County
—782 354	Hamilton County
—782 357	Clay County
—782 37	Nuckolls, Webster, Franklin Counties
	Class here *Republican River in Nebraska
—782 372	Nuckolls County
—782 374	Webster County
—782 377	Franklin County
—782 38	Harlan, Furnas, Gosper Counties
—782 382	Harlan County
—782 384	Furnas County
—782 387	Gosper County
—782 39	Phelps, Kearney, Adams Counties
—782 392	Phelps County
—782 394	Kearney County

*Class parts of this physiographic region or feature as instructed under —4–9

—782 397	Adams County
	Including Hastings [*formerly* —782398]
—[782 398]	Hastings
	Relocated to —782397
—782 4	Central counties
	Class here *Loup River
—782 41	Hall County
—782 42	Merrick and Nance Counties
—782 423	Merrick County
—782 425	Nance County
—782 43	Howard County
—782 44	Sherman County
—782 45	Buffalo County
—782 46	Dawson County
—782 47	Custer County
—782 48	Valley County
—782 49	Greeley County
—782 5	Northeast central counties
	Class here *Elkhorn River
—782 51	Boone County
—782 52	Platte County
—782 53	Colfax and Stanton Counties
—782 532	Colfax County
—782 535	Stanton County
—782 54	Madison County
—782 55	Antelope County
—782 56	Pierce County
—782 57	Wayne County
—782 58	Cedar County
—782 59	Knox County
—782 7	North central counties
	Class here *Niobrara River
—782 72	Boyd and Keya Paha Counties
—782 723	Boyd County

*Class parts of this physiographic region or feature as instructed under —4–9

—782 725	Keya Paha County
—782 73	Cherry and Brown Counties
—782 732	Cherry County
—782 736	Brown County
—782 74	Rock and Holt Counties
—782 743	Rock County
—782 745	Holt County
—782 76	Wheeler, Garfield, Loup Counties
—782 762	Wheeler County
—782 764	Garfield County
—782 767	Loup County
—782 77	Blaine, Thomas, Hooker Counties
—782 772	Blaine County
—782 774	Thomas County
—782 777	Hooker County
—782 78	Grant and Arthur Counties
—782 783	Grant County
—782 785	Arthur County
—782 79	McPherson and Logan Counties
—782 793	McPherson County
—782 795	Logan County
—782 8	Southwestern counties
—782 82	Lincoln County
—782 83	Hayes and Frontier Counties
—782 832	Hayes County
—782 835	Frontier County
—782 84	Red Willow and Hitchcock Counties
—782 843	Red Willow County
—782 845	Hitchcock County
—782 86	Dundy County
—782 87	Chase County
—782 88	Perkins County
—782 89	Keith County
—782 9	Northwestern counties (Panhandle)

—782 91	Deuel and Garden Counties
—782 913	Deuel County
—782 915	Garden County
—782 92	Sheridan County
—782 93	Dawes County
—782 94	Box Butte County
—782 95	Morrill County
—782 96	Cheyenne County
—782 97	Kimball and Banner Counties
—782 973	Kimball County
—782 975	Banner County
—782 98	Scotts Bluff County
—782 99	Sioux County
—783	South Dakota
—783 1	Northeastern counties
—783 12	Roberts County
—783 13	Marshall County
—783 14	Day and Brown Counties
—783 142	Day County
—783 144	Brown County
—783 15	Edmunds County
—783 16	McPherson County
—783 17	Campbell County
—783 18	Walworth County
—783 19	Potter County
—783 2	East central counties
—783 21	Faulk and Spink Counties
—783 213	Faulk County
—783 217	Spink County
—783 22	Clark County
—783 23	Codington County
—783 24	Grant County
—783 25	Deuel County
—783 26	Hamlin County

—783 27	Brookings, Kingsbury, Beadle Counties
—783 272	Brookings County
—783 273	Kingsbury County
—783 274	Beadle County
—783 28	Hand, Hyde, Sully Counties
—783 282	Hand County
—783 283	Hyde County
—783 284	Sully County
—783 29	Hughes County
	Including Pierre
—783 3	Southeastern counties
	Class here *Missouri River in South Dakota, *James River
—783 31	Buffalo County
—783 32	Jerauld County
—783 33	Sanborn County
—783 34	Miner County
—783 35	Lake County
—783 36	Moody County
—783 37	Minnehaha and neighboring counties
—783 371	Minnehaha County
	Including Sioux Falls
—783 372	McCook County
—783 373	Hanson County
—783 374	Davison County
—783 375	Aurora County
—783 38	Brule and neighboring counties
	Class here *Lake Francis Case
—783 381	Brule County
—783 382	Charles Mix County
—783 383	Douglas County
—783 384	Hutchinson County
—783 385	Turner County
—783 39	Lincoln and neighboring counties
	Class here *Big Sioux River

*Class parts of this physiographic region or feature as instructed under —4–9

—783 391	Lincoln County
—783 392	Union County
—783 393	Clay County
—783 394	Yankton County
—783 395	Bon Homme County
—783 4	Northwestern counties
—783 42	Harding County
—783 43	Butte County
—783 44	Meade County
—783 45	Perkins County
—783 5	Central counties
	Class here *Cheyenne River; *Lake Oahe
—783 52	Corson County
	Class here *Grand River
—783 53	Ziebach County
—783 54	Dewey County
	Class here *Moreau River
—783 55	Stanley County
—783 56	Haakon County
—783 57	Jackson and Jones Counties
—783 572	Jackson County
—783 577	Jones County
—783 58	Lyman County
—783 59	Gregory County
—783 6	South central counties
	Class here *White River
—783 61	Tripp County
—783 62	Todd County
—783 63	Mellette County
—783 64	Washabaugh County
—783 65	Bennett County
—783 66	Shannon County

*Class parts of this physiographic region or feature as instructed under —4–9

—783 9   Southwestern counties

          Class here *Black Hills

—783 91   Lawrence County

—783 93   Pennington County

          Including Badlands National Park

          Class Badlands National Park in Shannon County in —78366, in Jackson County in —783572

—783 95   Custer County

          Including Wind Cave National Park

—783 97   Fall River County

—784   **North Dakota**

—784 1   Red River Valley counties

          Class here *Red River of the North

—784 12   Richland County

—784 13   Cass County

          Including Fargo

—784 14   Traill County

—784 16   Grand Forks County

—784 18   Walsh County

—784 19   Pembina County

—784 3   Sheyenne River Valley and adjacent counties

          Class here *Sheyenne River

—784 31   Sargent and Ransom Counties

—784 314   Sargent County

—784 315   Ransom County

—784 32   Barnes County

—784 33   Steele County

—784 34   Griggs County

—784 35   Nelson County

—784 36   Ramsey County

—784 37   Cavalier County

—784 38   Towner County

—784 39   Benson County

*Class parts of this physiographic region or feature as instructed under —4–9

—784 5	James River Valley and adjacent counties
	Class here *James River in North Dakota
—784 51	Eddy and Foster Counties
—784 512	Eddy County
—784 516	Foster County
—784 52	Stutsman County
—784 53	La Moure County
—784 54	Dickey County
—784 55	McIntosh County
—784 56	Logan County
—784 57	Kidder County
—784 58	Wells County
—784 59	Pierce and Rolette Counties
—784 591	Pierce County
—784 592	Rolette County
—784 6	Souris River Valley counties
	Class here *Souris River
—784 61	Bottineau County
—784 62	McHenry County
—784 63	Ward County
—784 64	Renville County
—784 7	Counties north and east of Missouri River
	Class here *Missouri River in North Dakota
—784 71	Divide County
—784 72	Burke County
—784 73	Williams County
—784 74	Mountrail County
—784 75	McLean County
	Class here *Lake Sakakawea (Garrison Reservoir)
—784 76	Sheridan County
—784 77	Burleigh County
	Including Bismarck
—784 78	Emmons County

*Class parts of this physiographic region or feature as instructed under —4–9

—784 8	Counties south and west of Missouri River
	Class here *Little Missouri River
	For Badlands counties, see —7849
—784 81	McKenzie County
—784 82	Dunn County
—784 83	Mercer County
—784 84	Oliver and Stark Counties
—784 843	Oliver County
—784 844	Stark County
—784 85	Morton County
—784 86	Hettinger County
—784 87	Grant County
—784 88	Sioux County
—784 89	Adams County
—784 9	Badlands counties
—784 92	Bowman County
—784 93	Slope County
—784 94	Billings County
—784 95	Golden Valley County

>	—786–789 Rocky Mountains states
	Class comprehensive works in —78
	For Idaho, see —796
—786	Montana
	Class here *Missouri River in Montana
—786 1	North central counties
	Class here *Great Plains in Montana; *Milk River
	Use of this number for comprehensive works on Missouri River in Montana discontinued; class in —786
—786 12	Toole County
—786 13	Liberty County
—786 14	Hill County
—786 15	Blaine County
—786 16	Phillips County

*Class parts of this physiographic region or feature as instructed under —4–9

—786 17	Valley County
	Class here *Fort Peck Lake
—786 2	Northeastern and central plains counties
—786 21	Daniels and Sheridan Counties
—786 213	Daniels County
—786 218	Sheridan County
—786 22	Roosevelt County
—786 23	Richland County
—786 24	Dawson County
—786 25	Prairie County
—786 26	McCone County
—786 27	Garfield County
—786 28	Petroleum County
—786 29	Fergus and Chouteau Counties
—786 292	Fergus County
—786 293	Chouteau County
—786 3	Southeastern counties
	Class here *Yellowstone River
—786 31	Golden Valley, Musselshell, Treasure Counties
—786 311	Golden Valley County
—786 312	Musselshell County
—786 313	Treasure County
—786 32	Rosebud County
—786 33	Custer County
—786 34	Wibaux County
—786 35	Fallon County
—786 36	Carter County
—786 37	Powder River County
—786 38	Big Horn County
—786 39	Yellowstone County
—786 5	Northwest central counties
	Class here *Rocky Mountains in Montana

*Class parts of this physiographic region or feature as instructed under —4–9

—786 52	Glacier County

> Including Glacier National Park, Waterton-Glacier International Peace Park
>
> Class each specific part of Glacier National Park, of Waterton-Glacier International Peace Park, not provided for here with the part, e.g., in Flathead County —78682

—786 53	Pondera County
—786 55	Teton County
—786 6	Southwestern and central mountain counties
—786 61	Cascade, Meagher, Lewis and Clark Counties
—786 611	Cascade County
—786 612	Meagher County
—786 615	Lewis and Clark County

> Including Helena

—786 62	Judith Basin County
—786 63	Wheatland County
—786 64	Sweet Grass County
—786 65	Stillwater and Carbon Counties
—786 651	Stillwater County
—786 652	Carbon County
—786 66	Park and neighboring counties
—786 661	Park County
—786 662	Gallatin County
—786 663	Madison County
—786 664	Broadwater County
—786 67	Jefferson County
—786 68	Silver Bow County

> Including Butte

—786 69	Beaverhead County
—786 8	Northwestern counties

> Class here *Bitterroot Range

—786 81	Lincoln County
—786 82	Flathead County
—786 83	Lake and Sanders Counties

*Class parts of this physiographic region or feature as instructed under —4–9

—786 832	Lake County
	Class here *Flathead Lake
—786 833	Sanders County
—786 84	Mineral County
—786 85	Missoula County
—786 86	Powell County
—786 87	Deer Lodge County
—786 88	Granite County
—786 89	Ravalli County
—787	Wyoming
—787 1	Eastern counties
	Class here *Great Plains in Wyoming
—787 12	Campbell County
—787 13	Crook County
	Class here *Belle Fourche River
—787 14	Weston County
—787 15	Niobrara County
—787 16	Converse County
	Class here *North Platte River
—787 17	Platte County
—787 18	Goshen County
—787 19	Laramie County
	Including Cheyenne
—787 2	*Rocky Mountains in Wyoming
—787 3	Counties of *Big Horn Mountains
—787 32	Sheridan County
—787 33	Big Horn County
—787 34	Washakie County
—787 35	Johnson County
—787 4	Counties of *Absaroka Range
—787 42	Park County
—787 43	Hot Springs County
	Including *Owl Creek Mountains

*Class parts of this physiographic region or feature as instructed under —4–9

—787 5	**Yellowstone National Park and Teton County**
—787 52	Yellowstone National Park

> Class each specific part with the part, e.g., in Teton County, Wyoming —78755

—787 55	Teton County

> Including Grand Teton National Park; *Teton Range

> Class here *Snake River in Wyoming

—787 6	**Counties of *Wind River Range**
—787 63	Fremont County
—787 65	Sublette County
—787 8	**Southwestern counties**
—787 82	Lincoln County
—787 84	Uinta County

> Including *Bear River Divide

—787 85	Sweetwater County

> Including *Green River in Wyoming

—787 86	Carbon County

> Including *Pathfinder Reservoir

> Class here *Medicine Bow Range

—787 9	**Counties of *Laramie Mountains**
—787 93	Natrona County
—787 95	Albany County
—788	**Colorado**

> Class here *Rocky Mountains in Colorado

—788 1	**Northern counties of *Colorado Plateau**
—788 12	Moffat County

> Class here Dinosaur National Monument

> Class Dinosaur National Monument in Uintah County, Utah in —79221

—788 14	Routt County
—788 15	Rio Blanco County
—788 16	Garfield County
—788 17	Mesa County

> Class here *Colorado River in Colorado

*Class parts of this physiographic region or feature as instructed under —4–9

—788 18	Delta County
—788 19	Montrose County
—788 2	**Southern counties of Colorado Plateau**
—788 22	Ouray County
—788 23	San Miguel County
—788 25	San Juan County
—788 26	Dolores County
—788 27	Montezuma County

         Including Mesa Verde National Park

—788 29	La Plata County
—788 3	**Southern counties of Rocky Mountains**

         Class here *San Juan Mountains; *San Luis Valley; *Rio Grande in Colorado

         Use of this number for comprehensive works on Rocky Mountains in Colorado discontinued; class in —788

—788 32	Archuleta County
—788 33	Conejos County

         Use of this number for comprehensive works on San Luis Valley, on Rio Grande in Colorado discontinued; class in —7883

—788 35	Costilla County
—788 36	Alamosa County
—788 37	Rio Grande County
—788 38	Mineral County

         Use of this number for comprehensive works on San Juan Mountains discontinued; class in —7883

—788 39	Hinsdale County
—788 4	**West central counties of Rocky Mountains**

         Class here *Sawatch Range

—788 41	Gunnison County
—788 43	Pitkin County
—788 44	Eagle County
—788 45	Summit County
—788 46	Lake County
—788 47	Chaffee County

*Class parts of this physiographic region or feature as instructed under —4–9

—788 49	Saguache County
	Including Great Sand Dunes National Monument; *Sangre de Cristo Mountains
	Class Great Sand Dunes National Monument in Alamosa County in —78836
—788 5	East central counties of Rocky Mountains
—788 51	Huerfano County
—788 52	Custer County
—788 53	Fremont County
	Comprehensive works on Arkansas River in Colorado relocated to —7889
—788 55	Pueblo County
—788 56	El Paso County
	Class here Colorado Springs
—788 58	Teller County
—788 59	Park County
—788 6	Northern counties of Rocky Mountains
	Class here *Front Range
—788 61	Clear Creek County
—788 62	Gilpin County
—788 63	Boulder County
—788 65	Grand County
	Including *Rabbit Ears Range
—788 66	Jackson County
	Class here *Park Range
—788 68	Larimer County
—788 69	Rocky Mountain National Park
	Class each specific part with the part, e.g., in Larimer County —78868
—788 7	Northern counties of Great Plains
	Class here *Great Plains in Colorado; *South Platte River
—788 72	Weld County
—788 74	Morgan County
—788 75	Logan County
—788 76	Sedgwick County

*Class parts of this physiographic region or feature as instructed under —4–9

—788 77	Phillips County
—788 78	Yuma County
—788 79	Washington County
—788 8	**Central counties of Great Plains**
—788 81	Adams County
—788 82	Arapahoe County
—788 83	Denver County (Denver)
—788 84	Jefferson County
—788 86	Douglas County
—788 87	Elbert County
—788 89	Lincoln County
—788 9	**Southern counties of Great Plains**

Class here comprehensive works on *Arkansas River in Colorado [*formerly* —78853]

—788 91	Kit Carson County
—788 92	Cheyenne County
—788 93	Kiowa County
—788 94	Crowley County
—788 95	Otero County
—788 96	Las Animas County
—788 97	Bent County
—788 98	Prowers County
—788 99	Baca County
—789	**New Mexico**
—789 2	**Northeastern counties**

Class here *Great Plains in New Mexico

—789 22	Colfax County
—789 23	Union County
—789 24	Harding County
—789 25	Guadalupe County
—789 26	Quay County
—789 27	Curry County
—789 3	**Roosevelt and Lea Counties**

Class here *Llano Estacado in New Mexico

*Class parts of this physiographic region or feature as instructed under —4–9

—789 32	Roosevelt County
—789 33	Lea County
—789 4	Pecos Valley counties

        Class here *Pecos River in New Mexico

—789 42	Eddy County

        Including Carlsbad Caverns National Park

—789 43	Chaves County
—789 44	De Baca County
—789 5	Counties of Rocky Mountains
—789 52	Rio Arriba County
—789 53	Taos County
—789 54	Mora County
—789 55	San Miguel County
—789 56	Santa Fe County

        Class here Santa Fe

—789 57	Sandoval County
—789 58	Los Alamos County
—789 6	Basin and Range region counties

        Class here *Rio Grande in New Mexico

—789 61	Bernalillo County

        Class here Albuquerque

—789 62	Socorro County

        Including *Elephant Butte Reservoir

        Comprehensive works on Jornada del Muerto, on San Andres Mountains relocated to —78967

—789 63	Torrance County
—789 64	Lincoln County
—789 65	Otero County

        Including White Sands National Monument; *Sacramento Mountains; *Tularosa Valley

        Class White Sands National Monument in Dona Ana County in —78966

—789 66	Dona Ana County

*Class parts of this physiographic region or feature as instructed under —4–9

—789 67   Sierra County

                 Class here comprehensive works on *Jornada del Muerto, on *San
                 Andres Mountains [*both formerly* —78962]

—789 68   Luna County

—789 69   Grant and Hidalgo Counties

—789 692   Grant County

—789 693   Hidalgo County

                     Class here *Peloncillo Mountains

—789 8   Northwestern counties

—789 82   San Juan County

—789 83   McKinley County

—789 9   West central counties

—789 91   Cibola County [*formerly* —78992]

—789 92   Valencia County

                 Cibola County relocated to —78991

—789 93   Catron County

—79   **Great Basin and Pacific Slope region of United States   Pacific
             Coast states**

                 Class here new Southwest

                          SUMMARY

             —791   **Arizona**
             —792   **Utah**
             —793   **Nevada**
             —794   **California**
             —795   **Oregon**
             —796   **Idaho**
             —797   **Washington**
             —798   **Alaska**

—791   Arizona

—791 3   Colorado Plateau region

                 Class here *Colorado River

—791 32   *Grand Canyon National Park

—791 33   Coconino County

                     Class here *Painted Desert; *Little Colorado River

—791 35   Navajo County

*Class parts of this physiographic region or feature as instructed under —4–9

—791 37	Apache County
	Including Petrified Forest National Park
	Class Petrified Forest National Park in Navajo County in —79135
—791 5	Mountain region
—791 51	Greenlee County
—791 53	Cochise County
—791 54	Graham County
	Including *San Carlos Lake
—791 55	Gila County
—791 57	Yavapai County
—791 59	Mohave County
—791 7	Plains region
	Class here *Gila River
—791 71	Yuma County
	La Paz County relocated to —79172
—791 72	La Paz County [*formerly* —79171]
—791 73	Maricopa County
	Class here Phoenix
—791 75	Pinal County
—791 77	Pima County
—791 776	Tucson
—791 79	Santa Cruz County
—792	Utah
—792 1	Wyoming Basin region
—792 12	Cache County
—792 13	Rich County
—792 14	Summit County
	Including *Uinta Mountains
—792 15	Daggett County
—792 2	Rocky Mountains region
	Class here *Wasatch Range
—792 21	Uintah County
	Comprehensive works on *Green River relocated to —7925

*Class parts of this physiographic region or feature as instructed under —4–9

—792 22	Duchesne County
—792 23	Wasatch County
—792 24	Utah County
—792 25	Salt Lake County
—792 258	Salt Lake City
—792 26	Morgan County
—792 27	Davis County
—792 28	Weber County
—792 4	**Great Basin region**
—792 42	Box Elder County
	Class here *Great Salt Lake
—792 43	Tooele County
	Class here *Great Salt Lake Desert
—792 44	Juab County
—792 45	Millard County
—792 46	Beaver County
—792 47	Iron County
—792 48	Washington County
	Class here Zion National Park
	Class Zion National Park in Kane County in —79251, in Iron County in —79247
—792 5	**Colorado Plateau region**
	Class here comprehensive works on *Green River [*formerly* —79221]; *Colorado River in Utah
—792 51	Kane County
—792 52	Garfield County
	Including Bryce Canyon National Park
	Class Bryce Canyon National Park in Kane County in —79251
—792 53	Piute County
—792 54	Wayne County
	Including *Capitol Reef National Park
—792 55	Sevier County
—792 56	Sanpete and Carbon Counties
—792 563	Sanpete County

*Class parts of this physiographic region or feature as instructed under —4–9

—792 566	Carbon County
—792 57	Emery County
—792 58	Grand County

Including Arches National Park

—792 59	San Juan County

Including Canyonlands National Park; Glen Canyon National Recreation Area; *San Juan River; *Lake Powell

Class Canyonlands National Park in Wayne County in —79254; parts of Glen Canyon National Recreation Area not provided for here with the part, e.g., Glen Canyon National Recreation Area in Garfield County —79252

—793	Nevada
—793 1	Eastern region
—793 12	*Lake Mead National Recreation Area
—793 13	Clark County
—793 135	Las Vegas
—793 14	Lincoln County
—793 15	White Pine County

Including Great Basin National Park

—793 16	Elko County

Class here *Humboldt River

—793 3	Central region
—793 32	Eureka County
—793 33	Lander County
—793 34	Nye County
—793 35	Esmeralda County
—793 5	Western region
—793 51	Mineral County
—793 52	Churchill County
—793 53	Pershing County
—793 54	Humboldt County

Including *Black Rock Desert

—793 55	Washoe County

Including Reno

*Class parts of this physiographic region or feature as instructed under —4–9

—793 56	Storey County
	Including Virginia City
—793 57	Carson City
	Including *Lake Tahoe in Nevada
	Class here former Ormsby County
—793 58	Lyon County
—793 59	Douglas County
—794	**California**
—794 1	**Northwestern counties**
	Class here *Coast Ranges in California
—794 11	Del Norte County
—794 12	Humboldt County
	Including Redwood National Park
	Class Redwood National Park in Del Norte County in —79411
—794 14	Trinity County
—794 15	Mendocino County
—794 17	Lake County
—794 18	Sonoma County
—794 19	Napa County
—794 2	**Northeastern counties**
	Class here *Cascade Range in California
—794 21	Siskiyou County
	Including Lava Beds National Monument
	Class here *Klamath Mountains in California
	Class Lava Beds National Monument in Modoc County in —79423
—794 23	Modoc County
—794 24	Shasta County
	Including *Lassen Volcanic National Park
—794 26	Lassen County
—794 27	Tehama County
—794 29	Plumas County
—794 3	**North central counties**
—794 31	Glenn County
—794 32	Butte County

*Class parts of this physiographic region or feature as instructed under —4–9

—794 33	Colusa County
—794 34	Sutter County
—794 35	Yuba County
—794 36	Sierra County
—794 37	Nevada County
—794 38	Placer County
	Including *Lake Tahoe
—794 4	**East central counties**
	Class here *Sierra Nevada
—794 41	El Dorado County
—794 42	Amador County
—794 43	Alpine County
—794 44	Calaveras County
—794 45	Tuolumne County
—794 46	Mariposa County
—794 47	Yosemite National Park
	Class each specific part with the part, e.g., in Mariposa County —79446
—794 48	Mono County
—794 5	**Central counties**
	Class here *Central Valley (Great Valley), *Sacramento Valley; *Sacramento River
—794 51	Yolo County
—794 52	Solano County
—794 53	Sacramento County
	For Sacramento, see —79454
—794 54	Sacramento
—794 55	San Joaquin County
	Including Stockton [*formerly* —79456]
—[794 56]	Stockton
	Relocated to —79455
—794 57	Stanislaus County
—794 58	Merced County

*Class parts of this physiographic region or feature as instructed under —4–9

—794 6	West central counties
	Class here *San Francisco Bay Area
	See also —16432 for San Francisco Bay
—794 61	San Francisco County (San Francisco)
—794 62	Marin County
—794 63	Contra Costa County
—794 65	Alameda County
	For Oakland, see —79466; Berkeley, —79467
—794 66	Oakland
—794 67	Berkeley
—794 69	San Mateo County
—794 7	Southern Coast Range counties
—794 71	Santa Cruz County
—794 73	Santa Clara County
	For San Jose, see —79474
—794 74	San Jose
—794 75	San Benito County
—794 76	Monterey County
	Class here *Salinas River
	See also —16432 for Monterey Bay
—794 78	San Luis Obispo County
	Class here *Santa Lucia Range
—794 8	South central counties
	Class here *San Joaquin Valley; *San Joaquin River
—794 81	Madera County
—794 82	Fresno County
	Including Kings Canyon National Park
	Class Kings Canyon National Park in Tulare County in —79486
	For Fresno, see —79483
—794 83	Fresno
—794 85	Kings County
—794 86	Tulare County
	Including Sequoia National Park; *Mount Whitney

*Class parts of this physiographic region or feature as instructed under —4–9

—794 87	Inyo County
	Class here *Death Valley National Monument
—794 88	Kern County
—794 9	**Southern counties (Southern California)**
—794 91	Santa Barbara County
	Including Channel Islands National Park; *Santa Barbara Islands
	Class Anacapa Island in —79491
—794 92	Ventura County
—794 93	Los Angeles County
	Including Pasadena; *San Gabriel Mountains
	For Los Angeles, see —79494
—794 94	Los Angeles
—794 95	San Bernardino County
	Including *San Bernardino Mountains
	Class here *Mojave Desert
—794 96	Orange County
	Including *Santa Ana Mountains
—794 97	Riverside County
	Including Joshua Tree National Monument
	Class Joshua Tree National Monument in San Bernardino County in —79495
—794 98	San Diego County
—794 985	San Diego
—794 99	Imperial County
	Including *Salton Sea
	Class here *Imperial Valley; *Colorado Desert
—795	**Oregon**
	Class here Pacific Northwest; *Cascade and *Coast Ranges
	For Idaho, see —796; *Washington,* —797; *British Columbia,* —711
—795 2	**Southwestern counties**
	Class here *Klamath Mountains
—795 21	Curry County
	Class here *Rogue River
—795 23	Coos County

*Class parts of this physiographic region or feature as instructed under —4–9

—795 25	Josephine County
	Including *Siskiyou Mountains
—795 27	Jackson County
—795 29	Douglas County
	Class here Umpqua River
—795 3	**West central counties**
	Class here *Willamette Valley; *Willamette River
—795 31	Lane County
—795 33	Lincoln County
—795 34	Benton County
—795 35	Linn County
—795 37	Marion County
	Including Salem
—795 38	Polk County
—795 39	Yamhill County
—795 4	**Northwestern counties**
	Class here *Columbia River in Oregon
—795 41	Clackamas County
—795 43	Washington County
—795 44	Tillamook County
—795 46	Clatsop County
—795 47	Columbia County
—795 49	Multnomah County
	Class here Portland
—795 6	**North central counties**
—795 61	Hood River County
	Including *Mount Hood
—795 62	Wasco County
	Class here *Deschutes River
—795 64	Sherman County
—795 65	Gilliam County
—795 67	Morrow County
—795 69	Umatilla County

*Class parts of this physiographic region or feature as instructed under —4–9

—795 7	Northeastern counties
	Class here *Blue Mountains; *Snake River in Oregon
—795 71	Union County
—795 73	Wallowa County
	Including *Wallowa Mountains
—795 75	Baker County
—795 78	Grant County
—795 8	Central counties
—795 81	Wheeler County
—795 83	Crook County
—795 85	Jefferson County
—795 87	Deschutes County
—795 9	Southeastern counties
—795 91	Klamath County
—795 915	Crater Lake National Park
—795 93	Lake County
—795 95	Harney County
—795 97	Malheur County
—796	Idaho
—796 1	Southern Idaho
	Class here *Snake River
	Class specific counties in —7962–7965
—796 2	Southwestern counties
—796 21	Owyhee County
—796 23	Canyon County
—796 24	Payette County
—796 25	Washington County
—796 26	Adams County
	Including *Seven Devils Mountains
—796 27	Gem County
—796 28	Ada County
	Including Boise

*Class parts of this physiographic region or feature as instructed under —4–9

—796 29	Elmore County
	Including *Sawtooth Range
	Class comprehensive works on Sawtooth Mountains in —79672
—796 3	South central counties
—796 31	Camas County
—796 32	Blaine County
	Including *Pioneer Mountains
—796 33	Minidoka County
—796 34	Lincoln County
—796 35	Jerome County
—796 36	Gooding County
—796 37	Twin Falls County
—796 39	Cassia County
	Including *Goose Creek Mountains
—796 4	Southeastern counties
—796 41	Oneida County
—796 42	Franklin County
—796 44	Bear Lake County
	Including *Wasatch Range in Idaho
—796 45	Caribou County
—796 47	Bannock County
	Including *Bannock Range
—796 49	Power County
	Including *American Falls Reservoir
—796 5	Northeastern counties of southern Idaho
—796 51	Bingham County
—796 53	Bonneville County
—796 54	Teton County
—796 55	Madison County
—796 56	Fremont County
—796 57	Clark County
—796 58	Jefferson County

*Class parts of this physiographic region or feature as instructed under —4–9

—796 59	Butte County
	Including Craters of the Moon National Monument
	Class Craters of the Moon National Monument in Blaine County in —79632
—796 6	Central Idaho
	Class here *Bitterroot Range in Idaho
	Class specific counties in —7967–7968
—796 7	South central counties
	Class here *Salmon River Mountains
—796 72	Custer County
	Including *Lost River Range, *Sawtooth Mountains
	See also —79629 *for Sawtooth Range*
—796 74	Boise County
—796 76	Valley County
—796 78	Lemhi County
	Including *Beaverhead Mountains
	Use of this number for comprehensive works on Salmon River Mountains discontinued; class in —7967
—796 8	North central counties
—796 82	Idaho County
	Class here *Clearwater Mountains; *Salmon River
—796 84	Lewis County
—796 85	Nez Perce County
	Including *Clearwater River
—796 86	Latah County
—796 88	Clearwater County
—796 9	Northern Idaho
—796 91	Shoshone County
	Including *Coeur d'Alene Mountains
—796 93	Benewah County
—796 94	Kootenai County
—796 96	Bonner County
—796 98	Boundary County

*Class parts of this physiographic region or feature as instructed under —4–9

—797	Washington
	Class here *Columbia River
—797 2	Northeastern counties
—797 21	Pend Oreille County
—797 23	Stevens County
	Including *Franklin D. Roosevelt Lake
—797 25	Ferry County
	Class here *Kettle River Range
—797 28	Okanogan County
	Including *Sawtooth Ridge
—797 3	East central counties
—797 31	Douglas County
	Including *Grand Coulee
—797 32	Grant County
—797 33	Franklin County
—797 34	Adams County
—797 35	Lincoln County
—797 37	Spokane County
	Class here Spokane
—797 39	Whitman County
	Class here *Palouse River
—797 4	Southeastern counties
	Class here *Snake River in Washington
—797 42	Asotin County
—797 44	Garfield County
—797 46	Columbia County
	Including *Blue Mountains in Washington
—797 48	Walla Walla County
—797 5	Central counties
	Class here *Cascade Range in Washington
—797 51	Benton County
—797 53	Klickitat County

*Class parts of this physiographic region or feature as instructed under —4–9

—797 55	Yakima County
	Class here *Yakima River
—797 57	Kittitas County
	Including *Wenatchee Mountains
—797 59	Chelan County
—797 7	**Puget Sound counties**
	See also —16432 for Puget Sound
—797 71	Snohomish County
—797 72	Skagit County
—797 73	Whatcom County
	Including North Cascades National Park
	Class North Cascades National Park in Chelan County in —79759, in Skagit County in —79772
—797 74	San Juan County
—797 75	Island County
—797 76	Kitsap County
—797 77	King County
—797 772	Seattle
—797 78	Pierce County
—797 782	Mount Rainier National Park
	Class Mount Rainier National Park in Lewis County in —79782
—797 788	Tacoma
—797 79	Thurston County
	Including Olympia
—797 8	**Southwest central counties**
—797 82	Lewis County
	Class here *Cowlitz River
—797 84	Skamania County
—797 86	Clark County
—797 88	Cowlitz County
—797 9	**Coastal counties**
	Class here *Coast Ranges in Washington
—797 91	Wahkiakum County
—797 92	Pacific County

*Class parts of this physiographic region or feature as instructed under —4–9

—797 94	*Olympic Peninsula
	Class here *Olympic Mountains
—797 95	Grays Harbor County
—797 97	Mason County
—797 98	Jefferson County
	Class here Olympic National Park
	Class Olympic National Park in Mason County in —79797, in Clallam County in —79799
—797 99	Clallam County
	See also —16432 for Strait of Juan de Fuca
—798	Alaska
—798 2	Southeastern region (Panhandle)
	Including Haines, Ketchikan Gateway Boroughs; Juneau, Sitka; Glacier Bay National Park and Preserve, Misty Fjords National Park
—798 3	South central region
	Pacific Coast area from Icy Bay to Cape Douglas, inland to crest of Alaska and Aleutian Ranges
	Including Kenai Peninsula, Matanuska-Susitna Boroughs; Denali National Park and Preserve, Kenai Fjords National Park, Wrangell-Saint Elias National Park and Preserve; Kenai Peninsula; *Alaska Range
	Class Wrangell-Saint Elias National Park in southeastern region in —7982
	See also —16434 for Gulf of Alaska, Cook Inlet
—798 35	Greater Anchorage Area Borough
—798 4	Southwestern region
	Area from Cape Douglas to Stuart Island
	Including Bristol Bay, Kodiak Island Boroughs; Katmai National Park and Preserve; Yukon Delta National Wildlife Refuge; Aleutian, Kodiak Islands; *Aleutian Range, Taylor Mountains; *Kuskokwim River; Iliamma Lake
	See also —16434 for Bristol Bay

*Class parts of this physiographic region or feature as instructed under —4–9

—798 6	Central region

Area from the crest of Alaska Range to North Slope Borough

Including Fairbanks North Star, Yukon-Koyokuk Boroughs; Gates of the Arctic National Park and Preserve, Kobuk Valley National Park, Lake Clark National Park and Preserve; Seward Peninsula; *Kuskokwim Mountains

Class here *Yukon River

Class Gates of the Arctic National Park and Preserve in North Slope Borough in —7987

See also —16434 for Norton Sound

—798 7	North Slope Borough

Including Brooks Range

—8   South America

Class here Latin America, Spanish America, the *Andes

For Middle America, see —72

SUMMARY

—809 1	Regional treatment
—81	Brazil
—82	Argentina
—83	Chile
—84	Bolivia
—85	Peru
—86	Colombia and Ecuador
—87	Venezuela
—88	Guiana
—89	Paraguay and Uruguay

—[800 09]	Regional treatment

Relocated to —8091

—809 1	Regional treatment [*formerly* —80009]

Add to base number —8091 the numbers following —1 in —11–18 of this table, e.g., forest areas of South America —809152

—81   Brazil

—811	Northwestern region

Class here *Amazon River

—811 2	Acre state
—811 3	Amazonas state
—811 4	Roraima territory

Former name: Rio Branco territory

*Class parts of this physiographic region or feature as instructed under —4–9

—811 5	Pará state
—811 6	Amapá territory
—812	North central states
—812 1	Maranhão
—812 2	Piauí
—813	Northeastern region
—813 1	Ceará state
—813 2	Rio Grande do Norte state
—813 3	Paraíba state
—813 4	Pernambuco state
—813 5	Alagoas state
—813 6	Fernando de Noronha territory
—814	East central states
—814 1	Sergipe
—814 2	Bahia
—815	Southeastern states
—815 1	Minas Gerais
—815 2	Espírito Santo
—815 3	Rio de Janeiro

> Including former Guanabara
>
> Class here Rio de Janeiro

—816	Southern states

> Class here *Paraná River in Brazil

—816 1	São Paulo

> Class here São Paulo

—816 2	Paraná
—816 4	Santa Catarina
—816 5	Rio Grande do Sul
—817	West central region
—817 1	Mato Grosso do Sul [*formerly* —8172]
—817 2	Mato Grosso state

> Mato Grosso do Sul relocated to —8171

*Class parts of this physiographic region or feature as instructed under —4–9

—817 3	Goiás state
—817 4	Federal District
	Including Brasília
—817 5	Rondônia state
—82	**Argentina**
—821	South central region
—821 1	Federal Capital
	Including Buenos Aires
—821 2	Buenos Aires province
	See also —16368 for Bahía Blanca, La Plata estuary
—821 3	La Pampa province
—822	Mesopotamian provinces
	Class here *Paraná, *Uruguay Rivers
—822 1	Entre Ríos
—822 2	Corrientes
—822 3	Misiones
—822 4	Santa Fe
—823	Northeastern provinces
	Class here *Gran Chaco
—823 4	Chaco
—823 5	Formosa
—824	Northwestern provinces
—824 1	Jujuy
—824 2	Salta
—824 3	Tucumán
—824 5	Catamarca
—824 6	La Rioja
—825	North central provinces
—825 2	Santiago del Estero
—825 4	Córdoba
—826	Central Highland provinces
—826 2	San Luis

*Class parts of this physiographic region or feature as instructed under —4–9

—826 3	San Juan
—826 4	Mendoza
—827	Patagonian region
—827 2	Neuquén province
—827 3	Río Negro province

                     See also —16368 for Gulf of San Matias

—827 4	Chubut province

                     See also —16368 for Gulf of San Jorge

—827 5	Santa Cruz province

                     See also —16368 for Bahía Grande, Gulf of San Jorge

—827 6	Tierra del Fuego archipelago

         Class here comprehensive works on Tierra del Fuego island

         Class south Atlantic Ocean islands claimed by Argentina in —9711

            For Tierra del Fuego province of Chile, see —83646

—83   **Chile**

     This development reflects the political divisions established in 1973. Relatively minor changes between this development and the Edition 19 development, which reflects the previous political divisions, are not indicated

SUMMARY

—831	**Tarapacá, Antofagasta, Atacama regions**
—832	**Comquimbo and Aconcagua regions**
—833	**Central regions**
—834	**Bío-Bío and Araucania regions**
—835	**Los Lagos region**
—836	**Aisén del General Carlos Ibáñez del Campo and Magallanes y Antártica Chilena regions**

—831	Tarapacá, Antofagasta, Atacama regions
—831 2	Tarapacá region
—831 23	Arica province
—831 27	Iquique province
—831 3	Antofagasta region
—831 32	Tocopilla province
—831 35	El Loa province
—831 38	Antofagasta province
—831 4	Atacama region
—831 42	Chañaral province

—831 45	Copiapó province
—831 48	Huasco province
—832	Coquimbo and Aconcagua regions
—832 3	Coquimbo region
—832 32	Elqui province
—832 35	Limarí province
—832 38	Choapa province
—832 4	Aconcagua region

Class here former Aconcagua province

> For Quillota, Valparaíso, San Antonio provinces, see —8325; Easter Island, see —9618

—832 42	Los Andes province
—832 45	San Felipe province
—832 48	Petorca province
—832 5	Quillota, Valparaíso, San Antonio provinces

Class here former Valparaíso province

—832 52	Quillota province
—832 55	Valparaíso province
—832 58	San Antonio province
—833	Central regions
—833 1	Metropolitana region

Class here former Santiago province

—833 15	Santiago
—833 2	Cachapoal province

Class here Libertador General Bernardo O'Higgins region, former O'Higgins province

> For Colchagua province, see —8333

—833 3	Colchagua province
—833 4	Curicó province
—833 5	Talca province

Including northern part of former Maule province [*formerly* —8336]

Class here Maule region

> For Curicó province, see —8334; Linares province, —8337

—[833 6]   Maule province

> Northern part of former Maule province relocated to —8335, southern part of former Maule province to —8337

—833 7   Linares province

> Including southern part of former Maule province [*formerly* —8336]

—833 8   Ñuble province

—833 9   Concepción province

—834   Bío-Bío and Araucania regions

—834 1   Bío-Bío region

> *For Ñuble province, see —8338; Concepción province, —8339; Arauco province, —8342; Bío-Bío province, —8343*

—834 2   Arauco province

—834 3   Bío-Bío province

—834 5   Malleco province

—834 6   Cautín province

> Class here Araucania region
>
> *For Malleco province, see —8345*

—835   Los Lagos region

—835 2   Valdivia province

—835 3   Osorno province

—835 4   Llanquihue province

—835 6   Chiloé province

—836   Aisén del General Carlos Ibáñez del Campo and Magallanes y Antártica Chilena regions

—836 2   Aisén del General Carlos Ibáñ del Campo region

—836 22   Aisén province

> Including Chonos Archipelago

—836 25   General Carrera province

—836 28   Capitán Prat province

—836 4   Magallanes y Antártica Chilena region

—836 42   Ultima Esperanza province

—836 44   Magallanes province

> *See also —1674 for Strait of Magellan*

—836 46	Tierra del Fuego province
	Class comprehensive works on Tierra del Fuego archipelago in —8276
—836 48	Antártica Chilena province
—84	**Bolivia**
—841	Mountain region departments
—841 2	La Paz
	Class here La Paz, *Lake Titicaca
—841 3	Oruro
—841 4	Potosí
—842	Valley region departments
—842 3	Cochabamba
—842 4	Chuquisaca
	Including Sucre
—842 5	Tarija
—843	Santa Cruz department
	Class here plains region
—844	Amazon region departments
—844 2	El Beni (Beni)
—844 3	Pando
—85	**Peru**
—851	Northern departments
—851 2	Tumbes
—851 3	Piura
—851 4	Lambayeque
—851 5	Cajamarca
—851 6	La Libertad
—852	Central departments
—852 1	Ancash
—852 2	Huánuco
—852 3	Pasco
—852 4	Junín

*Class parts of this physiographic region or feature as instructed under —4–9

—852 5	Lima
	Class here Lima
—852 6	Callao
—852 7	Ica
—852 8	Huancavelica
—852 9	Ayacucho and Apurímac
—852 92	Ayacucho
—852 94	Apurímac
—853	Southern departments
—853 2	Arequipa
—853 4	Moquegua
—853 5	Tacna
—853 6	Puno
	Including Lake Titicaca in Peru
—853 7	Cuzco
—854	Eastern departments
—854 2	Madre de Dios
—854 3	Loreto
	Class here *Amazon River in Peru
—854 5	San Martín
—854 6	Amazonas
—86	**Colombia and Ecuador**
—861	Colombia
—861 1	Caribbean Coast region
—861 12	Córdoba
—861 13	Sucre
—861 14	Bolívar
—861 15	Atlántico
—861 16	Magdalena
—861 17	La Guajira
—861 2	Northwestern region
—861 23	El César
—861 24	Norte de Santander

*Class parts of this physiographic region or feature as instructed under —4–9

—861 25	Santander
—861 26	Antioquia
—861 27	Chocó
—861 3	North central region

For Casanare, Cundinamarca, Bogotá, see —8614

—861 32	Risaralda
—861 34	Quindío
—861 35	Caldas
—861 36	Tolima
—861 37	Boyacá
—861 38	Arauca
—861 39	Vichada
—861 4	Casanare, Cundinamarca, Bogotá
—861 43	Casanare
—861 46	Cundinamarca
—861 48	Bogotá
—861 5	South central region
—861 52	Valle del Cauca
—861 53	Cauca
—861 54	Huila
—861 56	Meta
—861 6	Southern region

For Amazonas, see —8617

—861 62	Nariño
—861 63	Putumayo
—861 64	Caquetá
—861 65	Vaupés
—861 67	Guainía
—861 7	Amazonas
—861 8	San Andrés y Providencia
	Islands in Caribbean Sea
—866	Ecuador
—866 1	Northern interior provinces
—866 11	Carchi

—866 12	Imbabura
—866 13	Pichincha
	Including Quito
—866 14	Cotopaxi
—866 15	Tungurahua
—866 16	Bolívar
—866 17	Chimborazo
—866 2	Southern interior provinces
—866 23	Cañar
—866 24	Azuay
—866 25	Loja
—866 3	Coastal provinces
—866 31	El Oro
—866 32	Guayas
	See also —1641 for Gulf of Guayaquil
—866 33	Los Ríos
—866 34	Manabí
—866 35	Esmeraldas
—866 4	Eastern provinces
—866 41	Napo
—866 42	Pastaza
—866 43	Morona-Santiago
—866 44	Zamora-Chinchipe
—866 5	Galapagos Islands (Colón)
—87	**Venezuela**
	Class here *Orinoco River
—871	Southwestern states
—871 2	Táchira
—871 3	Mérida
—871 4	Trujillo
—872	Northwestern states
—872 3	Zulia
	Class here *Lake Maracaibo

*Class parts of this physiographic region or feature as instructed under —4–9

—872 4	Falcón
	See also —16365 for Gulf of Venezuela
—872 5	Lara
—872 6	Yaracuy
—873	North central states
	Including Federal Dependencies
	For Federal District, see —877
—873 2	Carabobo
—873 4	Aragua
—873 5	Miranda
—874	Central states
—874 2	Apure
—874 3	Barinas
—874 5	Portuguesa
—874 6	Cojedes
—874 7	Guárico
—875	Northeastern states
—875 2	Anzoátegui
—875 3	Sucre
	See also —16366 for Gulf of Paria
—875 4	Nueva Esparta
—875 6	Monagas
—876	Southeastern region
—876 2	Delta Amacuro territory
—876 3	Bolívar state
—876 4	Amazonas territory
—877	Federal District
	Including Caracas
—88	**Guiana**
—881	Guyana
	Formerly British Guiana
—881 1	North West district
—881 2	Essequibo district
—881 3	Essequibo Islands district

—881 4   West Demerara district

—881 5   East Demerara district

                Including Georgetown

—881 6   West Berbice district

—881 7   East Berbice district

—881 8   Rupununi

—881 9   Mazaruni-Potaro district

—882   French Guiana (Guyane)

                Overseas department of France

                Contains Cayenne and Saint-Laurent du Maroni arrondissements

                Class here Inini

—[882 3]   Cayenne district

                Number discontinued; class in —882

—[882 4]   Inini district

                Number discontinued; class in —882

—883   Surinam

                Former name: Dutch Guiana

—883 1   Nickerie district

—883 2   Coronie district

—883 3   Saramacca district

—883 4   Para district

—883 5   Paramaribo district

                Class here Paramaribo

—883 6   Suriname district

—883 7   Commewijne district

—883 8   Marowijne district

—883 9   Brokopondo district

—89   Paraguay and Uruguay

—892   Paraguay

                Class here Paraguay River

—892 1   Oriental province

—892 12   South departments

—892 121   Capital District

                Including Asunción

—892 122	Central
—892 123	Paraguarí
—892 124	Ñeembucú
—892 125	Misiones
—892 126	Itapúa
—892 127	Caazapá
—892 128	Guairá
—892 13	North departments
—892 132	Alto Paraná
—892 133	Canendiyú
—892 134	Caaguazú
—892 135	Cordillera
—892 136	San Pedro
—892 137	Amambay
—892 138	Concepción
—892 2	Occidental province

Class here *Chaco Boreal

—892 23	Presidente Hayes
—892 24	Boquerón
—892 25	Nueva Asunción
—892 26	Chaco
—892 27	Alto Paraguay
—895	Uruguay

Class here *Uruguay River in Uruguay

—895 1	Coastal departments

See also —16368 for La Plata estuary

—895 11	Colonia
—895 12	San José
—895 13	Montevideo

Class here Montevideo

—895 14	Canelones
—895 15	Maldonado

*Class parts of this physiographic region or feature as instructed under —4–9

—895 16	Rocha
—895 2	Central departments
—895 21	Lavalleja
—895 22	Treinta y Tres
—895 23	Cerro Largo
—895 24	Durazno
—895 25	Florida
—895 26	Flores
—895 27	Soriano
—895 28	Río Negro
—895 3	Northern departments
—895 31	Paysandú
—895 32	Tacuarembó
—895 34	Rivera
—895 35	Salto
—895 36	Artigas

—9   Other parts of world and extraterrestrial worlds   Pacific Ocean islands

SUMMARY

—93	New Zealand
—94	Australia
—95	Melanesia New Guinea
—96	Other parts of Pacific Ocean Polynesia
—97	Atlantic Ocean islands
—98	Arctic islands and Antarctica
—99	Extraterrestrial worlds

>   **—93–96 Pacific Ocean islands**

Class comprehensive works in —9; each specific island or group of islands not provided for here with the subject, e.g., Japan —52

—93   New Zealand

—931   Specific islands

Use of this notation for comprehensive works on New Zealand discontinued; class in 93

—931 1   Outlying islands

Including Antipodes, Auckland, Campbell, Chatham, Pitt

For Cook Islands, see —9623

—931 2	North Island
—931 22	Auckland provincial district
	Contains Central Auckland, East Coast, Northland, South Auckland
	Including Hamilton
—931 23	Taranaki provincial district
—931 25	Hawke's Bay provincial district
—931 27	Wellington provincial district
—931 5	South Island and Stewart Island
—931 52	Marlborough provincial district
—931 53	Nelson provincial district
—931 54	Westland provincial district
—931 55	Canterbury provincial district
	Including Christchurch
—931 57	Otago provincial district
	Contains Otago, Southland
	Including Dunedin
—931 575	Stewart Island
—[932–937]	Melanesia
	Relocated to —95
—94	**Australia**
	Class here *Great Dividing Range

SUMMARY

—941	**Western Australia**
—942	**Central Australia**
—943	**Queensland**
—944	**New South Wales**
—945	**Victoria**
—946	**Tasmania**
—947	**Australian Capital Territory**
—948	**Outlying islands**

—941	Western Australia
—941 1	Perth metropolitan district
	Including Fremantle

*Class parts of this physiographic region or feature as instructed under —4–9

—941 2   Southwestern district

    Including Albany, Bunbury, Collie, Geraldton, Katanning, Manjimup, Merredin, Narrogin, Northam; Kalbarri, Nelson and Hay, Nornalup, Stirling Range National Parks; Darling, Stirling Ranges; Blackwood, Greenough, Swan Rivers

    For Perth metropolitan district, see —9411

—941 3   Northwestern district

    Including Carnarvon, Port Hedland; Barrow Island, Bernier and Dorre Islands, Cape Range National Parks; North West Cape; Dampier Archipelago; Dirk Hartog Island; Hammersley Range; Ashburton, Gascoyne, *Murchison Rivers; Lake Austin

—941 4   Kimberley district

    Including Broome, Derby, Wyndham; Bonaparte Archipelago; King Leopold Ranges; Fitzroy, Ord Rivers

—941 5   North central district

    Including Lake Nabberu

    Class here Gibson, Great Sandy, *Great Victoria Deserts

    Class Great Victoria Desert in South Australia in —94238

—941 6   South central district

    Including Coolgardie, Kalgoorlie, Wiluna; Lakes Barlee, Carey, Carnegie

—941 7   Southern district

    Including Esperance, Norseman; Cape Le Grand, Esperance National Parks; Archipelago of the Recherche

—942   Central Australia

—942 3   South Australia

—942 31   Adelaide metropolitan district

—942 32   Central district

    Including Angaston, Clare, Gawler, Mannum, Murray Bridge, Port Noarlunga, Port Pirie, Salisbury, Strathalbyn, Victor Harbour; Chaunceys Line Reserve National Park; Mount Lofty Ranges

    For Adelaide metropolitan district, see —94231

—942 33   Eastern district

    Including Barmera, Berri, Loxton, Renmark, Tailem Bend; Billiatt, Mount Rescue Conservation Parks; Lake Alexandrina

    Class here The Coorong

*Class parts of this physiographic region or feature as instructed under —4–9

—942 34   Southern district

      Including Bordertown, Kingston, Mount Gambier, Naracoorte; Canunda National Park; Messent Conservation Park

—942 35   West central district

      Including Kadina, Maitland, Moonta, Wallaroo; Flinders Chase National Park; Yorke Peninsula; Kangaroo Island

—942 36   North central district

      Including Peterborough, Quorn

—942 37   Northern district

      Including Leigh Creek; Sturts Stony Desert; Lakes Blanche, Callabonna, Frome; Wilpena Pound

      Class here *Flinders Ranges; *Coopers (Cooper) Creek; *The Warburton

—942 38   Western district

      Including Port Augusta, Port Lincoln, Whyalla; Hambridge, Hincks Conservation Parks; Lincoln National Park; Eyre Peninsula; Musgrave Ranges; the Alberga, the Neales; Lakes Eyre, Gairdner, Torrens

      Class here *Nullarbor Plain

—942 9   Northern Territory

      Class here northern Australia

      For Western Australia, see —941; Queensland, —943

—942 91   Southern district

      Including Alice Springs; Ormiston Gorge, Palm Valley, Uluru (Ayers Rock-Mount Olga) National Parks; Tanami Desert Wildlife Sanctuary; Davenport, Harts, Macdonnell, *Murchison, Petermann Ranges; Ayers Rock; Mount Zeil; Todd River

      Class here *Simpson Desert; *Finke River

—942 95   Northern district

      Including Daly Waters, Darwin, Katherine, Tennant Creek; Cobourg Peninsula, Katherine Gorge National Parks; Cobourg Peninsula Wildlife Sanctuary and Fauna Reserve; Daly River, Murgenella, Woolwonga Wildlife Sanctuaries; Arnhem Land; Bathurst, Elcho, Melville Islands; Sir Edward Pellew Group; Groote Eylandt; Newcastle Range; Daly, Roper, Victoria Rivers

      Class here *Barkly Tableland

      See also —16475 for Gulf of Carpentaria

—943   Queensland

      Class here Great Barrier Reef

*Class parts of this physiographic region or feature as instructed under —4–9

—943 1   Brisbane metropolitan district

—943 2   Southeastern district

> Including Beaudesert, Bundaberg, Gatton, Gympie, Ipswich, Kingaroy, Maryborough, Mundubbera, Nambour, Southport, Surfers Paradise, Wondai; Bunya Mountains, Cooloola, Lamington, Mount Barney National Parks; Fraser Island; *Bunya, Glasshouse Mountains; *McPherson Range; Burnett River

> Class here *Brisbane River

> *For Brisbane metropolitan district, see —9431*

—943 3   Downs district

> Including Chinchilla, Dalby, Goondiwindi, Inglewood, Miles, Millmerran, Oakey, Pittsworth, Stanthorpe, Texas, Toowoomba, Warwick; Granite Belt National Park; Darling Downs

—943 4   Southwestern district

> Including Charleville, Cunnamulla, Mitchell, Roma, Saint George; Channel Country; Moonie River

> Class here *Grey Range; *Paroo, *Warrego Rivers

—943 5   Central district

> Including Barcaldine, Biloela, Blackall, Clermont, Emerald, Gladstone, Longreach, Monto, Mount Morgan, Rockhampton, Winton, Yeppoon; Carnarvon, Dipperu, Isla Gorge, Robinson Gorge, Salvator Rosa National Parks; Northumberland Islands; *Connors Range; Barcoo, Fitzroy Rivers

> Class here *Eyre Creek; *Diamantina, *Georgina, *Thomson Rivers

—943 6   Northeastern district

> Including Atherton, Ayr, Bowen, Cairns, Charters Towers, Ingham, Innisfail, Mackay, Mareeba, Townsville, Tully; Bellenden Ker, Conway Range, Eungella, Hinchinbrook Island, Mount Elliott, Mount Spec, Whitsunday Island, Windsor Tableland National Parks; Swans Lagoon Fauna Reserve; Hinchinbrook, Whitsunday Islands; Clarke, Leichhardt Ranges; Burdekin River; Lake Barrine

—943 7   Northwestern district

> Including Cloncurry, Hughenden, Mary Kathleen, Mount Isa, Richmond; Simpson Desert National Park; Wellesley Islands; Selwyn Range; Gilbert, Leichhardt, *Mitchell Rivers

> Class here Flinders River

> *See also —16475 for Gulf of Carpentaria*

—943 8   Peninsula and Torres Strait Islands

> Including Cape York Peninsula; Murray Islands; Thursday Island; Archer, Normanby, Wenlock Rivers

*Class parts of this physiographic region or feature as instructed under —4–9

—944   New South Wales

> Class here *Australian Alps; *Murray River

—944 1   Sydney metropolitan district

> Including Hornsby, Liverpool, Parramatta, Penrith; Ku-ring-gai Chase National Park

—944 2   Lower north coast district

> Including Cessnock, Dungog, The Entrance, Forster, Gloucester, Gosford, Maitland, Muswellbrook, Newcastle, Port Macquarie, Scone, Singleton, Taree, Toronto, Woy Woy; Brisbane Waters National Park; Hawkesbury, Hunter Rivers

—944 3   Upper north coast district

> Including Ballina, Casino, Coffs Harbour, Grafton, Kempsey, Kyogle, Lismore, Murwillumbah; Gibraltar Range National Park; Point Lookout; Richmond River

> Class here *Clarence, *Macleay Rivers

—944 4   North central district

> Including Armidale, Barraba, Boggabri, Coonabarabran, Glen Innes, Gunnedah, Inverell, Moree, Murrurundi, Narrabri, Quirindi, Tamworth, Tenterfield; Mount Kaputar, New England National Parks; Nandewar, New England, Warrumbungle Ranges

> Class here *Gwydir, *Namoi Rivers

—944 5   Central district

> Including Bathurst, Cowra, Crookwell, Dubbo, Forbes, Gilgandra, Katoomba, Lithgow, Mudgee, Orange, Parkes, Wellington; Blue Mountains National Park; Curumbenya Fauna Reserve; *Blue Mountains; Jenolan Caves

—944 6   Upper south coast district

> Including Camden, Campbelltown, Mittagong, Moss Vale, Narellan, Port Kembla, Wollongong; Morton, Royal National Parks; Nepean, Wollondilly Rivers; Lake Illawarra

—944 7   Southeastern district

> Including Batemans Bay, Bega, Bomaderry, Bombala, Braidwood, Captains Flat, Cooma, Eden, Goulburn, Kiama, Moruya, Narooma, Nowra, Queanbeyan, Ulladulla, Yass; Kosciusko, Shoalhaven National Parks; Nadgee Fauna Reserve; *Mount Kosciusko; Yarrangobilly Caves; Shoalhaven River; Lake George

> Class here *Snowy Mountains; *Snowy River

> Class Australian Capital Territory in —947

*Class parts of this physiographic region or feature as instructed under —4–9

—944 8   Southern district

> Including Albury, Balranald, Cootamundra, Corowa, Deniliquin, Grenfell, Griffith, Gundagai, Hay, Junee, Leeton, Murrumburrah, Temora, Tumut, Wagga Wagga, Wentworth, Young; Cocoparra National Park; Edward, Tooma, Wakool Rivers; Lake Victoria

> Class here Murrumbidgee River

—944 9   Western district

> Including Bourke, Brewarrina, Broken Hill, Cobar, Condobolin, Coonamble, Nyngan, Walgett, Warren; Main Barrier Range; Barwon River; Menindee Lakes

> Class here *Castlereagh, *Darling, *Lachlan, *Macquarie Rivers

—945   Victoria

—945 1   Melbourne metropolitan district

—945 2   Central district

> Including Bacchus Marsh, Geelong, Healesville, Korumburra, Mornington, Pakenham, Queenscliff, Rosebud, Sorrento, Sunbury, Torquay, Werribee, Winchelsea, Wonthaggi; Kinglake National Park; French, Phillip Islands

> Class here Yarra River

> *For Melbourne metropolitan district, see —9451*

—945 3   North central district

> Including Alexandra, Broadford, Castlemaine, Creswick, Daylesford, Heathcote, Kilmore, Kyneton, Maldon, Maryborough, Seymour, Woodend, Yea

—945 4   Northern district

> Including Bendigo, Charlton, Echuca, Inglewood, Kerang, Kyabram, Nathalia, Numurkah, Rochester, Rushworth, Shepparton, Tatura, Yarrawonga

> Class here *Campaspe, *Goulburn, *Loddon Rivers

—945 5   Northeastern district

> Including Beechworth, Benalla, Corryong, Euroa, Mansfield, Mount Beauty, Myrtleford, Rutherglen, Tallangatta, Wangaratta, Wodonga; Mount Buffalo National Park; Mounts Bogong, Buffalo, Feathertop

> Class here Mitta Mitta, *Ovens Rivers

*Class parts of this physiographic region or feature as instructed under —4–9

—945 6   Gippsland district

> Including Bairnsdale, Lakes Entrance, Leongatha, Maffra, Moe, Morwell, Orbost, Sale, Traralgon, Warragul, Yallourn, Yarram; Ewings Morass, Lake Reeve, Nooramunga, Rocky Range Fauna Reserves; Mallacoota Inlet, Wilsons Promontory National Parks; Snake Island; Buchan Caves; Mitchell River; Lake Wellington

> Class here *La Trobe, *Macallister, Tambo Rivers

—945 7   Western district

> Including Ararat, Ballarat, Camperdown, Casterton, Colac, Coleraine, Hamilton, Mortlake, Port Fairy, Portland, Terang, Warrnambool; the Stones Fauna Reserve; Glenelg River; Lake Corangamite

—945 8   Wimmera district

> Including Dimboola, Donald, Horsham, Kaniva, Murtoa, Nhill, Saint Arnaud, Stawell, Warracknabeal; *The Grampians; *Lake Hindmarsh

—945 9   Mallee district

> Including Birchip, Hopetoun, Irymple, Merbein, Mildura, Ouyen, Red Cliffs, Robinvale, Sea Lake, Swan Hill; Hattah Lakes, Wyperfeld National Parks; *Wimmera River; Lakes Albacutya, Tyrell

—946   Tasmania

—946 1   Hobart metropolitan district

—946 2   Southern district

> Including Huonville, Kingston, New Norfolk, Port Cygnet; Hartz Mountains, Lake Pedder, Mount Field National Parks; Arthur, Frankland Ranges; Hartz Mountains; Hastings Caves; Bruny Island; Huon River

> Class here *Derwent River

> Port Davey relocated to —16576

> *For Hobart metropolitan district, see —9461*

—946 3   Central district

> Including Campbell Town, Deloraine, Longford, Oatlands, Perth, Poatina, Wayatinah, Westbury; Cradle Mountain-Lake Saint Clair National Park; Lyell Highway State Reserve; Cradle Mountain; Ducane Range; Mole Creek Caves; Great Lake; Lakes Crescent, King William, Saint Clair, Sorell

> Class here Great Western Mountains

—946 4   Eastern district

> Including George Town, Port Arthur, Rossarden, Scottsdale; Ben Lomond, Freycinet National Parks; Tooms Lake Wildlife Sanctuary; Ben Lomond; Freycinet, Tasman Peninsulas; Maria, Schouten Islands

> Class here *North Esk, *South Esk Rivers

*Class parts of this physiographic region or feature as instructed under —4–9

—946 5   Northwestern district

> Including Beaconsfield, Burnie, Devonport, Latrobe, Launceston, Penguin, Railton, Smithton, Somerset, Stanley, Ulverstone, Wynyard
>
> Class here *Arthur, *Forth, *Mersey, *Tamar Rivers

—946 6   Western district

> Including Queenstown, Rosebery, Zeehan; Frenchmans Cap National Park; *Eldon, Norfolk Ranges
>
> Class here *Gordon River

—946 7   Bass Strait Islands

> Including Furneaux Group (Cape Barren, Clarke, Flinders Islands); Hunter, King, Robbins, Three Hummock Islands

—947   Australian Capital Territory

> Including Tidbinbilla Nature Reserve

—947 1   Canberra

—948   Outlying islands

> Including Ashmore, Cartier, Christmas Islands
>
> *For Cocos Islands, see —699*

—948 1   Lord Howe Island

—948 2   Norfolk Island

—95   **Melanesia [*formerly also* —932–937]**   **New Guinea**

> Class here Oceania
>
> Class Polynesia, Micronesia in —96

\>   —951–957   New Guinea

> Class comprehensive works in —95

—951   Irian Jaya

> Former names: Irian Barat, Netherlands New Guinea, West Irian, West New Guinea

—953   Papua New Guinea   New Guinea region [*formerly* —955]

> Class here former German New Guinea, former territory of New Guinea
>
> Papuan region relocated to —954, Southern Highlands Province to —9561
>
> *For Highlands region, see —956; Momase region, —957; Bismarck Archipelago, —958; North Solomons Province, —9592*

*Class parts of this physiographic region or feature as instructed under —4–9

—954   Papuan region [*formerly* —953]

—954 1   Milne Bay Province

       Including Altotau, Samarai; D'Entrecasteaux Islands, Louisiade Archipelago, Muyua (Woodlark) Island, Trobriand Islands

—954 2   Northern (Oro) Province

       Including Popondetta; Didana Range, Kokoda Trail

—954 5   National Capital District

       Class here Port Moresby

—954 6   Central Province

       Including Abau, Bereina, Kupiano; Astrolabe Range

       Class here *Owen Stanley Range

—954 7   Gulf Province

       Including Kerema, Kikori, Malalaua

       Class here *Kikori, *Purari Rivers

—954 9   Western (Fly River) Province

       Including Balimo, Daru, Kiunga, Ok Tedi; Strickland River

       Class here *Star Mountains; *Fly River

—[955]   New Guinea region

       Comprehensive works on New Guinea region relocated to —953, Highlands region to —956, Momase region to —957

—956   Highlands region [*formerly* —955]

       Class here *Bismarck Range

—956 1   Southern Highlands Province [*formerly* —953]

       Including Mendi; Muller Range

—956 3   Enga Province

       Including Wabag

—956 5   Western Highlands Province

       Including Mount Hagen

       Class here Jimi, Waghi Rivers

—956 7   Simbu (Chimbu) Province

       Including Kundiawa

—956 9   Eastern Highlands Province

       Including Goroka

       Class here *Kratke Range

*Class parts of this physiographic region or feature as instructed under —4–9

—957   Momase (Northern coastal) region [*formerly* —955]

—957 1   Morobe Province

> Including Lae; Huon Peninsula; Bowutu Mountains; Siassi, Tami, Umboi Islands; Markham River

—957 3   Madang Province

> Including Bogia, Madang; Karkar, Long, Manam islands; Adelbert Range

> Class here *Finisterre, *Schrader ranges; Ramu River

—957 5   East Sepik Province

> Including Angoram, Wewak; Schouten Islands

> Class here *Prince Alexander Mountains; *Sepik, *Yuat Rivers

—957 7   West Sepik Province

> Including Aitape, Vanima; Torricelli Mountains

> Class here *Victor Emanuel Range

—958   Bismarck Archipelago

> Part of Papua New Guinea

—958 1   Manus Province

> Including Lorengau; Admiralty, Hermit, Ninigo islands

—958 3   New Ireland Province

> Including Kavieng; Lavongai (New Hanover) Island; St. Matthias Group

—958 5   East New Britain Province

> Including Kokopo, Pomio, Rabaul; Ulawun; Duke of York Group

> Class here comprehensive works on New Britain

> *For West New Britain Province, see* —9587

—958 7   West New Britain Province

> Including Kimbe; Whiteman Range; Vitu Islands

—959   Other parts of Melanesia

—959 2   North Solomons Province

> Part of Papua New Guinea

> Including Arawa, Kieta; Bougainville, Buka, Nukumanu islands; Nuguria Atoll

*Class parts of this physiographic region or feature as instructed under —4–9

—959 3	Solomon Islands
	Independent nation
	Former name: British Solomon Islands
—959 31	Western Province
—959 33	Guadalcanal Province
—959 35	Central Islands and Santa Isabel Province
—959 37	Malaita Province
—959 39	Makula and Temotu Province
—959 5	Vanuatu
	Former name: New Hebrides
—959 7	New Caledonia
	Including Loyalty Islands

—96   Other parts of Pacific Ocean   Polynesia

SUMMARY

—961	Southwest central Pacific Ocean islands, and isolated islands of southeast Pacific Ocean
—962	South central Pacific Ocean islands
—963	Southeast central Pacific Ocean islands
—964	Line Islands
—965	West central Pacific Ocean islands (Micronesia) Trust Territory of the Pacific Islands
—966	Federated States of Micronesia and Republic of Belau (Palau)
—967	Mariana Islands
—968	Islands of eastern Micronesia
—969	North central Pacific Ocean islands Hawaii

—961	Southwest central Pacific Ocean islands, and isolated islands of southeast Pacific Ocean
—961 1	Fiji
—961 2	Tonga (Friendly Islands)
—961 3	American Samoa
	Class here comprehensive works on Samoa
	For Western Samoa, see —9614
—961 4	Western Samoa
	Including Savai'i, Upolu
—961 5	Tokelau (Union Islands)
—961 6	Wallis and Futuna Islands
—961 8	Isolated islands of southeast Pacific Ocean
	Examples: Ducie, Easter, Henderson, Oeno, Pitcairn

—962	South central Pacific Ocean islands

Class here French Polynesia

For Marquesas Islands, see —9631; Tuamotu Islands, —9632

—962 1	Society Islands
—962 11	Tahiti
—962 2	Gambier and Tubuai (Austral) Islands
—962 3	Cook Islands

Part of New Zealand

For Manihiki Islands, see —9624

—962 4	Manihiki Islands

Part of Cook Islands

—962 6	Niue
—963	Southeast central Pacific Ocean islands

For isolated islands of southeast Pacific Ocean, see —9618

—963 1	Marquesas Islands

Part of French Polynesia

—963 2	Tuamotu Islands (Low Archipelago)

Part of French Polynesia

For Gambier Islands, see —9622

—964	Line Islands

Variant name: Equatorial Islands

Examples: Caroline, Flint, Jarvis, Kiritimati (Christmas), Malden, Starbuck, Tabuaeran (Fanning), Teraina (Washington), Vostok Islands; Kingman Reef

For Palmyra, see —9699

—965	West central Pacific Ocean islands (Micronesia) Trust Territory of the Pacific Islands

Including Wake Island

Class each specific island or group of islands with the island or group of islands, e.g., Marshall Islands —9683

—966	Federated States of Micronesia and Republic of Belau (Palau)

Including Senyavin, Truk Islands

Class here Caroline Islands

—967   Mariana Islands

>   Former name: Ladrone Islands

>   Class here Commonwealth of the Northern Mariana Islands

>   Examples: Guam, Saipan, Tinian

—968   Islands of eastern Micronesia

—968 1   Kiribati

>   Contains Banaba Island; Gilbert, Phoenix Islands

>   Tuvalu relocated to —9682

>   *For Line Islands, see —964*

—968 2   Tuvalu [*formerly* —9681]

>   Class here Ellice Islands

—968 3   Marshall Islands

>   Examples: Bikini, Eniwetok, Kwajalein Atolls

—968 5   Nauru (Pleasant Island)

—969   North central Pacific Ocean islands   Hawaii

>   —969 1–969 4 Hawaii

>   State of the United States of America

>   Class comprehensive works in —969

—969 1   Hawaii County (Hawaii Island)

—969 2   Maui County

—969 21   Maui Island

—969 22   Kahoolawe Island

—969 23   Lanai Island

—969 24   Molokai Island

>   Including Kalawao County (leper settlement)

—969 3   Honolulu County (Oahu Island)

—969 31   Honolulu

—969 4   Kauai County

—969 41   Kauai Island

—969 42   Niihau Island

—969 9   Outlying islands

>   Examples: Baker, Howland, Johnston, Midway, Palmyra Islands

—97   **Atlantic Ocean islands**

> Class each specific island or group of islands not provided for here with the island or group of islands, e.g., Azores —4699

—971   Falklands and Bouvet Island

—971 1   Falklands and dependent islands

> Examples: South Georgia; South Orkney, South Sandwich, South Shetland Islands

—971 3   Bouvet Island

—973   Saint Helena and dependencies

> Including Ascension Island; Tristan da Cunha Islands

—98   **Arctic islands and Antarctica**

>   **—981–988**   Arctic islands

> Class comprehensive works in —98; each Arctic island or group of islands not provided for here with the island or group of islands, e.g., Baffin region, Canada —7195

—981   Svalbard (Spitsbergen Archipelago)

—982   Greenland

—983   Jan Mayen Island

—985   Franz Josef Land

> Part of Arkhangelsk Region of Soviet Union

—986   Novaya Zemlya (New Land)

> Part of Arkhangelsk Region of Soviet Union

—987   Severnaya Zemlya (Northern Land)

> Part of Krasnoyarsk Territory of Soviet Union

—988   New Siberian Islands

> Part of Yakut Autonomous Soviet Socialist Republic of Soviet Union

—989   Antarctica

> Including Ellsworth, Enderby, Graham, Marie Byrd, Queen Maud, Wilkes Lands; Palmer Peninsula; South Pole

—99	**Extraterrestrial worlds**
	Worlds other than Earth
	Class space in —19
	See Manual at T2—19 vs. T2—99

>	**—991–994 Solar system**
	Class comprehensive works in —99
—991	Earth's moon
—992	Planets of solar system and their satellites
—992 1	Mercury
—992 2	Venus
—992 3	Mars and its two satellites
—992 4	Asteroids (Planetoids)
—992 5	Jupiter and its twelve satellites
—992 6	Saturn and its ten satellites
—992 7	Uranus and its five satellites
—992 8	Neptune and its two satellites
—992 9	Pluto and transplutonian planets
—993	Meteoroids and comets
—994	Sun

Table 3. Subdivisions for Individual Literatures, for Specific Literary Forms

Notation from Table 3 is never used alone, but may be used as required with the base numbers for individual literatures identified by * under 810–890. It is never used for individual literatures not identified by *; the number for works by or about individual or multiple authors in such literatures ends with the language notation, e.g., works of an author writing in Guaraní 898.3

Notation from Table 3 may also be used where instructed in 808–809

Table 3 is divided into three subtables:

Table 3–A for description, critical appraisal, biography, single or collected works of an individual author

Table 3–B for description, critical appraisal, biography, collected works of two or more authors; also for rhetoric in specific literary forms

Table 3–C for additional elements used in number building within Table 3–B and as instructed in 808–809

Turn to Table 3–A or 3–B for full instructions on building numbers for individual literatures, to 808 and 809 for other uses of Table 3–B and 3–C

See Manual at Table 3

Table 3–A. Subdivisions for Works by or about Individual Authors

Procedures for building numbers for individual authors:

1. Find the base number in the schedule 810–890. The base number may be identified in a note, e.g., at 820: "Base number for English: 82"; otherwise, it is the number given for the literature, e.g., Dutch-language literature 839.31. If there is a specific literary form, go to step 2; if not, go to the instructions under —8 in Table 3–A

2. In Table 3–A find the correct subdivision for the literary form, e.g., poetry —1. Add this to the base number, e.g., English poetry 821, Dutch poetry 839.311. If the literary form appears as a subdivision of —8 Miscellaneous writings, go to the instructions under —8 in Table 3–A; otherwise, go to step 3

(continued)

389

Table 3–A. Subdivisions for Works by or about Individual Authors (continued)

3.   Turn back to the appropriate number in the schedule 810–890 to see whether there is an applicable period table. If there is one, go to step 4; if not, complete the class number by inserting a point between the third and fourth digits, e.g., drama in English by a 20th-century New Zealand author 822, Khmer (Cambodian) poetry by a 20th-century author 895.9321

(Option: Where two or more countries share the same language, either [1] use initial letters to distinguish the separate countries, or [2] use the special number designated for literatures of those countries that are not preferred. Either option makes feasible the use of period tables for affiliated literatures, e.g., drama in English by a 20th-century New Zealand author NZ822.2 or 828.993322. Full instructions appear under 810, 819, 820, 828.99, 840.1–848.9, 848.99, 860.1–868.9, 868.99, 869, 869.899. If the option is used, go to step 4)

4.   Select the appropriate period number. Add this number to the number already derived; always insert a point after the third digit. The class number is complete (except for William Shakespeare), since standard subdivisions are never added for individual authors, e.g., Spenser's *Faerie Queene* 821.3 (821 English poetry + 3 Elizabethan period)

See Manual at Table 3–A; 800: Literary criticism

> ### —1–8 Specific forms

Unless other instructions are given, observe the following table of precedence for works combining two or more literary forms, e.g., drama written in verse —2 (*not* —1)

Drama	—2
Poetry	—1
Class epigrams in verse in —8	
Fiction	—3
Essays	—4
Speeches	—5
Letters	—6
Miscellaneous writings	—8

A single work of satire or humor, or a collection of satire or humor by an individual author in one form is classed with the form, e.g., satirical fiction —3. Satire or humor without identifiable form is classed according to the instructions at —8, with use of notation 07 from the table under —81–89 if there is an applicable period table. A collection of satire or humor by an individual author in more than one form is classed according to the instructions at —8, with use of notation 09 from the add table under —81–89 if there is an applicable period table

(continued)

> ## —1–8 Specific forms (continued)

Class comprehensive works (description, critical appraisal, biography, or collected works that cover two or more forms of literature by an individual author) with the form with which the author is chiefly identified, e.g., a biography that discusses the poetry and fiction of a mid-19th-century American writer known primarily as a novelist 813.3; or, if the author is not chiefly identified with any one form, class comprehensive works as instructed at —8, using notation 09 from the table under —81–89 if there is an applicable period table, e.g., the collected poetry and fiction of a mid-19th-century American writer not chiefly identified with any one form 818.309

(Option: Class description, critical appraisal, biography, single and collected works of all individual authors regardless of form in —8)

See Manual at Table 3–A

—1   Poetry

Class epigrams in verse in —8

See Manual at T3A—1, T3B—102 vs. T3A—2, T3B—2

—11–19   Poetry of specific periods

Add to —1 the notation from the period table for the specific literature in 810–890, e.g., earliest period —11; do not use standard subdivisions. If there is no applicable period table, add nothing to —1, e.g., poetry in English by an Australian author of the earliest period 821 (*not* 821.1)
(Option: Use the notation from the period table for an affiliated literature with either option given after step 3 at the beginning of Table 3–A, e.g., poetry in English by an Australian author of the earliest period A821.1 or 828.993411)

—2   Drama

Class here closet drama, drama written in poetry

See Manual at T3A—1, T3B—102 vs. T3A—2, T3B—2

—21–29   Specific periods

Add to —2 the notation from the period table for the specific literature in 810–890, e.g., earliest period —21; do not use standard subdivisions. If there is no applicable period table, add nothing to —2, e.g., drama in English by a New Zealand author of the earliest period 822 (*not* 822.1)
(Option: Use the notation from the period table for an affiliated literature with either option given after step 3 at the beginning of Table 3–A, e.g., drama in English by a New Zealand author of the earliest period NZ822.1 or 828.993321)

—3   Fiction

Class here novels, novelettes, short stories

Class graphic novels (cartoon or comic strip novels) in 741.5

—31–39   Specific periods

Add to —3 the notation from the period table for the specific literature in
810–890, e.g., earliest period —31; do not use standard subdivisions. If there is
no applicable period table, do not add anything to —3, e.g., fiction in French by
a Canadian author of the colonial period 843 (*not* 843.3)
(Option: Use the notation from the period table for an affiliated literature
with either option given after step 3 at the beginning of Table 3–A, e.g.,
fiction in French by a Canadian author of the colonial period C843.3 or
848.99233)

—4   Essays

—41–49   Specific periods

Add to —4 the notation from the period table for the specific literature in
810–890, e.g., earliest period —41; do not use standard subdivisions. If there is
no applicable period table, do not add anything to —4, e.g., essays in Spanish
by a 19th-century Mexican author 864 (*not* 864.2)
(Option: Use the notation from the period table for an affiliated literature
with either option given after step 3 at the beginning of Table 3–A, e.g.,
essays in Spanish by a 19th-century Mexican author M864.2 or 868.992142)

—5   Speeches

—51–59   Specific periods

Add to —5 the notation from the period table for the specific literature in
810–890, e.g., earliest period —51; do not use standard subdivisions. If there is
no applicable period table, add nothing to —5, e.g., speeches in Spanish by a
19th-century Colombian author 865 (*not* 865.2)
(Option: Use the notation from the period table for an affiliated literature
with either option given after step 3 at the beginning of Table 3–A, e.g.,
speeches in Spanish by a 19th-century Colombian author Co865.2 or
868.9936152)

—6   Letters

See Manual at T3A—6 and T3B—6

—61–69   Specific periods

Add to —6 the notation from the period table for the specific literature in
810–890, e.g., earliest period —61; do not use standard subdivisions. If there is
no applicable period table, add nothing to —6, e.g., letters in Portuguese by a
20th-century Brazilian author 869.6 (*not* 869.64)
(Option: Use the notation from the period table for an affiliated literature
with either option given after step 3 at the beginning of Table 3–A, e.g.,
letters in Portuguese by a 20th-century Brazilian author B869.64 or
869.899264)

—8   Miscellaneous writings

Only those forms named below

(Option: Class here description, critical appraisal, biography, single and collected works of all individual authors regardless of form; prefer —1–8)

Procedures for building numbers:

1.   To the base number add notation 8, e.g., miscellaneous writings in English 828. Go to step 2

2.   Turn back to the appropriate number in the schedule 810–890 to see whether there is an applicable period table. If there is one, go to step 3; if not, complete the class number by inserting a point between the third and fourth digits, e.g., miscellaneous writings in English by a 20th century New Zealand author 828, miscellaneous writings in Khmer (Cambodian) by a 20th century writer 895.9328
(Option: Where two or more countries share the same language, either [1] use initial letters to distinguish the separate countries, or [2] use the special number designated for literatures of those countries that are not preferred. Either option makes feasible the use of period tables for affiliated literatures, e.g., miscellaneous writings in English by a 20th-century New Zealand author NZ828.2 or 828.993382. Full instructions appear under 810, 819, 820, 828.99, 840.1–848.9, 848.99, 860.1–868.9, 868.99, 869, 869.899. If the option is used, go to step 3)

3.   Select the appropriate period number, e.g., the Victorian period in the English literature of Great Britain 8. Then follow the instructions under —81–89

—81–89   Specific periods

Add to —8 the notation from the period table for the specific literature in 810–890, e.g., earliest period —81; then add further as follows, but in no case add standard subdivisions:

02	Jokes [*formerly* 07], anecdotes, epigrams, graffiti, quotations
03	Diaries, journals, notebooks, reminiscences
07	Works without identifiable literary form

Class here experimental and nonformalized works

Jokes relocated to 02

08	Prose literature

Collections or discussions of works in more than one prose form

Class here collections and criticism of selected prose works of an individual author that do not include the author's main literary form, e.g., a collection of the prose works of an English Victorian poet 828.808, a collection of the stories and plays of an English Romantic essayist 828.708

Never class here comprehensive collections or criticisms of an author's work; class them in the author's main literary number, either with the predominant literary form or in 09 for individual authors not limited to or chiefly identifiable with one specific form

Class a specific form of prose literature with the form, e.g., essays —4; prose without identifiable literary form in 07

(continued)

—81–89   **Specific periods (continued)**

> 09   Individual authors not limited to or chiefly identifiable with one
> specific form
> > Class here description, critical appraisal, biography, collected
> > works
>
> If there is no applicable period table, add nothing to —8, e.g., prose literature in
> English by an Indian author of the later 20th century 828 (*not* 828.308)
> > (Option: Use the notation from the period table for an affiliated literature
> > with either option given after step 2 in the instructions under —8, e.g., prose
> > literature in English by an Indian author of the later 20th century In828.308
> > or 828.99358308)
>
> *See Manual at T3A—8 + 03 and T3B—803, T3B—8 + 03; T3B—7 vs.*
> *T3A—8 + 02, T3B—807, T3B—8 + 07, T1—0207*

Table 3–B. Subdivisions for Works by or about More than One Author

Table 3–B is followed and supplemented by Table 3–C, which provides additional
elements for building numbers within Table 3–B

Procedures for building numbers for works by or about more than one author, limited to
literatures of specific languages:

1.   Look in the schedule 810–890 to find the base number for the language. The base
number may be identified in a note, e.g., at 820: "Base number for English: 82";
otherwise, it is the number given for the literature, e.g., Dutch-language literature 839.31.
If there is a specific literary form, go to step 2; if not, skip to step 8

2.   In Table 3–B find the subdivision for the literary form, e.g., poetry —1. Add this
to the base number, e.g., English poetry 821, Dutch poetry 839.311. If the literary form
appears as a subdivision of —8 Miscellaneous writings, go to the instructions under —8
in Table 3–B. If the work deals with poetry, drama, fiction, or speech of specific media,
scopes, kinds for which there is special notation in Table 3–B, e.g., —1042 sonnets, go to
step 3. For other works that deal with or fall within a limited time period, skip to step 4;
for other works not limited by time period, skip to step 7

3.   Use the notation in Table 3–B for the kind of poetry, drama, fiction, or speech,
e.g., sonnets in English literature 821.042. Insert a point after the third digit. If the term
for the specific kind of literary form is neither identified by * nor appears in a class-here
note under a term identified by * the number is complete, e.g., collections of
English-language clerihews 821.07. If the term for the kind of literary form is identified
by * or does appear in a class-here note under a term so identified, follow the instructions
in the table under —102–108 in Table 3–B. Following these instructions will involve
using Table 3–C for literature of specific periods, literature displaying specific features or
emphasizing specific subjects, and literature for and by specific kinds of persons, e.g.,
collections of English sonnets 821.04208, collections of English sonnets about love
821.04208354

(continued)

Table 3–B. Subdivisions for Works by or about More than One Author (continued)

4.   Turn back to the appropriate number in the schedule 810–890 to see whether there is an applicable period table. If there is one, go to step 5; if not, complete the class number by inserting a point between the third and fourth digits, e.g., 20th-century drama in English by New Zealand authors 822, Khmer (Cambodian) poetry 895.9321

(Option: Where two or more countries share the same language, either [1] use initial letters to distinguish the separate countries, or [2] use the special number designated for literatures of those countries that are not preferred. Either option makes feasible the use of period tables for affiliated literatures, e.g., 20th-century drama in English by New Zealand authors NZ822.2 or 828.993322. Full instructions appear under 810, 819, 820, 828.99, 840.1–848.9, 848.99, 860.1–868.9, 868.99, 869, 869.899. If the option is used, go to step 5)

5.   Select the appropriate period number. Add this number to the number already derived, e.g., English poetry of the Elizabethan period 821.3; always insert a point after the third digit. Go to step 6

6.   Under the number for the literary form in Table 3–B, go to the subdivisions for specific periods, e.g., under —1 for poetry go to —11–19. Follow the instructions given there, which will lead to use of the table under —1–8. For literature displaying specific features, literature emphasizing subjects, and literature for and by specific kinds of persons, the instructions at —1–8 will lead to use of Table 3–C, e.g., critical appraisal of idealism in English Elizabethan poetry 821.30913

7.   If the work is not limited by time period, go to the first subdivisions under the particular form in Table 3–B, e.g., under —1 for poetry go to —1001–1009. Follow the instructions given there, which will lead to use of the table under —1–8. For literature displaying specific features, literature emphasizing subjects, and literature for and by specific kinds of persons, the instructions at —1–8 will lead to use of Table 3–C, e.g., collections of English poetry about war 821.0080358, collections of English poetry by rural authors 821.008091734

8.   If the work is not limited to a specific literary form, consult —01–09 in Table 3–B. Follow the instructions at the number selected, making use of Table 3–C when specified, e.g., collections of English literature in many forms about holidays 820.8033. Use period notation 08001–08009 and 09001–09009 only if there is an applicable period table

(continued)

Table 3–B. Subdivisions for Works by or about More than One Author (continued)

The procedures described above require the use of schedule 810–890, Table 3–B, and Table 3–C in varying order. Sometimes also other tables are used. Example:

82	English (810–890)
1	poetry (Table 3–B)
914	of later 20th century (810–890)
080	collections (Table 3–B)
32	about places (Table 3–C)
4253	Lincolnshire (Table 2)

Thus, collections of contemporary English-language poetry about Lincolnshire 821.914080324253

Note that literary form —8 Miscellaneous writings is arranged first by period and then by specific miscellaneous forms

Instructions in the use of notation from Table 3–B for rhetoric in specific literary forms, collections of literary texts from more than one literature, and history, description, critical appraisal of more than one literature are found in 808–809

See Manual at Table 3–B

SUMMARY

—01–09	[Standard subdivisions; collections; history, description, critical appraisal]
—1	Poetry
—2	Drama
—3	Fiction
—4	Essays
—5	Speeches
—6	Letters
—7	Satire and humor
—8	Miscellaneous writings

—01–07   Standard subdivisions

Standard subdivisions are used for general works consisting equally of literary texts and history, description, critical appraisal, e.g., a serial consisting equally of literary texts and history, description, critical appraisal of a variety of literature in English 820.5. Works limited to specific topics found in Table 3–C are classed in —08, with use of notation from Table 3–C

Class collections of literary texts in —08, history, description, critical appraisal in —09

—08   **Collections of literary texts in more than one form**

Add 0 to —08; then to the result add notation 001–99 from Table 3–C, e.g., collections of literary texts about holidays —08033

Use of this number for general works consisting equally of literary texts and history, description, critical appraisal of a specific literature discontinued; class in the base number for the literature, adding a 0 if necessary to make a three-digit number, e.g., texts and criticism of a variety of literary works in English 820 (*not* 820.8)

Works consisting equally of literary texts and history, description, critical appraisal of a specific literature are classed here if limited to specific topics found in Table 3–C, e.g., texts and criticism of English-language literary works about war 820.80358

Class history, description, critical appraisal of a specific literature in —09

See Manual at T3B—08

—09   **History, description, critical appraisal of works in more than one form**

Class here collected biography

Use —090001–090009 for standard subdivisions

See Manual at T3B—08

—090 01–090 09   Literature from specific periods

Add to —0900 the notation from the period table for the specific literature, e.g., the earliest period —09001. If there is no applicable period table, add nothing to —09, e.g., literature in Spanish by Argentine authors of the early 20th century 860.9 (*not* 860.90042) (Option: Use the notation from the period table for an affiliated literature, e.g., literature in Spanish by Argentine authors of the early 20th century A860.90042 or 868.9932090042. Full instructions appear under 810, 819, 820, 828.99, 840.1–848.9, 848.99, 860.1–868.9, 868.99, 869, 869.899)

—091–099   Literature displaying specific features or emphasizing subjects, and for and by specific kinds of persons

Add to —09 notation 1–9 from Table 3–C, e.g., history and description of literature on Faust —09351

> ## —1–8 Specific forms

Unless other instructions are given, observe the following table of precedence for works combining two or more literary forms, e.g., poetic drama —2 (*not* —1)

Drama	—2
Poetry	—1

    Class epigrams in verse in —8

Fiction	—3
Essays	—4
Speeches	—5
Letters	—6
Miscellaneous writings	—8
Satire and humor	—7

    Class collections of satire and humor in two or more literary forms as satire and humor
    (Option: Give precedence to satire and humor over all other forms)

When told to add as instructed under —1–8, add as follows:

1–7   Standard subdivisions
    Standard subdivisions are used for general works consisting equally of literary texts and history, description, critical appraisal, e.g., a serial consisting equally of literary texts and history, description, critical appraisal of poetry in English 821.005. Works limited to specific topics found in Table 3–C are classed in 801–809
    Class collections of literary texts in 8, history, description, critical appraisal in 9

8   Collections of literary texts
    General works consisting equally of literary texts and history, description, critical appraisal are classed in 1–7, in the number for the specific form, or the specific form plus literary period. Works limited to specific topics found in Table 3–C are classed in 801–809

8001–8007   Standard subdivisions

[8008]   With respect to kinds of persons
    Do not use; class in 808–809

[8009]   Historical, geographical, persons treatment
    Do not use; class in 9

801–809   Collections displaying specific features or emphasizing specific subjects, for and by specific kinds of persons
    Add to 80 notation 1–9 from Table 3–C, e.g., collections dealing with places 8032
    Works consisting equally of literary texts and history, description, critical appraisal are classed here if limited to specific topics found in Table 3–C

9   History, description, critical appraisal
    Class here collected biography
    Follow the instructions under 8 for works consisting equally of literary texts and history, description, critical appraisal

901–907   Standard subdivisions

(continued)

> ## —1–8 Specific forms (continued)

[908]	With respect to kinds of persons
	Do not use; class in 98–99
[909]	Historical, geographical, persons
	Do not use; class history and persons in 9, geographical
	treatment in 99
91–99	History, description, critical appraisal of texts displaying
	specific features or emphasizing specific subjects, for and by
	specific kinds of persons

> Add to 9 notation 1–9 from Table 3–C, e.g., critical
> appraisal of works by children 99282

Class comprehensive works on two or more forms in the base number for the individual literature, using notation 01–09 from Table 3–B if applicable, adding 0 when required to make a three-figure number, e.g., comprehensive works on English drama and fiction 820

—1   Poetry

See Manual at T3B—1

—100 1–100 9   Standard subdivisions; collections; history, description, critical appraisal

> Add to —100 as instructed under —1–8, e.g., collections of poetry
> dealing with places —1008032

>   —102–108   Specific kinds of poetry

Aside from additions, changes, deletions, exceptions shown under specific entries, add to notation for each term identified by * as follows:

01–07   Standard subdivisions

Standard subdivisions are used for general works consisting equally of literary texts and history, description, critical appraisal, e.g., a serial consisting equally of literary texts and history, description, critical appraisal of narrative poetry in English —10305. Works limited to specific topics found in Table 3–C are classed in 08, with use of notation from Table 3–C

Class collections of literary texts in 08, history, description, critical appraisal in 09

08   Collections of literary texts

Add to 08 notation 001–99 from Table 3–C, e.g., collections dealing with places 0832

Use of this number for general works consisting equally of literary texts and history, description, critical appraisal discontinued; class in the subdivision for the specific kind, e.g., texts and criticism of narrative poems —103 (*not* —10308)

Works consisting equally of literary texts and history, description, critical appraisal of the form in a specific kind are classed here if limited to specific topics found in Table 3–C, e.g., texts and criticism of narrative poems about war —10308358

09   History, description, critical appraisal

Class here collected biography

Add to 09 notation 001–99 from Table 3–C, e.g., critical appraisal of works by children 099282

Follow the instructions under 08 for works consisting equally of literary texts and history, description, critical appraisal

Class comprehensive works in —1, epigrams in verse in —8

See Manual at T3B—102–108, T3B—205, T3B—308 vs. T3C—1–3

—102   *Dramatic poetry

Example: dramatic monologues

See also —2 for poetic plays

See Manual at T3A—1, T3B—102 vs. T3A—2, T3B—2

*Add as instructed under —102–108

—103	*Narrative poetry
	Example: medieval metrical romances
	For ballads, see —1044
	See also —3 for prose versions of medieval romances
—103 2	*Epic poetry
—104	*Lyric and balladic poetry
	Examples: haiku, troubadour poetry
	Class dramatic lyric poems in —102
—104 2	*Sonnets
—104 3	*Odes
—104 4	*Ballads
—105	*Didactic poetry
—[106]	Descriptive poetry
	Number discontinued; class in —1
—107	*Satirical and *humorous poetry
	Example: clerihews
	Class satire and humor in two or more literary forms in —7
—107 5	*Limericks
—108	*Light and *ephemeral verse
	Examples: greeting card verse
	Class clerihews in —107, limericks in —1075

—11–19   **Poetry of specific periods**

Add to —1 the notation from the period table for the specific literature in 810–890, e.g., the earliest period —11; then add 0 and to the result add further as instructed under 1–8, e.g., collections from the earliest period dealing with places —1108032

If there is no applicable period table, add nothing to —1, e.g., collections of poetry in English by Australian authors of the earliest period 821 (*not* 821.108) (Option: Use the notation from the period table for an affiliated literature, e.g., collections of poetry in English by Australian authors of the earliest period A821.108 or 828.99341108. Full instructions appear under 810, 819, 820, 828.99, 840.1–848.9, 848.99, 860.1–868.9, 868.99, 869, 869.899)

Class specific kinds of poetry regardless of period in —102–108

*Add as instructed under —102–108

—2   Drama

Class here closet drama, drama written in poetry

See Manual at T3A—1, T3B—102 vs. T3A—2, T3B—2; T3B—2

—200 1–200 9   Standard subdivisions; collections; history, description, critical appraisal

Add to —200 as instructed under —1–8, e.g., collections of drama dealing with places —2008032

>   —202–205 Drama of specific media, scopes, kinds

Class comprehensive works in —2

>   —202–203 Drama for mass media

Class comprehensive works in —2

—202   For radio and television

—202 2   *For radio

—202 5   *For television

—203   *For motion pictures

—204   Drama of restricted scope

Class drama of restricted scope for mass media in —202–203

—204 1   *One-act plays

Including interludes [*formerly also* —2052], sketches [*formerly also* —2057]

—204 5   *Monologues

—205   Specific kinds of drama

Example: masques

Class specific kinds of drama for mass media in —202–203, specific kinds of drama of restricted scope in —204

See Manual at T3B—102–108, T3B—205, T3B—308 vs. T3C—1–3

—205 1   *Serious drama

Class here Nō plays

—205 12   *Tragedy

—205 14   *Historical drama

*Add as instructed under —102–108

—205 16	*Religious and *morality plays
	Not limited to medieval plays
	Class here miracle, mystery, passion plays
—205 2	*Comedy and melodrama
	Interludes relocated to —2041
—205 23	*Comedy
	Including farces
	Class satire and humor in two or more literary forms in —7
—205 27	*Melodrama
	Including modern detective and mystery (suspense) drama
—205 7	*Variety and miscellaneous drama
	Example: Punch and Judy shows
	Sketches relocated to —2041

—21–29   **Drama of specific periods**

Add to —2 the notation from the period table for the specific literature in 810–890, e.g., earliest period —21; then add 0 and to the result add further as instructed under —1–8, e.g., critical appraisal of drama of the earliest period —2109

Observe restrictions on use of period notation given at —11–19

Class drama of specific media, scopes, kinds regardless of period in —202–205

—3   Fiction

Class here novelettes and novels

Class graphic novels (cartoon or comic strip novels) in 741.5

See Manual at T3B—3

—300 1–300 9   Standard subdivisions; collections; history, description, critical appraisal

Add to —300 as instructed under —1–8, e.g., collections of fiction dealing with places —3008032

>   —301–308   Fiction of specific scopes and kinds

Class comprehensive works in —3

—301   *Short stories

Class short stories of specific kinds in —308

—[306]   Cartoon fiction

Relocated to 741.5

*Add as instructed under —102–108

—308   Specific kinds of fiction

Unless other instructions are given, observe the following table of
precedence, e.g., historical adventure fiction —3081 (*not* —3087)

Historical and period fiction	—3081
Adventure fiction	—3087
Love and romance	—3085
Sociological, psychological, realistic fiction	—3083

See Manual at T3B—102–108, T3B—205, T3B—308 vs. T3C—1–3

—308 1   *Historical and *period fiction

—308 3   *Sociological, *psychological, *realistic fiction

—[308 4]   Occupational fiction

Number discontinued; class in —3

—308 5   *Love and *romance

Modern romantic fiction

Medieval prose romances are classed in —3

See Manual at T3B—308729 vs. T3B—3085

—308 7   *Adventure fiction

Unless other instructions are given, observe the following table of
precedence, e.g., Gothic horror fiction —308729 (*not* —308738)

Science fiction	—308762
Gothic fiction	—308729
Western fiction	—30874
Detective, mystery, suspense, spy fiction	—30872
Ghost fiction	—308733
Horror fiction	—308738
Fantasy fiction	—308766

—308 72   *Detective, *mystery, *suspense, *spy, Gothic fiction

—308 729   *Gothic fiction

Class modern romantic fiction in which the supernatural has little
or no role in —3085

See Manual at T3B—308729 vs. T3B—3085

—308 73   Ghost and horror fiction

—308 733   *Ghost fiction

—308 738   *Horror fiction

—308 74   *Western fiction

—308 76   Science and fantasy fiction

—308 762   *Science fiction

—308 766   *Fantasy fiction

*Add as instructed under —102–108

—31–39   **Fiction of specific periods**

Add to —3 the notation from the period table for the specific literature in 810–890, e.g., earliest period —31; then add 0 and to the result add further as instructed under —1–8, e.g., critical appraisal of fiction of the earliest period —3109

Observe restrictions on use of period notation given at —11–19

Class specific scopes and kinds regardless of period in —301–308

—4   Essays

—400 1–400 9   Standard subdivisions; collections; history, description, critical appraisal

Add to —400 as instructed under —1–8, e.g., collections of essays dealing with places —4008032

—41–49   **Essays of specific periods**

Add to —4 the notation from the period table for the specific literature in 810–890, e.g., earliest period —41; then add 0 and to the result add further as instructed under —1–8, e.g., critical appraisal of essays of the earliest period —4109

Observe restrictions on use of period notation given at —11–19

—5   Speeches

—500 1–500 9   Standard subdivisions; collections; history, description, critical appraisal

Add to —500 as instructed under —1–8, e.g., collections of speeches dealing with places —5008032

>   **—501–506**   Specific kinds of speeches

Class comprehensive works in —5

—501   *Public speeches (Oratory)

Examples: after-dinner, platform, radio speeches; speeches and toasts for special occasions

For debates and public discussions, see —503

—503   *Debates and *public discussions

—504   *Recitations

—505   *Texts for choral speaking

—506   *Conversations

*Add as instructed under —102–108

—51–59   Speeches of specific periods

> Add to —5 the notation from the period table for the specific literature in 810–890, e.g., earliest period —51; then add 0 and to the result add further as instructed under —1–8, e.g., critical appraisal of speeches of the earliest period —5109
>
> Observe restrictions on use of period notation given at —11–19
>
> Class specific kinds regardless of period in —501–506

—6   Letters

> *See Manual at T3A—6 and T3B—6*

—600 1–600 9   Standard subdivisions; collections; history, description, critical appraisal

> Add to —600 as instructed under —1–8, e.g., collections of letters dealing with places —6008032

—61–69   Letters of specific periods

> Add to —6 the notation from the period table for the specific literature in 810–890, e.g., earliest period —61; then add 0 and to the result add further as instructed under —1–8, e.g., critical appraisal of letters of the earliest period —6109
>
> Observe restrictions on use of period notation given at —11–19

—7   Satire and humor

> Class here parody
>
> Because every other literary form takes precedence over satire and humor, this number is used only for collections and criticism of works in two or more literary forms
>
> *See Manual at T3B—7 vs. T3A—8 + 02, T3B—802, T3B—8 + 02, T3B—807, T3B—8 + 07, T1—0207; T3C—17 vs. T3B—7*

—700 1–700 9   Standard subdivisions; collections; history, description, critical appraisal

> Add to —700 as instructed under —1–8, e.g., collections of satire and humor dealing with places —7008032

—71–79   Satire and humor of specific periods

> Add to —7 the notation from the period table for the specific literature in 810–890, e.g., earliest period —71; then add 0 and to the result add further as instructed under —1–8, e.g., critical appraisal of satire and humor of the earliest period —7109
>
> Observe restrictions on use of period notation given at —11–19

—8 Miscellaneous writings

Only those forms named below

Procedures for building numbers:

1.   To the base number for the literature add notation 8, e.g., miscellaneous writings in English 828. If the work is limited to a specific time period, go to step 2; if not, go to step 4

2.   Turn back to the appropriate number in the schedule 810–890 to see whether there is an applicable period table. If there is one, go to step 3; if not, go to step 4

(Option: Where two or more countries share the same language, either [1] use initial letters to distinguish the separate countries, or [2] use the special number designated for literatures of those countries that are not preferred. This option makes feasible the use of period tables for affiliated literatures, e.g., miscellaneous writings in English by 20th-century New Zealand authors NZ828.2 or 828.993382. Full instructions appear under 810, 819, 820, 828.99, 840.1–848.9, 848.99, 860.1–868.9, 868.99, 869, 869.899. If the option is used, go to step 3)

3.   Select the appropriate period number, e.g., the Victorian period in the English literature of Great Britain 8. Then follow the instructions under —81–89

4.   If the work is not limited to a specific time period, or if there is no applicable period table, consider whether the work is limited to one of the forms of miscellaneous writing listed in —802–808. If it is limited to one of those forms, go to step 5; if not, complete the class number by inserting a point between the third and fourth digits, e.g., miscellaneous writings in Russian from many time periods 891.78, miscellaneous writings in English by 20th-century New Zealand authors 828, miscellaneous writings in Khmer (Cambodian) by 20th-century authors 895.9328

5.   Class the work in the appropriate number from the span —802–808, then complete the number by inserting a point between the third and fourth digits, e.g., prose literature in Russian from many time periods 891.7808, prose literature in English by 20th-century New Zealand authors 828.08, prose literature in Khmer (Cambodian) by 20th-century authors 895.932808

See Manual at Table 3–B: Number building

—800 1–800 9   Standard subdivisions; collections; history, description, critical appraisal

Add to —800 as instructed under —1–8, e.g., critical appraisal of miscellaneous writings from more than one period —8009

> —802–808 Specific kinds of miscellaneous writings

Class in each number without further subdivision history, description, critical appraisal, biography, collections of works of authors from more than one period

Class comprehensive works in —8

—802   Jokes [*formerly* —807], quotations, epigrams, anecdotes, graffiti

Class satire and humor in two or more literary forms in —7

> *See Manual at T3B—7 vs. T3A—8 + 02, T3B—802, T3B—8 + 02, T3B—807, T3B—8 + 07, T1—0207*

—803   Diaries, journals, notebooks, reminiscences

Interdisciplinary collections of diaries are classed in 900, diaries of nonliterary authors with the appropriate subject, e.g., the diary of an astronomer 520.92

> *See Manual at T3A—8 + 03 and T3B—803, T3B—8 + 03*

—807   Works without identifiable literary form

Class here experimental and nonformalized works

Jokes relocated to —802

> *See Manual at T3B—7 vs. T3A—8 + 02, T3B—802, T3B—8 + 02, T3B—807, T3B—8 + 07, T1—0207*

—808   Prose literature

Collections and discussions of works in more than one literary form

Class a specific form of prose literature with the form, e.g., essays —4; prose without identifiable literary form in —807

—81–89   **Miscellaneous writings of specific periods**

Add to —8 the notation from the period table for the specific literature in 810–890, e.g., earliest period —81; then add further as follows:

001–009	Standard subdivisions; collections; history, description, critical appraisal
	Add to 00 as instructed in the table under —1–8, e.g., collections 008
02	Jokes [*formerly* 07], quotations, epigrams, anecdotes, graffiti
	Class satire and humor in two or more literary forms in —7
0201–0209	Standard subdivisions; collections; history, description, critical appraisal
	Add to 020 as instructed in the table under —1–8, e.g., collections 0208
03	Diaries, journals, notebooks, reminiscences
0301–0309	Standard subdivisions; collections; history, description, critical appraisal
	Add to 030 as instructed in the table under —1–8, e.g., collections 0308
07	Works without identifiable literary form
	Class here experimental and nonformalized works
	Jokes relocated to 02
0701–0709	Standard subdivisions; collections; history, description, critical appraisal
	Add to 070 as instructed in the table under —1–8, e.g., collections of stream of consciousness writings 0708025

(continued)

−81–89   **Miscellaneous writings of specific periods (continued)**

     08   Prose literature

            Collections and discussions of works in more than one literary form

            Class a specific form of prose literature with the form, e.g., essays −4; prose without identifiable literary form in 07

     0801–0809   Standard subdivisions; collections; history, description, critical appraisal

            Add to 080 as instructed in the table under −1–8, e.g., collections 0808

If there is no applicable period table, class jokes, anecdotes, epigrams, graffiti, quotations regardless of period in −802; diaries, journals, notebooks, reminiscences regardless of period in −803; works without identifiable literary form regardless of period in −807; prose literature regardless of period in −808, e.g., collections of prose literature in English by Australian authors of the early 20th century 828.08 (*not* 828.20808)

(Option: Use the notation from the period table for an affiliated literature for either option given after step 2 under −8 in Table 3–B, e.g., prose literature in English by Australian authors of the early 20th century A828.20808 or 828.9934820808)

See Manual at T3A—8 + 03 and T3B—803, T3B—8 + 03; T3B—7 vs. T3A—8 + 02, T3B—802, T3B—8 + 02, T3B—807, T3B—8 + 07, T1—0207

Table 3–C. Notation to Be Added Where Instructed in Table 3–B and in 808–809

See Manual at Table 3–B: Order of precedence

SUMMARY

   −001–009   **Standard subdivisions**
   −01–09   **Specific periods**
   −1   **Literature displaying specific qualities of style, mood, perspective**
   −2   **Literature displaying specific elements**
   −3   **Literature dealing with specific themes and subjects**
   −4   **Literature emphasizing subjects**
   −8   **Literature for and by racial, ethnic, national groups**
   −9   **Literature for and by other specific kinds of persons**

−001–009   Standard subdivisions

−01–09   **Specific periods**

     Add to −0 the notation from the period table for the specific literature, e.g., the earliest period −01

> ### —1–3 Literature displaying specific features

> Do not use if redundant, e.g., description in descriptive poetry, science fiction about science
>
> Class comprehensive works in the appropriate number in Table 3–B
>
> *See Manual at T3B—102–108, T3B—205, T3B—308 vs. T3C—1–3*

—1   Literature displaying specific qualities of style, mood, perspective

Examples: dadaism, expressionism, radical writing, surrealism

Class literature displaying specific elements regardless of quality displayed in —2, literature dealing with specific themes and subjects regardless of quality displayed in —3

—12   **Realism and naturalism**

      Including determinism

—13   **Idealism**

—14   **Classicism and romanticism**

      Pastoral literature relocated to —321734

—142   Classicism

—145   Romanticism

      Including primitivism

—15   **Symbolism, allegory, fantasy, myth**

—16   **Tragedy and horror**

—17   **Comedy**

      Class satire and humor in two or more literary forms in —7 in Table 3–B

      See Manual at T3C—17 vs. T3B—7

—18   **Irony**

—2   Literature displaying specific elements

Class literature dealing with specific themes and subjects regardless of element displayed in —3

—22   **Description**

      Including setting

—23   **Narrative**

—24   **Plot**

—25   **Stream of consciousness**

—26	**Dialogue**
—27	**Characters**

Including the "double" (Doppelgänger) in literature

—3   Literature dealing with specific themes and subjects

—32   Places

Class here civilization of places

Add to —32 notation 1–9 from Table 2, e.g., pastoral literature —321734 [*formerly also* —14], the sea —32162, the American West —3278, California —32794

Class historical and political themes, historical events in specific places in —358

—33   Times

Examples: seasons, holidays; parts of day, e.g., dawn

—35   Humanity and human existence

Class here works dealing with contemporary perspectives

—351   Specific persons

Real, fictional, legendary, mythological

Examples: Abraham Lincoln, Faust, King Arthur, Odysseus, Pierrot

See also —352 for specific kinds of persons

—352   Specific kinds of persons

Examples: barbarians, fools or jesters, gentlemen, rebels

Add to —352 notation 03–99 from Table 7, e.g., women —352042

See also —351 for specific persons, —8–9 for literature for and by specific kinds of persons

—353   Human psychological and moral qualities and activities

Examples: chivalry, dreams, friendship, heroism, homosexuality, honor, insanity, justice, melancholy, personal beauty, pride, sentiment, snobbishness, success

Class crime in —355

For love, see —354

—353 8   Sex

Including erotic literature

Class here erotica

—354   Life cycle

Including birth, love, marriage, death

—355   Social themes

         Examples: costume or dress, commerce, crime, dancing, drugs, dwellings, economics, environment, food, law, occupations, recreation, school, sports, travel, violence

         Class here everyday life

         Class historical and political themes in —358

—356   Scientific and technical themes

         Examples: engineering, flight, medicine, science, ships

         Class physical and natural phenomena in —36

—357   Artistic and literary themes

         Examples: books, music, painting

—358   Historical and political themes

         Examples: nationalism, peace, war

         Class here historical events in specific places

—36   **Physical and natural phenomena**

         Examples: animals, fire, gardens, plants, weather

—37   **The supernatural, mythological, legendary**

         Examples: spiritualism, magic, witchcraft

         Class legendary and mythological persons in —351

—372   Places

         Example: Atlantis, Hades, utopia

         Class religious treatment of the netherworld in —382

—375   Beings

         Examples: fairies, ghosts, ogres, undines, vampires

—38   **Philosophic and abstract concepts**

—382   Religious concepts

         Examples: Christianity, the devil, God, hell

         Class persons connected with religion in —351, e.g., Moses

—384   Philosophic concepts

         Example: conscience, humanism, self-knowledge, transcendentalism

—4   Literature emphasizing subjects

Works not basically belles-lettristic discussed as literature

Add to —4 notation 001–999, e.g., religious works as literature —42, biography as literature —492

> ### —8–9 Literature for and by specific kinds of persons

Do not use if redundant, e.g., English-language poetry for and by the English

Unless other instructions are given, observe the following table of precedence, e.g., literature for or by Roman Catholic girls —92827 (*not* —9222 or —9287)

Persons of specific age groups	—9282–9285
Persons of specific sexes	—9286–9287
Persons occupied with geography, history, related disciplines	—929
Persons of other specific occupational and miscellaneous characteristics	—9204–9279
Persons of racial, ethnic, national groups	—8
Persons resident in specific continents, countries, localities	—93–99
Persons resident in specific regions	—91

Class comprehensive works in the appropriate number in Table 3–B; literature displaying specific features for and by specific kinds of persons in —1–3

—8   Literature for and by racial, ethnic, national groups

Add to —8 notation 03–99 from Table 5, e.g., literature by Africans and persons of African descent —896

—9   Literature for and by other specific kinds of persons

—91   For and by persons resident in specific regions

Not limited by continent, country, locality

Add to —91 the numbers following —1 in notation 11–19 from Table 2, e.g., literature by rural authors —91734

—92	**For and by persons of specific classes**
—920 4–927 9	Of specific occupational and miscellaneous characteristics

> Add to —92 notation 04–79 from Table 7, e.g., literature by painters —9275; however, class persons of specific age groups and sexes in —928
>
> *For persons occupied with geography, history, related disciplines, see —929*

—928	Of specific age groups and sexes

>	**—928 2–928 5 Age groups**

> Class comprehensive works in —928

—928 2	Children
—928 26	Boys
—928 27	Girls
—928 3	Young adults

> Aged twelve to twenty

—928 36	Young men
—928 37	Young women
—928 5	Persons in late adulthood

> Former heading: Adults aged 65 and over

>	**—928 6–928 7 Sexes**

> Class comprehensive works in —928

—928 6	Men
—928 7	Women
—929	Occupied with geography, history, related disciplines

> Add to —929 the numbers following —9 in notation 91–99 from Table 7, e.g., literature by archaeologists —9293

—93–99	**For and by persons resident in specific continents, countries, localities**

> (Do not use for literatures of specific countries if the literatures are separately identified in accordance with the options given under 810, 819, 820, 828.99, 840.1–848.9, 848.99, 860.1–868.9, 868.99, 869, 869.899)
>
> Add to —9 notation 3–9 from Table 2, e.g., literature (other than in Japanese language) by residents of Japan —952, Japanese-language literature by residents of Hokkaido 895.60809524
>
> *See Manual at T3C—93–99*

Table 4. Subdivisions of Individual Languages

The following notation is never used alone, but may be used as required with the base numbers for individual languages identified by * as explained under 420–490, e.g., English (base number 42) phonology (—15 in this table): 421.5. A point is inserted following the third digit of any number thus constructed that is longer than three digits. Notation from Table 1 is added to the notation in Table 4 when appropriate, e.g., —509 history of grammar, 425.09 history of English grammar

See Manual at 410

SUMMARY

—01–09	**Standard subdivisions**	
—1	**Writing systems and phonology of the standard form of the language**	
—2	**Etymology of the standard form of the language**	
—3	**Dictionaries of the standard form of the language**	
—5	**Structural system (Grammar) of the standard form of the language**	
—7	**Historical and geographical variations, modern nongeographical variations**	
—8	**Standard usage of the language (Prescriptive linguistics)**	**Applied linguistics**

—01   **Philosophy and theory**

—014   Language (Terminology) and communication

Class discursive works on terminology intended to teach vocabulary in —81

See Manual at T4—3 vs. T4—81

—014 1   Semiotics

Former heading: Communication

Class here content analysis, discourse analysis

Class a semiotic study of a specific subject with the subject, using notation 014 from Table 1, e.g., a semiotic study of science 501.4

For semantics, see —0143

—[014 2]   Etymology

Do not use; class in —2

—014 3   Semantics [*formerly* —2]

Class the history of word meanings in —2

See Manual at 401.43 vs. 412, 415, 306.44, 401.9

—[014 8]   Abbreviations and symbols

Do not use; class abbreviations and symbols as part of writing systems in —11, dictionaries of abbreviations and symbols in —31

—02   **Miscellany**

—03   **Encyclopedias and concordances**

Do not use for dictionaries; class dictionaries of the standard form of the language in —3, of historical and geographical variations, of modern nongeographical variations in the language in —7

—04   **Special topics**

—042   Bilingualism

Add to —042 notation 2–9 from Table 6 for the language that is not dominant in the area in which the linguistic interaction occurs, e.g., works dealing with the dominant language and English —04221

See also 306.446 for the sociology of bilingualism

—05–09   **Standard subdivisions**

See Manual at 407, T1—07 vs. 410.7, 418.007, T4—8007, 401.93

>   **—1–5 Description and analysis of the standard form of the language**

Class comprehensive works in the base number for the language (adding 0 when required to make a three-figure number), e.g., comprehensive works on phonology, etymology, dictionaries, grammar of standard French 440; standard usage, prescriptive and applied linguistics in —8

—1   **Writing systems and phonology of the standard form of the language**

—11   **Writing systems**

Examples: alphabets, ideographs, syllabaries

Including abbreviations, acronyms, capitalization, punctuation, transliteration

Class here paleography [*formerly* —17]

Class dictionaries of abbreviations and acronyms in —31; the paleography of historical and geographical variations, of modern nongeographical variations of the language in —7, e.g., the paleography of postclassical Latin 477

For spelling, see —152

—15   **Phonology**

Class here phonetics

For suprasegmental features, see —16

See also —3 for dictionaries

—152   Spelling (Orthography) and pronunciation

Class here description and analysis of the nature, history, and function of spelling and pronunciation

Class comprehensive works on writing systems in —11; specialized spelling and pronouncing dictionaries in —31; training in standard spelling and pronunciation in —81; speech training for public speaking, debating, conversation in 808.5

—16   **Suprasegmental features**

Vocal effects extending over more than one sound segment

Examples: juncture (pauses), pitch, stress

Class here intonation

See Manual at 808.1 vs. 414.6

—[17]   **Paleography and the study of early writings**

Use of this number for the study of early writings discontinued; class in the base number for the language (adding 0 when required to make a three-figure number)

Paleography relocated to —11

—2   **Etymology of the standard form of the language**

Semantics other than the history of word meanings relocated to —0143

—24   **Foreign elements**

Add to —24 notation 1–9 from Table 6, e.g., French words in the language —2441, French words in English 422.441

—3   **Dictionaries of the standard form of the language**

See Manual at T4—3 vs. T4—81

—302 8   Techniques, procedures, apparatus, equipment, materials

Class here lexicography

—31   **Specialized dictionaries**

Examples: dictionaries of abbreviations, acronyms, antonyms, clichés, collective nouns, eponyms, homonyms, idioms, paronyms, puns, synonyms; crossword-puzzle, picture, reverse dictionaries; spellers; word dividers

Class bilingual specialized dictionaries in —32–39, etymological dictionaries in —203

—32–39 **Bilingual dictionaries**

Add to —3 notation 2–9 from Table 6, e.g., dictionaries of the language and English —321, dictionary of French and English 443.21

A bilingual dictionary with entry words in only one language is classed with that language, e.g., an English-French dictionary 423.41. A bilingual dictionary with entry words in both languages is classed with the language in which it will be the more useful; for example, most libraries in English-speaking regions will find English-French, French-English dictionaries most useful classed with French in 443.21, Chinese-French, French-Chinese dictionaries with Chinese in 495.1341. If classification with either language is equally useful, give priority to the language coming later in the sequence 420–490, e.g., French-German, German-French dictionaries 443.31

See Manual at T4—32–T4—39

—5 **Structural system (Grammar) of the standard form of the language**

Historical and descriptive study of morphology and syntax

Class here comprehensive works on morphology, syntax, and phonology

For phonology, see —15

See also —8 for prescriptive grammar

—7 **Historical and geographical variations, modern nongeographical variations**

Examples: early forms; dialects, pidgins, creoles; slang

Subdivisions of —7 are given under some individual languages in 420–490

Use notation 7 only for works that stress differences among the forms of a language

Topics classed in —1–5 and —8 when applied to standard forms of the language are classed here when applied to historical and geographical variations, to modern nongeographical variations, e.g., the distinctive grammatical characteristics of a particular dialect

See Manual at T4—7

—8 **Standard usage of the language (Prescriptive linguistics)   Applied linguistics**

General, formal, informal usage

Class here works for persons learning a second language, works for native speakers who are learning the acceptable patterns of their own language

Use —8001–8009 for standard subdivisions

Class purely descriptive linguistics in —1–5

Topics of —8 applied to historical and geographical variations, to modern nongeographical variations of the language are classed in —7

For dictionaries, see —3; rhetoric, 808.04

See Manual at 407, T1—07 vs. 410.7, 418.007, T4—8007, 401.93; 410

—802 Translation to and from other languages

Class here interpretation

For works about translating from one language into another, use as base number the notation for the language being translated into; then add to —802 notation 2–9 from Table 6, e.g., translating from Chinese into English 428.02951

—81 **Words**

Meaning, pronunciation, spelling

Class formal presentation of vocabulary in —82, audio-lingual presentation of vocabulary in —83

See also —152 for nonprescriptive treatment of spelling and pronunciation, —3 for dictionaries

See Manual at T4—3 vs. T4—81

—82 **Structural approach to expression**

Formal (traditional) presentation of grammar, vocabulary, reading selections

Class here verb tables and inflectional schemata designed for use as aids in learning a language

For words, see —81; reading, —84

—824 For those whose native language is different

Add to —824 notation 2–9 from Table 6, e.g., the language for Spanish-speaking people —82461, English for Spanish-speaking people 428.2461

—83 **Audio-lingual approach to expression**

> Informal presentation through practice in correct usage
>
> Class here the "hear-speak" school of learning a language
>
> *For pronunciation, see —81*

—834 For those whose native language is different

> Class here bilingual phrase books
>
> Add to —834 notation 2–9 from Table 6, e.g., the language for Spanish-speaking people —83461, English for Spanish-speaking people 428.3461

—84 **Reading**

> *For readers, see —86*

—840 19 Psychological principles

> Class psychology of reading in 418.4019 unless there is emphasis on the specific language being read

—842 Remedial reading

> Correcting faulty habits and increasing the proficiency of poor readers

—843 Developmental reading

> Including the reading power and efficiency of good readers, speed reading

—86 **Readers**

> Graded selections with emphasis on structure and vocabulary as needed
>
> Class here texts intended primarily for practice in reading a language
>
> (Option: Class elementary readers in 372.412)

—862 Remedial readers

—864 For those whose native language is different

> Add to —864 notation 2–9 from Table 6, e.g., readers for Spanish-speaking people —86461, English readers for Spanish-speaking people 428.6461
>
> *See Manual at Table 4 T4—864 vs. Table 1 T1—014*

Table 5. Racial, Ethnic, National Groups

The following numbers are never used alone, but may be used as required (either directly when so noted or through the interposition of notation 089 from Table 1) with any number from the schedules, e.g., ethnopsychology (155.84) of the Japanese (—956 in this table): 155.84956; ceramic arts (738) of Jews (—924 in this table): 738.089924. They may also be used when so noted with numbers from other tables, e.g., notation 174 from Table 2

Except where instructed otherwise, and unless it is redundant, add 0 to the number from this table and to the result add notation 1–9 from Table 2, e.g., Germans in Brazil —31081, but Germans in Germany —31. Add notation from Table 2 if appropriate even when the group discussed does not approximate the whole of the group specified by the number in Table 5, if the number in Table 5 is limited to speakers of only one language, e.g., Bavarians in Brazil —31081, but the Maya in Guatemala —974

Except where instructed otherwise, give precedence first to ethnic group, second to nationality, last to basic races, e.g., United States citizens of Serbian descent —91822073 (*not* —13), United States citizens of the Caucasian race —13 (*not* —034073). In this table "ethnic group" most often means a group with linguistic ties, but it can also mean a group with cultural or racial ties. The numbers for basic races are used only for works treating races as extremely broad categories. Thus notation 036 Negro race is used for works treating Black peoples of African and Asian or Oceanian origin as belonging to the same race, but —96 is used for Black peoples of African origin

Except where instructed otherwise, when choosing between two ethnic groups, give precedence to the group for which the notation is different from that for the nationality of the people, e.g., a work treating equally the Hispanic and native American heritage of bilingual Spanish-Guaraní mestizos of Paraguay —983 (*not* —68892)

Except where instructed otherwise, when choosing between two national groups, give precedence to the former or ancestral national group, e.g., people from the Soviet Union who have become United States citizens —917073 (*not* —13)

See Manual at Table 5

—[01]   **Indigenes**

> Number and its subdivisions discontinued; class in 001–999 without adding notation from Table 5

—03   Basic races

Limited to the three basic races listed below

Races considered as narrower categories than basic races are classed with the appropriate ethnic groups, e.g., the Australoid race with the Australian native peoples —9915

See also —994 for the Polynesian race, —995 for the Melanesian and Micronesian races

—034   Caucasian race

Class here comprehensive works on Indo-European peoples

See also —9996 for peoples who speak, or whose ancestors spoke, Caucasian languages

—035   Mongoloid race

Use of this number is limited to works that discuss East Asians and American native peoples as belonging to one race

Class Asian Mongoloid races in —95, comprehensive works on North and South American native races in —97

—036   Negro race

Use of this number is limited to works that discuss Black peoples of African and Asian or Oceanian origin as belonging to the same race

Class the African Negro races in —96, the Aeta, Andamanese, Semang peoples in —9911

See also —9915 for the Australoid race

—04   Mixtures of basic races

Limited to works that emphasize the mixture of basic races

Class works about people of mixed blood that do not emphasize the mixture of basic races with the ethnic or national groups stressed in the works or with the groups with which the people are most closely identified

—042   Caucasians and Mongoloids

—043   Mongoloids and Negroes

—044   Negroes and Caucasians

—046   Caucasians, Mongoloids, Negroes

> ## −1–9 Specific racial, ethnic, national groups

By origin or situation

(Option: to give local emphasis and a shorter number to a specific group, place it first by use of a letter or other symbol, e.g., Arabs —A [preceding —1]. Another option is given at —1)

Class comprehensive works in 001–999 without adding notation from Table 5

See Manual at Table 5

—1   North Americans

(Option: To give local emphasis and a shorter number to a specific group, e.g., Sinhalese, class it in this number; in that case class North Americans in —2. Another option is given at —1–9)

For Spanish Americans, see —68; North American native peoples, —97

See Manual at T5—1

—11   Canadians

—112   Of British origin

—114   Of French origin

—13   People of the United States ("Americans")

For Afro-Americans, see —96073

—2   British   English   Anglo-Saxons

Class North Americans of British origin in —1, Anglo-Indians (Indian citizens of British origin) in —91411, people of Celtic (Irish, Scots, Manx, Welsh, Cornish) origin in —916

See Manual at Table 5; T5—201–T5—209 vs. T5—2101–T5—2109

—21   People of the British Isles

—23   New Zealanders

For Polynesians, see —994

—24   Australians

For Australian native peoples, see —9915

—28   South Africans of British origin

Class South Africans as a national group in —968

See also —2106891 for Zimbabweans of British origin

—3 **Nordic (Germanic) people**

> *For Anglo-Saxons, see —2*

—31 **Germans**

—35 **Swiss**

> Class here Swiss Germans, comprehensive works on the people of Switzerland
>
> Class the French-speaking Swiss in —410494, the Romansh-speaking Swiss in —5, the Italian-speaking Swiss in —510494

—36 **Austrians**

—39 **Other Germanic peoples**

> Example: Goths, Vandals

—392 Friesians

—393 Netherlandish peoples

—393 1 Dutch

—393 2 Flemings (Flemish)

> Class here comprehensive works on Belgians
>
> *For Walloons, see —42*

—393 6 Afrikaners

> Class South Africans as a national group in —968

—395 Scandinavians

> Class specific Scandinavian groups in —396–398
>
> *See also —94541 for Finns, —9455 for Lapps*

—396 West Scandinavians

—396 1 Icelanders

—396 9 Faeroese

—397 Swedes

—398 Danes and Norwegians

—398 1 Danes

—398 2 Norwegians

—4 **Modern Latin peoples**

> *For Italians, Romanians, related groups, see —5; Spanish and Portuguese, —6*

—41 **French**

> Class Canadians of French origin in —114
>
> *For Basques, see —9992; Corsicans, —58*

—42	**Walloons**
—49	**Catalans**

—5   **Italians, Romanians, related groups**

Example: Rhaetians

—51	**Italians**
—56	**Sardinians**
—57	**Dalmatians**
—58	**Corsicans**
—59	**Romanians**

—6   **Spanish and Portuguese**

—61   **People of Spain (Spaniards)**

> *For Catalans, see —49; Basques, —9992*

—68   **Spanish Americans**

Class here comprehensive works on Latin Americans

Class Latin American peoples not provided for here with the people, e.g., Brazilians —698

—687–688   National groups

Citizens of independent and partly independent jurisdictions having a Spanish-speaking majority or Spanish as an official language

Add to base number —68 notation 7–8 from Table 2, e.g., Puerto-Ricans —687295, Chileans —6883, Chileans in the United States —6883073; however, class comprehensive works on Spanish Americans in jurisdictions where they are a minority in —6807–6808, e.g., Spanish Americans in the United States —68073

—69   **Portuguese**

—691   People of Portugal

—698   Brazilians

Class here Brazilians of Portuguese origin, Brazilians as a national group

—7   **Other Italic peoples**

> *For Etruscans, see —9994*

—71   **Ancient Romans**

—79   **Osco-Umbrians**

Use of this number for other Italic peoples discontinued; class in —7

—[799]   Osco-Umbrians

Number discontinued; class in —79

—8   Greeks and related groups

For Macedonians, see —91819

—81   Ancient Greeks

Class here comprehensive works on ancient Greeks and Romans

For ancient Romans, see —71

—89   Modern Greeks and related groups

—893   Greek nationals

—895   Cypriots

Class here comprehensive works on the people of Cyprus

Class Turkish Cypriots in —943505645

—9   Other racial, ethnic, national groups

SUMMARY

—91	**Other Indo-European peoples**
—92	**Semites**
—93	**North Africans**
—94	**Peoples of North and West Asian origin or situation; Dravidians**
—95	**East and Southeast Asian peoples; Mundas**
—96	**Africans and people of African descent**
—97	**North American native peoples**
—98	**South American native peoples**
—99	**Aeta, Andamanese, Semang; Papuans; Australian native peoples; Malays and related peoples; miscellaneous peoples**

—91   Other Indo-European peoples

SUMMARY

—914	**South Asians**
—915	**Iranians**
—916	**Celts**
—917	**East Slavs**
—918	**Slavs**
—919	**Other East Indo-Europeans**

—914   South Asians

Class here Indo-Aryans; peoples who speak, or whose ancestors spoke, Indic languages

Class South Asians who speak, or whose ancestors spoke, languages closely related to East and Southeast Asian languages in —95

For Dravidians and Scytho-Dravidians, see —948

See Manual at T5—914 vs. T5—948

—914 1	**National groups**

Citizens of independent and partly independent jurisdictions of South Asia and of largely South Asian origin

Examples: Guyanese [*formerly* —969881], Maldivians, Mauritians

Class nationals of specific ethnolinguistic groups in —9142–9149, the Nepalese national group in —91495, Trinidadians of South Asian origin in —96972983, Fijians of South Asian origin in —995

See Manual at T5—9141

—914 11	Indians

Including Anglo-Indians (Indian citizens of British origin), post-1975 Sikkimese

Class comprehensive works on the Sikkimese in —91417

—914 12	Pakistanis and people of Bangladesh
—914 122	Pakistanis
—914 126	People of Bangladesh
—914 13	Sri Lankans (Ceylonese)

Class the Sinhalese as an ethnic group in —9148, the Tamil as an ethnic group in —94811

—914 17	Sikkimese

Class post-1975 Sikkimese in —91411

—914 18	Bhutanese

Class the Bhutia as an ethnic group in —954

—914 2	**Punjabis**
—914 3	**Hindis**
—914 4	**Bengali**

Class the Bengali of Bangladesh in —914126

—914 5	**Assamese, Bihari, Oriya**
—914 7	**Gujar, Gujarati; people who speak, or whose ancestors spoke, Rajasthani**
—914 8	**Sinhalese**
—914 9	**Other Indo-Aryan peoples**
—914 95	Nepali

Class here the Nepali as an ethnic group, comprehensive works on the people of Nepal

For Bihari, see —9145; Chepang, Newar and Tamang, —95

—914 96	Pahari
—914 97	Romany (Gypsy) people

—914 99	Dardic peoples
	Examples: Kashmiris, Kohistanis
	Including Nuri
	For Gypsies, see —91497
—915	Iranians
	Including Kushans, Scythians
—915 5	Persians
	Class here Persians as an ethnic group, comprehensive works on the people of Iran
	For other Iranian peoples, see —9159; Turkic peoples, —943
—915 9	Other Iranian peoples
	Examples: Baluchi, Galcha, Kurds, Ossets, Pamiri, Tajik
—915 93	Afghans (Pashtun)
	Class here Afghans as an ethnic group, comprehensive works on the people of Afghanistan
	For Turkic peoples, see —943
—916	Celts
	Example: Gauls
—916 2	Irish
—916 3	Scots
—916 4	Manx
—916 6	Welsh (Cymry)
—916 7	Cornish
—916 8	Bretons
—917	East Slavs
	Class here the people of the Soviet Union
	Class comprehensive works on Slavs in —918; a specific ethnic Soviet group with the group, e.g., Uzbek —943
—917 1	Russians
—917 14	Cossacks
—917 9	Ukrainians and Belorussians
—917 91	Ukrainians
—917 99	Belorussians

—918	Slavs
	For East Slavs, see —917
—918 1	Bulgarians and Macedonians
—918 11	Bulgarians
—918 19	Macedonians
—918 2	Yugoslavs
	For Macedonians, see —91819; Slovenes, —9184
—918 22	Serbs
—918 23	Croats
—918 4	Slovenes
—918 5	West Slavs Poles
	Example: Kashubs
	For Cossacks, see —91714
—918 6	Czechs
	Class here Czechoslovaks
	For Slovaks and Moravians, see —9187
—918 7	Slovaks and Moravians
—918 8	Wends (Sorbs, Lusatians)
—919	Other East Indo-Europeans
—919 2	Lithuanians
—919 3	Latvians (Letts)
—919 9	Miscellaneous East Indo-Europeans
	Limited to Hittites and the peoples provided for below
	Use of this number for other East Indo-Europeans discontinued; class in —919
—919 91	Albanians
—919 92	Armenians
—92	**Semites**
—921	Akkadians, Amorites, Assyrians, Babylonians, Chaldeans
—922	Aramaeans
—924	Hebrews, Israelis, Jews
	Class here Beta Israel
	Subdivisions may be added for any or all of the groups named above
	See also notation 296 in Table 7 for Jews as a religious group

—926	Phoenicians and Canaanites

> *For Amorites, see* —*921*

—927	Arabs and Maltese
—927 4	Palestinian Arabs
—927 5–927 6	National groups of Arabs

> Citizens of independent or partly independent jurisdictions having an Arab or Arabic-speaking majority or Arabic as the official language

> Add to base number —927 notation 5–6 from Table 2, e.g., Iraqis —927567, Sudanese —927624; however, class Arabs as a minority group in a country of Asia or Africa where Arabic is not the official language in —92705–92706, e.g., Arabs in Iran —927055; Mauritanians as a national group in —9661

—927 7	Maltese
—928	Ethiopians

> Including Amhara, Gurage, Harari, Tigrinya

> Class here comprehensive works on the people of Ethiopia

> Class Beta Israel in —924, the Oromo and other Cushitic peoples of Ethiopia in —935

—929	Mahri and Socotrans

> Class here South Arabic peoples

—93	**North Africans**

> Class here peoples who speak, or whose ancestors spoke, non-Semitic Afro-Asiatic languages

> *For Arabs, see* —*927; Ethiopians,* —*928*

—931	Ancient Egyptians
—932	Copts

> *See also notation 215 in Table 7 for Copts as members of the Coptic Church*

—933	Berbers and Tuareg
—935	Cushitic and Omotic peoples

> Examples: Oromo, Somali

> Class Beta Israel in —924, Djiboutians as a national group in —96771, the Somali as a national group in —96773

—937	Hausa

> Class the people of Niger as a national group in —96626

—94	**Peoples of North and West Asian origin or situation; Dravidians**

> Class Indo-Europeans of these regions in —91, Semites in —92

> *For Kushans, see* —*915*

—941	Tungusic peoples
	Examples: Goldi, Lamut, Manchu, Tungus
—942	Mongols
—943	Turkic peoples
	Examples: Azerbaijani, Kazaks, Kirghiz, Turkomans, Uighur, Uzbek, Yakut
	Class Chuvashes in —9456, Cossacks in —91714
—943 5	Turks
	See Manual at T5—9435
—944	Samoyed
—945	Finno-Ugrians
—945 1	Ugrians
	Examples: Ostyaks, Vogul
—945 11	Hungarians
—945 3	Permiaks, Votyak, Komi (Zyrian)
—945 4	Finnic peoples
	Examples: Karelians, Livonians, Veps
	For Lapps, see —9455; Mordvin, Cheremis, Chuvashes, —9456
—945 41	Finns
—945 45	Estonians
—945 5	Lapps
—945 6	Mordvin, Cheremis (Mari), Chuvashes
—946	Paleo-Asiatic (Paleosiberian) peoples
	Including the Ainu
—948	Dravidians and Scytho-Dravidians
	Examples: Maratha (Mahratta), Sindhi
	See also —914 for speakers of Indic languages who are not Scytho-Dravidians, —915 for Scythians
	See Manual at T5—914 vs. T5—948
—948 1	South Dravidians
	Example: Toda
	Class here peoples who speak, or whose ancestors spoke, South Dravidian languages
—948 11	Tamil
—948 12	Malayalis

—948 14	Kanarese
—948 2	Central Dravidians

      Examples: Gonds, Khond

      Class here peoples who speak, or whose ancestors spoke, central Dravidian languages

—948 27	Telugu
—948 3	North Dravidians Brahui

      Example: Kurukh

      Class here peoples who speak, or whose ancestors spoke, North Dravidian languages

—95   **East and Southeast Asian peoples; Mundas**

      Examples: Chepang, Karen, Miao (Hmong), Newar, Nosu, Tamang

      Class here the Asian Mongoloid races; South Asian peoples who speak, or whose ancestors spoke, languages closely related to East and Southeast Asian languages; comprehensive works on Asian peoples

      Class a specific Asian people with the people, e.g., Persians —9155

      For the Aeta and Andamanese, see —9911; Malays, —992

—951	Chinese
—954	Tibetans

      Class here the Bhutia as an ethnic group

      See also —91418 for the Bhutanese as a national group

—956	Japanese

      Including Ryukyuans

      Class here the Japanese as an ethnic group, comprehensive works on the people of Japan

      For the Ainu, see —946

—957	Koreans
—958	Burmese
—959	Miscellaneous southeast Asian peoples; Mundas

      Limited to the peoples provided for below

—959 1	Thai (Siamese), Lao, Shan, Khamti, Ahom

      Class here peoples who speak, or whose ancestors spoke, Thai (Tai) languages

      Use of this number for the Karen discontinued; class in —95

—959 2   Annam-Muong peoples   Vietnamese (Annamese)

> Class here peoples who speak, or whose ancestors spoke, Annam-Muong languages
>
> Class comprehensive works on Montagnards of Vietnam in —9593

—959 3   Mon-Khmer peoples   Khmer (Cambodians)

> Including comprehensive works on Montagnards of Vietnam
>
> Class here peoples who speak, or whose ancestors spoke, Mon-Khmer languages
>
> Class Montagnards of a specific ethnic group with the ethnic group, e.g., Rhade —9922
>
> *For the Semang, see —9911*

—959 5   Mundas

—**96**   **Africans and people of African descent**

> Class here African Negro races, African pygmies
>
> *For Arabs, see —927; Ethiopians, —928; North Africans, —93*

—960 73   Afro-Americans (United States Blacks)

> Add to base number —960730 notation 1–9 from Table 2, e.g., Afro-Americans in England —96073042

—961   Khoikhoi and San

—963–965   Peoples who speak, or whose ancestors spoke, Niger-Congo, Kordofanian, Nilo-Saharan languages

> Add to base number —96 the numbers following —96 in notation 963–965 from Table 6, e.g., the Zulu —963986

—966–968   National groups in Africa

> Citizens of independent and partly independent jurisdictions
>
> Add to base number —96 the numbers following —6 in notation 66–68 from Table 2, e.g., South Africans —968, Namibians —96881
>
> Class nationals of specific ethnolinguistic groups in —961–965, e.g., South African Zulu —963986
>
> *For South Africans of British origin, see —28; Afrikaners, —3936*
>
> *See also —9276 for national groups of African Arabs, e.g.,modern Egyptians —92762, Sudanese —927624; —928 for Ethiopians as a national group; —931 for ancient Egyptians as a national group*

—969   Other national groups of largely African descent

Citizens of independent and partly independent jurisdictions

Add to base number —969 notation 4–9 from Table 2, e.g., Haitians —9697294, Virgin Islanders —96972972; however, Guyanese relocated from —969881 to —9141

Class nationals of specific ethnolinguistic groups in —961–965; minority groups of African descent in —9604–9609, using notation from Table 2 as instructed at the start of Table 5 to show where the groups are located, e.g., persons of African descent in Canada —96071

—97   North American native peoples

Including the Tarascans

Class here North American native races; comprehensive works on North and South American native peoples, on North and South American native races

National groups of modern Central America are classed in —68728 even if the majority of their population is of North American native origin, e.g., Guatemalans as a national group —687281

For South American native peoples and races, see —98

—971   Inuit and Aleut

—972   Athapascan, Haida, Tlingit

Examples: Apache, Navaho, Chipewyan

—973   Algonkian, Muskogean, related peoples

Examples: Choctaw, Cree, Creek, Delaware, Ojibway

Class here peoples who speak, or whose ancestors spoke, Macro-Algonkian languages

—974   Azteco-Tanoan and Penutian

Examples: Chinook, Coos; Maya; Hopi, Ute; Kiowa

Class here peoples who speak, or whose ancestors spoke, Macro-Penutian languages

Class South American peoples who speak, or whose ancestors spoke, Penutian languages in —98

—975   Siouan, Yuman, Pomo, related peoples

Examples: Crow, Dakota; Cherokee, Huron, Iroquois

Including Yukian

Class here peoples who speak, or whose ancestors spoke, a Siouan or Hokan language

—976   Mangue, Mixtec, Popoloca, Zapotec, related peoples

Class here peoples who speak, or whose ancestors spoke, Macro-Otomanguean languages

—978   Matagalpan, Miskito, Sumo, related peoples

         Examples: Guaymi, Terraba

         Class here peoples who speak, or whose ancestors spoke, Misumalpan or other Macro-Chibchan languages in North America

         Class comprehensive works on peoples who speak, or whose ancestors spoke, Macro-Chibchan languages in —982

—979   Other North and Middle American native peoples

         Examples: Salishan, Wakashan

         Including peoples who speak, or whose ancestors spoke, Andean-Equatorial languages in North or Middle America, e.g., Antillean Arawak, Island Carib

         Class comprehensive works on peoples who speak or whose ancestors spoke, Andean-Equatorial languages in —983

—98   **South American native peoples**

         Including peoples who speak, or whose ancestors spoke, Penutian languages in South America, e.g., Araucanian

         Class here South American native races

         Class comprehensive works on peoples who speak, or whose ancestors spoke, Penutian languages in —974

         National groups of modern South America are classed in —688 even where the majority of their population is of South American native origin, e.g., Peruvians as a national group —6885

—982   Chibcha, Paez, Warrau, related peoples

         Example: Cuna

         Class here comprehensive works on peoples who speak, or whose ancestors spoke, Macro-Chibchan languages

         Class peoples who speak, or whose ancestors spoke, Macro-Chibchan languages in North or Middle America in —978

—983   Guaraní, Tupi, Quechua (Kechua), Yaruro, related peoples

         Class here comprehensive works on peoples who speak, or whose ancestors spoke, Andean-Equatorial languages

         Class peoples who speak, or whose ancestors spoke, Andean-Equatorial languages in North or Middle America in —979

—984   Gê, Panoan, Carib, related peoples

         Class here peoples who speak, or whose ancestors spoke, a Gê-Pano-Carib language

         See also —979 for the Island Carib

—99   **Aeta, Andamanese, Semang; Papuans; Australian native peoples; Malays and related peoples; miscellaneous peoples**

> Use of this number for other peoples discontinued; class in —9

—991   Aeta, Andamanese, Semang; Papuans; Australian native peoples

—991 1   Aeta, Andamanese, Semang

> Former heading: Negritos

—991 2   Papuans

> Class here peoples who speak, or whose ancestors spoke, Papuan languages; Papua New Guineans as a national group
>
> Class peoples of New Guinea who speak, or whose ancestors spoke, Austronesian languages in —995
>
> *For the Andamanese, see —9911*

—991 5   Australian native peoples

> Class here comprehensive works on the Australoid race
>
> Class peoples of Australia who speak, or whose ancestors spoke, Papuan languages in —9912; a specific people regarded as belonging to the Australoid race with the people, e.g., Papuans of New Guinea —9912

—992   Malays and related peoples

> Class here comprehensive works on peoples who speak, or whose ancestors spoke, Austronesian languages; comprehensive works on Malayo-Polynesian peoples
>
> *For Malagasy, see —993; Polynesians, —994; Melanesians and Micronesians —995*

—992 1   Filipinos

> Class the Aeta in —991

—992 2   Indonesians

> Including Jarai, Rhade
>
> Class here peoples who speak, or whose ancestors spoke, Indonesian languages
>
> Peoples who speak, or whose ancestors spoke, Malay (Bahasa Malaysia), and Malaysians as a national group are classed in —992
>
> Class comprehensive works on Montagnards of Vietnam in —9593
>
> *For Formosan native peoples, see —9925*

—992 5   Formosan native peoples

> Examples: Ami, Atayal, Bunun, Paiwan, Thao, Yami
>
> *See also —951 for the Chinese*

—993   Malagasy

—994   **Polynesians**

Examples: Maori, Western Samoans

Class here the Polynesian race; peoples who speak, or whose ancestors spoke, Polynesian languages; national groups of Polynesia

For Fijians, see —995

—995   **Melanesians and Micronesians**

Example: Fijians

Class here the Melanesian and Micronesian races; peoples who speak, or whose ancestors spoke, the Austronesian languages of Melanesia and Micronesia; national groups of Melanesia and Micronesia

Class Papua New Guineans as a national group and peoples who speak, or whose ancestors spoke, Papuan languages in —9912; peoples of Polynesian descent in —994

—999   **Miscellaneous peoples**

Limited to the peoples provided for below

Use of this number for other peoples discontinued; class in —9

—999 2   **Basques**

—999 3   **Elamites**

—999 4   **Etruscans**

—999 5   **Sumerians**

—999 6   **Georgians, Ingush, Chechen, Circassians, related peoples**

Class here peoples who speak, or whose ancestors spoke, Caucasic (Caucasian) languages

Table 6. Languages

The following notation is never used alone, but may be used with those numbers from the schedules and other tables to which the classifier is instructed to add notation from Table 6, e.g., translations of the Bible (220.5) into Dutch (—3931 in this table): 220.53931; regions (notation 175 from Table 2) where Spanish language (—61 in this table) predominates: Table 2 notation 17561. When adding to a number from the schedules, always insert a point between the third and fourth digits of the complete number

(Option A: To give local emphasis and a shorter number to a specific language, place it first by use of a letter or other symbol, e.g., Arabic language —A [preceding —1]. Option B is described at —1)

Unless there is specific provision for the old or middle form of a modern language, class these forms with the modern language, e.g., Old High German —31, but Old English —29

Unless there is specific provision for a dialect of a language, class the dialect with the language, e.g., American English dialects —21, but Swiss-German dialect —35

Unless there is a specific provision for a pidgin or creole, class it with the source language from which more of its vocabulary comes than from its other source language(s), e.g., Haitian Creole —41, but Papiamento —68

The numbers in this table do not necessarily correspond exactly to the numbers used for individual languages in 420–490 and in 810–890. For example, although the base number for English in 420–490 is 42, the number for English in Table 6 is —21, not —2

SUMMARY

—1	Indo-European (Indo-Germanic) languages
—2	English and Old English (Anglo-Saxon)
—3	Germanic (Teutonic) languages
—4	Romance languages
—5	Italian, Romanian, Rhaeto-Romanic
—6	Spanish and Portuguese
—7	Italic languages
—8	Hellenic languages
—9	Other languages

—1 Indo-European (Indo-Germanic) languages

Class here the Nostratic proto-proto-language

(Option B: To give local emphasis and a shorter number to a specific language, e.g., Ukrainian, class it in this number, and class Indo-European languages in —91. Option A is described in the introduction to Table 6)

For specific Indo-European languages, see —2–8

> ## —2–8 Specific Indo-European languages

Class comprehensive works in —1

For East Indo-European and Celtic languages, see —91

—2 English and Old English (Anglo-Saxon)

—21 English

Including dialects, pidgins, creoles of English

Class Old English in —29

—219 Middle English, 1100–1500

—29 Old English (Anglo-Saxon)

See also —219 for Middle English

—3 Germanic (Teutonic) languages

For English and Old English (Anglo-Saxon), see —2

—31 German

Class here comprehensive works on dialects of German

Class specific German dialects in —32–38, —394

See also —391 for Old Low German

—32 Franconian dialect

—33 Swabian dialect

—34 Alsatian dialect

—35 Swiss-German dialect

—37 Yiddish (Judeo-German)

—38 Pennsylvania Dutch (Pennsylvania German)

—39 Other Germanic languages

> —391–394 West Germanic languages

Class comprehensive works in —39

—391 Old Low Germanic languages

Examples: Old Frisian, Old Low Franconian, Old Low German, Old Saxon

> —392–394 Modern Low Germanic languages

Class comprehensive works in —39

—392	Frisian
—393	Netherlandish languages
—393 1	Dutch
	Class here Flemish [*formerly* —3932]
—[393 2]	Flemish
	Relocated to —3931
—393 6	Afrikaans
—394	Low German (Plattdeutsch)
—395	Scandinavian (North Germanic) languages
	For specific Scandinavian languages, see —396–398

>	—396–398 Specific Scandinavian languages
	Class comprehensive works in —395
—396	West Scandinavian languages
—396 1	Old Norse (Old Icelandic)
—396 9	Modern West Scandinavian languages
—396 91	Icelandic
	See also —*39699 for Faeroese*
—396 99	Faeroese

>	—397–398 East Scandinavian languages
	Class comprehensive works in —395
—397	Swedish
—398	Danish and Norwegian
—398 1	Danish
	Class Dano-Norwegian in —3982
—398 2	Norwegian (Bokmal, Riksmal)
	Class here Dano-Norwegian, comprehensive works on Norwegian
	For New Norse, see —*3983*
—398 3	Norwegian (New Norse, Landsmal)
	Class comprehensive works on Norwegian in —3982
—399	East Germanic languages
	Examples: Burgundian, Gothic, Vandalic

—4 Romance languages

For Italian, Romanian, Rhaeto-Romanic, see —5; Spanish and Portuguese, —6

—41 French

Including pidgins and creoles of French, e.g., Haitian Creole; Langue d'oc dialect

Class Provençal in —491

—49 Provençal and Catalan

—491 Provençal

—499 Catalan

—5 Italian, Romanian, Rhaeto-Romanic

—51 Italian

—56 Sardinian

—57 Dalmatian (Vegliote)

—59 Romanian and Rhaeto-Romanic

—591 Romanian

—599 Rhaeto-Romanic languages

Examples: Friulian, Ladin, Romansh

—6 Spanish and Portuguese

—61 Spanish

Including pidgins and creoles of Spanish

Class Judeo-Spanish (Ladino) in —67

For Papiamento, see —68

—67 Judeo-Spanish (Ladino)

—68 Papiamento

—69 Portuguese

Including Galician (Gallegan), pidgins and creoles of Portuguese

See also —68 for Papiamento

—7 Italic languages

For Romance languages, see —4

—71 Latin

Class comprehensive works on Latin and Greek in —8

—79   **Other Italic languages**

—794   Latinian languages other than Latin

> Examples: Faliscan, Lanuvian, Praenestian, Venetic

—797   Sabellian languages

> Examples: Aequian, Marrucinian, Marsian, Paelignian, Sabine, Vestinian, Volscian

—799   Osco-Umbrian languages

> Contains Oscan, Umbrian

—8   **Hellenic languages**

> Class here comprehensive works on classical languages
>
> *For Latin, see —71*

—81   **Classical Greek**

—87   **Preclassical and postclassical Greek**

> Including the language of Minoan Linear B; Biblical Greek, Koine (Hellenistic Greek); Byzantine Greek
>
> *See also —926 for Minoan Linear A*

—89   **Modern Greek**

> Examples: Demotic, Katharevusa

—9   **Other languages**

SUMMARY

—91	**East Indo-European and Celtic languages**
—92	**Afro-Asiatic (Hamito-Semitic) languages Semitic languages**
—93	**Non-Semitic Afro-Asiatic languages**
—94	**Ural-Altaic, Paleosiberian, Dravidian languages**
—95	**Languages of East and Southeast Asia Sino-Tibetan languages**
—96	**African languages**
—97	**North American native languages**
—98	**South American native languages**
—99	**Nonaustronesian languages of Oceania, Austronesian languages, miscellaneous languages**

—91   **East Indo-European and Celtic languages**

SUMMARY

—911	**Indo-Iranian (Aryan) languages**
—912	**Sanskrit**
—913	**Middle Indic languages (Secondary Prakrits)**
—914	**Modern Indic languages (Tertiary Prakrits)**
—915	**Iranian languages**
—916	**Celtic languages**
—917	**East Slavic languages**
—918	**Slavic languages**
—919	**Baltic and other Indo-European languages**

—911	Indo-Iranian (Aryan) languages

For Indic (Indo-Aryan) languages, see —912–914; Iranian languages, —915

>	**—912–914 Indic (Indo-Aryan) languages**
	Class comprehensive works in —911
—912	Sanskrit
	Including Vedic (Old Indic)
—913	Middle Indic languages (Secondary Prakrits)
	Class here comprehensive works on Prakrit languages
	Class tertiary Prakrits in —914
—913 7	Pali
—914	Modern Indic languages (Tertiary Prakrits)
—914 1	Sindhi and Lahnda
—914 11	Sindhi
—914 19	Lahnda
—914 2	Panjabi
—914 3	Western Hindi languages
—914 31	Standard Hindi
—914 39	Urdu
—914 4	Bengali
	Class Assamese in —91451
—914 5	Assamese, Bihari, Oriya
—914 51	Assamese
—914 54	Bihari
	Including Bhojpuri, Magahi, Maithili
—914 6	Marathi
	Including Konkani
—914 7	Gujarati and Rajasthani
—914 71	Gujarati
—914 79	Rajasthani
	Including Jaipuri, Marwari
—914 8	Sinhalese-Maldivian languages Sinhalese
	Example: Divehi (Maldivian)

—914 9	Other Indic (Indo-Aryan) languages
	Examples: Eastern Hindi, Nepali, Pahari
	Including Awadhi, Bagheli, Chattisgarhi
	See also —9549 for Himalayan languages, e.g.,Newari
—914 99	Dardic (Pisacha) languages
	Examples: Kashmiri, Khowar, Kohistani, Shina
	Including Nuristani (Kafiri), Romany (Gypsy)
—915	Iranian languages
—915 1	Old Persian
	Class here ancient West Iranian languages
	See also —9152 for Avestan language
—915 2	Avestan
	Class here ancient East Iranian languages
—915 3	Middle Iranian languages
	Examples: Khotanese (Saka), Pahlavi (Middle Persian), Sogdian
—915 5	Modern Persian (Farsi)
	Class Tajik in —9159
—915 9	Other modern Iranian languages
	Examples: Baluchi, Kurdish, Ossetic, Tajik, Yaghnobi
—915 93	Pamir (Galcha) languages Pashto (Afghan)
—916	Celtic languages
	Example: Gaulish
—916 2	Irish Gaelic
—916 3	Scottish Gaelic
—916 4	Manx
—916 6	Welsh (Cymric)
—916 7	Cornish
—916 8	Breton
—917	East Slavic languages
—917 1	Russian
—917 9	Ukrainian and Belorussian
—917 91	Ukrainian
—917 99	Belorussian

—918	Slavic languages
	Example: Common Slavic
	Class here comprehensive works on Balto-Slavic languages
	For East Slavic languages, see —917; Baltic languages, —919
—918 1	South Slavic languages
	For Serbo-Croatian, see —9182; Slovenian, —9184
—918 11	Bulgarian
—918 17	Old Bulgarian (Church Slavonic)
—918 19	Macedonian
—918 2	Serbo-Croatian
—918 4	Slovenian
—918 5	West Slavic languages
	Including Kashubian
	For Czech, see —9186; Slovak, —9187; Wendish, —9188; Polabian, —9189
—918 51	Polish
	Use of this number for Kashubian discontinued; class in —9185
—918 6	Czech
	For Moravian dialects, see —9187
—918 7	Slovak
	Including Moravian dialects
—918 8	Wendish (Sorbian, Lusatian)
—918 9	Polabian
—919	Baltic and other Indo-European languages

>	—919 1–919 3 Baltic languages
	Class comprehensive works in —919
—919 1	Old Prussian
—919 2	Lithuanian
—919 3	Latvian (Lettish)
—919 9	Other Indo-European languages
—919 91	Albanian
—919 92	Armenian

—919 93	Thraco-Phrygian and Illyrian languages
	Examples: Illyrian, Ligurian, Messapian, Phrygian, Thracian
—919 94	Tocharian language
	Including Agnean and Kuchean dialects [*both formerly* —91996]
—[919 96]	Agnean and Kuchean dialects
	Relocated to —91994
—919 98	Anatolian languages Hittite
	Examples: Luwian, Lycian, Lydian, Palaic
	See also —999 for Hurrian languages

—92   Afro-Asiatic (Hamito-Semitic) languages   Semitic languages

> *For non-Semitic Afro-Asiatic languages, see —93*

—921	East Semitic languages Akkadian (Assyro-Babylonian)
	Including Assyrian, Babylonian, Chaldean dialects of Akkadian
	See also —922 for Aramaic, —9995 for Sumerian

> —922–929 West Semitic languages

Class comprehensive works in —92

> —922–926 Northwest Semitic languages

Class comprehensive works in —92

—922	Aramaic languages
	For Eastern Aramaic languages, see —923
—922 9	Western Aramaic languages
	Former heading: Biblical Aramaic (Chaldee) and Samaritan
—923	Eastern Aramaic languages Syriac
—924	Hebrew
	Ammonite and Moabite relocated to —926
—926	Canaanite-Phoenician languages

Examples: Ammonite, Moabite [*both formerly* —924], Eblaite, Punic, Ugaritic, the language of Minoan Linear A

Class here comprehensive works on Canaanitic languages

> *For Hebrew, see —924*

> *See also —87 for Minoan Linear B, —9995 for Sumerian*

>	—927–929 Southwest Semitic languages
	Class comprehensive works in —92
—927	North Arabic languages Arabic
	Example: Maltese
	See also —929 for South Arabic languages
—928	Ethiopic languages
	Examples: Geez, Gurage, Harari, Tigre, Tigrinya
—928 7	Amharic
	Including Argobba dialect
—929	South Arabic languages
	Examples: Mahri, Qarawi, Shkhauri, Sokotri
	See also —927 for North Arabic languages
—93	**Non-Semitic Afro-Asiatic languages**
	Former heading: Hamitic and Chad languages
—931	Egyptian languages Egyptian
	Including Old, Middle, New, Demotic Egyptian
	For Coptic, see —932
—932	Coptic
—933	Berber languages
	Examples: Kabyle, Rif, Siwa, Tamashek (Tuareg)
—935	Cushitic and Omotic languages
	Examples: Beja, Oromo (Galla), Somali
—937	Chadic languages
	Example: Angas
—937 2	Hausa
—94	**Ural-Altaic, Paleosiberian (Hyperborean), Dravidian languages**
>	—941–943 Altaic languages
	Class comprehensive works in —94, Japanese in —956, Korean in —957
—941	Tungusic languages
	Examples: Even (Lamut), Manchu, Nanai (Goldi), Tungus

—942	Mongolic languages
	Examples: Buryat, Kalmuck, Mongolian
—943	Turkic (Turko-Tatar) languages
	Examples: Chagatai, Chuvash, Kazak, Kirghiz, Uighur, Uzbek, Yakut
—943 5	Turkish (Osmanli)
—943 6	Southwestern Turkic languages (Oghuz Turkic languages)
	Examples: Gagauz, Oghuz, Turkmen
	For Turkish, see —9435
—943 61	Azerbaijani

>	—944–945 Uralic languages
	Class comprehensive works in —94
—944	Samoyedic languages
	Examples: Nganasan, Ostyak Samoyed, Yenisei Samoyed (Enets), Yurak Samoyed (Nenets)
—945	Finno-Ugric languages
—945 1	Ugric languages
	Examples: Ostyak, Vogul
—945 11	Hungarian (Magyar)
—945 3	Permian languages
	Contains Votyak (Udmurt), Zyrian (Komi)
—945 4	Finnic languages
	Examples: Karelian, Livonian, Veps
	For Lapp, see —9455; Middle Volga languages, —9456
—945 41	Finnish (Suomi)
—945 45	Estonian
—945 5	Lapp
—945 6	Middle Volga languages
	Examples: Cheremis, Mordvin
—946	Paleosiberian (Hyperborean) languages
	Including Gilyak, Luorawetlin, Yeniseian, Yukaghir families; Ainu (relationship not clear)
	See also —971 for Inuit-Aleut languages

—948	Dravidian languages
—948 1	South Dravidian

        Examples: Kota, Toda

        Class here Dravida group

        Kurukh (Orâon), Malto relocated to —9483

—948 11	Tamil
—948 12	Malayalam
—948 14	Kannada (Kanarese)
—948 2	Central Dravidian

        Former heading: Andhra group

—948 23	Gondi
—948 24	Khond (Kandh)
—948 27	Telugu
—948 3	North Dravidian Brahui

        Examples: Kurukh (Oraon), Malto [*both formerly* —9481]

—95	**Languages of East and Southeast Asia** **Sino-Tibetan languages**

    Examples: Karen, Miao (Hmong), Yao

    Here are classed South Asian languages closely related to the languages of East and Southeast Asia

        For Malay languages, see —992

—951	Chinese
—951 1	Mandarin (Putonghua)
—951 7	Dialects

        Examples: Amoy, Cantonese, Foochow, Hakka, Pekingese (Beijing), Swatow, Wu dialects

—954	Tibeto-Burman languages

        Including the Bodo-Naga-Kachin, Kuki-Chin, Loloish groups

        For Burmese, see —958

—954 1	Tibetan
—954 9	Himalayan (Gyarung-Mishmi) languages

        Example: Newari

        See also —9149 *for Nepali*

—956	Japanese
—957	Korean
—958	Burmese

—959	Miscellaneous languages of Southeast Asia; Munda languages
	Limited to the languages provided for below
—959 1	Thai (Tai) languages
—959 11	Thai (Siamese)
—959 19	Other Thai (Tai) languages
	Examples: Ahom, Khamti, Lao, Shan
	Use of this number for Karen discontinued; class in —95
	For Annam-Muong languages, see —9592
—959 2	Annam-Muong languages
	Relationship to Thai and Austroasiatic languages not clear
—959 22	Vietnamese (Annamese)
—959 3	Mon-Khmer languages
	Examples: Khasi, Mon, Palaung, Sakai, Semang, Wa
	Class here Austroasiatic languages
	For Munda languages, see —9595; Annam-Muong languages, —9592
—959 32	Khmer (Cambodian)
—959 5	Munda languages
	Examples: Gadaba, Ho, Mundari, Santali
—96	**African languages**
	For Ethiopic languages, see —928; non-Semitic Afro-Asiatic languages, —93
—961	Macro-Khoisan languages
	Examples: Khoikhoi, San
—963	Niger-Congo and Kordofanian languages
—963 2	West-Atlantic languages
—963 21	Senegal group
	Example: Serer
	For Fulani, see —96322
—963 214	Wolof language
—963 22	Fulani (Fulah)
—963 3	Kwa languages
	Example: Gã
—963 32	Ibo (Igbo)
—963 33	Yoruba group Yoruba language

—963 37	Western group

> *For Volta-Comoe group, see —96338*

—963 374	Ewe group Ewe language
—963 38	Volta-Comoe group
—963 385	Central Volta-Comoe (Tano) subgroup Akan language

         Example: Anyi

         Class here Fante, Twi

—963 4	Mande (Mandingo) languages

         Examples: Bambara, Malinke, Mende

—963 5	Gur (Voltaic) languages

         Examples: Dagomba, Moré, Senufo

—963 6	Benue-Niger languages

         Examples: Bamileke, Sango

         Contains Adamawa-Eastern, Benue-Congo languages

         Class here Bantoid languages

         Use of this number for Kordofanian languages discontinued; class in —963

> *For Bantu languages, see —9639*

—963 9	Bantu languages

         Bantu proper (Narrow Bantu)

         Including Kari group

         Groups and zones of Bantu languages are based on Malcolm Guthrie's *Comparative Bantu; an Introduction to the Comparative Linguistics and Prehistory of the Bantu Languages*, 1967–1971

> *See also —9636 for Bantoid languages other than Bantu proper*
>
> *See Manual at T6—9639*

—963 91	Central Bantu languages Central eastern Bantu languages

         Contains Bena-Kinga, Gogo, Pogolo, Shambala, Zigula-Zaramo groups (from Guthrie's zone G); Bisa-Lamba, Fipa-Mambwe, Lenje-Tonga, Nyakyusa-Konde, Nyika-Safwa groups (from Guthrie's zone M); Manda, Senga-Sena, Tumbuka groups (from Guthrie's zone N)

> *For Swahili group, see —96392; central western Bantu languages, —96393*

—963 915	Bemba group Bemba language
—963 918	Nyanja group Nyanja language

         Class here Chichewa (Chewa)

—963 92   Swahili group   Swahili language

—963 93   Central western Bantu languages

> Contains Kimbala, Kimbundu, Kiyaka groups (from Guthrie's zone H); Kaonde, Luba, Lunda, Nkoya, Pende, Songe groups (Guthrie's zone L)

—963 931   Kikongo group   Kongo language

—963 94   Northern Bantu languages   Northeastern Bantu languages

> Contains Bembe-Kabwari, Bira-Huku, Konjo, Lega-Kalanga, Mbole-Ena groups (from Guthrie's zone D); Ilamba-Irangi, Sukuma-Nyamwezi, Tongwe groups (Guthrie's zone F)

> *For north northeastern Bantu languages, see —96395; northwestern Bantu languages, —96396*

—963 946   Ruanda-Rundi group

—963 946 1   Ruanda

—963 946 5   Rundi

—963 95   North northeastern Bantu languages

> Including Chaga (Shaka), Haya-Jita, Masaba-Luhya, Nyika-Taita, Ragoli-Kuria (Gusii) groups (from Guthrie's zone E)

—963 953   Kikuyu-Kamba group

> *For Kikuyu, see —963954*

—963 954   Kikuyu

—963 956   Nyoro-Ganda group

> Examples: Chiga, Nyankore

> *For Ganda (Luganda), see —96357*

—963 957   Ganda (Luganda)

—963 96   Northwestern Bantu languages

> Contains Bafia, Basa, Bube-Benga, Duala, Kaka, Lundu-Balong, Maka-Njem, Sanaga, Yaunde-Fang groups (Guthrie's zone A); Kele, Mbete, Myene, Njabi, Shira-Punu, Teke, Tende-Yanzi, Tsogo groups (Guthrie's zone B); Kuba, Mboshi, Mongo-Nkundu, Ngombe, Ngundi, Soko-Kele, Tetela groups (from Guthrie's zone C)

—963 968   Bangi-Ntumba (Ngala) group

—963 968 6   Losengo cluster   Lingala language

—963 97   Southern Bantu languages   Southeastern Bantu languages

> Contains Makua, Matumbi, Yao groups (Guthrie's zone P); Chopi, Tswa-Ronga (Tsonga), Venda groups (from Guthrie's zone S)

> *For Nguni group, see —96398*

—963 975   Shona group   Shona language

—963 977	Sotho-Tswana group
—963 977 1	Northern Sotho
	Class comprehensive works on northern and southern Sotho in —963977
—963 977 2	Southern Sotho
—963 977 5	Tswana language
—963 98	Nguni group
	Examples: Ndebele, Swazi (siSwati)
—963 985	Xhosa
—963 986	Zulu
—963 99	Southwestern Bantu languages
	Contains Chokwe-Luchazi, Lozi, Luyana, Subiya groups (Guthrie's zone K); Herero, Ndonga, Umbundu, Yeye groups (Guthrie's zone R)
—965	Nilo-Saharan languages
	Examples: Nilotic, Nubian languages; Luo, Songhai
	Class here Chari-Nile (Macrosudanic) languages
—[969]	Commercial languages
	Number discontinued; class in —96
—97	**North American native languages**
	Example: Tarascan
	Class here comprehensive works on North and South American native languages
	For South American native languages, see —98
—971	Inuit-Aleut languages
—972	Na-Dene languages
	Examples: Apache, Navaho; Chipewyan; Haida, Tlingit
	Class here the Athapascan-Eyak family
—973	Macro-Algonkian languages
	Examples: Choctaw, Creek [*both formerly* —975], Cree, Delaware, Ojibway
	Mosan languages (including Nootka) relocated to —979
—974	Macro-Penutian languages
—974 1	Penutian languages
	Examples: Chinook, Coos, Mixe, Tsimshian
	For Penutian languages of South America, see —98
—974 15	Mayan languages
	Examples: Kekchi, Maya, Quiche

—974 5   Uto-Aztecan languages

                Examples: Aztec, Hopi, Ute

                Class here comprehensive works on Aztec-Tanoan languages

                For Kiowa-Tanoan languages, see —9749

—974 9   Kiowa-Tanoan languages

                Class comprehensive works on Aztec-Tanoan languages in —9745

—975   Hokan and Siouan languages

                Examples: Pomo, Yuman; Crow, Dakota (Sioux); Cherokee, Huron, Iroquois

                Including Yukian

                Choctaw, Creek relocated to —973

—976   Macro-Otomanguean languages

                Examples: Manguean, Mixtec, Popoloca, Zapotec

—[977]   Tarascan language

                Number discontinued; class in —97

—978   Misumalpan and other Macro-Chibchan languages of North America

                Former heading: Miskito-Matagalpan languages

                Examples: Matagalpan, Miskito, Sumo; Guaymi, Terraba

                Class comprehensive works on Macro-Chibchan languages in —982

—979   Other North and Middle American languages

                Examples: Mosan languages (including Nootka) [*both formerly* —973], Cuitlatec

                Class Yukian in —975

—98   **South American native languages**

                Examples: Hishkaryana; Penutian languages of South America, e.g., Araucanian

                Class comprehensive works on Penutian languages in —9741

—982   Macro-Chibchan languages

                Example: Paez

                For Misumalpan and other Macro-Chibchan languages of North America, see —978

—983   Andean-Equatorial languages

                Examples: Esmeralda, Yaruro; Guaraní, Tupí

                Including Macro-Tucanoan languages

                Class Andean-Equatorial languages of North America in —97

—983 2	Andean languages
—983 23	Quechumaran (Kechumaran) languages Quechua (Kechua)
—984	Gê-Pano-Carib languages

Examples: Huarpe, Nambicuara, Taruma

—[985]   Hokan languages

Provision discontinued because without meaning in context of South America

—99   **Nonaustronesian languages of Oceania, Austronesian languages, miscellaneous languages**

Use of this number for other languages discontinued; class in —9

—991   Nonaustronesian languages of Oceania

—991 2   Papuan languages

See also —995 for Austronesian languages of New Guinea

—991 5   Australian languages

Aboriginal languages of Australia and related languages of adjacent islands

Class Papuan languages spoken in Australia in —9912

>   —992–995   Austronesian languages   Malayo-Polynesian languages

Class comprehensive works in —992

—992   Malay languages

Class here comprehensive works on Austronesian languages, on Malayo-Polynesian languages

Comprehensive works on Oceanic (Eastern Austronesian) languages relocated to —994

For Malagasy, see —993; Polynesian languages, —994; Austronesian languages of Melanesia and Micronesia, —995

—992 1   Philippine languages

—992 11   Tagalog (Filipino)

—992 2   Indonesian languages

Examples: Balinese, Madurese, Sundanese; Bornean languages

For Malay (Bahasa Malaysia), see —9928

—992 21   Indonesian (Bahasa Indonesia)

Class comprehensive works on Indonesian (Bahasa Indonesia) and Malay (Bahasa Malaysia) in —9928

—992 22   Javanese

—992 8	Malay (Bahasa Malaysia)

Examples: Melayu Asli (Proto-Malay) languages; Jakun

Class here comprehensive works on Malay (Bahasa Malaysia) and Indonesian (Bahasa Indonesia)

Class Sakai and Semang languages in —9593, Indonesian (Bahasa Indonesia) in —99221

—993	Malagasy
—994	Polynesian languages

Examples: Hawaiian, Maori, Samoan, Tahitian

Class here comprehensive works on Oceanic (Eastern Austronesian) languages [*formerly* —992]

For Austronesian languages of Melanesia and Micronesia, see —995

—995	Austronesian languages of Melanesia and Micronesia

Class comprehensive works on Oceanic (Eastern Austronesian) languages in —994

See also —*9912 for Nonaustronesian languages of Melanesia*

—999	Miscellaneous languages

Limited to Hurrian languages and the languages provided for below

Use of this number for languages not provided for elsewhere discontinued; class in —9

—999 2	Basque
—999 3	Elamite
—999 4	Etruscan
—999 5	Sumerian

See also —*926 for Eblaite language*

—999 6	Caucasic (Caucasian) languages

Examples: Chechen, Circassian, Georgian

—999 9	Artificial languages

Example: Afrihili

—999 92	Esperanto
—999 93	Interlingua

Table 7. Groups of Persons

The following notation is never used alone, but may be used as required with any appropriate number from the schedules, e.g., collections from more than one literature (808.8992) by Lutherans (notation 241 in this table): 808.8992241. They may also be used when so noted with numbers from other tables, e.g., chemistry (540) for (notation 024 from Table 1) dentists (notation 6176 from this table): 540.246176. Do not add from this table if the resultant concept is redundant, e.g., dentistry for dentists, Lutheran doctrine among Lutherans

SUMMARY

—01–09	[Persons by various nonoccupational characteristics; generalists, novices]
—1	Persons occupied with philosophy, parapsychology and occultism, psychology
—2	Persons occupied with or adherent to religion
—3	Persons occupied with the social sciences and socioeconomic activities
—4	Persons occupied with linguistics and lexicography
—5	Persons occupied with natural sciences and mathematics
—6	Persons occupied with applied sciences (Technologists)
—7	Persons occupied with the arts With fine and decorative arts
—8	Persons occupied with creative writing and speaking
—9	Persons occupied with geography, history, related disciplines and activities

—01   Individual persons

Class specific kinds of individuals in —03–99

—02   Groups of persons

Class groups of specific kinds of persons in —03–99

>   —03–08 Persons by various nonoccupational characteristics

Unless other instructions are given, class complex subjects with aspects in two or more subdivisions of this table in the number coming last in the table, e.g., gifted upper middle-class Jewish male young adults —0829 (*not* —0622, —055, —041, or —03924)

Class comprehensive works in base number

—03   Persons by racial, ethnic, national background

Add to base number —03 notation 01–99 from Table 5, e.g., North American persons —031

Class comprehensive works on members of nondominant racial, ethnic, national groups in —0693

—04   **Persons by sex and kinship characteristics**

>   **—041–042 Persons by sex**
>   Class comprehensive works in —04

—041   Males

—042   Females

>   **—043–046 Persons by kinship characteristics**
>   Class comprehensive works in —04

—043   Direct ancestors and their surrogates

—043 1   Parents
       Class here adoptive and foster parents; stepparents

—043 2   Grandparents
       Direct forebears other than parents

—044   Direct descendants and their counterparts

—044 1   **Sons and daughters**
       Class here adopted and foster children; stepchildren

—044 2   Grandchildren
       Direct descendants other than first generation

—045   Siblings
       Brothers and sisters by blood, adoption, foster care, remarriage of parents

—046   Collateral kinsmen
       Uncles, aunts, nephews, nieces, cousins, of all degrees

—05   **Persons by age**

—054   Children

—054 2   Infants
       From birth to age two

—054 3   Preschool children
       Ages three to five

—054 4   School children
       Ages six to eleven

—055   Young adults
       Ages twelve to twenty

—056	Adults
	Class adult males in —041, adult females in —042
—056 4	Middle adulthood
—056 5	Late adulthood
—06	**Persons by social and economic characteristics**
	Add to base number —06 the numbers following —086 in —0862–0869 from Table 1, e.g., members of nondominant racial, ethnic, national, socioeconomic, religious groups —0693; however, class members of specific nondominant racial, ethnic, national groups in —03; of specific nondominant religious groups in —2
—08	**Persons by physical and mental characteristics**
—081	By physical condition
—081 2	Healthy persons
—081 4	Ill persons
—081 6	Persons with physical disabilities
—081 61	Persons with impaired vision
	Class here blind persons, blind-deaf persons
—081 62	Persons with impaired hearing
	Class here deaf persons
—081 64	Persons with speech defects
—081 66	Persons with motor impairment
—082	By mental condition
—082 2	Healthy persons
—082 4	Ill and emotionally disturbed persons
—082 6	Persons with handicaps and deficiencies (Mentally retarded)
—082 9	Gifted persons
	Example: geniuses

>	**—09–99 Persons by various occupational characteristics**
	Class comprehensive works in base number
—09	**Generalists and novices**
	Generalists: persons occupied with several or many subjects and activities, or with specific subjects and activities of a general nature, as study, profession, vocation, hobby
—090 1	Scholars, academicians, researchers

—090 3	Persons occupied with systems
—090 4	Computer scientists
	Class here persons occupied with data processing
—090 9	Novices and amateurs
	Examples: laymen, dabblers, uninitiated, collectors
—091	Persons occupied with bibliography
—092	Persons occupied with library and information science
	For persons occupied with bibliography, see —091
—093	Encyclopedists
	Class lexicographers in —4
—096	Persons occupied with museology
—097	Persons occupied with publishing and journalism

>   **—1–9 Specialists**

Persons occupied with specific disciplines, subjects, activities as study, profession, vocation, hobby, affiliation

In a general way the notations from —1 through —9 have been developed from a reduction of numbers from the whole classification; however, the mnemonic matches are by no means perfect, and the table should not be used without consultation, e.g., local government personnel —354, not —352

Class comprehensive works in 001–999 without adding notation from Table 7, persons occupied with specific subjects or activities of a general nature in —09

—1   **Persons occupied with philosophy, parapsychology and occultism, psychology**

—11   **With philosophy**

—13   **With parapsychology and occultism**

Example: persons occupied with Rosicrucianism [*formerly* —3664]

—15   **With psychology**

—2   Persons occupied with or adherent to religion

Examples: founders, central and local administrative heads, clergy, missionaries, members of religious congregations and orders, saints, laymen

Class here persons occupied with or adherent to Christianity

SUMMARY

—21	With early church and Eastern churches
—22	With Roman Catholic Church
—23	With Anglican churches
—24	With Protestant churches of Continental origin and related bodies
—25	With Presbyterian churches, Reformed churches centered in America, Congregational churches
—26	With Baptist, Disciples of Christ, Adventist churches
—27	With Methodist churches; churches uniting Methodist and other denominations; Salvation Army
—28	With other churches
—29	With other religions

>   **—21–28 Persons occupied with or adherent to Christianity and Christian church**

Class comprehensive works in —2

—21   **With early church and Eastern churches**

—211   Apostolic Church

Including church fathers

—215   Eastern churches

For Eastern Orthodox churches, see —219

—219   Eastern Orthodox churches

—22   **With Roman Catholic Church**

Class modern Catholic schismatics in —248

—23   **With Anglican churches**

—24   **With Protestant churches of Continental origin and related bodies**

For Baptist churches, see —261; Church of the New Jerusalem, —284; Mennonite churches, —287

—241   Lutheran churches

—242   Calvinistic and Reformed churches of European origin

Class here comprehensive works on Calvinistic churches, on Reformed churches

For Huguenot churches, see —245; Presbyterian churches, —251; Reformed churches centered in America, —257

—243   Hussite and Anabaptist churches

—244   Albigensian, Catharist, Waldensian churches

—245	Huguenot churches
—246	Moravian churches

For Hussite churches, see —243

—248	Modern schisms in Roman Catholic Church
—249	Arminian and Remonstrant churches
—25	**With Presbyterian churches, Reformed churches centered in America, Congregational churches**

Including Puritanism

—251	Presbyterian churches
—257	Reformed churches centered in America
—258	Congregationalism
—26	**With Baptist, Disciples of Christ, Adventist churches**
—261	Baptist churches
—266	Disciples of Christ
—267	Adventist churches
—27	**With Methodist churches; churches uniting Methodist and other denominations; Salvation Army**
—28	**With other churches**
—281	Unitarian and Universalist churches
—283	Latter-Day Saints
—284	Church of the New Jerusalem (Swedenborgianism)
—285	Church of Christ, Scientist (Christian Science)
—286	Society of Friends (Quaker)
—287	Mennonite churches
—288	Shakers
—289	Others

Examples: Jehovah's Witnesses; Pentecostal churches

—29	**With other religions**
—291	Atheism, agnosticism, deism, theosophy
—292	Classical (Greek and Roman) religion
—293	Germanic religion
—294	Religions of Indic origin
—294 3	Buddhism
—294 4	Jainism

—294 5	Hinduism
	Class here Brahmanism
—294 6	Sikhism
—295	Zoroastrianism (Mazdaism, Parseeism)
—296	Judaism
—297	Islam and religions originating in it
	Class Sikhism in —2946
—297 1	Islam
—297 7	Black Muslim movement
—297 8	Babism
—297 9	Bahai faith
—299	Other religions
—299 1	Druidism
—299 5	Religions of East and Southeast Asian origin
—299 51	Chinese
—299 512	Confucianism
—299 514	Taoism
—299 56	Shintoism
—299 6	Religions originating among Black Africans and people of Black African descent
—299 7	Religions of North American native origin
—299 8	Religions of South American native origin
—299 9	Religions of other origin

—3   Persons occupied with the social sciences and socioeconomic activities

SUMMARY

—309	Sociologists
—31	Persons occupied with statistics
—32	Persons occupied with political science and politics
—33	Persons occupied with economics and related activities
—34	Persons occupied with law
—35	Persons occupied with public administration
—36	Persons occupied with welfare and public protection
—37	Persons occupied with education
—38	Persons occupied with commerce, communications, transportation
—39	Persons occupied with customs, etiquette, folklore

—[301]   Social scientists

         Number discontinued; class in —3

—309	Sociologists

Including ethnologists, ethnographers [*both formerly* —572], social ecologists, social anthropologists

—31	**Persons occupied with statistics**
—32	**Persons occupied with political science and politics**

For persons occupied with law, see —34; *with public administration,* —35

—321	Political scientists and theorists
—323	Civil rights workers
—328	Legislators
—329	Politicians

Other than legislators, public administrators, judges, legal officers

See also —351 *for heads of state and central governments*

—33	**Persons occupied with economics and related activities**
—331	Labor-oriented persons
—331 7	Workers

See also —0623 *for working class*

—331 8	Labor leaders
—332	Bankers and financiers
—333	Landowners and conservationists
—335	Communists, socialists, anarchists
—338	Entrepreneurs
—339	Economists
—34	**Persons occupied with law**
—341	Delegates to and employees of international organizations to promote peace and order
—342	Justices of supreme courts
—343	Judges

For justices of supreme courts, see —342

—344	Lawyers
—349	Local and auxiliary legal officers

Examples: justices of the peace, notaries public, bailiffs, coroners

See also —3632 *for police*

—35	**Persons occupied with public administration**

> Administrators as a high position in government is classed in —3523

—351	Heads of state and central governments
—351 1	Reigning monarchs and their regents
—351 2	Presidents and vice-presidents
—351 3	Prime ministers and premiers
—351 4	Dictators

> Class dictators occupying a specific position with the subject, e.g., presidents —3512

—351 8	Governors
—352	Other state and central government personnel

> *See also —355 for military personnel*

—352 1	Cabinet members and councilors of state
—352 2	Ambassadors and other envoys

> *For delegates to international organizations, see —341*

—352 3	Administrators and commissioners
—352 7	Civil service personnel

> Class civil service personnel occupied with a specific discipline, subject, activity with persons occupied with that discipline, subject, activity, e.g., economists —339

—354	Local government personnel

> Elected and appointed

—355	Military personnel

> Class here land forces personnel
>
> *For air and space forces personnel, see —358; naval personnel, —359*

—358	Air and space forces personnel
—359	Naval personnel
—36	**Persons occupied with welfare and public protection**

> Class socially disadvantaged persons in —0694

—361	With philanthropy, humanitarianism, social reform
—362	Social workers
—363	With public protection and utility services
—363 2	Police
—363 3	Fire fighters
—363 6	Persons occupied with public utility services

—364	With crime and delinquency
	Example: criminologists
	Class criminals and other offenders in —0692
	For persons occupied with law, see —34; with public protection, —363
—365	With administration of penal and related institutions
—366	Persons occupied with or belonging to esoteric associations and societies
—366 1	With Freemasonry
—366 2	With Knights of Pythias
—366 3	With Independent Order of Odd Fellows and International Association of Rebekah Assemblies
—[366 4]	With Rosicrucianism
	Relocated to —13
—366 5	With Benevolent and Protective Order of Elks
—367	Persons occupied with or belonging to general clubs
	Examples: social clubs, study clubs
—368	Persons occupied with insurance
—369	Persons occupied with or belonging to hereditary, military, patriotic, young people's societies; racial, ethnic, service clubs
—369 2	With hereditary, military, patriotic societies
—369 4	With young people's societies
	Example: Scouts
—369 5	With service clubs
	Examples: Kiwanis International, Lions International, Rotary International, Zonta International
—37	**Persons occupied with education**

>	—371–375 With specific educational activities
	Class comprehensive works in —37, persons associated with specific educational institutions in —379
—371	With school and college administration
—372	With teaching
—375	Students
—379	Persons associated with specific educational institutions
	Examples: administrators, teachers, students, alumni

—38	**Persons occupied with commerce, communications, transportation**
—381	With internal commerce (domestic trade)
	Examples: merchandisers, sales personnel [*formerly also* —658]
—382	With international commerce (foreign trade)
—383	With postal communication services
—384	With communication services
	Class here telecommunication services
	For persons occupied with postal communication services, see —383
—385	With railroad transportation services
—386	With inland waterway and ferry transportation services
	Including oceanic ferry transportation services [*formerly* —3875]
—387	With water, air, space transportation services
	For persons occupied with inland waterway and ferry transportation services, see —386
—387 5	Ocean (Marine) transportation
	Oceanic ferry transportation services relocated to —386
—387 7	Air transportation
—387 8	Space transportation
—388	With transportation services With ground transportation services
	For persons occupied with railroad transportation services, see —385; *with water, air, space transportation,* —387

—39   **Persons occupied with customs, etiquette, folklore**

—4   Persons occupied with linguistics and lexicography

—5   Persons occupied with natural sciences and mathematics

—51	**With mathematics**
—52	**With astronomy and allied sciences**
—521	Astronomy
—526	Geodesy, map making, surveying
—527	Celestial navigation
—529	Chronology
—53	**With physics**
—539	Nuclear physics

—54	**With chemistry and allied sciences**
—541	Chemistry
—548	Crystallography
—549	Mineralogy
—55	**With the earth sciences**
—551	Meteorology and climatology
—552	Petrology
—553	Geology
—56	**With paleontology**
—57	**With life sciences**
	Class persons occupied with paleontology in —56
—572	Physical ethnology
	Ethnologists, ethnographers relocated to —309
—573	Physical anthropology
—574	Biology
	Class persons occupied with botany in —58, with zoology in —59
—58	**With botany**
—[581]	General botany
	Number discontinued; class in —58
—589	Bacteriology
—59	**With zoology**
—[591]	General zoology
	Number discontinued; class in —59
—593	Protozoology
—595	Helminthology and entomology
—597	Herpetology [*formerly* —598] and Ichthyology
—598	Ornithology
	Herpetology relocated to —597
—599	Mammalogy

—6   Persons occupied with applied sciences (Technologists)

SUMMARY

—604	Persons occupied with technical drawing
—61	Persons occupied with medical sciences With medicine
—62	Persons occupied with engineering and allied operations, and manufacturing
—63	Persons occupied with agriculture and related technologies
—64	Persons occupied with home economics and family living
—65	Persons occupied with managerial services
—66	Persons occupied with chemical engineering and related technologies
—67	Persons occupied with manufacturing
—68	Persons occupied with manufacture of products for specific uses
—69	Persons occupied with buildings

—604   Persons occupied with technical drawing

—61   **Persons occupied with medical sciences**   **With medicine**

—613   With nursing and promotion of health

—614   With public preventive medicine

—615   With pharmacology, pharmacy, therapeutics, toxicology

> Class persons occupied with therapeutics of specific diseases or group of diseases in —616–618

—616   With specific medical specialities

> Use of this number for persons occupied with general medicine discontinued; class in —61

> Class persons occupied with surgery and related topics in —617; with gynecology, obstetrics, pediatrics, geriatrics in —618

—617   With surgery and related topics

> Example: anesthesiology

—617 1   Surgery

—617 6   Dentistry

—617 7   Ophthalmology

—617 8   Otology and audiology

—618   With gynecology, obstetrics, pediatrics, geriatrics

—618 1   Gynecology and obstetrics

—618 9   Pediatrics

—62   **Persons occupied with engineering and allied operations, and manufacturing**

> Including persons occupied with systems engineering

> Class comprehensive works on persons occupied with manufacturing in —67, with chemical engineering in —66

—620 1   With engineering mechanics and materials

—620 2   With acoustical engineering

—[620 7]   With systems engineering

         Use of this number discontinued; class in —62

—620 8   With biotechnology

—621   With applied physics

         Examples: mechanical, steam, hydraulic-power, pneumatic, cryogenic, tool engineering

—621 3   Electrical, electronic, magnetic, communications, computer engineering

—621 4   Heat engineering

         Example: solar engineering

—621 48   Nuclear engineering

—622   With mining and related operations

         Example: prospecting

—623   With military and nautical engineering

—623 1   Military engineering

—623 8   Nautical engineering and seamanship

—624   With civil engineering

         Examples: structural, tunnel, bridge engineering

         Class persons associated with other specific kinds of civil engineering in —625–629, with construction of buildings in —69

—625   With engineering of railroads, roads, highways

—627   With hydraulic engineering

—628   With sanitary and municipal engineering   With environmental protection engineering

—629   With other branches of engineering

—629 1   Aeronautical and aerospace engineering and operation

         Examples: pilots, copilots, navigators, aircraft engineers, air controllers

         Class persons occupied with astronautical engineering and operation in —6294

—629 2   Motor land vehicle engineering and operation

         See also —7967 for persons occupied with motor vehicle racing

—629 4	Astronautical engineering and operation
	Examples: astronauts and cosmonauts, vehicle engineers, ground-control personnel
—629 8	Automatic control engineering
—63	**Persons occupied with agriculture and related technologies**
—631	With farming
	Class persons occupied with specific kinds of farming in —633–638
—633	With field and plantation crop farming
—634	With fruit growing and forestry
—635	With horticulture and gardening
—636	With animal husbandry
	Class here persons occupied with stock raising
	Class persons occupied with raising dairy cattle in —637, culture of nondomesticated animals in —639
—637	With dairying
—638	With insect culture
—639	With hunting, fishing, conservation, related technologies
	Class persons occupied with sport hunting and fishing in —799
—639 1	Hunting and trapping
—639 2	Fishing, whaling, sealing
—639 3	Culture of cold-blooded vertebrates Of fish
—639 9	Conservation
—64	**Persons occupied with home economics and family living**
	Class here persons occupied with domestic arts and sciences
—641	Cooks and nutritionists
—642	Restaurateurs and caterers
—646	Seamstresses, cosmetologists, related occupational personnel
—646 4	Seamstresses and tailors
—646 5	Milliners and hatters
—646 7	Cosmetologists, hairdressers, barbers
—647	Hotel- and motelkeepers
—648	Launderers
—649	Homemakers

—65	**Persons occupied with managerial services**
—651	With office services

        Examples: bookkeepers, clerks, file clerks, office managers, secretaries, stenographers, typists

—657	With accounting

        For bookkeepers, see —651

—658	With management

        Merchandisers, sales personnel relocated to —381

        Class entrepreneurs in —338

—659	With advertising
—66	**Persons occupied with chemical engineering and related technologies**

        Class persons occupied with pharmacology in —615, with military applications in —6231, with pulp and paper technology in —676, with elastomer manufacturing in —678

—661	With industrial chemistry
—662	With technology of explosives, fuels, related products
—663	With beverage technology
—664	With food technology
—665	With petroleum and gas technology
—666	With ceramic technology
—669	With metallurgy
—67	**Persons occupied with manufacturing**

        Class persons occupied with manufactures not provided for here with the subject, e.g., automobile manufacturers —6292, furniture makers —684, millers —664

—671	With metal manufacture

        Class persons occupied with iron and steel manufacture in —672, with nonferrous metals in —673

—672	With iron and steel manufacture
—673	With manufacture of nonferrous metals
—674	With lumbering and manufacture of wooden products

        Class persons occupied with furniture manufacture in —684

—675	With leather and fur industries

        Examples: tanners, furriers

        Class persons occupied with leather goods in —685

—676	With pulp and paper technology
—677	With textiles

        Class persons occupied with manufacture of clothing in —687

—678	With rubber and elastomer manufacture
—679	With manufacture of other products of specific kinds of materials
—679 7	From tobacco

—68   **Persons occupied with manufacture of products for specific uses**

        Not provided for elsewhere

        Class here persons occupied with handicrafts

        Class persons occupied with artistic handicraft work in —745; with manufacture of products based on specific branches of engineering in —62

—681	With manufacture of precision instruments and other devices

        Example: calculating equipment

        See also —6213 for manufacture of electronic computers

—681 1	Watch- and clockmaking
—681 4	Optical work
—681 8	Manufacture of musical instruments
—682	With blacksmithing
—683	With lock- and gunsmithing and manufacture of household appliances
—684	With furniture manufacture
—685	With manufacture of leather goods and their substitutes

        See also —675 for persons occupied with manufacture of fur goods

—685 1	Saddlery and harness making
—685 3	Shoemaking and shoe repairing
—685 4	Glove and mitten making
—686	With printing and related activities
—686 2	Printing
—686 3	Bookbinding
—686 4	Photocopying (Photoduplication)
—687	With clothing manufacture

        Class persons occupied with shoemaking in —6853, with glove and mitten making in —6854

        For seamstresses and tailors, see —6464; milliners and hatters, —6465

—688	With manufacture of models and miniatures, costume jewelry, smokers' supplies, accessories for personal grooming, recreational equipment

—69   **Persons occupied with buildings**

Construction work and related occupations

—693   With construction work

> Examples: masonry, bricklaying, plastering, lathing, riveting
>
> Class persons occupied with carpentry in —694

—694   With carpentry

—695   With roofing

—696   With plumbing and pipe fitting

—697   With heating, ventilating, air conditioning

—698   With painting, glazing, paperhanging

—7   **Persons occupied with the arts**   **With fine and decorative arts**

For persons occupied with creative writing and speaking, see —8

SUMMARY

—71	**With civic and landscape art**
—72	**With architecture**
—73	**With sculpture and other plastic arts**
—74	**With drawing and decorative arts**
—75	**With painting**
—76	**With graphic arts**
—77	**With photography**
—78	**With music**
—79	**With recreational and performing arts**

—71   **With civic and landscape art**

—72   **With architecture**

—73   **With sculpture and other plastic arts**

—731   Sculpture

—736   Glyptics

—737   Numismatics

—738   Ceramic arts

—739   Art metalwork

—74   **With drawing and decorative arts**

—741   Commercial art

—743   Drawing

—745	Handicrafts
	Class persons occupied with textile handicrafts in —746, with glass in —748
—746	Textile arts
	Class here textile handicrafts
—747	Interior decoration
—748	Glass
—749	Furniture design
—75	**With painting**
—76	**With graphic arts**
	Example: printmaking
	Class persons occupied with a specific graphic art with the subject, e.g., painting —75
—77	**With photography**
—78	**With music**
—781	General principles
	Including music theory
—781 6	Traditions of music
	Examples: folk music, jazz, rock
—781 7	Sacred music [*formerly* —783]
—782	Vocal music [*formerly* —784]
	Examples: dramatic music, opera
	Persons occupied with stage presentations of dramatic music relocated to —7925
—[783]	Sacred music
	Relocated to —7817
—784	Instrumental ensembles and their music [*formerly* —785]
	Vocal music relocated to —782
	For chamber music, see —785
—785	Chamber music
	Instrumental ensembles and their music relocated to —784
—786	Percussion, mechanical, electrical instruments [*all formerly* —789], keyboard instruments and their music
—787	String instruments and their music
—788	Wind instruments and their music

—[789]	Percussion, mechanical, electrical instruments
	Relocated to —786
—79	**With recreational and performing arts**
	Class persons occupied with music in —78
—791	Public performances

Class persons occupied with stage presentations in —792, with magic in —7938

See also —78 for persons occupied with musical performances, —793–796 for persons occupied with sport and game performances

—791 3	Circus performance
—791 4	Motion picture, radio, television
—791 5	Puppetry
—792	Stage presentations

Class here theater

—792 1	Drama
—792 5	Opera

Class here persons occupied with stage presentations of dramatic music [*formerly* —782]

Class singers in —782

For musical plays, see —7926; variety shows, —7927

—792 6	Musical plays
—792 7	Variety shows
—792 8	Ballet and modern dance

Class here comprehensive works on persons occupied with dancing [*formerly* —7933]

For persons occupied with social, folk, national dancing, see —7933

—793	Indoor games and amusements

Class persons occupied with indoor games of skill in —794, with games of chance in —795

—793 3	Social, folk, national dancing

Comprehensive works on persons occupied with dancing relocated to —7928

—793 8	Magic
—794	Indoor games of skill

Class persons occupied with games combining skill and chance in —795

—794 1	Chess

—794 6	Bowling	
—794 7	Billiards and pool	
—794 8	Electronic games	Computer games
—795	Games of chance	

         Including card playing

         Class here gambling

—796	Athletics and outdoor sports and games

         Class persons occupied with aquatic and air sports in —797; with equestrian sports and animal racing in —798; with fishing, hunting, shooting in —799

—796 3	Ball games
—796 32	Basketball and volleyball
—796 33	Football, rugby, soccer
—796 34	Badminton, lacrosse, rackets, squash, table tennis, tennis
—796 35	Baseball, cricket, croquet, field hockey, golf, polo
—796 4	Weight lifting, track and field, gymnastics
—796 5	Hiking, mountaineering, spelunking
—796 6	Cycling
—796 7	Motor vehicle racing
—796 8	Combat sports

         Examples: boxing, fencing, jujitsu, wrestling

—796 9	Ice and snow sports
—797	Aquatic and air sports
—797 1	Boating
—797 2	Swimming and diving
—797 3	Surfing and water skiing
—797 5	Air sports

         Examples: stunt flying, gliding, soaring, skydiving

—798	Equestrian sports and animal racing
—799	Fishing, hunting, shooting
—799 1	Fishing
—799 2	Hunting
—799 3	Trapshooting, skeet and target shooting, archery

—8	**Persons occupied with creative writing and speaking**
—81	With poetry
—82	With drama
—83	With fiction
—84	With essays
—85	With oratory, debate, conversation
—86	With letter writing
—87	With satire and humor
—9	**Persons occupied with geography, history, related disciplines and activities**
—91	With geography and travel
—92	With biography
—93	With archaeology
—97	With history
—99	With genealogy

Relocations and Reductions

Here are brought together in two lists all the relocations and reductions since Edition 19, except relocations within the T2—711 British Columbia table from Table 2 and the 780 Music schedule—both of which have been completely revised.

The column headed *Edition 19* indicates in numerical order each number in that edition from which a topic or group of topics has been shifted; the column headed *Edition 20* indicates each corresponding number in the present edition to which those topics or groups of topics have been shifted. If two or more topics have been shifted from one number to two or more numbers, each separate shift is shown.

Numbers in the *Edition 19* column printed in square brackets are no longer in use; those not printed in brackets have lost part of their meaning through relocation or reduction, but still retain some of their original meaning.

Relocations

In a relocation one or more topics are shifted to a number differing from the old in respects other than length. If the relocation is partial, the original number remains valid; but if it is total, the original number is no longer used. Relocations are described and explained in the Introduction.

Relocations that have appeared previously in either *Dewey Decimal Classification Additions, Notes and Decisions* volume 4, *301—307 Sociology Expanded Version Based on Edition 19*, or *004—006 Data Processing and Computer Science and Changes in Related Disciplines* are indicated by * next to the Edition 19 number. Relocations that eliminate dual provision for the same topic or topics are indicated by † next to the Edition 19 number.

"Scatter" means that a topic has been split and relocated to so many numbers that it is not feasible to name them all.

For example, in Table 1 part of what was in T1—0724 has been relocated to T1—011; all that was in T1—[07401—07409] has been relocated to T1—0741—0749; all that was in T1—[073] has been relocated to eliminate dual provision, some to T1—0880909, some to T1—088375, and some to 331.55.

An indented number is an element of an add table. The number or span under which it is indented shows the location of the add table. For example, the 7 under 633—635 indicates that the 7 is an element of the add table at 633—635.

For details of the specific relocated topics the classifier should consult the appropriate entries in the tables and schedules.

Edition 19	Edition 20	Edition 19	Edition 20
[T1—016]†	016—	[T2—681]	T2—688
T1—028	T1—072	T2—682 3	T2—682 95
T1—028†	T1—078	T2—684 3	T2—684 91
T1—029	T1—05	T2—684 5	T2—684 91
T1—029†	332.6—	T2—694	T2—691
T1—072	T1—011	T2—694†	T2—696
T1—072†	T1—015 1	T2—694	T2—698 2
T1—072	T1—028 5	[T2—695]†	T2—696
T1—072	T1—028 7	[T2—700 09]	T2—709 1
T1—072 4	T1—011	[T2—714 12]	T2—714 115
[T1—073]†	T1—088 090 9	T2—714 17	T2—714 11
[T1—073]†	T1—088 375	[T2—714 212]	T2—714 13
[T1—073]†	331.55—	[T2—714 465]	T2—714 455
[T1—074 01—074 09]	T1—074 1—074 9	[T2—716 96]	T2—716 95
[T1—075 092]	T1—092	[T2—728 533]	T2—728 532
T1—076†	T1—078	[T2—745 3]	T2—745 1
[T1—088 04—088 08]	T1—081—087	[T2—747 63]	T2—747 62
T1—09	T1—021 8	[T2—747 76]	T2—747 75
T1—09	T1—022 1	[T2—747 79]	T2—747 78
T2—165 76†	T2—946 2	[T2—748 33]	T2—748 32
T2—168†	T2—479	[T2—748 76]	T2—748 75
T2—177*	T2—4	[T2—749 24]	T2—749 23
[T2—400 9]	T2—409 1	[T2—749 28]	T2—749 26
T2—411 62*	T2—411 65	[T2—749 37]	T2—749 36
[T2—416 23]	T2—416 21	[T2—749 38]	T2—749 36
[T2—416 62]	T2—416 61	[T2—749 67]	T2—749 65
T2—428 42*	T2—428 19	[T2—749 88]	T2—749 87
[T2—431 9]	T2—431 84	[T2—749 92]	T2—749 91
T2—434 2	T2—434 3	[T2—749 95]	T2—749 94
[T2—434 8]	T2—433	[T2—751 5]	T2—751 4
[T2—434 8]	T2—434 6	[T2—752 88]	T2—752 87
[T2—434 9]	T2—434 73	[T2—752 92]	T2—752 91
T2—435 9	T2—431 82	[T2—752 95]	T2—752 94
T2—444 8	T2—449	[T2—754 15]	T2—754 14
[T2—467 71]	T2—464 6	[T2—754 23]	T2—754 22
T2—494 3	T2—494 52	[T2—754 38]	T2—754 37
[T2—500 9]	T2—509 1	[T2—754 53]	T2—754 52
T2—521 9*	T2—521 87	[T2—754 58]	T2—754 57
[T2—521 91]*	T2—521 86	[T2—754 89]	T2—754 88
[T2—528 1]*	T2—522 9	T2—755 3	T2—163 47
T2—53	T2—569	T2—755 423	T2—755 422
T2—563	T2—496 1	[T2—756 386]	T2—756 385
T2—567 4	T2—567 2	[T2—756 396]	T2—756 395
[T2—600 9]	T2—609 1	T2—757 6	T2—757 8
[T2—629 2]	T2—625	[T2—758 795]	T2—758 794
[T2—660 097 521]	T2—660 917 521	[T2—758 865]	T2—758 864
[T2—660 097 541]	T2—660 917 541	T2—764 87	T2—764 88
T2—669 5	T2—669 6	T2—769	T2—77
T2—669 5	T2—669 7	[T2—769 865]	T2—769 864
T2—669 5	T2—669 8	[T2—774 18]	T2—774 17
[T2—669 9]	T2—671	T2—774 8	T2—774 923
T2—678 25	T2—689 7	[T2—775 12]	T2—775 11

*Previously published
†Eliminates dual provision

Edition 19	Edition 20	Edition 19	Edition 20
T2—775 3	T2—775 63	T7—782	T7—792 5
[T2—775 34]	T2—775 33	[T7—783]	T7—781 7
[T2—775 46]	T2—775 45	T7—784	T7—782
[T2—775 65]	T2—775 64	T7—785	T7—784
[T2—775 72]	T2—775 71	[T7—789]	T7—786
[T2—775 84]	T2—775 83	T7—793 3	T7—792 8
[T2—775 88]	T2—775 87	[001.424]	003
[T2—775 97]	T2—775 96	001.43	001.42
[T2—775 99]	T2—775 98	[001.5]	302.2
[T2—782 287]	T2—782 286	[001.53]	003.5
[T2—782 398]	T2—782 397	[001.533]	003.7
T2—788 53	T2—788 9	[001.534]	003.52
T2—789 62	T2—789 67	[001.534]*†	006.4
T2—789 92*	T2—789 91	[001.535]*	006.3
T2—791 71*	T2—791 72	[001.535]*†	511.3
T2—792 21	T2—792 5	[001.539]	003.54
[T2—794 56]	T2—794 55	[001.539]	025.04
[T2—800 09]	T2—809 1	[001.543 6]	652.8
T2—817 2*	T2—817 1	[001.6]*	004
[T2—833 6]	T2—833 5	[001.93]†	030
[T2—833 6]	T2—833 7	001.95*†	573.3
[T2—932—937]†	T2—95	011.31	016.091
T2—953	T2—954	011.34	016.05
T2—953	T2—956 1	011.42	016.093
[T2—955]	T2—953	011.44	016.094
[T2—955]	T2—956	017—019†	015
[T2—955]	T2—957	017—019	016.05
T2—968 1	T2—968 2	[021.001—.009]	021.01—.09
T3A—81—89	T3A—81—89	[022.33]	022.309
07*	02	[023.700 1—.700 9]	023.701—.709
T3B—205 2†	T3B—204 1	025.12	070.594
T3B—205 7†	T3B—204 1	025.349	025.344
[T3B—306]†	741.5—	025.47†	025.49
T3B—807*	T3B—802	025.524	Scattered
T3B—81—89	T3B—81—89	069	T1—075
07*	02	[069.7]	070.594
T3C—14†	T3C—321 734	[069.7]	686.2
[T4—17]	T4—11	[069.9]†	T1—074
T4—2	T4—014 3	[070.415]	808.066 07
T5—969 881	T5—914 1	070.444	070.449 613
[T6—393 2]	T6—393 1	070.444	070.449 641 5
[T6—919 96]	T6—919 94	070.502 94†	015
T6—924	T6—926	070.595†	070.509 753
T6—948 1	T6—948 3	152.182 8†	152.182 3
T6—973	T6—979	153.46	155.232
T6—975	T6—973	155.28	155.028 7
T6—992	T6—994	155.418 028 7	155.418 28
[T7—366 4]	T7—13	155.95†	155.93
T7—387 5	T7—386	[156.7]†	616.89
T7—572*	T7—309	[157]†	616.89
T7—598	T7—597	158.1†	155.904 2
T7—658†	T7—381	[170.202]	170.8

*Previously published
†Eliminates dual provision

Edition 19	Edition 20	Edition 19	Edition 20
174.24	179.7	306.7*	306.856
[181.095 12]	181.112	306.73*	306.77
[181.095 14]	181.114	[306.737]	306.874
[181.198]†	181.16	306.766†	305.906 64
[181.199]†	181.17	[306.777]	306.877
[197.1]	198.8	307.72†	306.349
207	268	307.740 9†	307.760 9
207.12	268.433	307.762−.764†	307.760 9
207.4−.9	268.433 094−.433 099	307.766−.768†	307.760 9
220.49	220.539 9	[312]*†	304.602 1
230.044	230.046	[312]*†	T1—021
[232.6]†	236.9	320.092	320.5
[232.7]†	236.9	[320.2]	320.011
[232.98]	229.8	320.4	320.8
[236.3]	236.9	321.5	321.6
241.6*†	241.3	[323.401]	323.01
241.6*†	241.4	[323.423]†	323.1
248.48	248.8	323.5†	324.62
[248.894 28]†	255	324.21	324.24−.29
[248.894 38]†	255.9	324.22	324.24−.29
[253.75]	259.5	324.23	324.24−.29
[259.7]†	253.7	324.24−.29	324.209
265	264.01−.09	324.268 03	324.268 083
[267.15]	287.96	324.268 04	324.268 08
[267.36]†	267.308	324.268 05	324.268 08
270.09†	270.072	324.268 07	324.268 06
271.1−.4*	270	[324.268 09]†	324.268 03−.268 08
[281.93]†	281.94−.99	324.9*	324.609
283.3†	283.4−.9	327.092†	327.209 2
283.3	287.94	327.209 2	327.3−.9
284.13†	284.14−.19	327.3−.9	327.123−.129
[284.23]†	284.24−.29	330.028†	330.015 195
285.83†	285.84−.89	330.155†	330.157
286.13†	286.14−.19	331.255	331.216 4
[287.97]	287.2	332.112†	332.114
[288]	289.1	332.12	332.175 2
291.64	291.2	332.56	332.46
297.14*†	297.211	332.645†	332.63
297.8†	297.9	[332.645 2]	332.632 28
299.809	299.89	333.1	333.717
[301.019]†	302	333.1†	333.73
302.072	302.015 195	[333.38]†	333.715
302.23	302.222	333.563*†	333.335 563
[304.65]†	363.91	333.72†	333.715 3
[304.662]†	363.92	333.75†	333.953 9
[304.664]†	363.91	333.82	333.793 2
304.82†	304.809	333.823 2†	338.476 655 382 7
305	302.230 8	333.910 4†	333.88
305.6*	305.92	333.912†	333.911 3
306†	305.8	333.917	333.918
306.08†	305	[334.506 8]†	658.870 7
306.1	306.4	336.343 5†	336.31

*Previously published
†Eliminates dual provision

Edition 19	Edition 20	Edition 19	Edition 20
338	333.79	[359.326 4]	359.985 3
338	368	[359.326 5]	359.985 3
[338.15]	338.17	[359.835 5]	359.948 35
338.174 9†	333.751 1	[359.835 7]	359.938 3
338.174 9†	333.751 3	[359.836]	359.985 83
338.27*†	333.8	359.982	359.985
338.604 1†	338.1−.4	[361.38]†	361.320 8
340.52	340.53	361.77*	361.763
341.242 2	341.242 4	362−363	
342−347	342−347	[75]†	363.1
[02633]*	002632	362.042 5*†	361.2
342.085 3	342.066 2	362.19*	362.104 25
343.052 3†	343.04	362.19*	362.175
[343.078 658 8]†	343.084	362.28	362.204 251
[343.078 659 1]†	343.082	362.292 86	362.292 7
[344.032 86]†	343.011	362.293	362.298
344.076 82	344.076 83	362.293 86	362.293 7
344.076 84	344.076 85	362.63*†	362.428 3
[348.06]	340.03	[362.704 4]†	362.708 6
[348.06]	348.003	[362.704 4]	362.708 694 5
[348.736]	348.730 3	[362.704 4]	362.73
351.2†	T1—025	[362.704 4]	362.76
[351.22]†	324.025	362.71	362.768
351.72*	351.003−.9	[362.792]	362.708 3
351.723 202 02*†	657.835 045	[362.793]	362.708 3
351.892†	327.202 5	362.82*	362−363
[351.000 76]†	351.3		3
351.003†	342.06	[363.284]†	363.45
351.003 4†	321	363.349 7*†	363.179 9
[351.003 7]†	320.404	[363.62]	333.793 2
351.007 5†	328.345 6	363.739†	363.738
353.034†	321.804 209 73	364.131†	364.164
353.913 4†	321.804 209 73	[364.46]†	363.23
353.97−.99†	321.804 209 74−.804 209 79	365.34*	365.45
34	Number for state	365.646†	365.66
353.996 903 4†	321.804 209 969	[368.001 51]	368.01
[355.002 8]†	355.8	[369.16]	369.15
[355.115]†	362.86	370.71†	371.146
[355.115 1]	331.252 913 55	[371.302 813]	649.68
355.34†	355.133 23	371.394 42	371.334
355.341†	355.6	[371.394 45]	371.334
355.42	355.43	372.193†	372.357 043
355.426†	363.32	372.3−.8	
355.71†	355.341	[0442]	649.68
358.3	355.26	372.8	372.358
358.3	358.22	373.246	T1—071 2
358.39	355.021 7	374.013†	T1—071 5
358.4	359.94	[374.02]	374.13
[359.002 8]†	359.8	[374.21]	374.22
359.31†	359.32	374.27	374.26
[359.325 5]	359.943 5	[380.141 029]†	630.209
[359.325 7]	359.933	[380.142 029]†	553.029

*Previously published
†Eliminates dual provision

Edition 19	Edition 20	Edition 19	Edition 20
[380.143 029]†	639.029	408.9	306.440 89
[380.143 102 9]†	639.029	409†	417.7
[380.3]	384	412	401.43
[380.5]	388	417.7	411.7
[381.410 29]†	630.209	[439.32]	439.31
[381.420 29]†	553.029	[481.7]	481.1
[381.430 29]†	639.029	[481.7]	487.1
[381.431 029]†	639.029	492.47	492.6
[382.410 29]†	630.209	509	500.8
[382.420 29]†	553.029	[512.33]	516.35
[382.430 29]†	639.029	512.5	512.75
[382.431 029]†	639.029	[512.522]	512.4
384.13	384.14	512.53	512.24
384.13	384.15	512.7	511.322
[384.4]*	384.1	512.72	512.75
384.543	384.544	512.94	512.4
384.543	384.545	513.2	513.55
384.545 3†	384.540 65	[513.93]	650.015 13
384.545 5†	384.540 65	515.235	515.7
384.554 3	384.554 4	515.722 3	515.782
384.554 3	384.554 5	[516.360 2]	516.363
[384.554 7]	384.555	[516.360 4]	516.362
384.555	384.556	[516.373]	516.374
[384.555 6]	384.554 6	[516.92]†	516.373
[384.555 7]	384.556	[516.93]	516.374
384.63	384.64	519.4	003.54
384.63	384.65	519.4*	004.015 1
[384.648]*	384.3	[519.535 2]	519.538
[384.7]†	363.107 2	[521.5]	520.1
385.1	385.2	[521.5]	523
385.1	385.3	[521.6]	523.980 1
386.1	386.2	[521.62]	523.301
386.1	386.24	[521.75]	523.510 1
386.1	386.3−.6	[521.76]	526.601
387.51	387.2	[521.8]	523.990 1
387.51	387.52	522.109†	522.19
387.51	387.54	522.29	522.209
387.51	387.58	522.5	523.702 8
385.71	385.72	[523.37]	523.302 87
385.71	385.73	[523.39]	523.302 12
385.71	385.74	[523.39]	523.302 22
388.049	388.041	[523.49]	523.402 12
388.049	388.042	[523.49]	523.402 22
388.049	388.044	[523.57]	523.510 287
388.11	388.12	[523.67]	523.602 87
388.11	388.13	[523.69]	523.602 12
388.404 2	388.413	[523.69]	523.602 22
[391.8]	Scattered	[523.77]	523.702 87
395.59†	395.3	[523.79]	523.702 22
[398.1]	398.01	[523.802 87]†	523.87
398.356†	398.36	[523.89]	523.802 12
401.9	306.44	[523.89]	523.802 22

*Previously published
†Eliminates dual provision

Edition 19	Edition 20	Edition 19	Edition 20
[523.890 3]	523.802 23	[537.9]	537.076
[523.890 8]	523.802 12	[538.2]†	538.4
[523.96]	523.92	[538.2]†	621.34
[523.97]	523.92	538.4	538.3
[525.6]†	551.470 8	[538.9]	538.021 2
[526.86]	526.022 1	[538.9]	538.076
[529.75]	389.17	539.721 7*	530.416
[529.78]†	681.11	539.754†	539.73
[530.028 7]†	530.8	539.754	539.757
[531.113 7]†	530.475	539.754	539.758
531.163	530.475	[539.9]	539.021 2
[531.7]†	530.415	[539.9]	539.076
[531.8]†	621.811	541.345	541.348 5
[531.9]	531.021 2	[541.345 3]	541.33
[531.9]	531.076	541.362	541.361
[532.057]†	530.425	[541.901]	541.24
[532.511]	532.510 1	547.842 5†	678.71
[532.6]†	530.427	[547.842 7]†	668.9
[532.7]†	530.425	[547.843 2]†	668.4
[532.9]	532.002 12	547.843 4	547.783
[532.9]	532.007 6	[547.85]†	677.4
533.1†	530.43	[548.1]	548.81
[533.13]†	530.43	548.9	530.429
533.5†	621.55	[550.154]†	551.9
[533.63]†	530.43	[551.015 4]†	551.9
[533.9]	533.021 2	551.14†	551.8
[533.9]	533.076	551.305†	551.41
[534.4]	620.21	551.305†	551.42−.45
[534.42]†	534.028 7	551.353	551.307
[534.9]	534.021 2	551.355	551.305
[534.9]	534.076	551.355†	551.42−.45
[535.33]†	681.4	551.44	551.21
[535.58]†	621.366	551.44†	551.397
[535.89]†	621.369 2	551.49†	551.23
[535.9]	535.021 2	[551.578 1]	551.577
[535.9]	535.076	552.5	549.67
[536.401]†	530.474	553.23	553.283
[536.443]†	530.474	553.282	553.283
536.56†	536.44	553.55†	553.87
[536.62]†	681.2	553.6†	631.4
[536.9]	536.021 2	553.7	333.88
[536.9]	536.076	553.9	553.6
[537.23]†	621.313	572*†	305.8
[537.242]†	621.315	574.072	574.015 195
537.534†	Scattered	[575.22]†	575.131
537.534 4†	621.381 336	576.64*	591.295
[537.535 3]†	621.381	582.046 3†	582.130 446 3
[537.535 5]†	621.381	[591.042]	591.529
537.61†	621.319 2	597.53	597.55
[537.63]†	621.31	[604.6]†	628.4
[537.63]†	621.319 2	[606.8]†	658
[537.9]	537.021 2	[607.33]†	331.55

*Previously published
†Eliminates dual provision

Edition 19	Edition 20	Edition 19	Edition 20
[607.33]	604.880 909	[621.381 73]	621.381 5
[607.33]	604.883 75	[621.381 73]†	621.395
609	604.8	[621.381 74]	621.381 531
610.73	615.507	[621.381 792]	621.389 28
[611.734]†	611.313	[621.381 95]*	621.39
[612.118 22]†	616.079	[621.381 952]*†	511.3
612.6	306.7	[621.381 959 4]*†	511.3
613.2	613.7	621.382†	621.383
[615.12]	615.13	621.384 133	621.384 12
615.364†	615.363	[621.384 136]	621.384 18
[615.65]	615.39	[621.384 165]	621.384 5
615.854†	615.328	[621.384 168]	621.384 5
615.856	Scattered	[621.384 17]	621.384 021 8
616.047 2	616.849 1	[621.384 17]	621.384 180 218
[616.072]	616.047	[621.384 17]	621.384 028 7
616.079†	616.97	[621.384 17]	621.384 180 287
616.079	616.978	[621.384 17]†	384.545 2
616.994†	616.993	621.384 2	621.382 35
617.472†	617.58	[621.384 3]	621.384 2
617.63*	616.992 314	[621.384 6]	621.384 5
617.63*	616.995 314	[621.388 332 028 8]	621.388 337
617.7*	616.992 84	[621.388 36]	621.388 8
617.7*	616.995 84	[621.388 7]	621.388 002 18
617.8*	616.992 85	[621.388 7]	621.388 002 87
617.8*	616.995 85	[621.389 336]	621.389 334
[618.028 7]	618.047 5	[621.389 6]	621.382 7
[618.33]	618.392	[621.393]*	333.793 2
[620.002 89]†	620.86	[621.394]*	621.319
620.112 3	620.112 6	[621.396]*	621.402 8
[620.15]	620.135	621.398 7	681.6
[620.32]	620.302 87	621.398 7	681.62
[620.72]	620.001 171	621.402 2*†	621.402 5
[620.72]	620.004 2	621.402 8	621.402 011
[620.85]†	628	[621.481]	621.483
[621.184]*	621.183	[621.567]	621.560 11
[621.312 52]	621.483	[621.692]	621.55
621.319†	621.317	[621.801 53]†	621.811
621.327	621.325	[621.802 88]†	621.816
[621.379]†	681.2	[621.943]	621.992
[621.380 282]	621.382 84	[621.945]	621.952
[621.380 283]	621.382 4	[621.994]	681.2
[621.380 4]	621.382	[622.187]*†	628.114
[621.380 44]	621.389 7	622.3	622.292
[621.381 043]	621.381 028 7	622.3	622.7
[621.381 1]	621.381 011	[622.31]	622.292
[621.381 37]	621.381 302 18	[622.32]	622.292 7
[621.381 37]	621.381 302 87	622.333	622.338 3
621.381 537†	621.395	622.338 2	622.338 3
621.381 548	621.381 502 18	[622.37]*†	628.114
621.381 548†	681.2	622.8	622.28
[621.381 7]	621.381 52	623.109†	623.19
[621.381 71]	621.381 52	[623.37]	623.737

*Previously published
†Eliminates dual provision

Edition 19	Edition 20	Edition 19	Edition 20
623.445	623.42	631.7†	631.587
623.451 4	Scattered	[631.819]	631.809
[623.459 5]	623.446	631.87	631.86
[623.459 6]	623.447	633−635	633−635
[623.48]	623.402 88	7	Scattered
[623.814]	623.84−.87	[633.002 8]	630.208
[623.814 4]	623.812	[633.002 8]	631
[623.820 8]	623.820 028 8	[633.08]	631
624.182	624.177 2−.177 9	[633.089]	632
[627.17]†	628.114	633.18	633.179
[627.35]†	623.83	[633.4]†	635.1
627.8	627.4	[633.49]†	635.2
[627.923]	623.828	[634.35]	634.304
628.114*†	627.56	634.83	Scattered
628.168	628.43	634.93†	621.319
[628.168 028 7]	628.161	[634.952]†	634.98
[628.168 6]	628.168 09	[634.954]	634.906 88
[628.168 8]†	363.739 46	634.97	634.97
[628.168 8]	628.168 09	7	Scattered
[628.17]*†	333.911 2	634.97	
[628.17]*†	333.911 3	[85−87]	634.985−.987
[628.17]*†	628.144 028 7	635.91	635.902 8
628.357	628.358	[636.001 575 1]†	636.082 1
[628.466]	625.763	[636.77]	636.700 22
[628.54]	628.4	[636.87]	636.800 22
628.7	628.509 173 4	[637.13]	637.14
[628.746 1]†	631.86	637.141 028 7†	637.127
[628.746 1]	668.636	639.091 6	639.8
[628.746 1]	628.746 6	639.091 62	639.8
[628.746 2]†	628.52	[639.200 1−.200 9]	639.201−.209
[629.132 509]†	629.130 9	[639.300 1−.300 9]	639.01−.09
629.132 524 042 2†	629.132 521 7	640.202	640.41
629.132 524 042 3†	629.132 521 6	[640.68]†	640.4
629.134 57†	629.133 021 8	[640.714]	640.715
[629.136 4]†	690.539	[641.508 82]	641.567
629.227 2	629.227 5	[643.604]	643.608 7
[629.460 44]	629.467	645†	747
[629.470 44]†	629.477	646.1*	646.302 8
629.804 3	629.89	646.6	648.1
[629.891]†	511.3	649.7†	291.44
630.257 51†	631.523	649.7†	248.845
631	630.208	[651.740 2]	808.066 65
[631.23]†	633.104 68	651.75	808.066 651
[631.23]†	633.208 68	658.045	658.152 24
[631.31]†	631.51	658.304 4	651.306 83
[631.33]†	631.53	[658.311 29]*†	T1−068 3
631.34†	Scattered	658.403 4	658.403 52
[631.35]†	631.55	[658.403 88]	658.403 801 1
[631.35]†	633.104 5	[658.456 2]†	060.68
[631.36]†	631.56	658.5†	624.068 5
[631.544]	631.583	658.568†	658.562 015 195
[631.545]	631.583	658.72	381.33

*Previously published
†Eliminates dual provision

Edition 19	Edition 20	Edition 19	Edition 20
[658.805]*†	658.848	[738.23]	738.09
[658.809]*†	T1—068 8	738.27	738.209
[658.838]*†	T1—068 8	738.270 9	738.209
[658.89]*†	T1—068 8	738.280 9	738.209
660.62	660.65	738.37	738.309
662.65	662.88	738.370 9	738.309
[663.220 4]	663.201—.209	738.380 9	738.309
[669.001]	669.01	741.092	751.5—.7
[669.002]	669.02	741.9*	741.5—.7
[669.003]	669.03	746	746
[669.005—.009]	669.05—.09	[0489]†	0288
[674.132]†	620.12	[0489]†	0289
[674.22]	674.202 8	748.202 88†	748.202 89
[676.26]	676.042	[750.28]†	751
678.533†	685.43	[756]†	758.99
[681.81—.83]	681.86—.88	[769.19]†	769.028 8
[686.212]†	686.282	769.5†	741.694
[686.217]	686.224	[770.28]†	771
[687.045]	687.112	778.534 4†	781.542
[687.110 42]	687.081	778.59†	781.546
[687.12]	687.082	782.1	792.5
[687.13]	687.083	[791.430 909]	791.436
[704.945]†	709.040 52	[791.435 3]†	070.18
721.2	721.41	[791.440 909]	791.446
722	720.95	[791.445]*†	070.194
722	720.9	[791.445]†	070.449 796
722	723	[791.450 909]	791.456
722	724	[791.455]*†	070.195
722.4	720.95	[791.455]†	070.449 796
722.4	720.954	793.3	792.8
[722.91]†	720.97	793.32	792.8
[722.91]†	720.98	[793.324]	792.7
724.1†	720.942 090 31	795.2	793.75
724.1†	720.942 090 32	[796.323 7]	796.323 6
724.1†	720.942 090 33	[796.332 7]	796.332 6
724.19†	720.946 090 32	[796.332 7]	796.332 079
724.19	724.16	[796.333 7]	796.333 6
724.5†	724.2	[796.334 7]	796.334 6
[724.8]	724.52	[796.335 7]	796.335 6
[724.91]	724.6	[796.352 7]	796.352 6
[726.523]†	726.51	[796.357 7]	796.357 6
727.38†	727.478	[796.358 7]	796.358 6
[728.69]	728.370 472	796.4†	613.71
[729.3]†	721.1—.8	796.41†	613.713
[729.9]†	726.529	796.41†	613.714
732.3—.9	730.95	796.41	796.44
732.3—.9	730.9	796.426	796.422
732.3—.9	734	[796.962 7]	796.962 6
732.3—.9	735	[797.17]*	797.3
732.4	730.95	808.02	808.06
732.4	730.954	808.887*	808.882
[732.91]*	733.093 91		

*Previously published
†Eliminates dual provision

Edition 19	Edition 20	Edition 19	Edition 20
830.1–.9	830.1–.9	972.830 3	972.830 2
1	21	972.830 4	972.830 51
3	22	972.830 51	972.830 52
[839.32]	839.31	972.840 2	972.840 1
894.81	894.83	972.840 3	972.840 2
895.1	895.1	972.840 4	972.840 51
1	22	972.840 51	972.840 52
2	3	972.850 2	972.850 3
900	133.430 9	972.850 4	972.850 51
900	306.4	972.850 51	972.850 52
[910.09]	910.91	972.860 3	972.860 2
[912.1001–.1899]	T1—022 3	[972.860 51]	972.860 44
913–919		[972.860 52]	972.860 44
04	Scattered	972.870 1	972.870 2
922.91	922.99	[972.870 4]	972.870 51
929.3	929.5	[972.870 52]	972.870 51
[929.799 9]	929.709	[973.42]	973.41
940.472	940.317	[973.45]	973.44
940.547 2	940.531 7	980.004*	981–989
943.703 3	943.730 33	[983.064 7]	983.065
945.09	945.084	987.04	987.03
946.08	946.073	987.05	987.04
946.08	946.074	989.505	989.504
949.405	949.404	[993.101–.103]	993.01–.03
956.103 5†	956.102 5	[993.2–.7]†	995
[956.940 01]	320.540 956 94		
958.101†	939.6		
960.23	960.312		
962.402	962.5–.9		
963.01	963.501		
[963.052]	963.043		
[966.901 3–.901 8]	966.91–.98		
[966.99]	967.1		
967.240 3	967.203		
967.301	967.31–.35		
967.510 1	967.511–.518		
[968.1]	968.8		
968.404	968.403 9		
968.703 3	968.703 2		
968.703 3	968.704 2		
968.801–.803	968.810 1–.810 3		
970.004*	971–979		
[971.501–.504]	971.510 1–.510 4		
972.02	972.018		
972.810 2	972.810 3		
972.810 4	972.810 51		
972.810 51	972.810 52		
972.810 53	972.810 52		
972.820 3	972.820 2		
972.820 4	972.820 3		
[972.820 51]	972.820 4		
[972.820 52]	972.820 4		

*Previously published
†Eliminates dual provision

Reductions

A reduction is the result of shifting one or more topics to a number shorter than the old but otherwise not differing from it. If all topics in a given number are thus shifted, the number is no longer valid. Reductions are described and explained in the Introduction.

In addition, several numbers have been dropped because their content in Edition 19 was meaningless within the context.

Reductions that have appeared previously either in *Dewey Decimal Classification Additions, Notes and Decisions* volume 4 or in *004–006 Data Processing and Computer Science and Changes in Related Disciplines* are indicated by * next to the Edition 19 number.

"Main number" means that the provision for the topic within a table has been discontinued to the schedule numbers to which the table number would previously have been added.

For example in Table 1, T1—[0141] and T1—[0147] have been discontinued and all of their content moved up to the broader number T1—014, while only part of the content of T1—0212 has been moved up to T1—21. For T1—0202, a part of the content has been discontinued from Table 1 to the schedule numbers to which the table number would previously have been added.

An indented number is an element of an add table. The number or span under which it is indented shows the location of the add table. For example, the 3 under 362–363 indicates that the 3 is an element of the add table at 362–363.

For details of the specific reduced topics the classifier should consult the appropriate entries in the tables and schedules.

Edition 19	Edition 20	Edition 19	Edition 20
[T1—014 1]	T1—014	T3B—102—108	
[T1—014 7]	T1—014	08	Main number
[T1—018]	T1—01	[T3B—106]	T3B—1
T1—020 2	Main number	[T3B—308 4]	T3B—3
T1—021 2	T1—021	[T4—17]	Main number
T1—028	Main number	[T5—01]	Main number
[T1—032—039]	T1—03	T5—79	T5—7
[T1—075 09]	T1—075	[T5—799]	T5—79
[T1—088 056]	Main number	T5—919 9	T5—919
[T1—088 081 2]	Main number	T5—959 1	T5—95
[T1—088 082 2]	Main number	T5—99	T5—9
[T1—092 4]	T1—092	T5—999	T5—9
[T1—092 6]	Main number	T6—918 51	T6—918 5
[T2—24]	T2—2	T6—959 19	T6—95
[T2—26]	Main number	T6—963 6	T6—963
[T2—467 73]	T2—467 7	[T6—969]	T6—96
[T2—528 5]*	T2—528	[T6—977]	T6—97
[T2—549 144]	T2—549 14	[T6—985]	Without meaning
[T2—549 145]	T2—549 14	T6—99	T6—9
[T2—567 3]	T2—567	T6—999	T6—9
T2—567 4	T2—567	[T7—301]	T7—3
T2—644	T2—64	[T7—581]	T7—58
[T2—671 12]	T2—671 1	[T7—591]	T7—59
[T2—671 13]	T2—671 1	T7—616	T7—61
[T2—714 215]	T2—714 21	[T7—620 7]	T7—62
[T2—714 263]	T2—714 26	[001.14]	001.1
[T2—714 265]	T2—714 26	011.3	011
[T2—714 281]	T2—714 28	[011.625 054]	011.62
[T2—714 466]	T2—714 46	[011.625 055]	011.625
[T2—719 9]	T2—719	[021.62]	021.6
T2—747 53	T2—747 5	[025.129]	025.12
T2—752 41	T2—752 4	[070.412]	070.41
T2—757 41	T2—757 4	070.433	070.43
T2—757 83	T2—757 8	[089.29]	089
T2—758 273	T2—758 2	[109.22]	109.2
T2—758 66	T2—758 6	[111.83]	111.8
T2—758 756	T2—758 7	128.5	128
[T2—759 121]	T2—759 12	133.324	133.3
T2—759 72	T2—759 7	[133.324 29]	133.324 2
T2—761 53	T2—761 5	[133.62]	133.6
T2—764 1	T2—764	[133.64]	133.6
T2—766 1	T2—766	135.4	135
T2—781 4	T2—781	[135.42]	135
T2—786 1	T2—786	[149.943]	149.94
T2—788 3	T2—788	[149.946]	149.94
T2—788 33	T2—788 3	150.192	150.19
T2—788 38	T2—788 3	[150.193 2—.193 3]	150.193
T2—796 78	T2—796 7	152.148	152.14
[T2—882 3]	T2—882	[152.42—.45]	152.4
[T2—882 4]	T2—882	152.8	152
T2—931	T2—93	[153.136]	153.13
T3B—08	Main number	[153.25]	153.2

*Previously published

Edition 19	Edition 20	Edition 19	Edition 20
[153.422−.423]	153.42	333.3	333
[153.734−.735]	153.73	[333.38]	333.3
[153.92]	153.9	[333.772]	333.77
[154.62]	154.6	[333.910 2]	333.91
154.72	154.7	333.914	333.91
[155.671]	155.67	[335.413]	335.41
[159]*	150	[335.436]*	335.43
[178.9]	178	335.5	335
[197.2]	197	338.82	338.8
[219]	210	341.488	341.4
[229.915]	229.91	343.099 45	343.099 4
[229.918]	229.91	[346.038 2]	346.038
[247.11−.18]	247.1	351.003	351
[247.3−.8]	247	351.003 1	351.003
261.832	261.8	355.021 5	355.02
[268.435]	268.4	355.021 7	355.02
268.6	268	355.021 8	355.02
[291.044]	291	[355.021 82]	355.02
291.178 32	291.178 3	[355.021 84]	355.021 8
291.7	291	[355.022]	355.02
301.7	301	[355.023]	355.02
[301.72]	301.7	355.033 2	355.03
[301.74]	301	355.134 9	355.134
304.28	304.2	355.343 4	355.34
[304.282]	304.28	355.415	355.41
305.5*	305	355.43	355.4
306.1	306	[355.430 5]	355.4
[306.778]	306.77	[355.430 7]	355.4
[306.779]	306.77	[355.430 7]	355.43
320.15	320.1	355.69	355.6
[320.156]	320.1	355.81	355.8
[320.157]	320.15	356.11	356.1
[320.17]	320.1	358.175	358.17
[320.2]	320	358.3	358
322.44	322.4	358.414 15	358.414
323.1	323	[358.414 3]	358.414
323.353	323	359.81	358.8
323.4	323	362−363	362−363
[324.268 2−.268 7]	324.268	3	Main number
[327.101 1]	327.101	362.293	362.29
327.11	327.1	[362.604]	362.6
328.2	328	[362.704]	362.7
328.3	328	[362.795]	362.7
[328.334 52−.334 54]	328.334 5	362.799	362.7
[328.365 2]	328.365	362.721−.727	363.72
331.12	331.1	363.738 4	363.738
331.125	331.1	[368.015]	368.01
331.889 6	331.889	[370.13]	370.1
331.892 6	331.892	[371.102 8]*	371.102
[332.420 422−.420 424]	332.420 42	[371.967 2]	371.967
332.55	332.5	[372.73]	372.7
[332.645 2]	332.645	373.23	370

*Previously published

Edition 19	Edition 20	Edition 19	Edition 20
378.053	378.05	[546.81−.87]	546.8
[384.554 56]	384.554 5	[547.862−.867]	547.86
[384.555 6]	384.555	551.470 22	551.470 2
[384.642]	384.64	564.19	564
[384.9]	384	567.94	567.9
[385.12]	385.1	[574.191 36]	574.191 3
[386.444]	386.44	574.522	574.5
[390.5]	390	574.873 223	574.873 22
[391.05]	391	[574.878]	574.87
[392.360 5]	392.36	[575.28]	575.2
[392.38]	392.3	[575.293]	575.29
395.59	395.5	[581.159 3]	581.159
491.857	491.85	[589.222 3]	589.222
495.919	495	[593.172]	591.17
499	490	594.19	594
[512.22]	512.2	594.71	594.7
[512.32]	512.3	595.764	595.76
[512.523]	512.52	604.24	604.2
[512.904]	512.9	612.49	612.4
[513.92]	513.9	612.801	612.8
[516.377]	516.37	613.83	613.8
521.1	521	[615.190 15−.190 18]	615.190 1
523	520	[615.191]	615.19
[526.982 3]	526.982	[615.537]	615.53
[531.322]	531.32	[615.61−.64]	615.6
[531.382 2]	531.38	[615.66−.67]	615.6
[531.382 3]	531.382	[615.704 3]	615.704
[531.382 5]	531.38	[615.851 52]	615.851 5
[531.552−.555]	531.55	616.075 72	616.075 7
[531.64]	531.6	[616.844]	616.84
[532.1]	532	616.849	616.84
[532.511]	532.51	[616.862]	616.8
[533.621−.629]	533.62	616.863	616.86
[534.203]	534.2	616.99	616.9
[534.205]	534.2	[617.605 9]	617.605
[534.206]	534.2	617.75	617.7
[534.207]	534.2	618.22	618.2
[534.33]	534.3	[620.004 22]	620
[534.34]	534.3	[620.004 25]	620.004 2
[534.35]	534.3	[620.7]	620
[535.58]	535.5	[621.184]	621.18
[536.401]	536.4	621.26	621.2
[536.443]	536.44	621.312 13	621.312 1
536.56	536.5	[621.312 56]	621.312 5
[537.245]	537.24	[621.321 5]	621.321
[537.246]	537.24	621.322	621.32
[538.743]	538.74	621.374	621.37
539.721	539.72	[621.381 042]	621.381
539.754	539.75	[621.381 336 1−.381 336 2]	621.381 336
541.345 1	541.345	621.381 5	621.381
[541.9]	541	621.381 51	621.381 5
[546.37]	546.3	[621.381 512 2−.381 512 8]	621.381 512

Edition 19	Edition 20	Edition 19	Edition 20
[621.381 513 2−.381 513 8]	621.381 513	629.895	629.89
621.381 53	621.381 5	630.202	630
[621.381 530 4]	621.381 5	631	630
[621.381 6]	621.381	[631.537]	631.53
[621.381 7]	621.381	631.81	631.8
[621.381 9]	621.381	632.94	632.9
621.384 1	621.384	633.895 9	633.895
621.384 16	621.384	634.52	634.5
[621.384 162−.384 164]	621.384	634.57	634.5
[621.384 166]	621.384 16	634.65	634.6
[621.384 185−.384 186]	621.384 18	634.92	634.9
[621.384 81]	621.384 8	634.928	634.92
621.388 1	621.388	634.972	634.97
[621.388 11]	621.388 1	[634.982]	634.98
[621.388 12−.388 13]	621.388	634.983	634.98
621.388 33	621.388 3	634.99	634.9
621.388 332	621.388 33	[634.999]	634.99
[621.388 85−.388 86]	621.388 8	635.952	635.9
[621.388 872−.388 874]	621.388 87	636.088 9	636.088
[621.388 9]	621.388	[636.088 92]	636
621.389 5	621.389	[636.088 99]	636.088 9
[621.389 52]	621.389	[636.413]	636.4
[621.389 53]	621.389 5	636.686	636.68
621.39*	621.3	636.686 9	636.68
[621.433 2]	621.433	[637.142 3]	637.142
[621.462]	621.46	[637.147 1−.147 2]	637.147
[621.481]	621.48	[637.23]	637.2
622.3	622	[637.33]	637.3
[623.12]	623.1	[639.411]	639.41
623.419	623.41	639.54	639.5
[623.419 4]	623.419	640.202	640
623.872	623.87	[640.68]	640
[624.52−.55]	624.5	641.222	641.22
[627.312−.313]	627.31	641.259	641.25
[627.35]	627.3	641.3	641
627.52	627.5	641.39	641.3
[628.119]	628.11	[641.573]	641.57
628.21	628.2	[641.575 2]	641.575
628.351	628.35	[641.575 4]	641.575
628.4	628	641.69	641.6
628.445 6	628.445	[643.604]	643.6
[628.462]	628.46	646.407	646.4
628.532	628.53	646.43	646.4
629.132 521	629.132 52	646.72	646.7
[629.136 13]	629.136	646.726	646.72
629.222 2	629.222	[649.552−.554]	649.55
[629.283 2]	629.283	649.64	649.6
629.29	629.2	[653.13]	653.1
[629.411 4]	629.411	[657.33]	657.3
[629.460 4]	629.4	658.311 2	658.311
[629.470 4]	629.47	658.42*	658.4
629.892	629.8	[658.456 3]	658.456

*Previously published

Edition 19	Edition 20	Edition 19	Edition 20
658.830 28	658.83	796.815 9	796.815
[659.132 2−.132 4]	659.132	[798.43]	798.4
659.136	659.13	798.8	798
659.2	659	[808.025]	808.02
660.2	660	[808.042 75]*	808.042 7
660.28	660	[808.59]	Without meaning
662.65	662.6	808.8	800
663.22	663.2	895.919	895
663.59	663.5	899	890
665.89	665.8	[910.453]	910.45
[674.134]	674.13	[940.441]	940.44
[674.22]	674.2	[940.544 1]	940.544
674.28	674.2	[972.820 52]	972.820 5
676.2	676	[972.820 53]	972.820 5
676.23	676.2	[972.860 52]	972.860 5
[676.26]	676.2	[972.860 53]	972.860 5
[677.57]	677.5	[989.505 5]	989.505
678.538	678.53	993.1	993
[683.402]	683.4		
[686.217]	686.2		
[686.232 6]	686.232		
686.303	686.3		
687.1	687		
687.11	687		
[687.110 4]	687.11		
687.25	687.2		
693.89	693.8		
[697.52]	697.5		
[724.9]	724		
728.3	728		
[728.67]	728.6		
728.82	728.8		
[729.83−.84]	728.8		
738.2	738		
[738.23]	738		
[738.24]	738		
738.382	738.38		
[738.383]	738.38		
[751.72]	750		
[757.9]	757		
[791.39]	791.3		
[791.435]	791.43		
[791.435 2]	791.43		
[791.445]	791.44		
[791.455]	791.45		
[792.090 9]	792.09		
792.82	792.8		
[793.324]	793.32		
794.2	794		
[794.22]	794.2		
796.426	796.42		
796.62	796.6		

*Previously published

Comparative Tables

As noted at their respective points in the schedules and tables, the developments for 780 Music and T2—711 British Columbia from Table 2 are new. The following lists, each arranged alphabetically by topic, show the number changes from Edition 19 to Edition 20 for a substantial number of topics. Usually only numbers for comprehensive works are given; however, some numbers are combinations, e.g.:

Topic	Edition 19	Edition 20
Rock	780.42	781.66
songs	784.54	782.421 66

This indicates that the comprehensive works number for rock has been changed from 780.42 to 781.66, and also that the number for rock songs has been changed to 782.42166, a number that has been built by combining, via instructions given in the schedule, the comprehensive works numbers for rock, 781.66, and for songs, 782.42. The abbreviation *T1* in these lists means Table 1 Standard Subdivisions, and *T2* means Table 2 Geographic Areas, Historical Periods, Persons.

Music

Topic	Edition 19	Edition 20
Accompaniment	781.66	781.47
Accordions	786.97	788.86
Aesthetics	780.1	781.17
Alto voices	784.8	782
children's	784.8	782.78
men's	784.8	782.86
women's	784.8	782.68
Anglican chants	783.5	782.322 3
Anthems	783.4	782.265
Anvils	789.4	786.884 3
Appreciation	780.15	781.17
Arabesques	781.5	784.189 4
piano music	786.42	786.218 94
Arrangement	781.64	781.37
Art music	780.43	781.68–.69
songs	784.3	782.421 68–.421 69
Bagpipes	788.92	788.49
Ballads	784.3	782.43
Ballet music	782.95	781.556
Band music	785.12	784.18

496

Topic	Edition 19	Edition 20
Bands	785.067	784
brass	785.067 1	784.9
jazz	785.067 2	784.165
marching	785.067 1	784.83
military	785.067 1	784.84
percussion	785.067 5	784.68
rhythm	785.067 5	784.68
wind	785.067 1	784.8
Banjos	787.7	787.88
Baritones (Horns)	788.44	788.975
Baritones (Voices)	784.8	782.88
Barrel organs	789.71	786.68
Bass voices	784.8	782.89
Bassoons	788.8	788.58
Bells	789.5	786.884 8
Bluegrass	780.42	781.642
Blues	781.573	781.643
songs	784.53	782.421 643
Bowed instruments	787.01	787
Brass bands	785.067 1	784.9
Brass instruments	788.01	788.9
Bugles	788.1	788.95
Canons	781.42	784.187 8
Cantatas	782.82	782.24
sacred	783.4	782.24
secular	782.82	782.48
Carillons	789.5	786.64
Carols	783.62−.63	782.28
Christmas	783.65	782.281 723
Cassations	781.5	784.185
orchestra music	785.31	784.218 5
Castanets	789.4	786.873
Celestas	789.6	786.83
Cellos	787.3	787.4
Chamber music	785.7	785
ensembles	785.068	785
Chamber orchestras	785.066 2	784.3
Chants	783.5	782.292
Anglican	783.5	782.322 3
Gregorian	783.5	782.322 2
Children's songs	784.624	782.420 83
Children's voices	784.8	782.7
Chimes	789.5	786.848
Choirs	784.106	782.506
sacred	783.8	782.522 06
Choral music	784.1	782.5
Chords	781.22	782.252
Christian sacred music	783.026	781.71
liturgical	783.21−.29	782.32
Christmas music	783.026	781.723
carols	783.65	782.281 723
liturgical	783.28	782.291 723

Topic	Edition 19	Edition 20
Classical music	780.43	781.68
Clavichords	786.222	786.3
Common of the mass	783.22	782.323 2
Composition	781.61	781.3
Concerti grossi	785.6	784.24
Concertinas	786.97	788.84
Concertos	785.6	784.23
Concerts	T1—073	T1—078
Concrete music	789.98	786.75
Conducting	781.635	781.45
Conservatories	780.72	780.71
Contralto voices	784.8	782.68
children's	784.8	782.78
women's	784.8	782.68
Cornets	788.1	788.96
Counterpoint	781.42	781.286
Countertenor voices	784.8	782.86
Country music	780.42	781.642
songs	784.52	782.421 642
Cymbals	789.2	786.873
Dance bands	785.066 6	784.48
Dance music (Form)	781.55	784.188
orchestral	785.41	784.818 8
piano	786.45	786.218 8
Dance orchestras	785.066 6	784.48
Dance suites	781.55	784.188 2
piano music	786.45	786.218 82
Divertimenti	781.5	784.185 2
orchestra music	785.31	784.218 52
Divine office	783.24	782.324
Double basses	787.41	787.5
Double-reed instruments	788.7—.8	788.5
Dramatic music	782	781.552
incidental	782.83	781.552
vocal	782	782.1
Drum and bugle corps	785.067 1	784.9
Drums	789.1	786.9
Duets		
chamber music	785.72	785.12
vocal	784.82	783.12
songs	784.306 2	783.124 2
Dulcimers	787.94	787.74
Ear training	780.77	781.424
Easter music	783.026	781.727
liturgical	783.28	782.291 727
Electronic instruments	789.9	786.7
organs	786.92	786.59
Electronic music	789.99	786.74
Embellishments	781.67	781.247
English horns	788.7	788.53
Ethnic music	781.72	781.62
Ethnomusicology	781.7	780.89

Topic	Edition 19	Edition 20
Études (Artistic)	781.5	784.189 49
piano music	786.47	786.218 949
Études (Exercises)		
piano	786.304 1	786.207 6
Euphoniums	788.44	788.975
Falsetto voices	784.8	782.86
Fifes	788.51	788.33
Film music	782.85	781.542
Film musicals	782.81	782.141 542
Flutes	788.51	788.32
Folk music	781.7	781.62
songs	784.4	782.421 62
Forms of music	781.5	781.8
French horns	788.41	788.94
Fugues	781.42	784.187 2
organ music	786.82	786.518 72
piano music	786.42	786.218 72
Glockenspiels	789.6	786.843
Gongs	789.4	786.884 3
Gregorian chants	783.5	782.322 2
Guitars	787.61	787.87
Harmonicas (Mouth organ)	788.9	788.82
Harmonicas (Musical glasses)	789.6	786.866
Harmony	781.3	781.25
Harps	787.5	787.9
Harpsichords	786.221	786.4
Home songs	784.61	782.421 535
Horns	788.4	788.94
Hymnals	783.952	782.27
Hymns	783.9	782.27
Improvisation	781.65	781.36
Improvisations	781.5	784.189 4
organ music	786.87	786.518 94
Incidental dramatic music	782.83	781.552
Instrumental ensembles	785	784
Instrumental sacred music	783.1	784.16
Instruments	781.91	784.19
Interludes	781.5	784.189 3
organ music	786.84	786.518 93
Intervals	781.22	781.237
Jazz	781.57	781.65
band music	785.42	784.165
bands	785.067 2	784.165
orchestras	785.066 7	784.416 5
Jew's harps	788.9	786.887
Kettledrums	789.1	786.93
Keyboard stringed instruments	786.1−.4	786
Lenten music	783.026	781.725
liturgical	783.27	782.291 725
Librettos		
treatises on	781.96	782.102 68
Litanies	783.26	782.292

Topic	Edition 19	Edition 20
Liturgical music	783.2	782.29
Lutes	787.67	787.83
Madrigals	784.12	782.43
Mandolins	787.65	787.84
Maracas	789.4	786.885
Marches	781.5	784.189 7
band music	785.13	784.818 97
piano music	786.44	786.218 97
Marching bands	785.067 1	784.83
Marimbas	789.6	786.843
Masques	782.9	782.15
Mass	783.21	782.323
Matins (Divine office)	783.24	782.324
Mazurkas	781.5	784.188 4
piano music	786.44	786.218 84
Melody	781.41	781.24
Membranophones	789.1	786.9
Memorizing	781.634	781.426
Men's voices	784.8	782.8
Meter	781.62	781.226
Mezzo-soprano voices	784.8	782.67
children's	784.8	782.77
women's	784.8	782.67
Military bands	785.067 1	784.84
Miniature scores		
treatises on	780.84	780.265
Motets	783.4	782.26
Mouth organs	788.9	788.82
Music boxes	789.8	786.65
Musical forms	781.5	781.8
Musical glasses	789.6	786.866
Musical plays	782.81	782.14
Musical saws	789.69	786.888
Musique concrète	789.98	786.75
National songs	784.71	782.421 599
Nomenclature	781.23	T1—014
Nonets		
chamber music	785.79	785.19
vocal	784.85	783.19
songs	784.306 7	783.194 2
Notations	781.24	T1—014 8
Oboes	788.7	788.52
Octets		
chamber music	785.78	785.18
vocal	784.85	783.18
songs	784.067	783.184 2
Offertories	781.5	784.189 92
organ music	786.86	786.518 992
Office hours	783.24	782.324
Operettas	782.81	782.12

Topic	Edition 19	Edition 20
Oratories	782.82	782.23
sacred	783.3	782.23
secular	782.82	782.48
Orchestras	785.066	784.2
chamber	785.066 2	784.3
dance	785.066 6	784.48
jazz	785.066 7	784.416 5
salon	785.066 2	784.4
string	785.066 3	784.7
symphony	785.066 1	784.2
with vocal parts	785.2	784.22
Ordinary of the mass	783.22	782.323 2
Organs	786.5—.8	786.5
barrel	789.71	786.68
electronic	786.92	786.59
reed	786.94	786.55
Overtures	781.5	784.189 26
orchestra music	785.5	784.218 926
Part songs	784.1	783.1
Passions	783.3	782.23
Patriotic songs	784.71	782.421 599
Percussion		
bands	785.067 5	784.68
instruments	789.01	786.8
Performance techniques	781.63	781.43
Performances	T1—073	T1—078
Pianos	786.21	786.2
player	789.72	786.66
Piccolos	788.51	788.33
Pitch	781.22	781.232
Player pianos	789.72	786.66
Plectral instruments	787.05	787.7
Pocket scores	780.84	780
treatises on	780.84	780.265
Polkas	781.5	784.188 44
piano music	786.44	786.218 844
Polonaises	781.5	784.188 4
piano music	786.44	786.218 84
Popular music	780.42	781.63
songs	784.5	782.421 63
Postludes	781.5	784.189 3
organ music	786.85	786.518 93
Preludes	781.5	784.189 28
organ music	786.83	786.518 928
Program music		
orchestral	785.32	784.215 6
Proper of the mass	783.23	782.323 5
Psychological principles	781.15	781.11
Quartets		
chamber music	785.74	785.14
vocal	784.84	783.14
songs	784.306 4	783.144 2

Topic	Edition 19	Edition 20
Quintets		
chamber music	785.75	785.15
vocal	784.85	783.15
songs	784.306 5	783.154 2
Radio music	782.86	781.544
Ragtime	781.572	781.64
Rattles	789.4	786.885
Recitals	T1—073	T1—078
Recorders (Wind instruments)	788.53	788.36
Recording music	789.91	781.49
Recordings		
treatises on	789.912	780.266
Reed instruments	788.056	788.4
organs	786.94	786.55
Requiem mass	783.21	782.323 8
Research	780.01	780.72
Rhapsodies	781.5	784.189 45
piano music	786.42	786.218 945
Rhythm (Musical element)	781.62	781.224
Rhythm bands	785.067 5	784.68
Rock	780.42	781.66
songs	784.54	782.421 66
Romantic music	781.5	784.189 6
orchestra music	785.31	784.218 96
piano music	786.43	786.218 96
Rondos	781.5	784.182 4
pianos music	786.41	786.218 24
Sacred music	783	781.7
instrumental	783.1	784.17
vocal	783.2−.9	782.22
Salon orchestras	785.066 2	784.4
Saxhorns	788.42	788.97
Saxophones	788.66	788.7
Scales	781.22	781.246
Scenarios	781.96	782.002 69
Schools	780.72	780.71
Scientific principles	781.1	781.2
Scores		
reading	781.633	781.423
treatises on	780.81−.84	780.262−.265
Secular cantatas	782.82	782.48
Secular oratorios	782.82	782.48
Secular songs	784.3	782.42
Septets		
chambers music	785.77	785.17
vocal	784.85	783.17
songs	784.306 7	783.174 2
Serenades	781.5	784.185 6
orchestra music	785.31	784.218 56

Topic	Edition 19	Edition 20
Sextets		
chamber music	785.76	785.16
vocal	784.85	783.16
songs	784.306 6	783.164 2
Solos vocal	784.81	783.2
songs	784.306 1	783.242
Sonatas	781.52	784.183
organ music	786.81	786.518 3
piano music	786.41	786.218 3
Sonatinas	781.52	784.183 2
organ music	786.81	786.518 32
piano music	786.41	786.218 32
Songs	784.3	782.42
art	784.3	782.421 68–.421 69
blues	784.53	782.421 643
country music	784.52	782.421 642
folk	784.4	782.421 62
for children	784.624	782.420 83
for home	784.61	782.421 535
for students	784.62	782.420 883 75
national	784.71	782.421 599
patriotic	784.71	782.421 599
popular	784.5	782.421 63
rock	784.54	782.421 66
sacred	783.6	782.25
secular	784.3	782.42
soul	784.55	782.421 644
Soprano voices	784.8	782.66
children's	784.8	782.76
women's	784.8	782.66
Soul music	780.42	781.644
songs	784.55	782.421 644
Sound	781.22	781.23
Spirituals	783.67	782.25
String orchestras	785.066 3	784.7
Stringed instruments		
bowed	787.01	787
keyboard	786.1–.4	786
plectral	787.05	787.7
Students' songs	784.62	782.420 883 75
Suites		
dances	781.5	784.188 2
piano music	786.45	786.218 82
general works	781.5	784.185 8
orchestra music	785.8	784.218 58
piano music	786.48	786.218 58
Swing	781.574	781.654
Symphonic poems	781.5	784.184
orchestra music	785.32	784.218 4
Symphonies	781.5	784.184
orchestra music	785.11	784.218 4
Symphony orchestras	785.066 1	784.2

Topic	Edition 19	Edition 20
Tambourines	789.1	786.95
Television music	782.87	781.546
Tenor voices	784.8	782.87
Theremins	789.99	786.73
Thorough bass	781.32	781.47
Timpani	789.1	786.93
Toccatas	781.5	784.18947
organ music	786.82	786.518 947
Tonalities	781.22	781.258
Transposition	781.642	781.436
Triangles	789.3	786.8842
Trios		
chamber music	785.73	785.13
vocal	784.83	783.13
songs	784.306 3	783.134 2
Trombones	788.2	788.93
Trumpets	788.1	788.92
Tubas	788.48	788.98
Twelve-tone system	781.3	781.268
Ukuleles	787.92	787.89
Variations	781.5	781.825
orchestra music	785.34	784.218 25
piano music	786.48	786.218 25
Vespers	783.24	782.324
Violas	787.2	787.3
Violins	787.1	787.2
Violoncellos	787.3	787.4
Viols	787.42	787.6
Vocal music	784	782
dramatic	782	782.1
sacred	783.2–.9	782.22
secular	784	782.4
Voice	784.9	783
Voluntaries	781.5	784.189 3
organ music	786.87	786.518 93
Whistling	784.949	782.98
Wind bands	785.067 1	784.8
Wind instruments		
brass	788.01	788.9
woodwind	788.05	788.2
Women's voices	784.8	782.6
Woodwind instruments	788.05	788.2
Xylophones	789.6	786.843
Zithers	787.8	787.7

British Columbia

Topic	Edition 19	Edition 20
Bulkley Mountains	T2—711 2	T2—711 85
Cariboo Mountains	T2—711 2	T2—711 7
Cascade Mountains	T2—711 3	T2—711 5
Central interior region	T2—711 2	T2—711 7–711 8
Chilliwack	T2—711 33	T2—711 37
Coast Ranges	T2—711 3	T2—711 1
Coastal region	T2—711 3	T2—711 1
Columbia River	T2—711 45	T2—711 6
Fraser River	T2—711 2	T2—711 3
Gulf Islands	T2—711 34	T2—711 28
Kamloops	T2—711 41	T2—711 72
Kelowna	T2—711 42	T2—711 5
Kitimat	T2—711 32	T2—711 1
Kootenay River	T2—711 45	T2—711 65
Lower coastal mainland	T2—711 33	T2—711 31
Mission City	T2—711 33	T2—711 37
Monashee Mountains	T2—711 44	T2—711 62
Nelson	T2—711 44	T2—711 62
Nicola River	T2—711 41	T2—711 72
Northern region	T2—711 1	T2—711 8
Northwest coastal region	T2—711 32	T2—711 1
Ocean Falls	T2—711 32	T2—711 1
Okanagan Valley	T2—711 42	T2—711 5
Penticton	T2—711 42	T2—711 5
Prince Rupert	T2—711 32	T2—711 1
Queen Charlotte Islands	T2—711 31	T2—711 12
Rocky Mountains	T2—711 45	T2—711
Selkirk Mountains	T2—711 43	T2—711 68
Similkameen River	T2—711 41	T2—711 5
Southern interior region	T2—711 4	T2—711 6
Thompson River	T2—711 41	T2—711 72
Trail	T2—711 44	T2—711 62
Vancouver Island	T2—711 34	T2—711 2
Vernon	T2—711 42	T2—711 5
Victoria	T2—711 34	T2—711 28

Equivalence Tables

The equivalence tables that follow lead in each Table A from Edition 19 numbers to Edition 20 numbers for use by persons familiar with the music and British Columbia numbers from Edition 19, in each Table B from Edition 20 numbers to Edition 19 numbers for classifiers whose libraries are remaining on Edition 19.

In most cases, the contents of an Edition 19 number will be assigned to the same Edition 20 number (and vice versa). If the topics are assigned to a different number, the topics will be listed separately in the Note column.

Music

Table A

Edition 19	Edition 20	Notes
780.01	780.72	
780.07	780.03	Relation to society
780.07	780.79	Financial support
780.08	780.07	Relation to arts
780.09	780.000 1–.099 9	
780.15	781.17	
780.42	781.63	
780.43	781.68	
780.72	780.71	
780.73	780.78	
780.77	781.42	Techniques for acquiring musical skills and learning a repertoire
780.81–.84	780	Music scores
780.81–.84	780.26	Treatises on music scores
781.1	781.2	
781.15	781.11	
781.22	781.23	
781.23	780.14	
781.24	780.148	
781.3	781.25	
781.32	781.47	
781.41	781.24	
781.42	781.286	Counterpoint
781.42	784.187 2	Fugue
781.42	784.187 8	Canon
781.5	781.8	
781.52	784.183	
781.55	781.554	
781.57	781.65	
781.572	781.64	
781.573	781.643	
781.61	781.3	
781.62	781.224	Rhythm
781.62	781.226	Meter

Edition 19	Edition 20	Notes
781.63	781.43	
781.63	781.46	Interpretation
781.635	781.45	
781.64	781.37	
781.65	781.36	
781.66	781.47	
781.67	781.247	
781.7	781.62	Folk music
781.71	780.863 3	
781.72	780.089	
781.73−.79	780.93−.99	
781.91	784.19	
781.96	780.268	
781.96	780.269	Scenarios
782	782.1	
782.81	782.12	Operettas
782.81	782.13	Singspiels
782.81	782.14	Musical plays
782.82	782.48	
782.83	781.552	
782.85	781.542	
782.86	781.544	
782.87	781.546	
782.9	782.15	Masques
782.95	781.556	
783	781.7	
783.026	781.71	
783.029	781.73−.79	
783.1	784.188 9	
783.2	782.29	Liturgical forms
783.2	782.3	Services
783.3	782.23	
783.4	782.24	
783.4	782.26	Motets, anthems
783.5	782.322 2	Gregorian chant
783.5	782.322 3	Anglican chant
783.6	782.25	
783.62−.63	782.28	Carols
783.8	782.522 06	
783.9	782.27	
784	782.−.-78 3	
784.1	782.5	Choruses
784.1	783.1	Part songs
784.2	782.5	
784.3	782.42	
784.4	782.421 62	
784.5	782.421 63	
784.52	782.421 642	
784.53	782.421 643	
784.54	782.421 66	
784.55	782.421 644	
784.6	782.421 5	

Edition 19	Edition 20	Notes
784.71	782.421 599	
784.75−.76	782.420 89	
784.8	782	
784.81−.85	783	
784.9	783	
785	784	
785.066	784.2	
785.066 2	784.3	
785.066 3	784.7	
785.066 6	784.48	
785.067	784	
785.067	784.8	Wind band
785.067	784.9	Brass band
785.068	784.3	
785.11	784.184	
785.12	784	
785.13	784.84	
785.2	784.22	
785.3	784.4	Music for salon orchestra
785.3	784.7	Music for string orchestra
785.31	784.189 6	
785.31	784.185	Cassations
785.31	784.185 2	Divertimenti
785.31	784.185 6	Serenades
785.32	781.56	
785.32	784.184	Symphonic poems
785.34	784.182 5	Variations
785.41	784.188	
785.42	784.165	
785.43	784.68	
785.5	784.189 26	
785.6	784.23	
785.7	785	
785.8	784.185	
786.1−.4	786.2−.4	
786.5−.8	786.5	
786.92	786.59	
786.94	786.55	
786.97	788.84	Concertinas
786.97	788.86	Accordions
787.1	787.2	
787.2	787.3	
787.3	787.4	
787.41	787.5	
787.42	787.6	
787.5	787.9	
787.61	787.87	
787.65	787.84	
787.67	787.8	
787.7	787.88	
787.8	787.7	

Edition 19	Edition 20	Notes
787.9	787.69	Hurdy-gurdies
787.9	787.75	Psalteries
787.92	787.89	
787.94	787.74	
788.01	788.9	
788.05	788.2	
788.056	788.4	
788.1	788.92	Trumpets
788.1	788.95	Bugles
788.1	788.96	Cornets
788.2	788.93	
788.41	788.94	
788.42	788.97	
788.44	788.975	
788.45	788.99	
788.48	788.98	Tubas
788.48	788.99	Instruments related to tuba
788.49	788.99	
788.5	788.3	
788.51	788.32	Flutes
788.51	788.33	Piccolos and fifes
788.53	788.35	Flageolets
788.53	788.36	Recorders
788.62	788.65	Bass clarinets
788.66	788.7	
788.7	788.52	Oboes
788.7	788.53	English horns
788.8	788.5	Heckelphones
788.8	788.58	Bassoons
788.9	788.5	
788.9	788.82	Mouth organs and harmonicas
788.92	788.49	
789.01	786.8	
789.1	786.9	
789.2	786.873	
789.3	786.884 2	
789.4	786.873	Castanets
789.4	786.884 3	Anvils and gongs
789.4	786.885	Maracas and rattles
789.5	786.64	Carillons
789.5	786.843	Chimes
789.5	786.884 8	Bells
789.6	786.8	
789.7	786.6	
789.8	786.65	
789.9	786.7	
789.91	781.49	
789.912	780.266	
789.98	786.75	
789.99	786.74	

Table B

Edition 20	Edition 19	Notes
780	780.81–.84	Music scores
780.000 1–.02	780.09	
780.030 1–.030 7	780.07	Music and society
780.031–.06	780.09	
780.07–.08	780.08	
780.090 1–.099 9	780.09	
780.14	781.23	Nomenclature
780.148	781.24	
780.26	780.81–.84	
780.266–.267	789.912	
780.268–.269	781.96	
780.28	781	
780.71	780.72	
780.72	780.01	
780.78	780.73	
780.79	780.07	Financial support
780.89	781.72	
780.93–.99	781.73–.79	Music composed or improvised in specific countries or localities
781.11	781.15	
781.12	781	
781.17	780.15	
781.2	781	
781.2	781.1	Scientific principles
781.224–.226	781.62	
781.23	781.22	
781.24	781.41	
781.247	781.67	
781.25	781.3	
781.286	781.42	
781.3	781.61	
781.36	781.65	
781.37	781.64	
781.42	780.77	
781.43–.44	781.63	
781.45	781.635	
781.46	781.63	
781.47	781.66	
781.47	781.32	Thorough bass
781.48	781.63	
781.49	789.91	
781.5	781	
781.542	782.85	
781.544	782.86	
781.546	782.87	
781.552	782.83	
781.554	781.55	
781.556	782.95	
781.56	785.32	
781.62	781.7	
781.63–.64	780.42	

Edition 20	Edition 19	Notes
781.65	781.57	
781.66	780.42	
781.68−.69	780.43	
781.7	783	
781.71−.72	783.026	
781.73−.79	783.029	
781.8	781.5	
782	784	
782	784.8	Collections
782.1	782	Dramatic music
782.12−.14	782.81	
782.15	782.9	
782.2	784	
782.22	783	
782.23	783.3	
782.24	783.4	
782.25	783.6	
782.26	783.4	
782.27	783.9	
782.28	783.6	
782.29	783.2	
782.3	783.2	
782.323	783.21	
782.324	783.24	
782.33−.39	783.029	
782.4	784	
782.42	784.3	
782.42	784.5	Popular songs
782.43	784.12	Madrigals
782.47	784.3	
782.48	782.82	
782.5−.9	784.1−.2	
783	784	
783	784.9	The voice
783.1	784.1	
783.12−.19	784.82−.85	Collections
783.2−.9	784.81	Collections
784	785	
784.182	785	
784.182 5	785.34	
784.183	781.52	
784.184	785.11	
784.184	785.32	Symphonic poems
784.185	785.8	
784.185	785.31	Cassations
784.185 2	785.31	
784.185 6	785.31	
784.186	785	
784.187	785	
784.187 2	781.42	
784.187 8	781.42	
784.188	785.41	

Edition 20	Editon 19	Notes
784.189	785	
784.189 26	785.5	
784.186	785.31	Romantic music
784.189 9	785.3	
784.19	781.91	
784.2	785	
784.2	785.066	Orchestra as type of organization
784.22	785.2	
784.23−.28	785.6	
784.3	785.066 2	
784.4	785.066	Type of organization
784.4	785.3	Music
784.6	785.067	
784.68	785.0675	Type of organization
784.68	785.43	Music
784.7	785.0663	Type of organization
784.7	785.3	Music
784.8	785.067	
784.9	785.067	
785	785.068	Chamber music ensembles
785	785.7	Chamber music
786.2−.4	786.1−.4	
786.5	786.5−.8	
786.55	786.94	
786.59	786.92	
786.6	789.7	
786.64	789.5	Carillons and mechanized bells
786.65	789.8	Music boxes
786.7	789.9	
786.74	789.99	Electronic music
786.75	789.98	Concrete music
786.8	789.01	General works
786.8	789.6	Miscellaneous instruments
786.843	789.5	Chimes
786.873	789.2	Cymbals
786.873	789.4	Castanets
786.8842	789.3	Triangle
786.884 3	789.4	Anvils and gongs
786.884 8	789.5	
786.885	789.4	Maracas
786.9	789.1	
787.2	787.1	
787.3	787.2	
787.4	787.3	
787.5	787.41	
787.6	787.42	Viols
787.69	787.9	
787.7	787.8	Zithers
787.74	787.94	Dulcimers
787.75	787.9	

Edition 20	Editon 19	Notes
787.8	787.67	
787.84	787.65	
787.87	787.61	
787.88	787.7	
787.89	787.92	
787.9	787.5	
787.92−.93	787.9	
788.2	788.05	
788.3	788.5	
788.32−.34	788.51	
788.35	788.53	Flageolets
788.36	788.53	
788.4	788.056	
788.49	788.92	
788.5	788.056	General works
788.5	788.9	Miscellaneous instruments
788.5	788.8	Heckelphone
788.52	788.7	
788.53	788.7	
788.58−.59	788.8	
788.65	788.62	
788.7	788.66	
788.8	788.9	
788.84−.86	786.97	
788.9	788.01	
788.92	788.1	
788.93	788.2	
788.94	788.41	
788.95−.96	788.1	
788.97	788.42	
788.975	788.44	
788.98	788.48	
788.99	788.4	
788.99	788.45	Ophicleides and key bugles
788.99	788.48	Instruments related to tuba
788.99	788.49	Alpenhorn

British Columbia

Table A

Edition 19	Edition 20	Notes
T2—711 1	T2—711 8	
T2—711 2	T2—711 7–711 8	
T2—711 2	T2—711 31	Squamish-Lillooet Regional District
T2—711 3	T2—711 1	Northern coastal region
T2—711 3	T2—711 31	Southern coastal region
T2—711 31	T2—711 12	
T2—711 32	T2—711 1	
T2—711 33	T2—711 31–711 37	
T2—711 34	T2—711 2	
T2—711 4	T2—711 5–711 7	
T2—711 41	T2—711 5	Similkameen River valley
T2—711 41	T2—711 72	Thompson and Nicola River valleys
T2—711 42	T2—711 5	
T2—711 43	T2—711 62	Lower Selkirk Mountains
T2—711 43	T2—711 68	Comprehensive works on Selkirk Mountains
T2—711 44	T2—711 62	
T2—711 45	T2—711 65	

Table B

Edition 20	Editon 19	Notes
T2—711 1	T2—711 32	
T2—711 12	T2—711 31	
T2—711 2	T2—711 34	
T2—711 28	T2—711 34	
T2—711 31	T2—711 3	
T2—711 31	T2—711 31	Squamish-Lillooet District east of Coast Mountains
T2—711 37	T2—711 3	
T2—711 5	T2—711 41	Similkameen region
T2—711 5	T2—711 42	Okanagan Valley
T2—711 62	T2—711 43	Selkirk Mountains region
T2—711 62	T2—711 44	Area between Monashee and Selkirk Mountains
T2—711 65	T2—711 45	
T2—711 68	T2—711 2	Area north of 51°N
T2—711 68	T2—711 43	Selkirk Mountains region
T2—711 68	T2—711 44	Area between Monashee and Selkirk Mountains
T2—711 68	T2—711 45	Upper Columbia River Valley
T2—711 7	T2—711 2	
T2—711 72	T2—711 41	Valleys of Thompson and Nicola Rivers
T2—711 8	T2—711 1	
T2—711 82	T2—711 2	Central interior region

The 20th edition of the Dewey Decimal Classification was designed by Lisa Hanifan of Albany, New York. Edition 20 is the first edition to be generated from an online database. Database design, technical support, and programming for this edition were provided by John J. Finni and Cora M. Arsenault from Inforonics, Inc., of Littleton, Massachusetts. Composition was done in Times Roman and Helvetica on a Linotronic L100 under the supervision of Inforonics, Inc. The book was printed and bound by Hamilton Printing Company of Rensselaer, New York.